LITTLE WHITE HOUSES

ARCHITECTURE, LANDSCAPE, AND AMERICAN CULTURE SERIES
Katherine Solomonson and Abigail A. Van Slyck, Series Editors

*Medicine by Design: The Architect
and the Modern Hospital, 1893–1943*
Annmarie Adams

*Little White Houses: How the Postwar
Home Constructed Race in America*
Dianne Harris

*Manhood Factories: YMCA Architecture
and the Making of Modern Urban Culture*
Paula Lupkin

*Fallout Shelter: Designing for
Civil Defense in the Cold War*
David Monteyne

*Women and the Everyday City:
Public Space in San Francisco, 1890–1915*
Jessica Ellen Sewell

*194X: Architecture, Planning, and Consumer
Culture on the American Home Front*
Andrew M. Shanken

*A Manufactured Wilderness: Summer Camps
and the Shaping of American Youth, 1890–1960*
Abigail A. Van Slyck

*The Architecture of Madness:
Insane Asylums in the United States*
Carla Yanni

LITTLE WHITE HOUSES

How the Postwar Home Constructed Race in America

DIANNE HARRIS

Architecture, Landscape, and American Culture Series

University of Minnesota Press
Minneapolis • London

This book is supported by a grant from the Graham Foundation for Advanced Studies in the Fine Arts.

The University of Minnesota Press gratefully acknowledges financial assistance provided for the publication of this book from the University of Illinois Campus Research Board.

A version of chapter 3 was published as "Clean and Bright and Everyone White: Seeing the Postwar Domestic Environment in the United States," in *Sites Unseen: Landscape and Vision,* ed. Dianne Harris and D. Fairchild Ruggles (Pittsburgh: University of Pittsburgh Press, 2007), 241–62. A version of chapter 4 appeared previously as "Race, Class, and Privacy in the Ordinary Postwar House, 1945–1960," in *Landscape and Race in the United States,* ed. Richard H. Schein (London/New York: Routledge, 2006), 127–56.

Every effort was made to obtain permission to reproduce material in this book. If any proper acknowledgment has not been included, we encourage copyright holders to notify the publisher.

Published by the University of Minnesota Press
111 Third Avenue South, Suite 290
Minneapolis, MN 55401-2520
http://www.upress.umn.edu

Library of Congress Cataloging-in-Publication Data
Harris, Dianne Suzette.
Little white houses : how the postwar home constructed race in America / Dianne Harris.
(Architecture, landscape and American culture series)
Includes bibliographical references and index.
ISBN 978-0-8166-5332-4 (hardback) — ISBN 978-0-8166-5456-7 (pb)
1. Architecture and race—United States. 2. Mass media and architecture—United States.
3. Architecture, Domestic—United States—History—20th century. 4. Whites—Race identity—United States—History—20th century. I. Title.
NA2543.R37H37 2013
728.01'030973—dc23   2012036292

Printed in Canada on acid-free paper

The University of Minnesota is an equal-opportunity educator and employer.

20 19 18 17 16 15 14 13   10 9 8 7 6 5 4 3 2 1

For my family

Contents

Preface

In 1933, my maternal grandparents, Rudolf and Eva Weingarten, left their home and family in Germany, embarking on a journey that would eventually see them established and recognized as American citizens. As a Jew, my grandfather had already found his career possibilities restricted in Germany. Trained as an engineer, he traveled to Tel Aviv (then Palestine), where he worked for four years before emigrating with his family to the United States. By that time, their family had expanded to include two young daughters. After a brief stay with family in New York, Rudy and Eva moved to Los Angeles, where my grandfather found employment with a company called Gateway to Music, a job that allowed him to follow his deep interest in stereophonic engineering. But by 1941, classified by the U.S. govern-ment as an "enemy alien" and perhaps considered especially suspicious because of his knowledge of shortwave radio technology, Rudy found his freedom, once again, severely restricted. For the duration of the U.S. involvement in World War II, Rudy Weingarten could not drive beyond a five-mile radius from his house, and he could move beyond that boundary only with special permission from government officials. Despite the fact that he was a Jew fleeing a repressive and violent regime, FBI agents interrogated him in his home on a periodic basis for the duration of the war.[1]

Like many others who immigrated to the United States, my grandparents—who were fluent in both German and Hebrew—mostly stopped speaking their native languages. They obtained citizenship as quickly as possible, and they did everything they could to assimilate, to become unobtrusive, to become as ethnically "white" and American as possible.[2] Owning a home of their own was an important goal for them, as it was for millions of other postwar Americans, and I think it is fair to speculate that homeownership symbolized much for them, as it did for millions of others. To own a home was to have a sense of permanence, of investment; it represented the ownership not just of real property but of a crucial piece of the American Dream. Then, as now, that dream was not equally available to all. A primary factor in determining access to the dream of homeownership was a white identity.

As I will detail in this book's introduction, the postwar period was one in which cultural notions of whiteness shifted, and the relationship of Jews to whiteness was particularly in flux. I do not believe my grandparents regularly or consciously pondered their racial identity in the cultural terms I explore in this book, but I do think it is fair to say that they were aware of conforming to a set of residential expectations that may have been linked to their sense of themselves as immigrants who desired to be seen as Americans according to the terms they fashioned for themselves and their family. Their inherent personalities dictated that their house would be immaculately kept and that they would comport themselves unobtrusively and quietly in public. That these traits also served to enforce their appearance as solidly white, middle-class citizens was coincident with the norms enforced by the mass media in the United States, as I will demonstrate in the pages that follow. Yet it is interesting to consider also how media representations created a set of definitions and expectations for the identities of postwar homeowners, and how those parameters were internalized by the millions of new homeowners from various cultural backgrounds across the United States between 1945 and 1960. As media and rhetoric scholar Cara Finnegan has noted, there is, and always has been, a powerful relationship between seeing and knowing.[3] This book began as my way of trying to understand how seeing, reading, thinking about, and living in postwar domestic environments helped my grandparents and many others of their generation know what it meant to be a new citizen of the United States and how they navigated the waters of belonging in a country that appeared to offer, but clearly did not offer, equal opportunity for all.

As immigrants who had rented a series of apartments and houses, they were without a baseline of American knowledge to inform their later experience of homeownership. Like many other immigrants and upwardly mobile blue-collar and working-class Americans, they performed the cultural work required to establish solidly white identities. To be seen as other than white could be perilous and costly in a climate of nationwide and institutionalized racism, where anyone seen as "other" could be denied housing, services, and societal benefits. As Karen Brodkin observes, "The alternatives available to nonwhite and variously alien 'others' has been either to whiten themselves or to be consigned to an animal-like, ungendered underclass unfit to exercise the prerogatives of citizenship."[4] This was a condition my grandparents and many other immigrants from many other parts of the world clearly wished to avoid, and their houses became important symbols of their attainment of both citizenship and its attendant privileges.

My grandparents purchased their first house in Southern California's San Fernando Valley in 1955, and it was the home they occupied for the rest of their lives. Theirs was a nonrestricted neighborhood—such areas were available in some abundance in that geographic region of the Los Angeles basin. As the single largest purchase they made in their lifetime, the house became a focus of much of their attention. It was scrupulously maintained, fastidiously clean, carefully furnished and decorated. Like thousands of other Americans, my grandparents read newspaper and magazine articles that focused on house design and interior decoration; they watched television shows that focused on domestic life; and they both adopted the spatial practices and forms they viewed and simultaneously found opportunities to preserve (if modestly) subtle cues to their personal identity. Their house serves as a leitmotif for this book, just as my memories of them are nearly inseparable from my memories of their house. Those memories helped me create the plan of their house that appears in this book, as well as the short vignettes that appear at the beginnings of the chapters. As Richard White has so brilliantly demonstrated, memory is not history; indeed, "history is the enemy of memory."[5] But memories, which for me are always profoundly spatialized, provide important portals for asking questions about the past. While they can "mislead as well as lead," I hope that in this instance my memories of a particular house have fruitfully led to the formation of a new perspective on the way we understand the history of postwar housing in the United States.

Introduction

Between 1945 and 1960, a pervasive iconography of white, middle-class domesticity circulated widely in various media and became instantiated in millions of new homes across the United States. This book examines the ways textual and visual representations of those houses continuously and reflexively created, re-created, and reinforced midcentury notions about racial, ethnic, and class identities—specifically, the rightness of associating white identities with homeownership and citizenship. By looking carefully at house form and at representations of house form, I seek to understand the ways in which postwar domestic environments became poignant ciphers for whiteness, affluence, belonging, and a sense of permanent stability. The house and garden, and their representations, therefore appear as the material dimensions through which racial and class identity and difference are recursively constructed, assumed, and negotiated.

Much (but not all) of the material that forms the basis for the analysis in this book is utterly commonplace, ubiquitous, and accessible: mass-circulation magazine and catalog articles and images; builders', architects', and trade journals; advertisements; ordinary household objects and artifacts; and the kinds of ordinary houses and gardens seen in nearly every suburb and small town in the United States. They constitute an enormous body of seemingly mundane representations and material forms that are (or were) often encountered, viewed, and experienced as part of the ordinary activities of everyday life—"seamlessly sutured into the material

FACING
An ordinary postwar house, Urbana, Illinois. Date and architect unknown. Photograph by the author.

practices of ordinary life," as Robert Hariman and John Lucaites put it.[1] And because they are so pervasive and seemingly ordinary as to become critically unobserved, these representational and material forms constitute powerful ideological devices. They have much to tell us, not only about the ways such representations, objects, and sites constructed and reinforced specific national policies and economic and social structures, but also about how they served as justification and substantiation for ways of imagining Americans of various racial, ethnic, and class backgrounds at midcentury.

I am particularly interested here in understanding how these familiar images, words, objects, and sites operated—and perhaps continue to operate—to construct a sense of the raced and classed past, present, and even future. As W. J. T. Mitchell wrote nearly twenty years ago, we must ask not simply what representations *mean* but "what they *do* in a network of social relations" in order to understand more fully the ways representations "work in our culture." Mitchell urges us to understand all representations as "relay mechanisms in exchanges of power, value, and publicity" and to consider in our analyses the roles played by the knowledge industries that produce these representations.[2] That is one particular goal of this study.

This book focuses exclusively on houses and representations produced during the fifteen-year period bracketed by the end of World War II and the beginning of the 1960s. Many of the issues I examine—concerns for domestic privacy, cleanliness, order, and family togetherness, to name a few—are not unique to this period. In fact, most have roots that can be traced to at least the nineteenth century if not earlier, and numerous architectural historians have indeed studied those issues in relation to American house form in the nineteenth and early twentieth centuries.[3] However, significant changes in the economy and culture of the immediate postwar period make this fifteen-year span ripe for a focused study that examines the particular ways in which those concerns were renewed and played out within the context of the private single-family home. The postwar economic boom and the federal financing and mortgage insurance programs that made that housing available to millions of first-time homeowners created fertile ground for a renewed and often rearticulated focus on the links among homeownership, citizenship, and racial and class identity. They also led to a significant rise in the production of representations related to the iconographic field that is my focus here. In the chapters that follow, I examine the houses made possible by those federal programs, and I also examine the reasons behind the rearticulation of specific values and ideals.

The fifteen-year period that frames this study is also especially well suited to an examination of the links among houses, representations, and race, for this was a time of significant shifts in racial thinking. Throughout this book, I use the term *race* to indicate a set of socially constructed categories that are, like the built environment, based in human experience, historically contingent, and rooted to questions about the formation of identities. In examining these issues, I join a growing number of scholars who study the connections that exist between the spatial world/built environment and the construction of race and white identities. Like them, I seek to understand the ways in which power and injustice operate so that I can contribute to dismantling them. I do this for several reasons. First, I believe, as does Matthew Jacobson, that "racism, as Alexander Saxton writes, is 'fundamentally a theory of history.' . . . It is a theory of . . . who belongs and who does not, of who deserves what and who is capable of what." If, as Jacobson insists, it is the historian's task "to discover which racial categories are useful to whom at a given moment, and why," then we might productively ask ourselves what whiteness meant, what it stood for, and what it embodied in the postwar housing market.[4] Like Jacobson, I also believe that because "race is a public fiction" (in the sense that it is a highly fluid social construction) that is also "a kind of social currency," evaluations of the ways race is defined, expressed, and represented in the public sphere become crucial to an understanding of the persuasive power and influence of the iconographic fields that pertain to race and whiteness.[5] To borrow the words of Michael Omi and Howard Winant, it is not possible "to acknowledge or oppose racism without comprehending the sociohistorical context in which concepts of race are invoked."[6] I seek here to elucidate one such sociohistorical context. I will say more about this in the text that follows.

Second, I engage these very charged questions about race and whiteness because I believe that architecture and the visual world always belong to and circulate within—indeed construct—the political, economic, and social worlds in which we live. Architecture is not benign, even (and sometimes especially) when it is spectacularly beautiful or when it is so ordinary we hardly notice it. And architecture is about race even (and perhaps especially) when it is situated in an all-white suburb—a fact that architectural historians have tended to overlook completely. I therefore write against these beliefs, but also against the strong current of discourse that continues to be produced in many professional schools of design that encourages future architects, planners, and landscape architects to ignore issues pertaining to social justice and the built environment and to relegate questions about race and its social, economic, and political implications to the outer peripheries or completely outside their classrooms, studios, and practices. If it seems to some readers that I see race everywhere in this study, perhaps my view can serve as a necessary corrective to the extensive body of architectural histories that have seen race nowhere.

THE ORDINARY POSTWAR HOUSE

Although numerous studies have focused on the history of housing segregation and the history of suburban planning in which those practices are embedded, no previous studies have addressed the specific ways in which ideas about the racialization of such houses were communicated and circulated or their potential impact on the construction of American culture. This book does so, by examining a range of published texts, images, media forms, and houses themselves, mining the wealth of information embedded in such sources. Unlike the typical narratives of architectural history, which normally include well-known architects, wealthy clients, and sensational houses, this book takes an approach that is far less glamorous but certainly more relevant to a broad spectrum of American lives. I focus here primarily on ordinary houses—that is, houses that were not designed by architects as custom homes but were instead designed and built by merchant builders or developers for a mass audience or by homeowners for themselves. Instead of adopting a regional focus, I have chosen a national scope for this study, using a set of broad themes to structure my analysis. I do this because, as stated earlier, I am interested in understanding the formation of an American iconography of race and class as it related to postwar houses and homeownership and as it circulated in various forms of mass and popular media. This iconography, as I will show, was not regionally specific, but existed and circulated in media intended for a nationwide audience.

Certainly, a regionally specific study would yield important findings. It might engage the ways in which specific local immigrant communities influenced house form and housing markets, and it might also elucidate some important ways in which racial categories—including whiteness—might be inflected by regional histories. But that is not my task here. Although California, for example, was a veritable laboratory of experimentation in postwar house and garden design, new housing appeared nationwide after 1945, and some of the most interesting developments that were truly intended for a mass audience (as opposed to experiments in high-style design, paid for by wealthy patrons or museum sponsorship) happened all over the country. The Midwest, for example, was an important location for the development of new housing ideas for the average buyer. The participants in the University of Illinois Small Homes Council produced an extraordinary number of experimental houses and studies of postwar dwellings, and they disseminated plans both locally through circulars and nationally through magazines such as *Popular Mechanics*.[7] As a result, experimental houses were constructed throughout Chicago's hinterlands, and readers across the United States purchased plans from magazines and followed their do-it-yourself construction

the PM Modern

This contemporary home with low-slung roof and sweeping lines provides 1344 square feet of living area. It has three intriguing courts. The facade gives no hint that it is a split-level home

the PM Traditional

Picturesque and inviting is this modified Cape Cod farmhouse design. It has 1850 square feet of living area with three bedrooms on the second floor. Modern touches include family room

guides. Moreover, research villages constructed in Illinois and Michigan and publicized in national shelter and women's magazines spread innovative construction ideas throughout the region, and early suburbs such as Park Forest, Illinois, gained acclaim and publicity for a range of innovations that received coverage in the national media, including television.

Merchant builders such as the Levitts published their designs in both popular and trade magazines. Their designs and construction ideas circulated rapidly throughout the country, and they were used and adapted by builders nationwide.[8] Indeed, builders relied on these magazines to help them learn about the most significant housing trends in various regions, which they then replicated in their own locales. The houses they produced may not have appeared as identical replicas of those they aimed to copy, but the ideas about houses circulated nationally. Those ideas—those rhetorical strategies—are my focus in this book. Because interesting developments in ordinary house construction occurred nationwide, I avoid concentrating on any particular region.

My criteria for including houses in this study are as follows: they had to have been at least intended for an imagined mass audience of middle-class homeowners, and they had to have been priced within reach of most middle-class Americans during the fifteen-year period examined. The price ranges for such ordinary houses varied to some extent and depended primarily on location, just as they also increased over the period of the study. The U.S. census for 1950 found that the national median value of urban and rural nonfarm dwellings was $7,354. By 1960, the median value of a similarly located home owned by whites rose to $12,900, but the median value for a "nonwhite" home in the same period was only $6,700.[9] The Census Bureau's figures can serve as a fair guide for the price ranges for the houses considered in this book, except for those built by architects as part of special developments or projects that were meant as experiments that would eventually translate to a mass housing market. The census figures also bluntly indicate the vast disparity in property values that existed between homes owned by whites and homes owned by anyone identified as nonwhite.

Instead of avant-garde plans and dramatic settings, I examine plans for common houses and dwellings intended to be common houses. I look at the clever ways ordinary builders and homeowners found to store all the new items families acquired for their modest dwellings and the cultural dimensions and significance of taste and display as upwardly mobile citizens adapted their living conditions to the new and largely optimistic consumer world of the 1950s. Instead of high-style design, then, I largely examine the ways ordinary house form and its representations served as an index of identity, authenticity (however constructed), and belonging during a time of cultural transition vis-à-vis notions of race/ethnicity and middle-class identity.

An ordinary postwar house, Urbana, Illinois. Date and architect unknown. Note the picture window and the storage wall that supports the shed roof of the carport. Photograph by the author.

Although I intend this primarily as a study of ordinary houses, this book also includes some examples of dwellings that were designed by well-known architects and that were a cut above what could be strictly designated as ordinary. Custom-designed houses were and still are the exception in the American cultural landscape, and most Americans of the postwar period could not afford them. However, the ideals presented in popular publications, on television, and through tours of custom-designed houses affected the ways Americans considered and understood their own, more ordinary dwellings and their own racial and class identities. Custom-designed houses thus have a place in this book, especially those that were intended to serve as models

This dream home in stuccoed masonry, consisting of cabinet kitchen, two bedrooms, living room, bathroom and utility room, complete with laundry and heating plant, is yours for less than $3650 if you build it yourself. Block construction is within the ability of an average man

Concrete block house, 1949. Immediate postwar models frequently included less than 1,000 square feet of space and had traditionally configured plans. Courtesy of *Popular Mechanics*; originally published in the May 1949 issue.

for mass community builders. But I also examine houses built from stock plans that could be purchased through the mail from magazines or lumber companies. Occasionally, therefore, the names of well-known architects appear, especially those who were truly and persistently interested in building homes for the masses.

Despite the suburban locations of most of the houses

and gardens that form this book's subject, this is not a history of suburban planning and development; that subject has received significant scholarly attention elsewhere.[10] I also largely avoid the usual subjects of suburban vernacular histories simply because they too have already received the attention of scholars of midcentury domesticity: William Levitt's housing tracts thus receive less attention here, but houses by unknown developers, lawns, television programs, magazine advertisements, and questions about the storage and display of material artifacts receive more.

Ubiquitous though they may be in the North American suburban landscape, postwar houses have been the subject of very few studies, especially from the perspective I take here. The corpus of scholarly literature that examines the specific material qualities of ordinary postwar houses is surprisingly small, and studies that include analyses of the race and class dimensions I privilege here are virtually nonexistent.[11] Indeed, the real paucity of rigorous scholarly studies that focus on the history of ordinary postwar houses posed a significant challenge as I conducted research for this book. Because so little scholarship exists on ordinary postwar dwellings, I have made efforts to elucidate the forms and spaces typical of so many of these homes. Although recent scholarship by historians has included extensive discussion of the social production of space, few historians have actually looked at the concrete nature of space itself in that production process. In this book I examine the spaces, surfaces, materials, forms, and enclosures of our everyday lives and the ways they, along with their representations, contribute to cultural constructions of racial and class identities. Moreover, in examining the visual culture related to postwar housing and interiors, I have found that issues related to class, race, and gender are central. Identity politics is a hallmark of post-

war American life, and to ignore this issue within the context of the midcentury house seems, at least to me, impossible.

THE CULTURAL WORK OF REPRESENTATIONS

This book examines the cultural work performed by houses and domestic artifacts intended for a middle-class audience and by textual and visual representations of those houses that entered mainstream culture between 1945 and 1960 in the United States. As such, it is intended as a contribution to various fields of inquiry that examine the production of American (U.S.) cultural iconography and its impact on American cultural formations. Questions about residential architecture remain at the book's core, but this is not a traditional architectural history of postwar houses in the United States, although I hope it might point to some new directions for the production of scholarship in that field. Instead, this book examines the roles of the visual and material fields related to postwar houses in constituting and reinforcing ideas about race, ethnicity, and class in American postwar culture as they related to ideas about homeownership.

Like some scholars working in the fields of American studies, visual culture studies, material culture studies, communication, and rhetoric (among others), I am particularly interested here in the symbolic practices, iconographic formations, and rhetorical strategies embedded in the visual field created between 1945 and 1960 that included houses as a primary subject. The idea that the visual and material fields possess constitutive power related to the formation of identities (personal, family, community, national) that are deeply linked to the construction of race, class, and gender has become an acknowledged commonplace among scholars in the above-listed fields during the past decade.[12]

As with other rhetorical forms, such as public discourse, I use the evidence marshaled herein to understand—as have scholars such as Robert Hariman and John Louis Lucaites—the ways that cultural ideals circulate through "structures of representation that can be labeled rhetorical, ideological, aesthetic, political, and more. Public texts are complex mediations of experience. In every case the focus is on how the material practice enables and constrains actors and audiences alike as they try to acquire knowledge, apply values, and otherwise do the work of making agreements and building public consent."[13] In short, this book aims to understand how these images, texts, objects, and sites functioned in the creation and substantiation of specific forms of U.S. culture and cultural life in the second half of the twentieth century.

Studies that link visual culture to rhetorical suasion are, in general, more easily found and perhaps more well-known than studies that include analyses of buildings and designed landscapes as rhetorically powerful tools that actively shape history and culture. However, studies of the latter type are not absent, and a significant corpus of scholarship on the architectural history of all periods, produced in the past thirty years (and even earlier), points toward the importance of the built environment in shaping public opinion, perception, and belief about a range of cultural conditions. We might profitably call these studies in "spatial rhetoric(s)," but they all fall neatly within the purview of the increasingly methodologically capacious field of architectural history. The approach I take in this book builds on and contributes to this tradition of scholarship, using ordinary houses and gardens as the focus for understanding the rhetorical work performed by the built world instead of examining more elite spaces such as palaces, villas, grand estates, churches and cathedrals, national capitals, and municipal and government buildings. I do not contend that buildings/houses are experienced in the same ways as visual or textual representations—indeed, they are seen, experienced, and understood in highly complex and multiple ways that are likewise historically contingent—but I examine them here as material facets of a complex iconographic field that also includes visual and textual representations of houses.

Given this focus, readers will rightfully ask questions about the specific ways various audiences may have received and understood these multiple forms. How much can we really assume or know about the impacts of sets of images (for example) on specific or even vaguely defined audiences of midcentury Americans? As Hariman and Lucaites note: "This issue will always remain a matter of debate . . . [one] that should be happening continually. Healthy democracies are those where citizens are accustomed to arguing thoughtfully about how they are influenced." Multitudes of individual responses may be impossible to recover, but they are also not necessarily relevant to my task. Instead, I seek to understand the operation of the evidence I have herein marshaled in the formation of a U.S. public culture. I want to know, as do Hariman and Lucaites, how these multiple forms

> reproduce ideology, communicate social knowledge, shape collective memory, model citizenship, and provide figural resources for communicative action. . . . What is important in this view is to recognize how the dominant codes articulate dominant social relationships and that the distinctive ideological effect is the formation of subjective identity consistent with that social structure. . . . the combination of mainstream recognition, wide circulation, and emotional impact is a proven formula for reproducing a society's social order.[14]

Midcentury Americans may or may not have questioned the pervasive whiteness of the subjects portrayed in association with mass-circulated images of houses, for example, and they may or may not have embraced the various practices that resulted in a largely segregated midcentury housing market. But they certainly viewed those images within the complicated historical context of the pre–civil rights United States. My point is not that all viewers shared a common perception of these images, but that, as Martin Berger has recently noted, "they built their distinctive visions on a shared racial bedrock that few whites questioned."[15] Americans most certainly viewed their world variously, yet it was also commonplace at midcentury (as it in some respects remains) for them to construct their world around the then accepted social, economic, and political constructions of race. It is therefore safe to say that the ways Americans read images of all kinds was influenced not just by what they saw on the page or on the television screen but also by their own racial values and by the historical circumstances of their moment.

I am, therefore, specifically interested in the mechanics of the operation of this ideological field. Instead of the more common theoretical formulations that posit the necessity for unveiling or unmasking ideologies that are imagined to be hidden in completely naturalized, and therefore invisible, cultural forms, I adopt instead Slavoj Žižek's notion of ideological cynicism. Žižek essentially formulated a critique of Marx's well-known statement about ideology from *Capital* ("They do not know it, but they are doing it."). For Žižek, Marx's ideological framework depends on a subjective naïveté that can neither see nor recognize the supposed reality that is being manipulated or distorted. He claims that later critics of Marx, such as members of the Frankfurt School, productively complicated Marx's formulation by emphasizing the importance of not simply "throwing away the distorting spectacles of ideology; the main point is to see how the reality itself cannot reproduce itself without this so-called ideological mystification. The mask is not simply hiding the real state of things; the ideological distortion is written into its very essence."[16] Žižek, however, takes this one step further in his formulation of ideological cynicism, which is based, in part, on the writings of Peter Sloterdijk. Žižek writes:

> The cynical subject is quite aware of the distance between the ideological mask and the social reality, but he none the less still insists upon the mask. The formula, as proposed by Sloterdijk, would then be: "they know very well what they are doing, but still, they are doing it." Cynical reason is no longer naïve, but is a paradox of an enlightened false consciousness: one knows the falsehood very well, one is well aware of a particular interest hidden behind the ideological universality, but still one does not renounce it.[17]

And he later states: "Belief supports the fantasy which regulates social reality."[18]

In this book, then, I employ Žižek's theoretical framework to examine the ways a specific ideological and rhetorical field regulated the social realities of race and class as they intersected with the realm of postwar domesticity and the residential sphere. I assert and attempt to demonstrate in the pages that follow that a pervasive iconography of white, middle-class domesticity that circulated widely in various media and that became instantiated in thousands of houses nationwide served to reinforce and to continuously and reflexively create and re-create midcentury notions about racial and class identity, and specifically about the rightness of associating white identities with homeownership and citizenship. Like Sloterdijk and Žižek, I do not presume that Americans were naive or completely unable to see or recognize the exclusionary rhetoric that was embedded in these cultural forms. Instead, I work from a belief that the vast majority of midcentury Americans knew and deeply understood the economic value, political authority, and social clout invested in white identities; that white Americans of European descent were likewise so committed to the national formulation of whiteness that they saw it everywhere, acknowledged it only in exceptional instances, and participated in the privileges it conveyed largely without question; that they understood the racial logic of the segregated housing market and its long-term implications for themselves and their families; that, in short, "they knew very well what they were doing, and still, they were doing it."[19]

I do not state this as an indictment, or as an assumption that all Americans were or are openly or even consciously racist, although many scholars who study race claim that to live as a white person in the United States is to be unable to escape a range of fundamentally racist practices. What I do assert, following the work of those same scholars, is that white Americans have tended not to see, think about, or acknowledge their unearned privileges, nor have they tended to examine the ways in which their white identities are socially constructed and culturally reinforced. In short, white Americans have seen themselves as entirely unracialized, their spaces as race-neutral. This book aims to contribute to the literature that examines the social construction of white identities and the vast and complicated implications that dismantling whiteness holds for the attainment of social, economic, and political justice in the United States.

RACE/ETHNICITY AND SPACE

It may seem strange to search for the spatial cues of racial/ethnic construction in the banal, and seemingly benign, setting of the ordinary house. Moreover, some historians will find the analysis of racial and class formation that I attempt here uncomfortable, as much of what I examine is, to some extent, literally invisible, as with the absence of nonwhites in mass-media images of newly constructed postwar houses. Yet that very invisibility, as I have mentioned above, is one of the key signals that indicates the operation of racialization in the popular consciousness.[20] If historians have too rarely examined space and the built environment as critical agents in the formation of culture, architectural and landscape historians have far too seldom considered race in the development of their historical narratives. That space is constitutive of culture is now a widely accepted notion among scholars in the humanities; by extension, space is equally significant in the construction of ideas about race and identity, since these are cultural products as well. This line of inquiry has become the focus of important works by geographers and by scholars in the fields of American studies and ethnic studies. Scholars in all fields who study race now follow the model for understanding racial formation that is perhaps best known from the work of Michael Omi and Howard Winant, who assert that race must be understood as

an unstable and "decentered" complex of social meanings constantly being transformed by political struggle. . . . *race is a concept which signifies and symbolizes social conflicts and interests by referring to different types of human bodies.* Although the concept of race invokes biologically based human characteristics (so-called "phenotypes"), selection of these particular human features for purposes of racial signification is always and necessarily a social and historical process. . . . there is no biological basis for distinguishing among human groups along the lines of race. Indeed, the categories employed to differentiate among human groups along racial lines reveal themselves, upon serious examination, to be at best imprecise, and at worst completely arbitrary.

Omi and Winant posit their theory of racial formation "as the sociohistorical process by which racial categories are inhabited, transformed, and destroyed."[21]

Geographers such as David Delaney, Audrey Kobayashi, Linda Peake, Laura Pulido, Richard Schein, Owen Dwyer, Laura Barraclough, James Duncan, and Nancy Duncan have all contributed to our understanding "of how space works to condition the operation of power and the constitution of relational identities . . . [and to] help to highlight the critical importance of racialized space to other aspects of American life."[22] These scholars have examined at multiple scales the complex relationships that exist between space and the construction of race, but it is more usual to see such studies conducted at the scale of the nation, the state, or the city. This book aims instead, and somewhat unusually, to focus on both the microscale of the house and its material artifacts and the macroscale of the nationwide circulation of ideas about race and housing.

Although my focus here is on houses of the postwar era, by 1945 the connections forged among homeownership, white identities, and citizenship had existed for decades in the United States, with the precise alignment of white identities and ideas about home shifting according to both time and locale. A fairly large body of multidisciplinary scholarship already exists that links design, construction, homeownership, and home furnishing to identity formation. Scholars in fields such as cultural geography, anthropology, and environment/behavior research acknowledge that, as James Duncan and David Lambert have written, "homes . . . are primarily sites in which identities are produced and performed in practical, material and repetitively reaffirming ways."[23] The representations I examine here both announced and replicated these. And the idea that residence is a crucial site for racial identity formation is borne out by the work of scholars such as David Freund, who has examined the links between homeownership and white identities, and Karyn Lacy, whose middle-class black subjects in her ethnographic study all believed that "black social spaces and residential places [are] crucial sites for the construction of black racial identities."[24] With the increase in popular media directed at new and prospective homeowners, the media and homeowners became mutually related actors: media informed and homeowners/builders performed ideas related to race and class that were recursive and mutually constitutive.

If homeownership was historically the single most important symbol of achievement and belonging, it was not always or necessarily symbolic of middle-class identity, but was instead more deeply connected to notions of security for earlier immigrants and working-class Americans of the late nineteenth and early twentieth centuries. Homeownership served as a safeguard against the vicissitudes of unfair landlords, unpredictable rents, and homelessness. A home of one's own could also serve as a predictable and safe bank, an investment that represented security against uncertain times. Owning a house was the surest way to cement one's (and one's family's) inclusion in the nation.[25] But the race riots that took place in cities such as Detroit and Chicago in the 1910s and 1920s indicate that ideas about homeownership as an exclusively white privilege were already deeply embedded in the American consciousness by those early decades of the twentieth century; indeed, Americans were by that time willing to resort to violence to protect that notion.[26] As David Roediger has indicated, racially restrictive covenants that barred anyone not identified as white from purchasing homes in specific neighborhoods existed from the 1870s. They arose largely from

> a specific fear of black residents and exempted new immigrants from restrictions. . . . Under law, the vast majority of new immigrants were secure in their Caucasian identities. . . . The principal exception in this regard was the exclusion of Jews, especially from some new suburban developments and

rental properties. . . . By far the most important feature of the covenant was its firm linking of white racial status with property. . . . It was precisely in the automatic connection of white and neighbor that restrictive covenants, and Jim Crow housing generally, most poisoned new immigrant attitudes regarding race.[27]

No study of postwar domestic environments in the United States should exclude race, even if racial difference is seldom actually pictured in representations of domesticity from the period. Its very absence speaks remarkably loudly, once we begin to look and read more carefully. Anyone who spends any time at all examining the literature from the period must come away with a powerful sense of the consistent character of the subjects depicted. Over and over, the houses and gardens are peopled by well-dressed, well-groomed whites. This is, of course, not surprising since, with relatively few exceptions, whites were the only people with access to new suburban housing in this period. Advertisers and publishers understandably targeted the market they understood to be cultivable, expandable. As advertising specialist Arthur Dix wrote in 1957, "Advertising should be directed at those who buy."[28] And those who bought new houses were largely white. Some new housing did exist for inner-city nonwhites as the result of slum clearance associated with urban renewal

ABOVE The cover illustration for the October 1957
issue of *Popular Mechanics* depicts white homeowners
with their property. Courtesy of *Popular Mechanics*.
RIGHT The cover illustration for the October 1954 issue of *Popular Mechanics* features white homeowners. Courtesy of *Popular Mechanics*.

programs. These programs led to large-scale minority housing displacement across the country and the subsequent "solution" of new housing in high-rise public housing projects. Moreover, examples existed of black housing developments that were constructed during the postwar period, along with scattered developments that were unrestricted.[29] But the spatialized American Dream of the single-family detached home remained primarily, to use Roediger's terms, "white, unless marked otherwise."[30]

HOUSING AND RACE

The fifteen-year period that frames this study is especially well suited to an examination of the links between housing and race. The years leading up to the civil rights movement saw the emergence and ascendancy of the idea of ethnicity as at least a partial replacement for some racial categories, specifically those pertaining to Jews.[31] As Omi and Winant have noted, ethnicity theory emerged in the 1920s, challenging the then prevailing notions of race that were based in biological arguments and in social Darwinist theories.[32] But the postwar period saw the decisive shift toward ethnicity as a substitute for these older models of race thinking, resulting in part from U.S. reactions to the Holocaust.[33] Ideas about race and ethnicity are fluid, but this specific shift is significant because it resulted in what Matthew Jacobson has called "a compelling

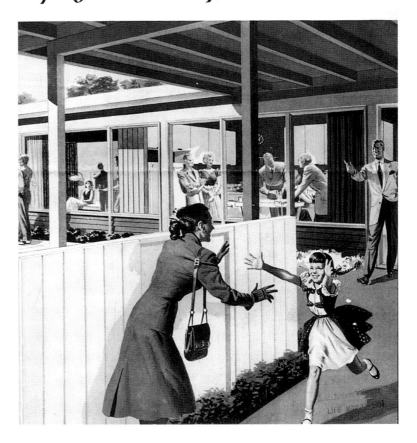

An advertisement for Ranger homes in 1954 features white homeowners and their guests. Courtesy of the D'Arcy Collection of the Communications Library of the University of Illinois at Urbana–Champaign.

indeterminacy" to some racialized questions. Instead of a United States shaped exclusively by a black/white binary, Jacobson's work proposes a more complicated, nuanced, and fluctuating white/other binary. Indeed, the production and constitution of racial binaries in the United States is both ongoing and messy, but what matters for this study is the role played by houses and the material and visual culture attendant to houses in the production of racial thinking. As recent scholarship indicates, whiteness is not defined by skin color alone, since appearance has not always determined racial identity in the United States or elsewhere. For example, members of the working classes and immigrant European workers were once regarded as other than white and as biologically different. Moreover, as Karen Brodkin has demonstrated, Jews were not considered "white" in the United States until sometime after the immediate postwar period. The ability to own a home in the suburbs was a sign of belonging to the middle class, and to belong to that class was to be further bleached. Indeed, Brodkin positions the suburbs as the site in which Jews learned "the ways of whiteness" through the help of "radio, magazines, and the new TV."[34] But they also learned those lessons from the spaces of the houses and gardens in which they lived every day. Houses, and the literature and media representations surrounding them, coached immigrants in the assimilation and whitening process. They defined expectations to live by

through the spaces of daily domestic life and the objects and surfaces that filled those spaces. Representations of houses joined the houses themselves to provide articulations of the expected and hoped-for occupants for postwar housing. That Jews and some other ethnic groups were newly identified as white during the 1950s was not the result of any broad societal acceptance of difference; rather, it was related to the groups' ability and desire to assimilate and blend—to become white.[35] As I show in the chapters that follow, the issues that resulted from this identity shift were clearly legible in the literature, marketing, and forms of ordinary houses and gardens.

If the formulation of whiteness varies according to time and space, it is nearly always constructed against and through a set of imaginary notions of what it might mean to be "other." As Stuart Hall has written, racism is a "structure of knowledge and representations" that are based on ideas about and that are used to generate understandings of a fixed "us" in opposition to and in a separate space from "them."[36] Identity construction is a complex process, but it relies, at least in part, on "negotiations with representational economies" and determinations about what one is not.[37] Since all identities remain in flux, any such determination depends on the creation of stereotypical images, of an "ethnic absolutism" that defies individuation and ultimately defies rights to human dignity.[38] For example, for cen-

An ordinary postwar house, Urbana, Illinois. Date and architect unknown. Photograph by the author.

turies blackness was both imagined and represented in specific ways (described in chapter 1) that were likewise linked to material, spatial, and of course corporeal attributes.[39] My point is that the spectrum of signifiers through which whiteness is created and re-created depends on the ability of whites to identify what they are not in equal measure to deciding what they are, and that these signifiers have existed in the spatial and visual realm for centuries.

Overwhelmingly, the evidence collected and examined by historians in a range of fields now indicates that the private single-family home on its own lot in an exclusive suburb signaled a specifically formulated kind of racial and class identity that was likewise inextricably linked to cultural authority. As David Freund has demonstrated, "advocates of racial exclusion regularly used the terms 'homeowner,' 'citizen,' 'voter,' and 'white' interchangeably," and this conflation of the terms came about in the postwar United States as a result of carefully constructed government housing and economic policies.[40]

HOUSES AND CLASS

Although questions about the formation of racial/ethnic identity are central to this book, questions about class structure and development are equally significant. In his important 1963 text on suburbia, sociologist William Dobriner took class as a given—indeed, as the central category for analysis of postwar suburban life. He asserted that suburbs are highly variable communities and that the only meaningful analysis to be constructed is one based on class. Significantly for this study, he also noted that "hardly any aspect of material culture or social relationships escapes the omnipresent and searching eye of evaluation. Religions, races, cities, names, neckties, families, occupations, neighborhoods, colleges, accents, manners, cars, haircuts, speech—all are ranked on a subjective continuum of social values."[41]

What Dobriner's generation of scholars had yet to realize or articulate fully was the extent to which race and class are deeply intertwined. Indeed, as Stuart Hall and Paul Gilroy have written, "race is the modality in which class is lived," and "gender is the modality in which race is lived."[42] Race, class, and gender are mutually constitutive categories in identity formation, and each can serve as an amplifier for the others. Being poor, or female, for example, frequently amplifies and multiplies the racist practices enacted against persons of color.[43] In this book, I show how houses and the visual and textual representations about houses served these modalities that continuously and reflexively linked race, class, and gender. As Susan Ruddick has written, shifting our

> view of gender, race, and class as separate and distinct systems to intersecting systems has moved scholarship away from arid, endless debates that attempted to identify which system was predominant in the final instance. Scholars in black and cultural studies and black feminist writers have moved this analysis one step further, from an understanding of how gender, race, and class *intersect within* individuals in the structuring of social identities to an analysis of how these positions *interlock between* individuals, as notions of the appropriate roles and behaviors of different social groups have evolved in relation to one another, in what they call *interlocking systems of oppression*.[44]

Gender constructions are highly racialized, and in my analysis of space I aim to consider them consistently as such. The gendered aspect of domestic environments has received far more attention than issues pertaining to class and especially to race, and this book's focus is not specifically on gender. However, women were the primary daytime occupants of postwar houses, and, as such, they are implicitly key players throughout this book.

Much like race, class is an inherently unstable category for analysis. U.S. census data suggest that social class and occupation (blue-collar versus white-collar) are equivalent and correlated to income. However, class formation and definitions of class in the postwar United States were far more complex and fluid than these data might suggest. Although occupation, income, and homeownership serve as significant markers of both class and race in the United States, none of these constitute determining factors for class identity, because both class and race were and are social constructions forged through a range of complex everyday practices and group relationships, economic structures, and material artifacts that serve as indexes of social status. In the postwar era especially, definitions of what it meant to be "middle-class" changed along with a general increase in economic security for whites, an increase in disposable income that led to greater access to material possessions that conveyed social status, and increased access to homeownership.[45] Homeownership alone constituted a specific means for establishing status, and though it did not necessarily provide an immediate ticket to middle-class identity, it certainly conferred a strong connection to at least the promise of upward mobility and of acceptance into the dominant and growing economic majority.[46] For those who were leaving behind blue-collar and/or immigrant backgrounds, the house became a potent symbol of acceptance and an instrument of aspiration to a broader range of opportunities. The configuration, decor, possessions, and maintenance of the house (and the labor involved in that maintenance) all provided opportunities to convey a range of images and lifestyles. Inner-city apartment dwelling, noise, crowding, smells, and manual labor all spoke of a working-class past and ethnic origins. Little proclaimed whiteness, class stability, and citizenship quite like a house of one's own in the suburbs.

In this book, then, I also examine the ways ordinary houses were intended to transcend and even sometimes obscure middle-majority Americans' lower-economic, working-class, and ethnic or racial roots, and/or their efforts never to return to their prewar lives and conditions. By looking carefully at house form and at representations of house form, I seek to understand the extent to which postwar domestic environments were a poignant cipher for whiteness, at least modest affluence, citizenship, and a sense of permanence. The house and garden, and their representations, therefore appear as the material dimension through which racial and class identity and difference are recursively constructed, assumed, and negotiated.

Because class is an inherently fluid category—one that is constantly being renegotiated and reconfigured by individuals and by the societies and cultures in which they are immersed—it is also inherently difficult to discuss or analyze in concrete terms. As Barbara Ehrenreich has indicated in her study of American class formation:

> Class is a notion that is inherently fuzzy at the edges. When we talk about class, we are making a generalization about large groups of people, and about how they live and make their livings. Since there are so many borderline situations, and since people do move up and down between classes, a description like middle class may mean very little when applied to a particular individual. But it should tell us something about the broad terrain of inequality, and about how people are clustered, very roughly, at different levels of comfort, status, and control over their lives.[47]

Class also tells us about aspirations, about how people conceptualize their identities, and about the distribution of power at various scales. Martha Gimenez theorizes that it is "the connections between class and experiences that gave rise to identity politics," and she notes Weber's emphasis on property ownership as key to "class situations" and the importance of "status situations." Of Weber's theory, Gimenez writes that it is at the level of appearances and practices that "people spontaneously become conscious of their place in the structures of inequality that produce and reproduce those appearances and shape their lives. Most people in the United States seem to be Weberians from birth, understanding class differences mainly in terms of 'lifestyles' made possible by their socioeconomic status . . . and membership in status groups such as gender, race, and ethnicity."[48] In this book, by focusing on the house and its representations, I hope to elucidate some essential aspects of class formation and its links to these lifestyles and appearances, along with its links to racial and ethnic identity at the scale of the individual (though this is treated generically), the neighborhood, and the nation.

According to Richard Polenberg, 1950s critics of suburban life such as William Whyte believed that the suburbs were places where "class distinctions dissolved and ethnic attachments evaporated." Polenberg notes that "class distinctions did not disappear in the suburbs. The range of classes was considerably narrower, however, and the means of telling them apart somewhat more difficult." Although "suburbs exhibited no single pattern with respect to ethnic adaptation . . . [they were] typified by a narrowing of the range of ethnic groups but not by any diminution of an awareness of differences within that range."[49] Indeed, and contrary to Whyte's assertion, awareness of differences could be categorized as acute in the suburban postwar context, whether that awareness extended to class, gender, sexuality, or ethnic and racial distinctions.

A NOTE ON SOURCES

Despite my inclusion of descriptions of my grandparents' house, which I use to provide a detailed sense of one particular postwar house and because I believe my grandparents' experience adds a degree of nuance to the black/white binary that characterizes many studies of race and housing and helps to illustrate the contingencies of Jewish identities with regard to whiteness in this period, this book should not be mistaken for an ethnographically based study, nor is it an economic analysis of postwar housing. Trained as an architectural historian, and having spent much of my career analyzing prints, drawings, and photographs as well as spaces, I have reached into a range of disciplines—as noted above—to obtain answers to the complex questions I have formulated about postwar houses and the iconographic field attendant to those houses. We certainly need ethnographic studies of postwar houses, just as we could benefit from some rigorously conducted economic analyses of houses and the housing market in the same period. However, I am trained neither as an ethnographer nor as an economist, and my skills are best put to use in the examination of the visual, material, and built worlds. I therefore rely here primarily on those forms of evidence and leave it to future scholars with expertise that extends beyond my own to create studies based on ethnographic and economic data.

Ordinary house plans and documents about such houses rarely find their way into archives, so the traditional sources on which architectural historians typically rely are seldom available for those who wish to study these forms. As examined in detail in the chapters that follow, a range of nationally circulating publications intended for both specialized and mass audiences serve as important sources for this study, especially since I am concerned with the construction of an American iconography of race and class and its impact on the formation of U.S. culture. Although those primary sources are important to this study, I have also made use of a wide range of archives and other resources for this project, including papers and collections maintained by the National Association of Home Builders; the Museum of Television and Radio/Paley Center for New Media, New York; the National Museum of American History Archives Center; the Horticultural Division of the Archives of American Gardens at the Smithsonian Institution; the Chicago History Museum; the Wisconsin Historical Society Archives/ NBC Collection; the College of Environmental Design Archives at the University of California, Berkeley; the

Huntington Library Photographic Collection; the Francis Loeb Library Special Collections at Harvard University; the Sackler Museum Archives; the Ryerson and Burnham Archive at the Art Institute of Chicago; the U.S. Gypsum Corporate Archives; the A. Quincy Jones archives in the private collection of Elaine Sewell Jones (consulted before her death); the Clare Barrows papers (in the private collection of her family); government documents related to trading stamp regulation; and the Building Research Council Archives at the University of Illinois. Some of these collections contain drawings, pamphlets, and clippings related to postwar houses; others contain documentation about editorial processes at shelter magazines; some house rare film (now converted to video or to digital formats) of early television programming concerning postwar houses and gardens; still others contain information about the intersection of corporate interests and the building industries with the questions I ask here.

The inaccessibility of the corporate archives for some of the journals used in this study, such as *House Beautiful* and *Popular Mechanics*, made answering some questions a real challenge. Fortunately, I was able to locate some important primary source documents pertaining to editorial and managerial decisions in alternative locations. *House Beautiful*'s editor, Elizabeth Gordon, for example, corresponded with photographers such as Maynard Parker and with landscape architects such as Thomas Church, so their archives also contain limited Gordon correspondence. Gordon left a very small collection of her papers to the archives of the Sackler and Freer Galleries of Art/Smithsonian Institution, and these also proved useful.

Houses themselves constituted important sources of information as well, and I have drawn on built examples whenever it made sense to do so. Although cultural and social historians are accustomed to regarding textual documents alone as authoritative sources of evidence, historians of visual culture and the material environment also regard buildings, artifacts, and visual representations as key forms of evidence. House plans, for example, have much to tell us about cultural values; so do household objects, gardens, advertisements, and the myriad products of the shelter and advertising industries. Moreover, the ubiquitous and ordinary forms of the visual and material world convey an enriched dimension to the histories of housing inequality and segregation in the United States. Through these forms of evidence, we can begin to understand not only the more commonly studied historical structures that governed the postwar housing market (banks, government agencies, real estate boards, construction industries) but also—and equally important—the everyday forces that shaped and reinforced the ongoing acceptance of a system marked by deep inequality. By looking closely at what some might consider the detritus of everyday life, we learn about the ways in which everyday acts of participation in a dominant culture are formulated, taken for granted, rehearsed, and enacted, and how the structures are reinforced.

I wrote this book while working and living in Urbana, Illinois, which is a virtual laboratory of postwar house design. Every trip to the grocery store or walk to my office became an opportunity to look at and ponder the variations displayed along the roadside. Writing this book has helped me see that cultural landscape differently. I hope the readers of this book will patiently consider the history I present here, even if it offers an uncomfortable view of their own neighborhoods, and perhaps even of their own houses.

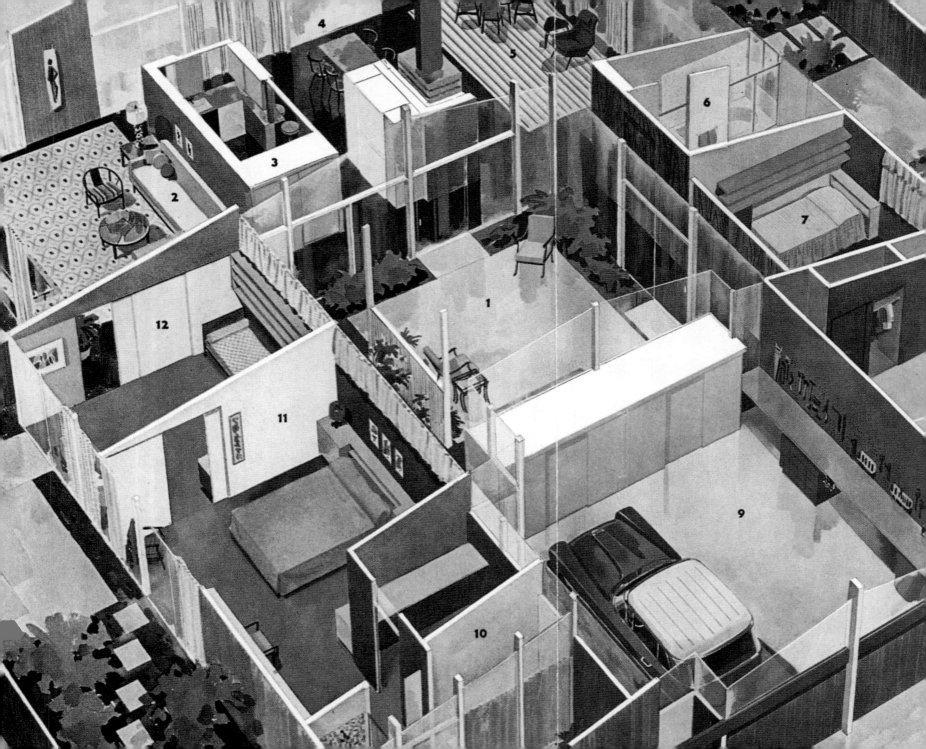

1

THE ORDINARY POSTWAR HOUSE

It can sometimes be difficult to imagine that very ordinary, ubiquitous aspects of the built environment hold rhetorical power. The field of spatial rhetoric, in fact, is a fairly new one, emerging since the 1980s along with the ascendancy of semiotic theory and its movement into humanities disciplines outside English. The idea that visual and textual productions hold rhetorical and persuasive power is a much older and well-accepted one, and despite several decades of scholarly investigations into the social and political history of architecture, it still does not go without saying that buildings, landscapes, and city spaces may also be persuasive and rhetorically powerful. Darryl Hattenhauer posited a semiotic approach to the analysis of architecture in 1984 when he wrote: "Architecture is rhetorical because it induces us to do what others would have us do. Architecture, then, is a persuasive phenomenon."[1] And in her study of apartment plots in film and television, Pamela Wojcik has pushed Hattenhauer's statement further, asserting that, "like props, characters, and other semantic elements, space and place are more than just one lexical choice among many; they are imbricated in signifying structures that are historically determined and that carry tremendous connotative and ideological weight related to issues of sex, gender, class, race, the body, individuality, family, community, work, pleasure, and more."[2] So, too, the particular characteristics of ordinary postwar houses matter in the signification of ideas about race, class, gender, and belonging, just as I have already asserted is true for

FACING
View of the "California style" house (*detail, see p. 52*).

The home of Rudolf and Eva Weingarten, circa 1955. Collection of the author.

visual and textual representations of those houses. Understanding the basic forms and spaces of such houses lies at the core of this investigation, so I begin here with a description and assessment of the configuration of a typical postwar dwelling. Once again, I look to my grandparents' house as a point of departure, since it was, in many respects, a typically modest postwar ranch house. My grandparents' experience as homeowners also provides an entrée into a more detailed examination of the political, cultural, and economic forces that shaped the racialized housing market of the postwar era.

CONSTRUCTING WHITE NEIGHBORHOODS

When Rudy and Eva Weingarten purchased their home in the San Fernando Valley of Los Angeles in 1955, it was the first and last piece of real estate they would ever own. With both of their daughters attending college and their own hi-fi and electronics store successfully launched, Rudy and Eva joined the vast ranks of Americans who were able to cease living their lives as renters by purchasing a small, single-story house. Situated at the corner of two side streets in Van Nuys, the house sat on land once occupied by citrus orchards and was conveniently located near major arterials and freeways that conveyed traffic in numerous directions but most importantly to the south, toward Los Angeles's primary business districts. Part of a tract development, the neighborhood appears to have remained unrestricted to Jews, Italians, and some other immigrant Americans (though I don't remember any blacks or Latino/as in the neighborhood in its early years). As Laura Barraclough's recent study of the San Fernando Valley indicates, the rapid construction of housing developments in the Valley in the 1950s meant that developers and merchant builders followed the racially exclusive practices required to qualify for federally insured financing. As Barraclough notes, "Only 3.3 percent of federally subsidized suburban housing units constructed in Southern

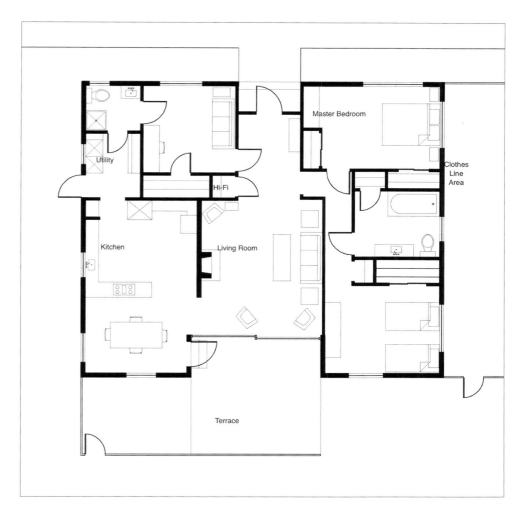

A plan diagram of the Weingarten residence.
Drawing by Matthew Zelensek.

California's 1950s housing boom were made available to nonwhites."[3]

The Valley was intentionally constructed as a white region where developers exploited rural myths and pastoral aesthetics in an attempt to create exclusive neighborhoods of privilege. But it also seems to have been a welcoming environment for Jews, who by this time were already becoming an accepted ethnic group in suburban developments nationwide, even as their presence could cause concern about the nature and construction of white identities. As George Sanchez has reported, about twenty-two thousand Jewish families lived in the San Fernando Valley by 1950; only five thousand black families lived there at that same time. The new color line in the Valley "placed Jews decidedly into the 'white race' but continued to exclude Blacks, Asians, and probably most Mexicans," and Jewish builders also began to construct homes for this market.[4] In 1955, a client of my grandfather's informed him about a new Valley development that was under construction, and my grandparents quickly made an offer on the house, happy to be able to pick the interior and exterior paint colors, the carpeting and linoleum, the Formica for countertops, and fixtures for the not-yet-completed home. If they worried about finding a neighborhood that would accept them, they did not openly speak about their fears. Instead, as my mother remembers, they simply understood which neighborhoods to avoid because they would not be welcome there.

Neither the fact of my grandparents' Jewish identity nor their understanding of the sociopolitical dynamics of the region's housing market is incidental to this narrative. To be a Jewish immigrant in search of housing was to possess a highly specific (if largely unspoken and unacknowledged) sense of one's status as a newly (and provisionally) white individual in the United States. But if my grandparents and others like them understood the factors that shaped their opportunities in the 1950s, architectural historians have tended to overlook whiteness as a critical factor in the shaping of spatial histories.

Notions of the social construction of race have been in currency for some time, and "whiteness studies" emerged as a field around 1988 with the appearance of key studies by Richard Dyer, Aldon Lynn Nielsen, Peggy McIntosh, and David Roediger, among others.[5] In this field led by ethnic studies, scholars of whiteness explore the idea that whiteness, like all other racial categories, remains a social construction. Examining white culture and the ways it asserts its dominance while essentializing, minoritizing, and discriminating against all others, scholars in a range of disciplines have directed our attention to that which is so pervasive it is almost invisible: the apparent ineffability of white privilege in its myriad forms—what Roediger calls the ability of white identity and white privilege to hide in plain sight.[6] He claims that whiteness is manifestly "able to hide in plain sight" because it "remains at times ineffable and multiple. . . . Our task is thus almost never to say that something 'is really all about race.' It is to show how whiteness exists in a complex history and a multiply inflected present."[7] Moreover, whiteness itself is constructed variously and is never monolithic, so that even those considered irrefutably "white" have multiple experiences and backgrounds.

This quality of "hiding in plain sight" pertains equally to a range of ideologies that are embedded in the spaces that surround us. Landscapes are particularly well suited to the masking of such constructions because they appear to be completely natural, God-given, and therefore neutral and because they serve as unnoticed background to our everyday lives. But landscapes, and indeed architecture, are never neutral. They are always powerful symbols and containers of cultural values, just as they simultaneously work to construct culture. Given this equivalence of invisibility between the ideologies of constructed space and constructions of race, domestic form and ideologies of whiteness become more than usually complicit in the manufacturing of societal norms. Again, however, we must remember Žižek's theoretical framework: the masking is complete only if the participant/viewer truly does not see it. Instead, I propose that ideological postwar cultural landscapes were effective precisely because their ubiquitous and quotidian qualities could render them simultaneously invisible and visible: they could be seen and seemingly ignored even as Americans completely understood and inhabited their economic, political, and cultural logics.

The idea that white privilege comprises a spatialized set of practices is becoming more widely examined, and scholars have formed significant consensus around this notion. In the past fifteen years, scholars have begun to outline clearly the indelibly drawn connections between race and space and between white identities and access to land, freedom of geographical movement, and property rights—something the legal scholar Cheryl Harris has called "whiteness as property."[8] The monetary value attached to whiteness has been measured significantly in terms of homeownership, which in turn is linked to notions of citizenship and national belonging.[9] I will examine these connections in some detail in later parts of this book, but I will also focus on the more general notion put forth by David Delaney that "race is what it is and does what it does precisely because of how it is given spatial expression."[10] Far from being tangentially connected, the construction of race and the built environment that surrounds us are joined by ties that are in fact fundamental to the constitution of racial and ethnic categories.

The stakes surrounding ideas about who is and is not white were significant in the postwar period, and they remain so today: white identities afforded homeownership, access to good schools and health care, proximity to outlets selling varieties of healthful foods, relative distance from toxic factories and other dangerous sites, and varying degrees of financial security. In the postwar era, and in recognition of those stakes, the occlusion of ethnic identities became essential for social conformity, and the images of postwar homes that were reproduced everywhere in the mass media instructed viewers about containing ethnic difference and attaining class status. The images were remarkably consistent—clean, tidy, orderly, shiny, brightly lit, and uncluttered. Taken together with magazine and newspaper articles, television programs, advertisements, and even the houses themselves, they defined for viewers and inhabitants the contours of residential conformity: how to look like everyone else and, essentially, how to be white. Still, as Karen Brodkin notes, Jews of the 1950s were identified as "somewhere between wannabes and nouveau arrivistes, accepted as white, but not securely."[11] Like some other nonwhites and those recently of the lower economic classes, they were out of the ghetto and into the suburbs, but seldom "to the manor born." Worse still, their presence as potential "passers" generated specific concerns for some homeowners.

Matthew Jacobson has focused specifically on questions related to neighborhood belonging for postwar Jews, citing an indeterminacy to their sense of belonging that is linked to what he also calls "the vicissitudes of whiteness—the cultural and historical contingencies of looking Jewish and seeing Jews."[12] Because some racial categories became new categories of ethnicity, and because Jews could be newly categorized as white, perceptions of whiteness became ever more pressing, ever more destabilized, generating greater levels of concern than may have existed previously for whites who sought (for various reasons) to establish their own identities more definitively. The probationary whiteness of Jews and some other ethnic groups at midcentury created tensions over race among other groups whose differences were not always visible or easily discerned. Films such as *Lost Boundaries* (1949), *Imitation of Life* (1934 and 1959), and *I Passed for White* (1960) all took "passing" as their central subject, and their popularity and/or critical acclaim indicate the extent to which the topic occupied a significant degree of public attention in this period.

As a group, then, Jews became a specific kind of register for racial anxiety in the United States at midcentury. Jews were dispersed geographically during the postwar era with increased U.S. industrialization and suburbanization, and they had access to housing in some newly constructed postwar suburbs even as they were restricted from purchasing in others and in many urban areas. In restricted areas, Jews could also sometimes "pass" if they wished to do so.[13] But if Jews became white, Jewishness also persisted as a visual category, something many Americans believed could be seen and recognized in the physiognomy of individuals. It could also, by extension, be seen and recognized in house design and material culture, and in decorating and design preferences, as I will explain in later chapters. After World War II, Americans were perhaps more keenly attuned to these perceptual differences than ever before. Novels such as Laura Hobson's *Gentleman's Agreement* (1947) and Arthur Miller's *Focus* (1945), and later Philip Roth's *Goodbye, Columbus* (1959), emphasized the visual and perceptual bases of Jewish identity and connected them (to varying degrees) to allegories that could be detected in the design and decoration of the home. The erasure of race as a category attached to Jews led, perhaps inevitably, to a greater awareness and focus on the visual and perceptual bases of white identities. This, then, is another important reason to study these issues at midcentury.

I have asserted above that the landscape of postwar housing was one marked by segregation and inequality, but to what extent was this the case? U.S. census data demonstrate with some precision the situation vis-à-vis the distribution of housing as it related to race. The 1950 "Census of Housing" included categories for both "Occupancy Characteristics" and "Race and Color of Occupants." For the latter, households were categorized as either white or nonwhite, with nonwhites including heads of households who were identified as "Negro," "Indian," "Japanese," "Chinese," or "Other." Heads of households of Mexican ancestry or birth who were not Indian or another nonwhite race were classified as white. The Census Bureau noted, "The concept of race as it has been used by the Bureau of the Census is derived from that which is commonly accepted by the general public."[14] The housing census of 1950 counted primarily occupancy of dwellings. It did not collect detailed information about dwellings or their design characteristics, and it recorded only sketchy information about condition. The census data indicate that in 1950, 39,043,595 whites occupied dwelling units (with a total U.S. white population of 134,942,028); the total number of occupied dwellings owned by nonwhites for that same year was 3,782,686 (with a total U.S. nonwhite population of 15,755,333). According to the Census Bureau: "About 1 out of 11 occupied dwelling units in the United States in 1950 was occupied by a nonwhite household. A great majority of these were Negro. . . . Since 1890, the number of nonwhite households increased at a slower rate than white households, dropping from 11.3 percent of all households in 1890 to 8.8 percent in 1950." Occupancy statistics, however, do not indicate ownership. More telling are those statistics that indicate that in 1950, 22,240,970 U.S. whites owned their own homes, compared with 1,252,103 blacks. The total number of houses owned by all "others" was a mere 66,893. The proportions varied by region and state, but the key here is that nonwhites owned significantly fewer residences everywhere in the United States.[15] It should also be noted that only about one-third of all dwelling units occupied by nonwhites in 1950 had both hot and cold piped running water inside the structure, and another third had no running water at all. Close to 2,000,000 of these had no access to either a shared or private conventional toilet in the dwelling, and more than 2,000,000 had no bathtub or shower.[16]

By 1960, black household occupancy numbers had increased and the Census Bureau noted that in terms of occupancy, "between 1950 and 1960, the number of nonwhite households increased at a faster rate than white households." However, the increase in occupancy (not homeownership) for nonwhite households occurred entirely within central-city areas that the Census Bureau designated as Standard Metropolitan Statistical Areas. Outside the urban core, in the newly built and growing suburban areas, nonwhite households experienced a slight decrease in occupancy for the same period. By 1960, nearly 31,000,000 U.S. dwellings were owned by whites; only about 2,000,000 were owned by nonwhites. The rates for nonwhite homeownership were highest in the West and lowest in the Northeast.[17] But overall, the differences in both rates of homeownership and the quality of house amenities (if we consider indoor plumbing an amenity rather than a necessity) were stark, demonstrating the vast economic, political, and social disadvantages accorded to those identified as nonwhite.

Despite the fact that some groups were finally admitted to the postwar housing market through racial reassignment or because they could pass for white, blacks, Asians, Native Americans, and Latinos were largely excluded from homeownership in most of the nation's new neighborhoods. The primary responsibil-

ity for this condition lies squarely on the shoulders of the federal government, which institutionalized racist housing policies and practices in the offices of the Federal Housing Administration (FHA) with practices initiated by the Home Owners' Loan Corporation (HOLC) in 1933.[18]

The FHA consistently acted to reinforce racially exclusive neighborhoods and to create urban ghettoes through the application of a policy of "minority containment." Using justifications related to market and developer demands, the FHA cloaked its actions in the verbiage of good intentions and compliance with federal law while consistently restricting access to housing by refusing to insure mortgage loans to any but white Americans. Its well-known redlining practices created cartographies of spatial inequality that mapped housing injustice into the American landscape. As a result, between 1932 and 1964 the FHA and the Veterans Administration (VA), through the GI Bill, "financed more than $120 billion worth of new housing, but less than 2% of this real estate was available to nonwhite families, and most of that small amount was located in segregated areas."[19] As Clarence Mitchell of the National Association for the Advancement of Colored People (NAACP) declared in a 1951 speech, "What the courts have forbidden state legislatures and city councils to do and what the Ku Klux Klan has not been able to accomplish by intimidation and violence, federal policy is accomplishing through a monumental program of segregation in all aspects of Housing which receive Government aid."[20] Such indictments begin to tell the true history of postwar housing: a history that was controlled to a large extent not by architects and their fashions, or even necessarily by consumer desires, but instead by extremely conservative and powerful government agencies, banks, and real estate agents.

Architects remained largely outside these sociopolitical debates, but the federal government did have an impact on the profession of architecture by influencing the kinds of houses that were built. The failure of architectural modernism as a style to be adopted on a mass scale was in large part the result of FHA conservatism: the modernist aesthetic held little appeal for an agency insuring mortgages for loans to builders whose construction estimates were based on traditional house types and forms. Anyone who wished to build less conventional homes quickly discovered that the FHA refused to provide mortgage insurance for their loans, since untested house types and forms were deemed high-risk investments. The FHA frowned on difference of any kind, whether in house form and style or in the identities of houses' occupants. Still, a frank analysis of the inequalities of the postwar housing market cannot excuse architects and their profession. Despite the fact that architects and design critics of the period emphasized avant-garde solutions and even the search for a "democratic architecture," very few postwar building professionals engaged consistently or deeply with issues of social, economic, and political justice. Then as now, design professionals tended to imagine the consideration of race and class as falling outside the purviews of their respective professional realms. At a 1949 conference titled "Building for Modern Man," none of the environmental design professionals who participated explored the possibilities of changed social conditions. In fact, Thomas Creighton, who was the editor of *Progressive Architecture* during the period, openly acknowledged this point in the conference's published proceedings, stating that "we must operate within our existing social structure."[21] The "progressiveness" indicated by the title of Creighton's magazine referred to stylistic and formal inventions rather than a commitment to progressive social reforms. Despite their vanguard design rhetoric, the majority of postwar designers imagined the domestic realm within the existing social box, one that accepted racially restrictive covenants and the social, political, and economic armature of the pre–civil rights era.

Despite the 1948 U.S. Supreme Court ruling in *Shelley v. Kramer* that outlawed racially restrictive covenants, the FHA and the real estate industry continued to enact segregationist policies and practices such as redlining for decades. The covenants and the practices based on them constituted a sometimes subtle, pernicious, and (at least to whites) invisible form of racism that "hides behind a color-blind rhetoric of privatism and free-market advocacy."[22] Charles Abrams wrote as early as 1955 that the "FHA adopted a racial policy that could well have been culled from the Nuremberg laws. From its inception FHA set itself up as the protector of the all white neighborhood. It sent its agents into the field to keep Negroes and other minorities from buying houses in white neighborhoods."[23] And, as Karen Brodkin and others have demonstrated, FHA underwriting manuals openly insisted on racially homogeneous neighborhoods. The FHA insured mortgages on loans only in white neighborhoods, using a rating system in which the highest ratings were assigned to all-white neighborhoods, second-grade status was given to Jewish and white working-class areas, and the third and lowest grade went to racially mixed neighborhoods (this situation has changed little over the past fifty years).[24] Attempts at integration frequently resulted in riots and other forms of hostility. Clearly, the stakes were high for those who would and could pass or assimilate, although exclusion could be preferable to the violence they were likely to experience if their true identities were discovered.

Moreover, the National Association of Home Builders (NAHB) was also complicit in the racialization of the housing market throughout the postwar era. Formed in reaction to governmental intervention in the housing industry in the postwar period, the NAHB became a strong economic force and a powerful lobbying organization for the massive development of single-family dwellings. Public housing was not among the NAHB's interests, and the organization interfered with the construction of such housing whenever possible. Renowned for its annual convention and trade show, with massive exhibit halls that sometimes included model home designs that were featured on television programs, the NAHB communicated with the trades through its own publication (*House and Home* magazine). Members of the NAHB included real estate lobbyists, merchant builders, and groups such as the U.S. Chamber of Commerce, the United States Savings and Loan League, the National Association of Retail Lumber Dealers, and the Mortgage Bankers Association. The NAHB exerted significant power in the world of private real estate development. Although it was not a governmentally supported organization, it formed strong alliances with construction industry executives and with civic organizations such as the New Face of America program and the American Council to Improve Our Neighborhoods. Working together, these groups advocated urban renewal and the remodeling of older inner-city housing, thereby keeping nonwhites in older unrestricted neighborhoods while simultaneously appearing to do the "good work" of saving areas from becoming "slums."[25] Even the market for remodeled houses in older urban neighborhoods was highly discriminatory; whites could buy such houses with no down payments, yet nonwhites could get nothing better than fifteen-year loans with down payments of 50 percent.[26] Linked to the FHA, on which its members relied for mortgage insurance on loans to developers and builders, the NAHB was therefore complicit in the redlining and racist practices of the FHA.[27]

Not only were postwar houses available to and therefore intended primarily for whites, but they were also built primarily by whites. As Thomas Sugrue has demonstrated, the construction industries were substantially dominated by white workers from 1945 through 1969. Ironworkers, plumbers, pipe fitters, steamfitters, sheet metal workers, electrical workers, roofers, and elevator construction workers were nearly all white. Although some housing developers, such as the Levitts, refused to hire union workers and therefore heavily relied on immigrant laborers who were willing to pick up work wherever they could, much of the construction industry was dominated by union labor. Blacks could not gain entry into the unions that regulated labor in the construction trades, and those who worked in construction ended up in only the lowest-level jobs, which were most vulnerable to layoffs; this was particularly true for construction in suburban and rural areas. As a result, Sugrue notes, the construction industry was "notorious for racial homogeneity."[28]

As noted above, the U.S. Supreme Court made housing discrimination illegal in 1948, but the practice quickly went underground and remained widespread. In some cases, the embedded codes were explicit, as in the activities of real estate boards and agents, and financing and mortgage insurance agencies. In others, they were hidden or rendered "invisible," as in the vocabulary used by tastemakers, who seldom overtly intended racist discourse but engaged in it unconsciously because whiteness and WASP culture were the acknowledged standards. For example, real estate industry literature drew explicit connections between racial stereotypes and property values. Kevin Fox Gotham notes:

> In many property deeds, racial minorities frequently found themselves described as nuisances and threats because of their perceived negative impact on a residential area. . . . [Stereotypes] associated black residence with declining property values, deteriorating neighborhoods, and other negative consequences. . . . This segregationist real estate ideology was buttressed by local housing reformers and social workers who equated black neighborhoods with violent crime, disease, and other negative vices. . . . [The image of black neighborhoods was that they were] pathological, disorganized, and deviant. . . . [In FHA and real estate industry rhetoric] race became coded as culture . . . [and the industry used] various racially coded symbols and imagery to circumvent accusations of racism while maintaining the racial homogeneity of settlement space.

Homogeneous neighborhoods were called "secure" or "stable" and were noted for possessing "integrity."

Other racial code words included "culture," "crime," "school quality," "property values," and "private."[29]

The cultural currency of these codes was both powerful and pervasive, such that a distinctive set of adjectives came to possess racial corollaries. For example, black spaces were typically imagined as cramped, crowded, dirty, unhygienic, and not private. In the white imagination, black residential life included multigenerational and mixed-gender sleeping arrangements and social activities carried out on the front stoop, in the street, and in the alley instead of inside the private home or in the private backyard. Deteriorating and ramshackle construction marked by unglazed window openings, furnishings assembled from salvage sites, and unkempt surroundings might complete a stereotypical and essentializing image of black domestic life. It was an image white Americans experienced in sections of nineteenth-century cities; it was what they saw and read about in New Deal photographs of urban poverty; what they read about in fiction such as Flannery O'Connor's midcentury depiction of Atlanta in "The Artificial Nigger" (1955). As the white grandfather and grandson who are the main characters in that short story wander lost through the city streets, O'Connor describes their experience: "They walked on for some time on streets like this before he remembered to turn again. The houses they were passing now were all unpainted and the wood in them looked rotten; the street between was narrower. Nelson saw a colored man.

Then another. Then another. 'Niggers live in these houses,' he observed."[30]

Likewise, the spaces depicted at the beginning of the film version of *Goodbye, Columbus* (1969) provide an interesting example that correlates residential spatial characteristics with the racial/ethnic identities of occupants. When the main character, Neil Klugman, leaves the house he shares with his aunt Gladys and his uncle Max in their working-class New Jersey neighborhood to see his assimilated Jewish girlfriend in the affluent suburbs, the architectural contrast is striking. Gladys and Max live in what we are to presume is an urban ethnic neighborhood; their wood-frame house is small, crowded, and worn, and the front porch supports furnishings that would never be found in front of a house in the affluent suburb (the nouveau riche decor of the suburban affluent Jews in this film is equally instructive). These contrasts—clean/dirty, spacious/crowded, private/public, tidy/cluttered—facilitated the establishment of white identities by creating their opposite.

Thus white immigrants were deemed "clean" and "thrifty," in opposition to the definition of blacks as "shiftless, indolent, lazy, criminals, immoral, pleasure-seeking, negligent, ignorant, careless and unsanitary."[31] Cleanliness and ideas about hygiene held particular currency as codes, just as they had for decades in both Europe and the United States, resulting in what Anne McClintock has called the "soft-soaping of empire," in which imagined and visualized cleanliness and cleaning products and practices are deeply intertwined with images of and ideas about race.[32] Immigrants to the United States had been regarded as dirty and in need of an assimilating cleanse since at least the nineteenth century; indigenous peoples and anyone else identified as nonwhite were believed not only unhygienic but also possibly diseased. Nineteenth-century handbooks that focused on the idealized home focused specifically on hygienic principles, as such handbooks continued to do for decades.[33] Postwar notions of the connections that bound white identities to specific norms of hygiene and in turn to ideas about domesticity—and the intricate if not always subtle codes that conveyed these ideas—must therefore be seen as outgrowths of these historically bound yet continuous notions.

So widespread were these ideas that connected white identities to specific house forms and codes that the popular literature on housing used them extensively and without question. Integrated into narratives that were intended to assist working-class and middle-class Americans who hoped to own their own homes, these publications rehearsed the rhetoric that articulated specific residential forms and codes as linked to white, middle-class identities. For example, a 1946 book by Mary Catlin and George Catlin titled *Building Your New House* reveals the life that postwar homeowners were leaving behind and the range of class concerns that were embodied in homeownership. Written for families of modest means who wanted to build homes of their own, the book tells the story of a couple who lost their livelihood during the Great Depression, detailing the hardships they endured as they suffered without electricity on an Iowa farm. Though they longed to build their dream house, it remained just that through the Depression years of 1933–37. When George decided to return to college to earn a degree, they sold the farm and bought what Mary called a "depression-born house on wheels, the trailer."[34] She writes of the terrible cold they endured during the Iowa winter in the trailer, heated as it was by a tiny coke-burning stove that did little to combat the frigid temperatures, so that a thick layer of ice accumulated on the interior walls for weeks at a time. This passage is significant, because it rehearses a strong prejudice against trailer living, long identified as lower-class, nonwhite (or "white trash"), and to be avoided whenever possible.

When the Catlins had built their first and smallest house, two college boys roomed with them, reducing their privacy at home, and they continued to take in college boarders to help cover costs. Mary complained about these boarders, "two strangers waiting for the meal I was going to cook for them for money. I had never sold a meal in my life before."[35] Again, this work signaled lower-class conditions, especially the "menial" task of cooking meals for others in the home for pay, work that was typically relegated to nonwhite workers in upper-class homes.

Over the years, Mary and George steadily improved

their living accommodations by buying lots in ever more affluent neighborhoods and building larger homes. They moved from campus cottage to Cape Cod colonial to Sunset Drive to Wood Street to Country Club Boulevard, moving "up in the world" with each house change.[36] Mary recommended that her readers build Cape Cod houses because they are compact, efficient, stylish, and tasteful and because the plan "rates excellent on privacy."[37] The Catlins' story was a fairly common one for white families, a tale of upward mobility that emphasized what they had left behind—a lack of privacy, noise, crowding, and Depression-era privations—conditions that no Americans wanted to return to if they could help it.

In keeping with FHA guidelines, Mary advised that a new home builder find as exclusive a neighborhood as possible:

> For peace of mind all around, don't buy in a neighborhood which is socially "spotty," with some undesirable families mixed in with desirable ones. This is especially true if you have children, for it is almost certain that there will be some roustabouts with whom you don't want your offspring to play. . . . Children's playmates have an important bearing on later life as well as present happiness. The mother who has been reading the latest figures on juvenile delinquency and who wants her children to grow up

to be a credit to the community will certainly pay attention to the neighbors she will have.[38]

Furthermore, Mary warned her readers that when building "an attractive home in an absolutely undeveloped section, a person sometimes finds that those who follow throw up tar-paper shacks, leave the jalopy sitting alongside the house as a permanent feature, and build smelly chicken pens and rabbit hutches out back."[39] Her meaning is not difficult to discern; to avoid these lower-class problems that signal nonwhite identities, she once again advocated buying in restricted districts and in subdivisions that had deed restrictions that accompanied the purchase of the lot and that stipulated setbacks, hiding clotheslines from view, and so on.[40] Thus the Catlins communicated the consequences of not conforming to middle-class norms of behavior. Their book, compared to others of the period, is not unusual. Indeed, its contents were completely unremarkable to readers of the day, appearing as yet another helpful guidebook for the construction of one of the most desirable and rare postwar necessities: a house of one's own.

I examine these codes and rhetorical strategies in greater detail in the chapters that follow, but given the cultural currency they enjoyed, the tastemaking and design literature from the postwar era must be viewed in an entirely new light. Reception of these codes cannot

FACING
A composite of illustrations of the houses built by the Catlins.
From Mary Catlin and George Catlin, *Building Your New House* (1946).

FIGURE 1. "We Were Actually Building"

FIGURE 5. First-floor Plan Campus Avenue Cape Cod

FIGURE 2. Campus Avenue House

SECOND FLOOR

FIRST FLOOR

FIGURE 10. Original Plan—Beech Avenue House

FIGURE 4. Our Campus Avenue Houses

FIGURE 9. Beech Avenue House

FIGURE 8. Our Country Club House

FIGURE 7. Our Sunset Drive House

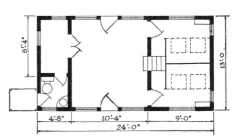

FIGURE 3. Original Plan of Campus Cottage

Porch

Kitchen

Living Room

Hall

Bed Room

Bath

Hall

Cl. Cl. Cl.

Bed Room

Cl.

Deck

Roof

Closet

Bunk

Roof

Closet

Bunk

Stove

Bed

Closet

Kitchen

Fuel

Dining Rm.

H.

Cl.

Garage

Living Room

be strictly quantified, and I am not asserting that they were uniformly received. Instead, they must be seen as constituting a set of broadly dispersed social practices that were adopted in mass media, by the building trades, and by the design community in their efforts to address an audience they associated already with a white imaginary. These practices instructed the audience in and reinforced a set of dominant cultural values that likewise circulated in visual and textual representations of and about housing. The codes were part of the broad, ideologically charged discourse about housing. As such, media and market obsessions with household order and cleanliness become not simply an aesthetic or health preference; rather, they are equally significant as part of the constellation of signifiers for whiteness. Terms such as *privacy, ease, luxury, freedom, informal-*

Hiding clotheslines from view became a common design trend in the postwar era, and the requirement to do so was even written into some development covenants. Here a laundry line is hidden by a fence to create a separate drying yard not easily seen by guests or neighbors. Photograph by Maynard L. Parker. Courtesy of the Huntington Library, San Marino, California.

ity, order, cleanliness, and spaciousness (among others) appeared consistently in the sales and advertising literature—in print and on television—related to postwar house design and decoration. Federal and private interests were therefore involved, delivering a seamless message predicated on text and images that together worked to restrict the availability of new housing while simultaneously reinforcing the notion that homeownership was largely a privilege for middle-class whites. In the chapters that follow, I examine the spatial and material ramifications of these codes to reveal their significance as tools for identity formation.

Although much of this study examines the ways in which houses and their representations worked to produce white, middle-class subjectivity, it must be acknowledged that large numbers of Americans who were identified as white were equally excluded from the suburban housing market. As Thomas Sugrue cautions, the untold stories of "poor whites, migrant farmers, . . . displaced industrial workers, and intellectual and cultural dissenters" remain outside the suburban narratives typically constructed for the postwar era.[41] Working-class whites, he notes, had become newly assertive with so much at stake, and this group fought integration especially fiercely. Moreover, the population on which I focus in this book—middle-class whites who purchased new homes that were largely in suburban locations in the fifteen years that immediately followed World War II—was actually a small but highly visible segment of the American population; the people who make up this group cannot be taken to represent all of American culture in that period or monolithically to represent whiteness as it is understood in the United States. Despite the consumer surges that characterized the enormous economic expansion of the immediate postwar era, we must remember that the period also saw up to one-third of the population living below the poverty line, especially in the South.[42] We also have to remember that whiteness meant many things, that as a category it is multiple, and mutable, its complex definitions continually reformulated through time. The postwar affluence signaled by the houses discussed herein was therefore a restricted affluence, if one that nevertheless significantly changed the appearance of the U.S. cultural landscape. And the whiteness of its imagined and intended occupants was one largely formulated through a range of cultural forces that included the house and its representations.

It is also important to note that developers, builders, and government officials were not oblivious to the problem of minority housing. The federal Housing and Home Finance Agency produced pamphlets for builders and developers to inform them about the ramifications of the Housing Act of 1949 (Title I), which called for integrated residential neighborhoods and stated the goal of providing decent housing for all Americans. Aimed at slum clearance and urban renewal projects, the act recognized slums as a national problem and addressed the need to replace homes lost to removal efforts.[43] Perhaps unsurprisingly, there was a major increase in attention to this issue starting in 1954, when the housing market experienced a slight slump. In 1955, for example, *House and Home* noted: "More builders are starting to build for the biggest untapped market. They are still hobbled by land, financing problems, but spurred by the threat of compulsory open occupancy in FHA, VA projects." The NAHB saw minority home construction as a way to forestall what the organization's 1955 president, Dick Hughes, called "the worst crisis we've ever had." By 1954, groups such as the NAACP (with its attorney Thurgood Marshall) and the National Urban League were successfully pressuring the government to bar FHA and VA loans to houses not for sale to blacks and other people of color. As a result, a significant, if still relatively small, group of articles on the topic of housing for nonwhites began to appear in the shelter magazines after this date.[44]

Although the postwar era is largely regarded as one of economic prosperity, the 1954 slump was not the only recession experienced in the period. The housing market dipped during four brief recessions in the fifteen-year period of this study, the longest of which lasted only eleven months, and all were fairly mild economic downturns. However, the housing market was so robust during this time and the economy so dependent on new housing starts that even relatively modest downturns caused the kind of alarm noted above. The ten-month recession that lasted from July 1953 until May 1954 resulted by the end of 1954 in an increase in government-assisted expansion of the housing market. As one economist wrote, housing starts increased by the end of that year, owing mainly "to the general easing of credit and to an unusually strong response by the financial system to that policy." And when a more significant economic downturn occurred in 1958, *Time* magazine credited housing starts with leading the economy out of the recession.[45] Clearly, powerful ties bound the U.S. economy to the iconography examined herein.

THE SPATIAL CONTOURS OF WHITENESS

The house my grandparents purchased was stylistically nondescript, completely unobtrusive. Nothing about its cream-colored stucco exterior was remarkable or memorable for passing strangers, which made it absolutely ideal for a couple who wanted to quietly fit in. But a careful analysis of their home and its spaces provides an understanding of some of the key physical as well as social dimensions of ordinary postwar domesticity.

At about 1,250 square feet, Rudy and Eva's house was comfortable and remarkably well built: the modest one-story structure sat over a crawl space and included two bedrooms, two bathrooms, a wood-paneled den, a living room, a kitchen with a dining area, and a small pantry/utility room. A detached garage created the edge for a modest courtyard/garden space. A narrow space along one side of the lot contained a clothesline, carefully concealed from both street and neighbors by a tall fence so that drying underclothes could not be seen—a design device intended to eliminate from view the appearance of this form of labor and the lower-class appearance of the laundry line, an aspect of middle-class houses examined in some detail in later chapters.

The rear garden itself was divided into three spaces: a paved patio, a rectangle of lawn bordered by shrubs and small trees, and the clothesline along the side. Despite the house's corner location, and despite the fact that it had entrances off both streets, the visual focus was inward—either to the internal life of the house or to the garden, which was completely enclosed by a tall fence and (originally) shaded by an overhead lattice that spanned the distance between the garage and the house over the paved patio. Mowed, edged, and clipped, the front and rear gardens never had a leaf out of place or a weed invading the borders. Hypermaintained first by my grandparents and later by a hired gardener, the yard could only be described as "clean." So fastidiously maintained were its lawns that a small strip of dirt frequently showed between the strenuously clipped edge of the lawn and the sidewalk paving. Like fingernails trimmed to the quick or a severe military haircut, the tidy lawns and hedges seemed to reveal a self-conscious desire to appear neat, groomed, upstanding.

Inside, the house combined traditional forms with the emerging, if modest, fashions of postwar domesticity. Although it was not an open-plan configuration, only the range countertop separated the kitchen and dining area, and an opening allowed movement to flow from dining room to living room, from which entry to the garden could be gained through sliding glass doors. The window over the kitchen sink looked out onto the street, as did larger windows in the den and in the master bedroom on the other side, but these were usually partially covered with blinds, sheers, or drapes. Only the kitchen window remained frequently uncovered, serving as the primary aperture to the street.

Like so many first-time homeowners, my grandparents lavished care on their modest home. They selected linoleum patterned with multicolored flecks to cover the kitchen floor. Boomerang-patterned Formica covered the kitchen countertops, surrounding the built-in stainless steel electric stove, with its four burners and built-in griddle (for cooking pancakes, but my grandmother used it for making matzo brei and latkes—each time she did so, she may have been reminded that her house was designed for a generically conceived white, non-Jewish occupant). The matching oven was mounted in a nearby wall (I discuss this important postwar invention in a later chapter). The original house plans called for an indoor barbecue located next to the oven, but my grandparents eliminated this feature during the construction phase. Given their background, they doubtless had little experience at that time with grilled foods (in later years they appreciated their outdoor grill and used it frequently), and the idea of cooking over an open flame indoors must have seemed to them a bit foreign. The pantry/utility room eventually contained both washing machine and dryer (though it would be some years before my grandparents could afford the dryer), as well as cabinets for food and small appliance storage. It was here that my grandmother kept her extra set of dishes (some were also stored in other closets) and cooking implements for use when family members who kept kosher came to visit—a storage requirement not anticipated by the home builder and one that cost her much-needed storage space, and that again perhaps reminded her that she was not the designer/builder's imagined occupant.

The living room was the most spacious room in the house. The floors were originally covered by wall-to-wall carpet (thereby eliminating the "old-fashioned" need for waxing floors), but my grandparents eventually pulled the carpet away to reveal the hardwood beneath throughout the house. Since my grandparents favored the modernist designs my grandfather had seen generated by the Bauhaus in Germany, and because they had a friend who worked for the Herman Miller furniture company from whom they could purchase furnishings at a discount, their house contained chairs and cabinets designed by Charles Eames and George Nelson—decorating choices that marked them as stylish but also, and

perhaps unknown to them, as both Jewish and foreign, as I will explain in the following chapters. From my grandfather's point of view, the living room was little more than a personalized space for listening to chamber music on his elaborate high-fidelity sound system, and the hardwood floors improved the acoustical setting. He spent many hours listening to recorded music played through an excellent and carefully made speaker system of his own design. His elaborately outfitted stereo system was housed in a hall closet that he had customized to become a hidden chamber of technological wizardry. That the components of his hi-fi system were not displayed to guests is not incidental, and analysis of the ways in which such luxuries were concealed or displayed—and the reasons for such determinations—serves as the subject of a later chapter.

In the den, which doubled as a guest room, my grandfather constructed a desk with a special cabinet that would eventually contain a color television. He also built a television into the wall of their bedroom, high above my grandmother's closet. It was the first remote-controlled television I had ever seen, and watching TV from their bed, changing channels with the remote control, seemed the height of luxury to me as a child. Eventually, my grandfather would wire the entire house (all 1,250 square feet of it) for an intercom system that allowed communication between the rooms (a rather absurd addition, since it was easy to hear voices calling between spaces) and connected to the two porches at both house entrances to provide security from outsiders. If the editors of *Popular Mechanics* had known about Rudolf Weingarten, they would certainly have considered his house for a feature article on one of their favorite topics: electronic gadgetry built into the home.

If Rudy and Eva Weingarten's house was unremarkable to outsiders, it was also a fairly typical model for 1955. Indeed, its primary features varied little from the examples recommended in a 1951 *Life* magazine article that included eight house designs commissioned with the magazine's cosponsor *Architectural Forum*. According to the article, the key new features of postwar homes were "open floor plans, sliding partitions, radiant heat, large windows, fine details and workmanship." In addition, many included carefully planned outdoor terraces and landscaping that accommodated activities for specific family members of varied age groups.[46] Despite the magazine's claim, most tract houses were not notable for their fine craftsmanship, given that they were constructed rapidly and with inexpensive materials to reduce costs. My grandparents' house was, however, surprisingly well constructed (one of the reasons they purchased it), but it was also somewhat more expensive than homes of comparable square footage built elsewhere in the Los Angeles basin in the mid-1950s. Although they had forced-air rather than radiant heating, they did possess the requisite sliding glass doors and

large windows, and the house's plan configuration was a bit more open than earlier models might have been. As we will see, these features could be interpreted variously, and inclusion of even a few served as a mark of class distinction and modernity. I will detail the significance of each in the chapters that follow.

For the most part, ordinary postwar houses were very small, though they steadily increased in square footage over the fifteen-year period that is the focus of this book. Many Americans who had struggled to find housing in the immediate postwar market were thrilled to find affordable houses, even if they often did not exceed 1,000 square feet of living space and were sometimes as small as 750 square feet. The FHA "minimum house" standard, after all, required only that a house be approximately 540 square feet in order to qualify for government-backed financing.[47] A common configuration included two bedrooms, one bathroom, a living room, and a kitchen that might include a small area for dining. Compared to today's "McMansions," these houses seem even smaller than they might have to their original inhabitants—families that often included at least two children and who were accustomed to apartment dwelling. Even if they were happy to be housed in homes of their own, many families were nonetheless concerned with the image, if not the fact, of the cramped living they experienced every day. Cramped quarters conjured lower-class and nonwhite lifestyles and Depression-era conditions, as I will demonstrate in the chapters that follow. Decorating to increase at least the appearance of space, if not the spatial reality of the home, became a central concern expressed repeatedly in popular magazines.

A *Life* magazine article that featured William Levitt's 1952 houses for his Pennsylvania development (which cost $9,000 each) called attention to the problem of house size, noting that the average home had shrunk by 200 square feet since 1942.[48] By 1953, an article in the same magazine optimistically proclaimed that "the square footage in the average development home has increased from 700 in 1948 to almost 1,000 square feet; that two-thirds of builder houses now have three bedrooms; that storage space is ample, averages 10% of the area of the house."[49] Correlating this change in house size with the baby boom and the increasing numbers of families with three and four children, the author's rosy view of what must certainly have been a very cramped situation indicates, to some extent, the degree to which American spatial expectations have changed since mid-century. Although the article was no doubt intended to boost housing sales, it also likely represented the different expectations that postwar families had for their spatial needs. Still, customer satisfaction with small houses was short-lived, and the market-driven pressure to increase house size was both practically and socially motivated.

The split-level house gained in popularity as developers sought house forms that allowed more living space without substantially increasing construction costs or lot sizes. Although initially designed to accommodate sloping lot conditions, split-level houses soon appeared on flat lots across the country, looking a bit like two-story houses that had been cut off at the knees. Although they required more excavation than houses constructed at grade, they allowed for multilevel living that still conformed in appearance with the majority of the ranch houses then under construction. Although less common than other forms, the split-level became synonymous with the stereotypical discontent, anomie, and hyperconformity of suburban postwar life, primarily because of the 1960 publication of *The Split-Level Trap*.[50] That book's generalizations may have had little to do with the actual conditions of the specific split-level house form, but as Alan Ehrenhalt has described, lack of privacy was a problem in a 1957 split-level; its owners liked the modern look of the house, but there was no wall separating the bedroom corridor on the second floor from the living area below, so that acoustics were a constant source of irritation to inhabitants. Nonetheless, the split-level became an icon of middle-class aspirations and resulted in larger dwellings. As Ehrenhalt notes: "In 1953, 88 percent of the new houses built in America had still been ranch houses, many of them Levittown-style slabs or slabs plus a crawl space like those in Emery Manor. Three years later, split-levels had overtaken them. . . . Because of the trend to

A split-level house, Urbana, Illinois. Date and architect unknown. Photograph by the author.

split-levels, the average size of the newly built American home was increasing rapidly. In 1950, the average had been 983 square feet—12 percent less than before the war. By mid-decade, as the split-levels came in, the average grew closer to 1,200 square feet."[51]

Between 1945 and 1960, ordinary houses grew incrementally larger, their plans responding to a range of social and technological changes.[52] Every room of the American house would expand to accommodate changes in family needs and structure, to allow for new technologies, to encompass increasing numbers of material possessions, but also to conform with a range of social pressures that were linked to emerging values. For example, bathrooms became larger in postwar houses because Americans began to spend more time in them than ever before. Certainly bodily requirements had not changed, nor had fixtures and plumbing changed enough to warrant enlargement of spaces rarely occupied by more than one person at a time. But the 1950s witnessed increased levels of societal interest in personal hygiene and body smells, perhaps a result of increases in the televised marketing of hygiene and personal grooming products. Wini Breines sees the bathroom as the site where family members assuaged their fears about being socially acceptable.[53] In this sense, the bathroom too becomes a crucial space of conformity, since it is the site where physical appearances are modified, tamed, or transformed.

A key structural and spatial difference between houses constructed previously and many newly constructed postwar houses was the absence of basements and attics in some parts of the country. Data from the 1960 U.S. census indicate that although 54 percent of all housing units nationwide included basements, 46 percent were structures built on concrete slabs or with foundations that included crawl spaces. But some of this varied regionally, such that many more structures in the Northeast included basements than did structures in the West.[54] For example, 1960 census figures indicate that 89 percent of units in the Northeast were constructed with basements, while only 74 percent of houses built in the North Central Region had them; in the South, only 19 percent of structures included basements, and in the West only 27 percent had them.[55]

Although many houses in some geographic regions continued to include basements, it was cost-effective for developers to eliminate these spaces, and they could do so because of the invention of the small, clean-running furnace that could fit into a compact space on the ground floor of a house. Manufacturers also began to produce water heaters that were greatly reduced in size, so these utilities could fit neatly into ground-floor closets, often located next to kitchens or in hallways. By eliminating the need for basement excavation, these technological advances allowed builders to construct houses on concrete slabs on grade or over crawl spaces, which was far less costly and far more efficient. Slab-on-grade houses could also be quickly mass-produced, much in the manner of the Levitts' houses.[56] Eliminating attics also reduced construction times and costs, though unfinished "expansion attics" were commonly found in mass developments such as those produced by the Levitts. Thus many postwar houses became vertically compressed, without the deep roots of the basement or the lofty reaches of the attic. The fact that many of these houses lacked basements and attics is significant. Basements and attics are typically spaces that contain artifacts that trigger memories, nostalgic longings, and clues to ancestral origins. Without these spaces, families in the postwar era were less likely than their predecessors to retain those artifacts, and even if they did so, those spaces, so keyed to literary notions of memory, were absent. Many postwar houses therefore became (though perhaps incidentally) more efficient frameworks for forgetting past lives—a fundamental requirement for assimilation.[57]

Another ramification of the disappearance of the basement and attic was a resultant lack of storage space. In December 1952, *Life* magazine called space "the number one problem of the average household."[58] All pieces of furniture were suddenly expected to do double or triple duty, to have fold-out or slide-out storage spaces. Room dividers doubled as bookshelves, and sofas appeared designed with storage shelves hanging off their backs. The problem was made even worse in houses with truly open plans, because partition walls that formerly accommodated shelf space were now absent and closet space was limited.[59] As a result, the garage began to perform double duty, housing the new automobile but also serving as a much-needed storage space for bicycles, scooters, games, garden furniture, lawn mower, power tools, rakes and other garden tools, and various supplies.[60] Since the houses were de facto designed to accommodate families presumed to be white, middle-class, Christian, and heterosexual, builders never considered a range of storage needs that might differ depending on race or ethnicity, or on the need to keep from view any objects that might reveal alternate sexual orientations or gender performances. As I will demonstrate in the chapters that examine consuming and displaying, storage became a primary concern for postwar homeowners, and the solutions they found and that were promoted in the mass media reveal a great deal about cultural identity, subject formation, and self-fashioning.

By October 1958, *Popular Mechanics* featured a

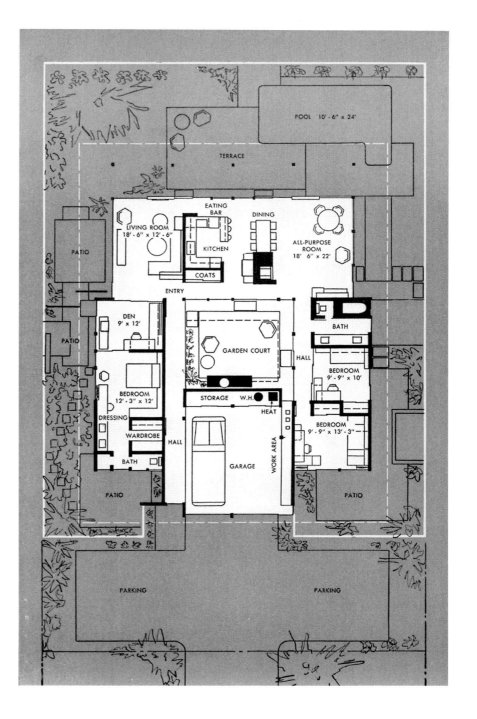

A "California style" house designed by A. Quincy Jones and Frederick Emmons for *Popular Mechanics*. This plan includes all the elements for an idealized postwar house. Courtesy of *Popular Mechanics*; originally published in the October 1958 issue.

three-bedroom, two-bathroom house that can be viewed as paradigmatic for the times. The magazine's editors had asked the California architects A. Quincy Jones and Frederick Emmons to design a house for their readers "with all the best features of what has become nationally known as 'California Style' and that could be adapted for the rest of the country." Jones and Emmons were a natural choice, since they were the architects for some of merchant builder Joseph Eichler's renowned developments in California. With an open plan and organized around a glazed interior garden court, the $25,000 house that Jones and Emmons designed for *Popular Mechanics* contained nearly every feature considered desirable at the time. The primary living spaces had an indoor/outdoor feeling, with views and access to the outdoors from every room, including the bathrooms; at the same time, there was privacy for the bedroom areas and for the family from the street. Outdoor areas included five "private" patios, a service yard, and a rear terrace. The family room and dining/living areas achieved connections with the outdoors through the use of glass walls and sliding glass doors. The kitchen was equipped with an island, built-in modern appliances, and a barbecue fireplace; a wall of the family room contained built-in TV and hi-fi cabinets. A private den offered a retreat for the parents. The master bedroom featured a walk-in wardrobe and built-in dressers, and the children's bedrooms were located on the opposite side of the house for additional privacy. The children's

compartmented bath contained a washing machine and dryer. This laundry–bath combination opened onto a service yard that allowed access to clothes-drying and play areas and was "handy for adult gardeners who may want to clean up before going into living areas of the house." The two-car garage was outfitted with a storage wall, accommodation for water heater and furnace, and a workshop with a pegboard wall above it.[61]

These features became standard in many houses after 1960, and they indicate the degree to which houses had grown since the first years after the cessation of the war. The features are also essential in that they form the basis for an understanding of the houses discussed in the chapters that follow. Each feature signified (or was intended to signify) an important, new, and distinctly American form of dwelling. The exception, of course, is the look of the house, its style. Jones and Emmons designed houses for Eichler that were stylistically modern, but acceptably so, the soft modernism that maintained signs of the traditional (hipped roofs, the use of wood and stone) but combined them with new, more open spatial configurations. Despite the popularity of their Eichler houses, most ordinary postwar houses did not include even this moderate or middling form of modernism. As Philip Nobel has written, the design and housing market in the postwar United States is best described as "stubbornly inertial" when it came to accepting the forms of stylistic or high-style architectural modernism.[62] The reasons for this are varied, and

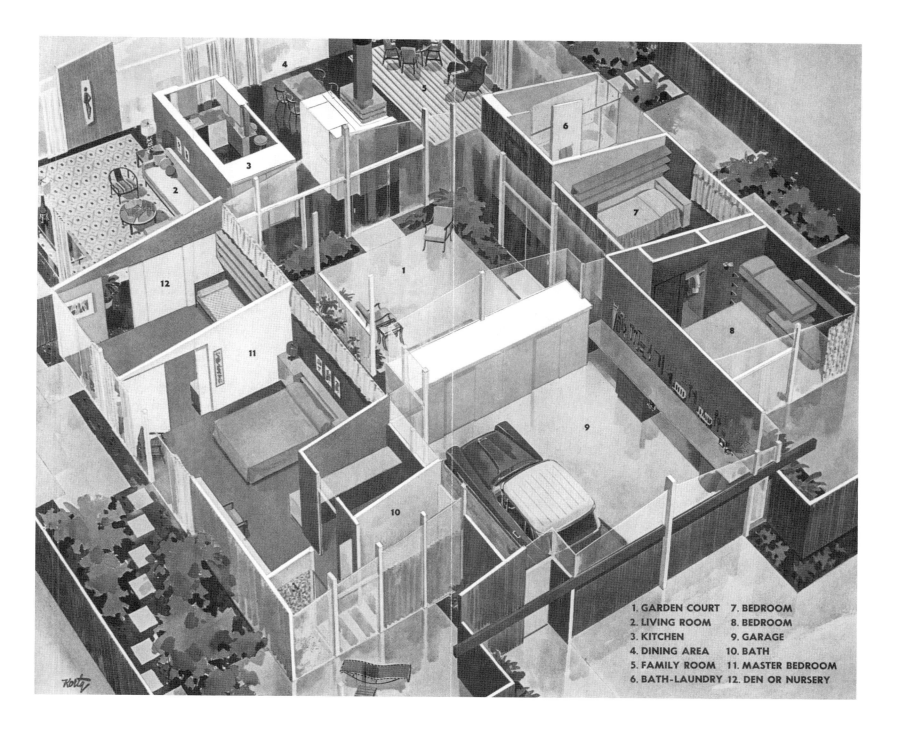

1. GARDEN COURT 7. BEDROOM
2. LIVING ROOM 8. BEDROOM
3. KITCHEN 9. GARAGE
4. DINING AREA 10. BATH
5. FAMILY ROOM 11. MASTER BEDROOM
6. BATH-LAUNDRY 12. DEN OR NURSERY

some explanations appear in the chapters that follow. Still, despite the stylistic variable, the features found in the Jones and Emmons house were the same as those desired by thousands of American families for their postwar homes, no matter the external appearance. In the outlines of those houses, we see the shadows of the houses constructed in the United States today. They also provide a blueprint for the spatial requirements of white, middle-class, and heteronormative domesticity.

POSTWAR HOUSES AND IDENTITY FORMATION

Inside and outside their home, my grandparents lived a contained life. The only outwardly displayed sign of my grandparents' Jewish identity was the carefully placed mezuzah at the front-door threshold; inside, a large silver Seder plate hung prominently over the fireplace mantel in the living room. Many Jewish homes in the United States similarly displayed Seder plates as prominent items of household decor, not only because such plates were often exceptionally large and attractive, but also because, as one scholar has postulated, Seder was the most accessible aspect of Judaism for American gentiles, since it could be understood as analogous to the Last Supper.[63] The dining room cabinet held a few pieces of Judaica. Still, their house always looked European to me, somehow not American. Despite their clear desire to assimilate, their proclivity for modern-

ist furnishings alone marked them as different. Yet all the other signs of their Jewish identity remained largely concealed: the matzo in the cupboards, the rendered chicken fat in the refrigerator, the meat grinder used for making chopped liver stored in the cabinet, my grandfather's yarmulkes and tallis kept in a drawer, and, of course, that extra set of dishes. Like most Jewish homes of the period, theirs was "essentially devoid of explicitly Jewish markers, especially when compared to earlier tenements." According to Jenna Weissman Joselit, the shelter and women's magazines played a role in this, since the average Jewish woman "had read one full year's back issues of *House Beautiful* and *American Home*. She knew what she wanted. . . . Making do with inherited Judaica, few homes had anything but the barest of Judaica collections: Brass candlesticks and perhaps a menorah and mezuzah appear to have been the norm." Although Judaism flourished in some of New York's postwar suburbs, it was an increasingly secularized, personal form of observance.[64]

The programmatic and design disjunctures that existed between my grandparents' house and their daily requirements were slight compared to some. Recent studies of immigrant housing clearly indicate the range of cultural differences that American house form tends to negate. For example, a study of Chinese immigrants who purchased suburban houses in Madison, Wisconsin, found that expectations for accommodation of multigenerational and extended kinship living styles are thwarted by American house form.[65] Chinese houses typically have less room specialization, such that a single interior space may serve multiple functions. The spaces therefore accommodate greater capacity, defined by Renee Chow as the flexibility inherent to the design of a house that allows its residents a variety of uses and living patterns without necessitating structural changes.[66] Moreover, Chinese houses are generally enclosed by high walls for privacy and protection, and gardening in China is geared primarily to food production, whereas American yards typically focus on ornamentals, particularly in front yards, where growing vegetables is considered forbidden. American kitchens are not well suited to Chinese cooking practices, which rely on gas ranges more powerful than typical American ranges to cook traditional Chinese food well; these ranges also require more efficient exhaust hoods to ventilate fumes and smoke. Moreover, typical American kitchen cabinets are not big enough to store the very large bags of rice many Chinese families purchase. Therefore, many Chinese immigrants in the United States convert their laundry rooms or garages into auxiliary kitchens to prevent oily fumes and smoke from entering the main living spaces of their houses and to store additional food products. Because of their desire to conform, Chinese immigrants tend not to alter the exteriors of their homes, instead maintaining signs of their ethnicity only on the inside.[67] What is significant here is the rhetorical and persuasive power the house holds over its occupants. In order to accommodate cultural differences, homeowners must frequently subvert the social order imposed by the forms of their houses and by the designers of those houses.

My grandparents were not alone in their understanding of the relationships that existed between their identities and their house, its maintenance, and its furnishings. To the contrary, postwar Americans were keenly aware of the ways in which their houses and furnishings signaled specific clues about their race, class, and status. In addition to sociologists, cultural anthropologists, cultural geographers, and urban historians, the authors of suburban fiction have deeply understood and explored the connection between suburban house form and identity formation, and their texts have likewise reinforced specific cultural norms.

Richard Yates's 1961 novel *Revolutionary Road* provides an excellent example. The book begins with a young couple searching for a new home. They consider themselves too urbane and sophisticated for suburban living, yet they are unable to afford the space their family requires in the city. In a series of passages, Yates clarifies the psychological discomfort the couple experiences as they deliberate about the selection and purchase of their first home—an ordinary postwar house. As they drive toward the suburban location of the new house, Yates describes their dismay and the manner in which they justify the move to themselves: "Economic circumstances might force you to live in this environment, [but] the important thing was to keep from being contaminated. The important thing, always, was to remember who you were." The real estate agent who leads them to the house identifies each neighborhood with a specific class of occupant:

> "Now of course it isn't a very desirable road down at this end," she explained. . . . "As you see, it's mostly these little cinder-blocky, pickup-trucky places—plumbers, carpenters, little local people of that sort. . . . *eventually* it leads on up and around to a perfectly dreadful new development called Revolutionary Hill Estates—great hulking split levels, all in the most nauseous pastels . . . but the place I want to show you has absolutely no connection with that. One of our nice little local builders put it up right after the war, you see, before all the really awful building began. It's really rather a sweet little house and a sweet little setting. Simple, clean lines, good lawns, marvelous for children."

As Frank and April first glimpse the house, April notes that it is

> small and wooden, riding high on its naked concrete foundation, its outsized central window staring like a big black mirror. "Yes, I think it's sort of—nice, don't you darling? Of course it does have the picture window; I guess there's no escaping that."

"I guess not," Frank said. "Still, I don't suppose one picture window is necessarily going to destroy our personalities."

Frank and April later decide that

> their solid wall of books would take the curse off the picture window; a sparse, skillful arrangement of furniture would counteract the prim suburban look of this too-symmetrical living room.[68]

If a picture window could destroy a personality, and bookshelves could be imagined as the antidote to such identity destruction, it is not hard to imagine the extent to which houses and their representations constituted essential elements in the establishment of personal and family identities. At the very least they were *imagined* as essential to the process. A bookcase, a set of properly displayed artful objects, the correct number and placement of tasteful furnishings—all these signaled very specific and widely understood markers of race and class that likewise conveyed specific notions of privilege and belonging.

The chapters that follow provide further examination of the connections that existed then and now between specific objects, residential forms, texts, images, and notions of identity. But novels such as Yates's demonstrate the ways in which domestic space and its representations created a spatial and visual rhetorical framework for citizenship as it was linked to specifically configured notions of property. Along with the houses occupied by Americans like my grandparents, they served to reinforce and continually restate the presumed whiteness of postwar residential property owners in the United States.

That postwar suburbs became racially segregated is not news, and numerous excellent studies have traced the phenomenon of uneven social and economic development in cities such as Detroit, Chicago, and Kansas City, to name a few.[69] As Kevin Fox Gotham observes, the conjoining of race and space "continues to underlie the construction of knowledge and social reality among many Whites at the same time that racial ideologies, beliefs, and institutional practices have become more invisible and covert."[70] But it is exactly this invisibility that signals its significance. Excluding individuals and families that appeared nonwhite was only a small part of the housing story, only a fraction of the means by which new housing was made to seem inherently and exclusively the domain of whites who were likewise middle-class. The rest of the story—or a significant portion of it—belongs to the everyday encounters Americans had with their stove tops, their curio cabinets, their bookshelves, their gardens, and their neighbors; it belongs to the books they read, the magazines they browsed, and the television programs they watched. It is a story that belongs—whether or not we wish to claim it—to all of us.

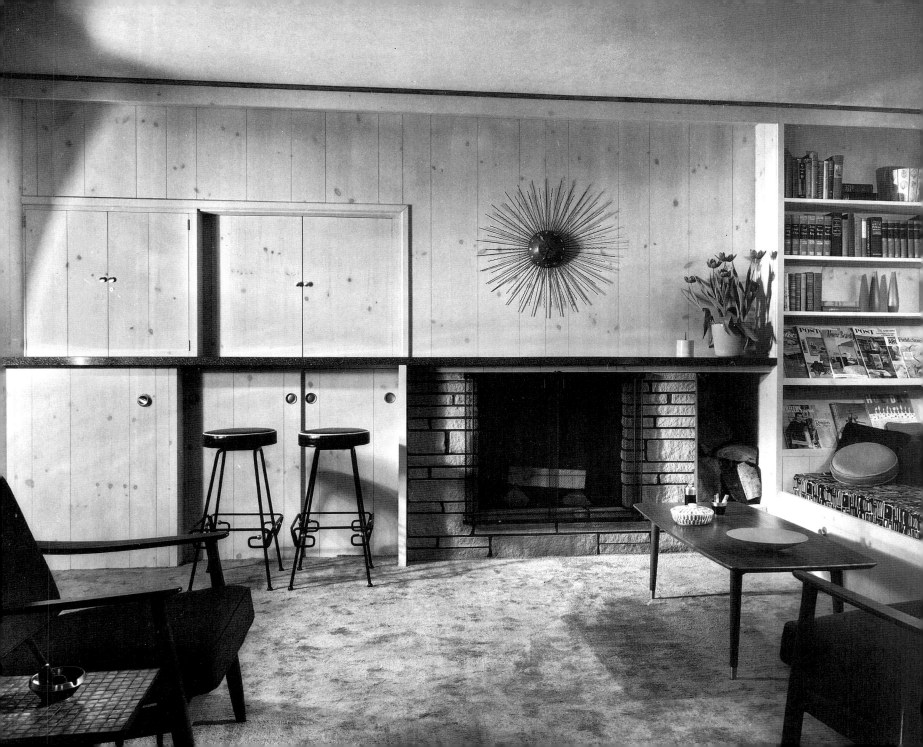

2

MAGAZINE LESSONS

Publishing the Lexicon of White Domesticity

As a very young child, I eagerly awaited the monthly arrival by mail of my mother's copy of *McCall's* magazine. I could not yet read, but the periodical's text mattered little to me. Instead, I coveted the "Betsy McCall" paper doll that was included toward the back of each issue. Cutting out the doll and the smartly designed accompanying outfits was fun; each new magazine signaled the arrival of a new toy. The paper doll also kept me, and thousands of children like me, busy for at least a short period of time so that my mother could read the magazine. But for my mother, and for the millions of women like her throughout the United States in the postwar era, subscriptions to monthly magazines brought much more than a brief respite from child care and housework. As they carried their magazines from mailbox to home interior, American women—and men who read their own magazines—imported ideas from experts and from advertisers that created aspirations and expectations about taste, culture, appropriate living, and the importance of consuming. These magazine lessons, packaged for readers who were sometimes insecure about their social, class, and racial status—perhaps also about their sexuality—became much more than simple recreational diversions. They carried the weight of authority for new homeowners and for those who aspired to buy new homes, offering definitions for an ever-growing audience of readers about the right way to live and, more subtly, about those who might rightfully consider the privilege of homeownership. Because popular

FACING
Living room
(*detail, see p. 66*).

magazines are among several important and sometimes complicated sources of evidence I cite in support of the arguments I make in this book, I begin this chapter by explaining their significance and by examining the ways scholars might consider these magazines as legitimate forms of evidence for architectural and cultural histories. A later chapter examines architectural drawings that appeared in popular magazines, demonstrating the ways in which those representations cultivated and substantiated specific ideas about race, class, and homeownership in the United States.

In his book *Imagined Communities*, Benedict Anderson notes that the readers of mass-circulation publications such as newspapers are "continually reassured that the imagined world is visibly rooted in everyday life . . . fiction seeps quietly and continuously into reality, creating that remarkable confidence of community in anonymity which is the hallmark of modern nations." He also remarks on the power of print capitalism to encourage rapidly growing numbers of people to self-consciously imagine themselves and their identities in relationship to others in important and new ways, and, in so doing, to formulate a nationally imagined community.[1] Likewise, I contend that visual and textual representations, artifacts of domestic material culture, and houses all constitute a cultural system that plays a fundamental role in establishing ideas about citizenship and belonging. To use Anderson's words, they are a "mode of apprehending the world" that allows us to "think the nation."[2] The notion that houses and their representational systems might help us think the nation is no stretch when we consider the deep historical significance of housing to the U.S. national and global economy now, as in the past.

The print culture I examine here—primarily shelter and popular magazines and books about house design and home decoration—is remarkable for the tremendous consistency of content that appears throughout the fifteen-year period examined in this book. Publishers repeatedly printed a set of messages constituting a rhetorical language with spatial and visual ramifications for the creation of an acceptable lifestyle while simultaneously contributing to the production of subject identities for those at whom the texts and images were aimed. Words such as *informality, casual lifestyle, leisure, individuality, privacy, uncluttered,* and even *clean* constituted a lexicon for whiteness and middle-class identity. The images that accompanied these words and articles formed an iconography of whiteness that reinforced and sometimes substituted for the verbal lexicon. In shelter and lifestyle magazines, as well as in the design literature from the period, whiteness remains, as Valerie Babb has demonstrated for a range of texts in American literature, so "obvious and pervasive" that the racial aspect remains "essentially invisible," though I also contend that white Americans saw whiteness everywhere and questioned it rarely.[3] This lexicon and iconography were not truly invisible to whites and others who consumed these texts and images. Instead, and again following Žižek's theory of ideological cynicism, Americans both recognized and deeply understood this iconography of race and class even if they seldom questioned its role in the creation of cultural formations. Significantly, *Ebony* magazine is most useful in this study for its poignant scarcity of housing features, which were otherwise ubiquitous in a wide range of magazines and books that were aimed at an audience of assumed white readers. Publishers and authors implicitly assumed and expected that new houses were designed and built for middle- and upper-middle-class whites—a reality that was both self-reinforcing and assured by government policies, as detailed in chapter 1. As Martin Berger has noted, photographers and editors of the northern white press took society as they found it. Using "long-standing norms of racial identity to move their white audiences in productive ways . . . the white press relied on . . . legible and comfortable formulations" to persuade Americans about a range of midcentury issues.[4]

Just as the architecture and furnishings of late nineteenth-century settlement houses assisted in the assimilation of immigrants, so the postwar house and its attendant literature created a structure and a set of norms for the bleaching of difference. As Babb notes, "Ethnic identity—the holidays, cultural rituals, language, dress, cooking, folklore, and religious practices of a people—was consigned to being a thing of the past, part of a life to be left as one advanced toward a future identity that would be secured through adopting the practices and values of a 'better type' (read middle- and upper-class white) of Americans."[5] Her research indicates, as does the work of Dolores Hayden, Gwendolyn Wright, and many other historians of American domestic environments, that the American house has always served to some degree as a framework for assimilation.[6] But in the years between 1945 and 1960, the drive to domestic conformity assumed some new dimensions. Moreover, single-family homeownership became a reality for more Americans than ever before, so this particular form of a spatially configured push to conformity affected a larger percentage of the population.

Postwar America may well have been "the era of the expert," in which the popularity of advice literature indicated a prevailing faith in expertise.[7] Yet Americans had long turned to such books and magazines for advice on how to cook, behave, dress, raise children, garden, and decorate the home, among other things. As Dell Upton has noted, such literature was a commonplace element in nineteenth-century domestic life, typically connecting middle-class identity with "possessions and the ability to select and use them knowingly. Thus, they tied class to consumption."[8] Women's and shelter magazines have also traditionally played a significant role in assimilation, offering instruction to immigrants and their children in a particularized image of American identity and class structure by describing and illustrating appropriate modes of participation—that is to say, according to a very specific set of norms—in American culture.

Essentially, popular, women's, and shelter magazines valorized mainstream, middle-class values through the repetition of images that portrayed whiteness and its prerogatives, such as homeownership, as equivalent with American identity. With each issue's instructions in cooking, home decorating, and homemaking, the publishers, editors, and authors defined a correct way of living that, if followed, promised implicitly to erase potentially damaging traces of an immigrant, ethnic, or nonwhite past. The magazines created an imaginary world of idealized Americans—especially of American women—who all happened to be white, heterosexual, beautiful, clean, well organized, and financially comfortable. That this was a narrowly constructed and largely fictitious middle-class world was not lost on everyone, and many readers certainly discerned the ridiculously monolithic nature of the portrayals of domestic life and inhabitants. In 1962, for example, the architectural writer Kate Ellen Rogers critiqued media representations of women in the home, writing that the homemaker portrayed in television and in advertisements was

> an awe-inspiring creation made up of wise and secure mother, sage counselor, discerning psychologist, creative interior designer, exciting companion, intelligent partner, charming hostess, brilliant conversationalist, expert cook, as well as housekeeper par excellence. That all of this is accomplished on a shoestring is taken for granted, for she is also a shrewd manager. This homemaker is usually pictured in such magazine articles and advertisements as young, pretty, and impeccably dressed.[9]

Still, the repetition of conventional images that featured elegantly groomed white women and their families in meticulously decorated and cleaned houses constantly reinforced a message about the rightful owners and occupants of such dwellings. As Valerie Babb has written, because "whites are the only personifications of privilege, social mobility, economic security, and cultural refinement, experiences and products that appear race-neutral are implicitly racialized."[10] The very fact that nearly every image about the home that appeared in a magazine or on a television show included whites alone meant that the possessive investment in whiteness was continually reinforced.[11] In many cases, such representational choices were not consciously constructed, but were instead taken for granted as the only possible norm in the racially divided, Jim Crow era of the 1950s. Nonwhites, it was assumed, had little access to surplus income or homeownership, and were therefore invisible to and rendered invisible by advertisers, publishers, or network executives. Yet the formulaic repetition of images in the press ultimately both shaped and reinforced the widely held notion that the privately owned house occupied by a single nuclear family was equivalent with white ownership and occupancy, and it was likewise seen as inherently valuable and as the most desirable kind of setting in which to live.[12]

With the rise of picture magazines (magazines that extensively featured photography) in the 1930s and 1940s, American readers became increasingly receptive to and skilled in (if not always sophisticated at) reading visual narratives.[13] The magazines and the representations that appeared in them constitute forms of documentary evidence whose circulation made them both rhetorically powerful and historically fluid because of their very potential for geographic and temporal flow. It comes as no surprise, then, that *Life* magazine explicitly stated its purpose: "To see and be instructed."[14]

In fact, print magazines hold rhetorical power that is potentially greater than that of television or newspapers because they often remain in readers' homes for months and even years.[15] The consistently reproduced images of whiteness in connection with images and ideas about houses and domesticity that appeared in the magazines functioned as a set of discursive conventions that performed specific ideological tasks. Does this mean that

In this National Homes advertisement, a white husband and wife proclaim that the house illustrated in the ad is "for us!" Postwar houses were almost exclusively available to the white audience pictured in this illustration, so that "This is for us!" must be read as carrying multiple meanings. The cartoon couple proclaims the house as being for them, but the caption also and perhaps more subtly pertained to a broad national audience that was presumed to look like those featured in the ad.
Life magazine, September 13, 1954, 139.

media representations *determined* the ways Americans understood the relationships among race, class, and homeownership? I do not seek to make such an argument here, but instead follow the course that media and communications scholars have followed for decades, one that views media and their representations as powerful historical and cultural agents that "shape people's perceptions about their world."[16] The magazines did not necessarily determine reader perspectives, but they did aim continually to persuade and reinforce the deep connections between homeownership and whiteness, between property and citizenship, because that was the known and understood cultural condition. They did not challenge social conventions, but instead bolstered those that already existed. As magazine historian Theodore Peterson observed in 1956, magazine advertising may have contributed to the improvement of material life, but it also "tended to be a force for conservatism in the realm of ideas. Business and industry were understandably anxious to protect the system under which they flourished and to safeguard the large investment in the machinery of production and distribution which had raised the material welfare. Advertising tended to promote allegiance to the existing system" in ways that were about free enterprise and free competition and that catered to a majority that advertisers did not wish to offend or alienate.[17] Peterson noted further that "in fiction and in articles, commercial magazines were inclined to maintain the status quo . . . [and] actu-

ally perpetuated minority stereotypes, approved caste lines, and, in the words of Joseph T. Klapper, pictured 'a world where the highest income is reserved for white, American-born gentiles who practice the Protestant ethic.'"[18] Magazines such as *Life* did occasionally include features about blacks and members of other underrepresented groups, but my focus here is not on those exceptional articles; I am concerned with the massive corpus of representations associated specifically with houses and homeownership.[19]

In recent years, it has become somewhat fashionable within the realm of cultural studies to dismiss the use of popular magazines as primary source evidence because, according to some critics, these publications merely reflect elite tastes and therefore cannot be used as evidence of true middle- or working-class values, tastes, attitudes, desires, or actions. In this book, the problem is made more complex because I variously critique/analyze such journals and rely on them as a form of primary evidence to discern the forms of some postwar houses and as an essential aspect of postwar domestic visual culture.[20] However, following from the scholarship of Richard Ohmann and Nancy Walker, I see such magazines as serving a far more important role than the critics recognize.

In his study of magazines, markets, and class at the turn of the century, Richard Ohmann demonstrates that, to some extent, magazines shape their readerships through consistency of message, voice, and advertisements. Nineteenth-century magazines such as *Godey's Lady's Book* and *Ladies' Home Journal* published hundreds of patterns for houses, and these "made the vocabulary of home design familiar to millions of people thinking about how to organize their material lives and build their cultural capital." The images in these magazines provided readers with a sense that home design mattered for both families and for society, and they contributed to a late nineteenth-century discourse about individuality as a dominant ideal and the "house as a projection of its owner's taste."[21] Ohmann links the mass circulation of these popular magazines with the emergence of what he calls a "professional-managerial class" or PMC, which was likewise linked to the acquisition of suburban space as a means of purchasing identity. The PMC built social identity around "consumption, location, homogeneity of family presentation, autonomy," and magazines helped them cultivate those ideals by shaping audiences around common needs or interests that were directly related to profit. The magazines, therefore, both charted PMC social space and guided it, entering "similar homes everywhere, and [they] were part of what made those homes similar. And of course magazines helped shape the values and interests of PMC people, including an interest in the brand named commodities advertised there." Indeed, the magazines themselves became brand-name commodities whose consumption and display conferred distinction.[22] Maynard Parker's photographs for *House*

Beautiful, for example, frequently included magazines prominently displayed on living room racks and on coffee tables, their titles clearly visible. As such, the magazines became status symbols that conferred distinction on the owner who possessed the taste, literacy, and, of course, the income to be able to afford multiple subscriptions.

Nancy Walker's study of women's magazines between 1940 and 1960 indicates that these publications had the "potential to both reflect and influence women's lives" with their large circulation. Walker's argument therefore merits quoting at some length:

> While it would be impossible to know precisely what role any of these magazines played in the lives of American women during and after World War II, there are several important indications that they had a significant part in defining women's aspirations regarding work and family, appearance, health, and happiness. One indicator is the magazines' expanding readership. . . . despite criticism to the contrary, the editors of women's magazines did not make choices about the contents of the magazines in a vacuum; indeed, the relationship between the editors and readers of many of the magazines was remarkably interactive, so that editors' decisions about regular features, special articles, and format were informed at least in part by expressed reader preferences. Some of the magazines regularly

An unidentified living room with magazine shelves at far right, circa 1950. Photograph by Maynard L. Parker. Courtesy of the Huntington Library, San Marino, California.

conducted polls of readers on selected topics. . . . Magazines that were read by millions of women allow us to understand what society expected of them and, to a more limited degree, what women hoped for from life in American culture.[23]

As further evidence of the cultural impact of the magazines, Walker cites the numerous critiques of women's

magazines that appeared in the postwar period. The attention they received from critics testifies, at least in part, to the significance of the magazines in midcentury culture, and she reminds us that the magazines had more impact in the immediate postwar era because, along with radio, they were the primary media outlets in homes before television became pervasive after about 1957.[24] Magazines such as *McCall's* and *Good*

Housekeeping, it must be remembered, had circulation levels between two million and eight million, with actual readerships that were larger because women shared the magazines.[25]

Magazine subscription and circulation rates doubled, and in some cases tripled during the fifteen-year period of this study, along with a rise in the number of magazines published.[26] Newsstand sales remained brisk, but subscription rates rose more dramatically as the paper rationing and shortages of the war years gave way to increased stability and economic prosperity. The relatively rapid rise of suburban homeownership also stimulated subscription sales, particularly for women's and shelter magazines.[27] Blockbuster general-interest magazines such as *Life* saw particularly significant increases in subscription rates, from under 2.5 million in 1945 to nearly 6 million by 1960. But circulation figures for what the industry termed "mechanics and science" publications such as *Popular Mechanics,* for "women's" magazines such as *Ladies' Home Journal,* or for "home" magazines such as *House Beautiful, Better Homes and Gardens,* and *House & Garden* also soared to triple and quadruple their 1945 rates.[28] One study found that in 1938, a single magazine copy passed through multiple hands, so that the average issue of *Life* reached 17 million people.[29] Though this was surely an inflated estimate, it is clear that advertisers understood the power of the medium.

Magazines displayed under a table in California architect Cliff May's home, circa 1950s.
Photograph by Maynard L. Parker. Courtesy of the Huntington Library, San Marino, California.

Postwar advertisers were keenly aware of these circulation increases, just as they also understood that specific magazines were meant for specific audiences whose consuming patterns varied according to gender but also according to economic and social status. They therefore sought precise information about the social and economic identities of the audiences who purchased each magazine so that their clients could derive the greatest impact—and therefore the greatest value—for their advertising dollars. To this end, they commissioned studies that examined the economic and education levels of the readers of particular periodicals, along with their employment status, their possessions, their drinking habits, and their status as pet owners. But, as James Baughman has pointed out, "generally speaking, a majority of those in the bottom income categories did

Popular and shelter magazines displayed on a table in the living room of a Barker Brothers Furnishings model home, circa 1950s. Photograph by Maynard L. Parker. Courtesy of the Huntington Library, San Marino, California.

not read periodicals. Simply put, they lacked the discretionary income and the free time of the middle and upper classes."[30]

One such study included four national weeklies (*Collier's, Life, Look,* and *Saturday Evening Post*), four women's magazines (*Good Housekeeping, Ladies' Home Journal, McCall's,* and *Woman's Home Companion*), and one home magazine (*Better Homes and Gardens*). Subscribers to all the magazines in the study were evenly distributed throughout the United States, a fact that is significant for this book because it illustrates the national framework in which these representations of domestic life and architecture circulated.[31] The study found that *Life* attracted an audience split neatly between men and women, and that, compared with other magazines, it attracted readers with higher education levels and slightly higher income levels. *Life* readers were also about 10 percent more likely to be employed in so-called blue-collar jobs and to be homeowners than were readers of the other magazines in the study, with readers of *Collier's* and *Better Homes and Gardens* appearing to have lower rates of homeownership and lower-paying jobs.[32] Although not included in this particular study, magazines such as *House Beautiful,* with its lower circulation rates and higher-end product advertisements, clearly targeted a slightly more elite audience, including professionally trained architects and landscape architects. But despite these differences, the readers of general magazines did not typically earn high incomes. Instead, the median annual family income for 1957 readers of *Life, Look,* and the *Saturday Evening Post* hovered between $5,040 and $5,460.[33] The average *House Beautiful* reader may have earned somewhat more, and the average *Popular Mechanics* reader may have earned somewhat less, but the advertisers understood the general economic range of the majority of readers, and from their statistics they compiled a clear sense of reader identity.

House designs that appeared in *House Beautiful,* then, tended to be larger and more elaborate than those that appeared either in *Life* or in *Popular Mechanics* because the *House Beautiful* readership was known to be at least somewhat more wealthy and because the latter attracted a crossover audience of design professionals who were interested in the somewhat more elaborate architectural works that appeared there. *Popular Mechanics* tended to feature a greater number of "Do-It-Yourself" or "Build-It-Yourself" articles and plans for more modest homes that suited the economic status of its largely male readership. Nevertheless, all the magazines featured the same themes for home design that appear as the structure for this book, no matter the size of the house or the income level of its owner.

If advertisers collected data about the socioeconomic status of readers, they firmly believed (though not necessarily correctly) that white readers read white magazines and newspapers, and black readers read black magazines and newspapers. An ad in a 1950 issue

of *Printer's Ink* (a leading journal for the advertising industry) declared, "The Negro Market is Terrific! 15 million American negroes spend 10 billion dollars a year!" The ad suggested that advertisers should aim to reach this "big buying public . . . through Negro newspapers and magazines," which the advertisers could find by contacting Interstate United Newspapers, Inc.[34] Recalling Arthur H. Dix's 1957 statement that "advertising should be directed to those who buy," it is not surprising that the visual content of mass-circulation magazines of the period was overwhelmingly characterized by the whiteness of everyone and everything depicted.[35] After all, advertisers were simply directing their work toward those they knew were most likely to participate in the consumption of postwar housing and its attendant material culture: middle- and upper-middle-class whites. But the overwhelming reproduction of white images also continually enforced the public's sense of the powerful connections that existed between whiteness and middle-class housing.

It is also important to note that general magazines, shelter magazines, women's magazines, and mechanics/science magazines constitute specific genres intended to promote specific and differentiated cultural forms and norms (masculinity/outdoor sports, femininity/domesticity, self-regulation and self-management, and so on). Yet the inclusion of matters related to house design

An unidentified living room with
magazine display shelves, circa 1950s.
Photograph by Maynard L. Parker. Courtesy of the
Huntington Library, San Marino, California.

and construction and to home decorating cut across all these genres in the postwar era, since housing was one of the most vigorous sectors of the national economy and houses were among the most desired acquisitions for postwar Americans. The magazines of the various genres were different from one another, but their inclusion of house- and housing-related features created a consistency among a large number of popular postwar periodicals.

The shelter, women's, and general magazines also sometimes provide important information about what individuals specifically desired in their homes. For example, *McCall's* published a report on the "Second Congress on Better Living," held in Washington, D.C., in 1957, during which women were asked about their preferences in house design. The women reported that they liked colonial-style houses with low-maintenance interiors and exteriors, lots of wiring so they could keep adding appliances without blowing a fuse, no picture windows, and more space, including more storage. They thought builders' model homes typically featured too-small bedrooms, and they wanted more mature trees and brand-name appliances.[36] Although such articles appear less frequently in these magazines than a historian might wish, their occasional presence should not be taken lightly. Readers also made their opinions known in letters to the editor, and they swayed magazine features and advertising patterns through the power of their purchasing choices. The magazines thus

record a dialogue between editorial persuasion and consumer opinion and desire that is far from simple.[37]

A structure that perpetuated reader dependence amplified the persuasive power of the magazines. The more a housewife read the magazines, the less sure she was of her own ability to make correct decisions, since the editors and authors constantly reinforced the notion that their expert advice was essential. As mentioned above, such magazines flourished, as they had for decades, because they relied on authoritative voices—a culture of expertise—to convey specific forms of information. But the source of that authority varied depending on the type of magazine. In some cases, the voice of expertise emanated from an editor, as with *House Beautiful's* Elizabeth Gordon, who for two decades positioned herself as an arbiter of taste for the nation. Since feature writers were sometimes anonymous, their expertise extended from the authority of the editor, but carefully selected licensed architects and landscape architects also contributed to all these periodicals, lending their professional credibility to the consistently reproduced content, which likewise reflected editorial control. In magazines such as *Popular Mechanics*, the author was sometimes a homeowner whose expertise derived from his having "done-it-himself" and who served as the voice of experience, a peer passing along much-needed information. Letters to the editor also provided specific forms of peer-to-peer content. But the voices of advertisers and of the products they advertised were particularly pronounced in these magazines because advertising influenced virtually every aspect of the publications. Advertising revenue kept magazines alive, and editors necessarily responded accordingly, shifting content to reflect and to help create shifting market trends.[38] Again, what is remarkable for this study is that these varying expert voices reiterated such consistent messages, replicating an unswerving ideology that linked white identities, middle-class status, and homeownership.

Editors understood that their audience of new and first-time homeowners was hungry for information on how to be tasteful, how to be sophisticated, how to belong to the assimilated middle class, and they catered to that audience very successfully.[39] The producers of tastemaking literature were automatically set up as distinct from their readers, who needed their advice—a hierarchy was built into the system of editor, author, and reader so that the reader could never be assured of having the cultural capital possessed by the magazine's producers. As long as the reader must rely on the expert's advice, an audience is assured, and the success of such publications must be attributed at least in part to this dependence model.

Despite the mass popularity of the shelter and women's magazines, not everyone uniformly appreciated these publications. The architectural press maintained a particularly uneasy relationship with the popular magazines because the latter frequently overlooked the architect's professional expertise in favor of do-it-yourself plans or the works of merchant builders. For example, a 1955 *Architectural Forum* essay discussed the role played by women editors of shelter magazines as liaisons or interpreters between ordinary citizens and architects or merchant builders. The author described "a special tribe of women editors. . . . to listen to some of them speak of 'my public' is a remarkable experience. Many a prototype or exhibition house is designed in their busy minds." He then disparaged the editors and their publications as mere indicators of popular (rather than highbrow) taste.[40] Female architects were very rare during this period in the United States, and in its specific derision of female editors the *Forum* article betrays the rampant sexism that existed (and still exists) in the architectural profession.

House Beautiful's Elizabeth Gordon was the most widely known of these editors at the time, and the architectural profession maintained a measured distance from her that betrayed a balance of respect and disdain. During her tenure as editor in chief (1939–64) at what was arguably the most influential shelter magazine of the period, Gordon earned a reputation as a dogmatic proponent of "soft modernism" over International Style modernism; indeed, she claimed that the latter would lead to the demise of American democracy.[41] As she wrote in her unpublished résumé, Gordon decided to devote entire issues of her magazine to single subjects, such as Scandinavian design or the Japanese design concept of *shibui*, so that she could "counter the influence of the Museum of Modern Art, who was promoting the Bauhaus school of design—which I never approved of."[42] Yet she contributed significantly to promoting the careers of numerous designers, including Thomas Church, Douglas Baylis, John Yeon, A. Quincy Jones, Gardner Dailey, William Wurster, Harwell Hamilton Harris, and (most famously) Frank Lloyd Wright, by repeatedly featuring their designs in the magazine. And Gordon herself wrote that she used *House Beautiful* as "a propaganda teaching tool—to broaden people's 'thinking-and-wanting' apparatus. To make them think broader than locally. To make them want to travel internationally. I did it even in the cooking and food departments."[43] She also described the magazine as "a class publication catering to people who could afford an architect."[44] Even if most of her readers could not afford architects, they aspired to the status conveyed by both the publication itself and the products promoted within its pages, including houses that were a cut above what most middle-class Americans could afford. Despite the disdain some felt for her, Gordon could not be ignored because she wielded considerable power with her pen, and she was eventually named an honorary member of the American Institute of Architects for having made *House Beautiful* into a "serious architectural influence."[45] An uncomfortable tension therefore existed among magazines such as *House Beautiful*, architects, and high-style tastemakers who understood the power of the journals if they did not entirely respect their contents.

One architect and writer, Robert Woods Kennedy, exemplified the attitude held by many of his colleagues. Calling the journals "Dream Magazines," and specifically addressing *Better Homes and Gardens, American Home, House Beautiful*, and *Arts and Decoration*, he criticized what he believed were the unrealistic and unattainable visions the magazines put into his clients' heads, as well as the trend toward "do-it-yourselfism."[46] He wrote:

This is the antithesis to the creative approach to design. At the present time none of the dream magazines provides the prospective homeowner with much of a clue to the connections between living and style. The editors themselves are usually only dimly aware of the issues involved. Furthermore their purpose is not to prepare people to build. It is to sell magazines. . . . The editor of one such magazine specifically tells the architects he commissions to design a house catering to the readers' desires, rather than to their economic capabilities. Thus any reasonably photogenic house for the upper three per cent in terms of income will be published. . . . With such devices the magazines build up a picture of an architecture which by and large does not exist. . . . Thus the problem is to persuade the client involved in the dream magazine myth that beauty and livability are experienced in time and space rather than in pictures.[47]

Despite the objections of some architects and high-style tastemakers, the magazines enjoyed tremendous popularity and had a significant impact on ordinary house design and construction. Aware of the trend, a 1955 issue of the builders' magazine *House and Home* advised readers:

> Each month, more than 50 million U.S. magazine readers learn to like (and want) quality design. . . . Do you know that this month, also, those same 50 million—all of them potential home buyers—are being further sold on the idea that storage should come in walls, that most furniture ought to be built in, that more than half of their living space should be out-of-doors (and that the outdoors should be planned for that purpose), and that such modern devices as metal fireplaces, flat roofs, plastic skylights, and family rooms are as natural a part of any good house as the front door? These millions of course, are the readers of U.S. consumer magazines—and they are your best customers.

The article concluded that builders, architects, and mortgage bankers should prepare themselves to deal with a newly discriminating public, whose tastes were as up-to-date as their own, and that they had better be ready to give the customers what the magazines had taught them to want. With examples culled from *Life, American Home, Ladies' Home Journal, Parents, Good Housekeeping, Better Homes, Living, House Beautiful, Holiday, Sunset, House & Garden,* and *Companion,* and circulation figures provided for each magazine, the article provided a compelling argument. It noted finally: "*House & Home* feels that the consumer magazines are such an important barometer of what the home buying public is going to want—and going to get—that we will, henceforth, publish a monthly pictorial review of what consumers are finding on their newsstands. We hope that this feature will help builders to gauge accurately the demand for better design that is being created throughout the US."[48]

In keeping with this conviction, *House and Home* consistently included articles informing its readers of the importance of such press coverage. For example, a 1955 issue included a double-page ad for the *Better Homes and Gardens* "Idea Home of the Year" that called it "an Idea Home for promotion-wise builders." The model received special endorsement at that year's annual NAHB convention. The ad also noted that the house would first be shown to the public in the September issue of *Better*

Homes and Gardens, which would be read by four million families, "guaranteeing that tremendous throngs of top prospects will view the homes locally. . . . Lists of builders, addresses of their home, and names of home furnishers will be featured in a colorful two-page advertisement. . . . In addition, builders will be supplied with a complete package of promotional aids (most of them at no cost) including: copies of the magazine, newspaper materials, radio and TV spots, publicity and news releases, special display and directional pieces, miniature *Better Homes & Gardens* cover folders . . . IN SHORT, EVERYTHING THE BUILDER WILL NEED FOR A MOST SUCCESSFUL PROMOTION!"[49] The editors of *Fortune* likewise agreed that popular magazines played an essential role in determining patterns of consumption, and they specifically identified suburban readers as not only avid consumers but also trendsetters. After all, they wrote, "it is the suburbanite who starts the mass fashion—for children, hard-tops, culottes, dungarees, vodka martinis, outdoor barbecues, functional furniture, picture windows, and costume jewelry. . . . Moreover, the consumer is getting ideas from fashion, home, and 'consumer' magazines, whose circulation has boomed."[50]

Later that same year, *House and Home* included an article titled "Twelve Top Merchandising Techniques" that laid out methods that builders could use to help ensure rapid house sales. In addition to the obvious requirements of well-designed houses placed in good locations and reasonably priced, the article recommended that builders provide adequate parking at model home sites; that they tastefully and completely furnish the houses; that visitors to the sites be provided with professionally designed sales literature and brochures illustrated with professionally made photographs of the houses; that specially produced signage be implemented in the houses to point out key features; that recorded music and sales pitches be used throughout the interiors; and that realtors and educated salesmen deliver sales talks at the sites. The article also advised "cashing in on brand-name products," since manufacturers spend thousands of dollars on ads for their products to cultivate name recognition in the public. By listing the products used in their houses in promotional material and signage, builders could benefit from the ads the corporations had already paid for and placed in magazines and on television. For extra benefit, builders were instructed to link their houses to magazine house projects whenever possible and to time their openings to coincide with home shows that were advertised in local newspapers and on television.[51] This interweaving of advertising sales among magazines, model home exhibits, newspapers, and television came to characterize a newly savvy industry that exploited these media tools to their full potential.

Magazine-sponsored house-building projects became important features that appeared throughout the postwar decades and facilitated the intersection of corporate strategies, consumer desire, and house construction. In turn, the houses served as three-dimensional, full-scale advertisements for builders, products, materials, appliances, furnishings, architects (occasionally), and, perhaps most important, specific lifestyles. Among the best known of these were the so-called Case Study Houses sponsored by *Arts and Architecture* magazine under the editorial guidance of John Entenza.[52] This program featured designs by more than twenty architects, most of whom built a single model house based on a specific set of concerns. The steel-framed house designed by Charles and Ray Eames, for example, was constructed with off-the-shelf, prefabricated materials and parts that were intended to be inexpensive and easily obtained. Like most of the program's houses, however, it became an isolated example that never reached a mass market for a variety of reasons, among them the difficulty of obtaining large quantities of precut steel during that period and the overt modernity of the house's form, which likely caused hesitation and resistance from both builders and the FHA. Moreover, *Arts and Architecture* targeted an elite and limited audience of architects, artists, designers, and tastemakers and did not reach the mass audience that could be claimed by the popular and shelter magazines.[53]

Although they have received less attention from historians than has Entenza's project, house plans and magazine-sponsored model homes filled the pages of popular magazines during the postwar era. Most of these were far more ordinary than the Case Study Houses, and they were far more likely to be built by readers who could purchase the plans for—in some cases —as little as five dollars. The number of houses built from such plans is difficult to gauge, but the plans were published with great frequency. The architectural historian Thomas Hine has suggested that the "magazine-sponsored program that probably came closest to dealing with the real concerns of postwar home-seekers" was the "*Better Homes and Gardens* Five Star Home Series," which had appeared since the 1930s. The houses were designed by an architect, and the blueprints could be purchased for five dollars a set. According to Hine, "In 1947 the magazine boasted that every 57.6 seconds, a family obtained a set of drawings for a Five Star Home."[54] The estimate likely reflects the editor's tendency toward hyperbole, and even if a set of plans truly sold every minute, it is impossible to know how many of the houses were actually built. Whether the houses were constructed or not, the blueprint sales were certainly brisk for such projects, indicating the enthusiasm with which some members of the public greeted these magazine-sponsored programs.

Such projects appeared in magazines well before the war ended, creating a pent-up demand for new houses and anything with which they were connected. For example, from 1938 to 1940, *Life* magazine featured eight new homes designed each year, with prices ranging from two thousand dollars to ten thousand dollars. Like most of these projects, the editors stated that their purpose was to demonstrate "important advances that have been made in the past decade in the design and technology of house building," even if the true goal was largely related to advertising and sales revenue.[55] By the time of the 1940 issue, seventy-three builders in twenty-seven states were building or had built *Life* houses, and the most expensive of the 1940 houses was to be given away in a promotional raffle.[56] These houses would have been in enormous demand, since relatively few housing starts occurred during this period. Given that the magazines were not in direct competition with each other, *Architectural Forum* (read primarily by architects) featured advertisements for the 1938 *Life* houses. For example, U.S. Gypsum and Certain-teed products (which included roofing and siding, insulating board, wallboard, and gypsum products) both advertised in *Architectural Forum* with slogans tied to the *Life* house; Certain-teed's ad stated, "*Life* builds a home for modern living, Certain-teed keeps it modern for years to come."[57] Likewise, Westinghouse proclaimed "*Life* house . . . Any house . . . Every house Needs a Westinghouse Elec-tri Center Kitchen," and advised readers that they could obtain kitchen plans by mailing in the coupon provided. Moreover, the Westinghouse ad included an illustration of the "Planned Electric Laundry" to accompany the *Life* house designed by the well-known architect Royal Barry Wills.[58] Through an intricate se-

ries of links and interlacing modes of publicity, houses, magazines, and corporations became woven into the culture of consumption that was likewise essential to the formation of personal and family identity.

The magazine house was not a new idea in the postwar era, then, and consumers had been able to purchase model home kits and blueprints from magazines for decades. But after the end of World War II, when materials became more widely available and FHA-insured mortgages made purchases possible for many, the pace and variety of such projects grew dramatically. Almost every popular and shelter magazine that was aimed at a white audience included house designs and plans that could be purchased, many of which were sponsored by major appliance or materials corporations. The annual "parade of homes" issue became a standard for most magazines, though the title varied depending on the publication. *Popular Mechanics,* for example, included numerous build-it-yourself models with plans that could be purchased, and these appeared consistently throughout the fifteen-year period that followed the end of the war. Monthly features with detailed coverage of the entire construction process for a plywood ranch house, for example, showed readers how an average man built the house from the magazine's plans with relative ease and within a reasonable time frame. Tom Riley, the owner/builder of the plywood ranch house and author of the articles, became familiar to readers through his serialized features, and his everyday discussion of the process helped them imagine themselves building *Popular Mechanics* houses for their families.[59]

It should be clear by now that the women's, shelter, and popular magazines were created by editors who carefully calculated the presentation of text and images, and who understood—or at least imagined—that their readers gave equally careful attention to the pages they read. The iconography of the images contained in their pages received intense consideration and must therefore be evaluated accordingly. An example taken from correspondence between *House Beautiful* editor Elizabeth Gordon and photographer Maynard Parker makes the point. Parker was one of the primary *House Beautiful* photographers during Gordon's editorial tenure,

The plywood ranch house featured in *Popular Mechanics*. Readers could purchase plans for the house from the magazine, which published serialized monthly accounts of owner Tom Riley's experience constructing the house.

Courtesy of *Popular Mechanics*; originally published in the November 1950 issue.

This is the architect's drawing of the new PM plywood house which Tom Riley is building in Portland, Ore.

I'm Building the POPULAR MECHANICS
PLYWOOD RANCH HOUSE

and she sent him traveling across the United States in search of houses that might be featured in the magazine's pages. In a letter dated October 9, 1942, Gordon suggested to Parker that the front door of the Gruell house in Ventura, California, would make a good cover shot, "especially if you could plan an action in it like a child playing or a mother and baby." For that same house, she suggested to Parker that "when they have rounded up a mother model and two little girls or a little girl and little boy outfitted with the right color garments, you will pilot the party to Ventura to take the shot. I think it important that the models be wearing brilliant yellow, as that is one of the main colors missing in the house and its surrounding planting."[60] A cover that was meant to appear "candid," then, was completely staged, fabricated. Instead of the house's actual occupants, the featured "mother" and "children" were models, chosen to create the best composition and outfitted in colors that best complemented the scene. Using models instead of homes' real families was not uncommon; for the U.S. Gypsum Research Village located in Barrington, Illinois, and constructed in 1955–56, photographs created by the Chicago architectural photography firm of Hedrich Blessing likewise relied on hired models, and shelter magazines were used to promote the project.[61] By using models instead of house occupants, the magazine editors could carefully select people who were intended to represent ideal homeowners and whose age, gender, race, hair color, attire, and affect could be completely and carefully controlled.

Controlling the display of household objects was of equal concern for magazine editors. For a photo shoot at the Avery Rennick house, Gordon reminded Parker, "We will send the accessories for the table top in the foreground. Everything else is up to you."[62] The photographs of house interiors were often highly staged, the owners' personal art and artifacts removed in favor of objects carefully selected by the editor and her staff. It should come as no surprise, then, that *House Beautiful* often appeared on coffee tables in these photographs; Gordon used every opportunity to promote her magazine as an essential accessory for stylish homes, though it should be noted that the magazine's appearance in photos may sometimes have reflected the fact of the owner's subscription. Gordon also made sure to include carefully placed accessories, such as floral arrangements that were purchased for the photo shoot, decanters, glasses, table settings, trays, and in one instance a riding crop—an accessory intended to convey the gentility and Gentile-ity of a house's horse-owning and equestrian-active occupants.[63] Each photo shoot involved the coordination of a team that included florists, the photographer, the homeowner, models, and stylists.[64] With experts at the ready, photographs of house interiors were anything but candid, casual, or impromptu, and they seldom reflected the daily and material realities of middle-class postwar families.

That such photographs were carefully calculated and that they contained a complexly formulated iconography can be seen in the example of a *House Beautiful* photo shoot of the Havens house in Berkeley, California, designed by Harwell Hamilton Harris in 1939. In advance of the photo shoot, Gordon sent a letter to the owner, John Weston Havens, addressing a delicate issue. Gordon wanted to have models interacting with Havens in various parts of the house and garden, "to show the house in use, with people and living activities going on." She wrote to Havens:

> I am very hopeful that you will be in all these pictures, for the owner always interests people more than model nonentities. And I hope, too, that you can get some friends of yours to cooperate as the other models. The girl on the front cover probably ought to be a professional model, however, unless you can get some friend who is a whiz of a beauty and very on the thin side (as photography thickens people up). . . . That brings me to a sort of delicate point, on which you will have to be arbiter: We would rather the girl at the table with you be wearing a morning coat or hostess coat, for the simple reason that it lets us get more square inches of color into the composition than would be possible in any other costume. However, we realize that it implies you are married, which, I understand, you are not. If this composition is not to your liking, then we will bow to your feelings, and have the girl wear black slacks and a fuchsia blouse, making it appear that perhaps she came to play badminton with you—or what have you. For purely selfish reasons of color, we hope you'll let her wear a housecoat of the color indicated. It is a modern color, and we want the flower color on the piano arrangement to coordinate with it.[65]

Evidence indicates that Havens was gay, and it seems likely that Gordon was aware of that fact.[66] Her instructions to have a woman present in the photographs may well have been an effort to disguise Havens's sexual orientation from her readers. It was equally an effort to reinforce the heteronormative expectations for residential occupants. As the letter indicates, such photographs contained an intricate iconographic system that, at least in the editor's mind, was available to all her readers. Editors such as Gordon were deeply aware that their readers looked carefully at such images and that they could decode an iconography of race, class, gender, sexuality, and domesticity. The mere presence of a morning or hostess coat indicated the marital status of those photographed—a point that might be lost on twenty-first-century readers. That the subjects were always white meant that race was constantly and evenly articulated and, as such, demanded little attention from readers. As Nancy Walker notes, because the magazines were always about and aimed at white, middle-class women, they "provide chilling evidence of the economic power of racism"—and, in this particular instance, of homophobia—in their complete exclusion of blacks, since the content of the magazines was driven to a very large degree by advertising.[67]

My aim in this chapter has been to demonstrate the rhetorical power of these magazines and their content. The postwar shelter, builders', and design magazines form a critically important source of evidence, a vast and significant archive for understanding the cultural work performed by houses and house interiors, as well as the representations of those sites. On their pages, the editors and magazine writers instructed, persuaded, and ultimately constructed an audience of homeowners and potential home buyers—readers who purchased consumer durables, household objects, and houses according to the dictates presented within the magazines' pages. As they did so, they also purchased identities that were necessary to the accumulation of wealth and that guaranteed them homes in locations that afforded good schools and a specific (if often fictive) sense of security. Some readers also defied the dictates of the texts and images presented month after month, looking elsewhere for representational models as they fashioned lives that required them to move outside of a system that was not designed for nonconformists, for blacks, for Latinos, for Asians, or for those who were not heterosexual. Alternative models were, however, difficult to locate as the mainstream press became the overwhelming producer of texts and images related to postwar domesticity.

3

RENDERED WHITENESS
Architectural Drawings and Graphics

Visual representations of postwar houses, interiors, and landscapes have a surprisingly uniform appearance. They typically favor the perspective or axonometric view and feature pastel colors, biomorphic garden forms, and well-dressed and neatly coiffed women in high-heeled shoes. This is a graphic style we have come to associate readily with the 1950s, and these images sometimes seem comical now for their contrivance and naïveté. Although they appeared commonly in popular publications of the period, these images—considered here as part of the vast archive of postwar architectural history and visual culture—have not received the attention of architectural historians or art historians, or even scholars of visual culture. Produced for mass audiences, these images bore mul-

tiple imperatives: they had to exhibit enough technical proficiency to imply professional credibility for the architects and landscape architects whose designs they portrayed; they had to be easily legible, decipherable, for a mass audience not always accustomed to reading architectural drawings; and, perhaps most important, they had to be persuasive. These were their obvious purposes, but their persuasive or rhetorical function deserves particular attention for the purposes of this study.

The anthropologist Karen Brodkin has written of the development of a "public iconography of white nuclear family bliss" in this period, and American images of the postwar house contributed significantly to this representational system, one predicated on a consumerist

FACING
An aerial perspective drawing for a house designed by architect Cliff May, circa 1950s. Photograph by Maynard L. Parker. Courtesy of the Huntington Library, San Marino, California.

vision intended to appeal to an overwhelmingly white middle-class majority of new or soon-to-be first-time homeowners.[1] An essential aspect of these images was their depiction of racial and class distinctions, as well as the repetition of heteronormative ideals of domesticity and of specific gender roles. As noted in the introduction to this volume, the 1950s were a period in which racial and ethnic reassignment and class mobility saw some increased fluidity, and the stakes involved in such assignments could be quite high. An article in a 1955 issue of *Ebony*, for example, reported on a white family in Florida that suffered a sheriff's racist policies; the children of the family were barred from public school when they were accused of actually being black.[2] An article in another 1955 issue of *Ebony* addressed the difficulties that mixed-race couples encountered in the housing market.[3] These were fairly commonplace discriminatory practices for the period, unremarkable if still deeply troubling to those who experienced them, but the *Ebony* articles are telling in regard to the real and spatialized ramifications for individuals' life opportunities of the systemic racism that existed in the immediate postwar era. To be identified as white and to be among the middle majority was to benefit from a range of societal privileges that included access to housing and to FHA-insured mortgages and advantageous bank loans. To be identified as nonwhite was to have that access, among many others liberties, denied.[4]

What role did visual representations of postwar houses play in literally rendering the whiteness of postwar housing natural for a national audience of Americans who read various forms of the popular press? How did they contribute to the formation of an iconography of middle-class whiteness and domesticity linked to citizenship and belonging? In particular, what kinds of cultural work did architectural renderings and views of house interiors do to help inform Americans and to verify their expectations about the rightful occupants of postwar housing? How might these representations have functioned as part of the recursively reflexive processes of cultural production enacted by the millions of viewers who engaged with this particular form of visual culture? Because such representations are ubiquitous, and because they seem to function as documentarily objective portrayals of houses and the domestic sphere, it is easy to overlook much that they include and easier still not to notice what is missing from them, especially when they are considered within the context of the times they represent. Conspicuously absent are significations and images of anything *other* than white middle- or upper-class environments. All others are excluded—completely erased or controlled through selective omission.

This chapter examines popular representations of the postwar house and garden derived primarily from shelter and women's magazines to demonstrate the ways they contributed to an iconography of racially/ethnically based spatial exclusion in the residential sphere.

FACING
"A fine outdoor sitting area" from *House Beautiful*, July 1950, 49.

Drawn images of houses had been appearing in popular, women's, and shelter magazines since the nineteenth century, and many of the conventions that were in place in 1850 for depicting domestic environments, such as the use of perspective and of tightly framed views of house and garden that excluded surrounding context, persisted in 1950. As I will demonstrate, however, newly pervasive conventions, such as the use of the axonometric and aerial views, began to characterize popular postwar representations of houses. In the analysis that follows, I explain the significance of this shift in representational technique and analyze the meanings these images held for postwar audiences. As noted in chapter 2, the magazine images are especially significant for this study because of the large, nationwide audience they reached.

Like numerous scholars in the field of visual culture studies and visual rhetoric, Richard Dyer has noted that representations deeply affect our feelings, thoughts, and cognition of and about that which is represented.[5] Popular representations of houses and gardens that circulated to a nationwide audience likewise confirmed and valorized accepted norms associated with race, class status, and gender and offered lessons (sometimes subtle, sometimes not) for new and aspiring first-time homeowners, who may also have been newly identified as "white" or middle-class. The drawings provided a kind of promise, depicting spaces that, if emulated in built form, could also help to strengthen the iden-

A drawing for a three-bedroom, two-bath Greenbriar "Custom-Line" home, National Homes Corporation. *Life* magazine, January 17, 1955.

tity and status many viewers and homeowners had so recently attained. These popular representations of spaces were a lens through which notions of class and race could be identified, established, or reaffirmed. I am not, however, asserting that such renderings were uniformly received. Indeed, there is little evidence concerning the reception of such images. It is my argument that these drawings were based in the deployment of a uniform set of representational practices that created a framework for viewing among the magazine-reading public, and they likewise reflected and contributed to a set of dominant cultural values about race, class, and gender in the postwar United States. Despite individual viewers' beliefs or particular perceptions, these dominant cultural values provided a consistent background against which American visual culture of all kinds was produced, and therefore—at least to some extent—consumed.

All architectural renderings, whether presented to individual patrons or to mass audiences in serial publications, are intended to explicate and persuade—as architects are fully aware. The architect produces drawings or models that will most clearly convey his or her ideas, incorporated with solutions intended to meet the client's needs and desires, with the goal of persuading the client to proceed with the project. Because this is nearly always done in the most time- and cost-efficient manner possible, embellishments—such as depictions of human figures, artifacts of material culture, pets,

neighbors, and even plantings—are generally kept to a minimum and carefully selected. Architectural renderings derive their persuasive powers, in part, from their apparently guileless nature and their appearance of documentary objectivity; any ideological content remains, or is intended to remain, largely hidden and may even be unconsciously reproduced by the renderings' creators. In this way, architectural renderings are very much like maps and some forms of landscape representation.[6]

Architectural and landscape drawings are a specific form of two-dimensional representation. Unlike artists' paintings or drawings, which may engage the emotions, architectural drawings are meant to prompt us to imagine the spaces of the rendered homes and gardens as if we were their inhabitants—a mental projection that is seldom dispassionate or disconnected from desire, and that is at once spatial and acquisitive. Our eyes cannot simply play across the surface of the page (which holds little or no interest), nor does looking at or into the image necessarily reveal an artistic agenda, because the architect generally suppresses artistic goals of self-expression in favor of a particularized mode of descriptive mapping. Instead, we enter a cognitive realm that is in equal parts map and dreamworld. We imagine ourselves, our family members, our neighbors, and a newly acquired and idealized life that is completely dependent on an image of a space and its surroundings. Inclusion and exclusion of people and things is implicit in the dream as we mentally envision a desired environment. It is nearly impossible to "shop" for house plans without projecting a hoped-for life and lifestyle. As the eye moves over the plan, the imagination conjures and catalogs the space, and desire takes hold.

Again, architects and builders had published drawings of houses and house plans for decades before 1945. The elevations, perspective views, and measured floor plans of nineteenth-century and early twentieth-century houses filled the pages of contemporary magazines, pattern books, catalogs, and journals. Section drawings appeared occasionally, especially in catalogs advertising mail-order houses, since buyers needed to see and understand construction details and instructions that were best portrayed in section. Typically drawn at eye level and from the street, and generally excluding representations of people, house renderings sometimes included a limited repertoire of landscape features, though exceptional examples such as the renderings produced by Marion Mahony Griffin for Frank Lloyd Wright and for Walter Burley Griffin included significant landscape embellishment, as did some others, such as the renderings produced by Bernard Maybeck for his clients.[7] But the usually tight frames and close focus of these earlier drawings provided opportunities to display the abundance of architectural details and embellishments that existed on many Victorian houses, to depict materials, and perhaps even to make visible construction techniques, though these could be conveyed in only the most general sense. Elevations and plans often appeared on the same page (one over the other) or next to each other on adjacent pages so that readers could view the two forms of spatial representation with relative ease and assemble for themselves more complete mental images of the advertised house. Rear yards seldom appeared in such images, a fact owed in part to the late development of ornamental backyards as common elements in the American cultural landscape (more about this in chapter 8) and in part to the conventions of representation—elevation and ground-level perspective—which made it difficult to provide a comprehensive view of the house and its entire lot. Most significant, these earlier representations seldom included people, whether real or imaginary, so the iconography of ideal ownership/occupancy was more flexible even if the owners/occupants were largely presumed to be white.

In the 1930s and 1940s, however, with the national economy, the war effort, and national morale predicated to a large extent on the need for a robust rebound in the housing industry, popular representations of housing in magazines began to shift. Many magazine features on houses of this period continued to include drawings rather than photographs because they could be more selective and because they frequently depicted unbuilt designs. Photography was preferred for displaying built works, particularly high-style or architect-designed houses, but it did not lend itself well to the representation of ordinary small houses and gardens. Whereas the interiors of 1,000-square-foot houses were particularly difficult to portray to advantage through photography, drawings permitted a degree of spatial distortion and a sense of spaciousness in which credibility and fantasy could coexist. Increasingly, magazines began to publish drawings of houses that included depictions of white GIs and the women they hoped to marry, shown together in visual narratives constructed to buttress the promise of single-family homeownership as an American ideal worth fighting for.[8]

Even by the 1920s, however, representational conventions had already begun to shift within the design community, as architects and landscape architects increasingly embraced aerial perspectives and the axonometric view as symbolic of cultural modernity. As Dorothée Imbert has noted, the "reductive precision" of the axonometric drawing, combined with its facilitation of a viewpoint that is both "everywhere and nowhere," made it a representational form ideally suited to the depiction of modernist spaces and forms that likewise appeared rational and inevitable because of their technically produced visual logic.[9] Aerial perspectives and axonometric views were ideal because they facilitated perceptual legibility while also lending a sense of aesthetic and perhaps technological modernity because they demanded an extra layer of professional expertise in their construction.

Plans and blueprints are notoriously difficult to read, especially for those not well acquainted with architectural or visual culture.[10] But aerial and axonometric views portray space with the illusion of dimensionality and are therefore easier for the average viewer to decipher. They provide the supposed realism of a constructed model yet can be made even more persuasive because of their inherent possibility for manipulation. In addition, aerial or bird's-eye views signal privilege and authority, since they provide a commanding view from above.[11] In the postwar era, they provided potential consumers with a visual language of freedom in which the eye was unconstrained by either a single viewpoint or any boundary other than the edge of the page. Moreover, the aerial perspective or axonometric view assumes a universal viewer for whom vision is monolithically and homogeneously conceived. No viewer is defined or specified, because the assumed viewer is white and middle-class, an assumption of unitary/collective identity that suppresses alternatives.

The drawings conveyed the key principles of designs to a mass audience, and modernity was one of the most important aspects of the drawings. Despite the fact that aesthetic preferences among the majority of Americans favored traditional architectural forms and styles, and despite the fact that the FHA made it difficult for would-be buyers to receive federally insured mortgages for houses that were nontraditional in form and appearance, most of the magazines promoted at least "soft modern" house styles.[12] The postwar house

renderings therefore conveyed a sense of the new, the exciting, and the comfortably modern.

Yves-Alain Bois has clarified the possible ideologies of axonometry facilitated by the abolition of the fixed viewpoint of perspective renderings. Bois points out that axonometric drawings are useful tools for seeing the modern because there is "no limit or stopping point of space," and this results in a feeling of visual "liberation."[13] The overhead, hovering axonometric or aerial view grants the viewer the perceptual command of space, which—implicitly in the drawings and explicitly in the everyday life of the 1950s pre–civil rights era—was a privilege reserved primarily for whites. Unrestricted movement, whether of the eye or the body, was implicitly linked to whiteness and class identity, so that axonometric representations not only conveyed aesthetic and architectural modernity but also subtly reinforced racial constructs, as did the very aesthetic of modernity, with its emphasis on cleanliness, spaciousness, and lack of clutter (as detailed below).

In the renderings of postwar houses, as in those of houses from earlier decades, the fence is the property boundary and empty space surrounds the dwelling—a convention that helps to focus the viewer's attention on the subject being depicted. Neighboring buildings are rarely included, in part because the focus of the rendering is the single-family dwelling and because too-close neighbors could recall prewar apartment living.[14] In reality, many postwar suburban houses were constructed very close together on small lots. But in the 1950s culture of containment, neighbors were to be kept at bay, on the other side of a fence that ensured family privacy and insularity, reinforcing the ideal of nuclear family togetherness and its counterpart, exclusion of outsiders.[15] The house and garden are therefore never depicted as part of a neighborhood or shown in any sort of broader physical context. Unlike drawings from earlier decades, however, in which the front elevation dominated, a front view of the house is sometimes (not always) included, since that was the view intended for the evaluative gaze of neighbors and passing strangers.

Advertisers and real estate agents might refer to the careful arrangement of residential renderings as the development of "eye appeal"—the simple act of determining and implementing those aspects of the built environment that appeal to the consumer's eye. But in the process of crafting eye appeal, postwar architects and architectural draftsmen produced drawings that also "crafted white settings," hoping to sell attractive houses to Americans who were eager to gain entrée to the white middle majority.[16] For some, the architect's drawing has become itself a symbol of spatial exclusion. The geographer David Sibley, for example, describes a British documentary film about a shopping mall in which the consumers were "all apparently white, middle-class nuclear families, the kind of public which populates architects' sketches."[17] In parallel with historian Annie Gilbert Coleman's analysis of the visual

FACING
An aerial perspective drawing of the Shainwald residence. Wurster, Bernardi, and Emmons, architects; Thomas Church, landscape architect. *House Beautiful*, November 1950, 205.

Rendered Whiteness | 91

Whatever your need, your desire...there's a

NEW NATIONAL

HOME *for you!*

Two-level Hollybrook "Custom-Line"
—4 bedrooms, 2 baths, activities room, carport. Many design variations available in
this model, as in all National homes.

Birchbrook "Custom-Line"—3 bedrooms and basement, glass-walled living-
dining area. Hip roof.

The Ambassador—a spacious "Custom-
Line" home, with fireplace . . . 4 bedrooms
. . . 2 baths . . . 2-car garage.

In this advertisement, the houses appear as
though completely isolated from any surrounding
neighborhood context. *Life* magazine, January 17, 1955.

culture of skiing, house and garden representations "idealized a particular construction of whiteness . . . that
[drew] attention to itself and placed people of color on
the periphery" through total exclusion.[18]

In addition to depicting the forms of domestic
worlds, the drawings are images of a white culture that
privileged spaciousness, cleanliness, order, leisure, and
the fashionable appeal of aesthetic/architectural modernism. Not only did the drawings make house and garden attractive, but they also subtly offered a persuasive
visual rhetoric about the purchase of a culturally constructed white identity.[19] Images of stylistically modern homes (even if of the middling modernist variety)
were therefore equally about containing and eliminating the signs of ethnic difference and attaining class
status. The appearance of the drawings is remarkably
homogeneous: clean, tidy, orderly, shiny, and bright,
they broadcast the symbolism of sameness, safety, and
assimilation. The textual descriptions are likewise very
consistent. Words such as *informality, casual lifestyle, leisure, individuality, privacy,* and *cleanliness* served as a lexicon and as metaphors for an identity that was clearly
white and clearly middle-class, and I examine the use
of a number of these words in the chapters that follow.

As a rule, the housing advertisements that appeared
in shelter and women's magazines of the period did not
depict or include people of color—everything was displayed in the homes of and surrounded by white families. Indeed, it could be argued that a very limited rep-

A child plays in an unusually tidy room.

From *Contemporary Houses Developed from Room Units* (Urbana: University of Illinois, Small Homes Council, 1951), 43.

resentational tradition existed for depicting blackness related to the domestic sphere in the white/national press, one used primarily to depict images of slaves, servants, victims, or minstrels in blackface. In white residential settings, images of racial alterity appeared seldom, and typically only through the presentation of material culture artifacts of those same slaves, servants, and minstrels, but configured as cups, planters, salt and pepper shakers, maple syrup containers, and so on—black "figures" made to serve in some capacity and to substitute for the absence of actual slaves and servants of color.

On the rare occasions that images of nonwhites appeared in postwar shelter publications, they frequently

Now...

MENGEL DOORS

with

MATCHING

GOLD COAST CHERRY PANELS

It had to happen! The tremendous response to Mengel Doors in rotary-cut Gold Coast Cherry demanded matching plywood panels.

Now they're here—satin-smooth panels with all the beauty of this exciting wood imported from Mengel's exclusive African concession—*but still priced lower than many other hardwoods!*

See for yourself—ask your dealer to show you samples.

Door Department, The Mengel Company, Louisville 1, Kentucky.

Mengel Doors equal or exceed the requirements of Bureau of Standards specifications CS 200-55

CUT FROM OUR OWN EXCLUSIVE TIMBERING CONCESSIONS

appeared as stereotypes that valorized and reinforced racist beliefs. For example, an advertisement for Mengel cherrywood doors that appeared in the builders' magazine *House and Home* in 1956 includes a cartoon-like drawing of a diminutive African man in blackface dressed in only a loincloth and holding what appears to be some sort of shield as he stares from the side of a "Gold Coast Cherry" door.[20] A small map of Africa appears in the lower right corner with a circle indicating the location from which the wood for the door was derived, a location the Mengel Company proclaims (with no trace of imperialist irony) as "Our own exclusive timbering concessions." To the left of the cartooned man is a drawing of a comparatively tall woman of indeterminate race/ethnicity whose appearance is both exoticized and hypersexualized through her attire (a tiny, strapless, micro-minidress), visible cleavage, multiple ankle and wrist bracelets, large hoop earrings (probably intended to appear "ethnic"), and a hairstyle that includes an animal bone used as a decorative element. These absurdly cartooned figures reproduced for the viewers of 1956 the antithesis of white subjectivity, helping them to know whiteness through the depiction of its opposite, which in this case was a stereotypical depiction of the primitive, tribal, hypersexualized person of color, and understood through the well-known representational traditions of minstrelsy and exotic entertainment. In the white postwar press related to the housing and building industries, depictions of black-

Advertisement for Mengel Doors.
House and Home, November 1956, 25.

ness appeared within a very limited expressive repertoire, a condition that therefore limited opportunities
for the construction of alternative imaginaries among
the white public, but also perhaps among publics of
color. Whiteness was constructed against its opposite,
then, in very narrowly defined visual terms.

It is probably true that nearly all architectural renderings (then and now) have a "whiteness" to them,
since they are produced mostly by white male architects
for actual or imagined white patrons.[21] But this aspect
of the images assumes new poignancy in the postwar
period, in which the absence of architectural features in
black magazines speaks eloquently of the limited place
for people of color in the burgeoning housing market.
For the entire decade of the 1950s, women's magazines,
shelter magazines, and even popular periodicals such
as *Life, Look,* and *Popular Mechanics* published regular
features on housing developments, house design, do-
it-yourself housing, and stock plans that could be purchased for as little as five dollars. Indeed, few issues of
these magazines were published that did not feature
housing in some manner. But in *Ebony* very few articles
on houses or housing appeared in the 1950s. From 1954
through 1956, for example, the magazine featured only
one house, the elaborate and costly modern residence
of a successful black physician—an example that was
well outside the reach of the vast majority of the *Ebony*
readership.[22] *Ebony,* which began publication in November 1945, was dedicated to promoting a positive image
of black lifestyles in America; as the editors put it, the
magazine aimed "to mirror the brighter side of Negro
life."[23] In doing so, it included mostly images of blacks
who had accepted white codes of behavior, appearance,
and status. In order to focus on black achievements,
Ebony for the most part had to ignore the housing question. Although African American suburbs and housing
tracts developed in specific circumstances and settings,
such as those surrounding historically black university
campuses, they were nonetheless rare, and obtaining
decent housing remained a primary concern for nonwhites in the postwar era.[24]

Aside from using axonometric and aerial views,
what additional visual cues did draftsmen and architects insert in their representations that obscured
blue-collar or ethnic roots to produce an iconography
of whiteness? Using a system of signs and/or representational techniques to create an atmosphere of desirable
domesticity, architectural renderers produced drawings
for publication that captured or encapsulated the American Dream by using a series of simple ideograms and
graphic formulas that likewise seized upon a set of cultural codes for racial and class identity formation. The
representations themselves were clean and bright, rendered carefully with ink line drawings or with appealing pastel and color washes. Ironically, if the houses
and representations could affirm racial whiteness, the
drawings, like the houses themselves, frequently contained great numbers of brightly colored products and

surfaces. The white-wall aesthetic of high modernism seldom appeared in ordinary postwar domestic settings, where instead bright colors conveyed attributes such as hygiene, novelty, sophistication, and individual distinction.

The parts of the drawings were often clearly displayed and labeled for consumption to avoid confusion: everything was impeccably neat. Nothing was out of place, as though every house were occupied by an obsessively tidy owner, an attribute made more visible by the careful placement of a single child, playing with a single toy; a parent taking care of the lawn with a single tool. Nothing was ever lying about, overgrown, or out of place. The houses and gardens were portrayed as clutter-free environments, when in actuality they were jammed full of new consumer goods, causing storage to become one of the primary design considerations for ordinary small houses from 1945 onward. Cluttered and untidy environments signaled lower-class and ethnic identity for the occupants, and so the reality and the ideal were at odds with each other. As geographer David Sibley has noted, "Exclusionary discourse draws particularly on colour, disease, animals, sexuality, and nature, but they all come back to the idea of dirt as a signifier of imperfection and inferiority, the reference point being the white, often male, physically and mentally able person." He observes further: "In the same system of values, whiteness is a symbol of purity, virtue and goodness and a colour which is easily polluted. . . .

Thus, white may be connected with . . . an urge to clean, to expel dirt and resist pollution, whether whiteness is attributed to people or to material objects."[25]

Moreover, Jewish social reformers from the first half of the twentieth century attempted to establish "the parameters of domesticity" for new immigrants by concentrating primarily on "issues of personal and environmental cleanliness . . . [and they] focused almost exclusively on the cultural ramifications of dirt. As they understood it, the elimination of dirt was by no means an exclusively physical act but one fraught with profound social and cultural meaning, intrinsic to the process of integration. When seen from this perspective, housekeeping itself was nothing less than civic virtue."[26] The tastemaking and housekeeping literature therefore advised Jewish immigrants to "keep decoration to a minimum" and to aim for simplicity in home design and decor. These were reactions against the typical tenement, which was "replete with colored wallpaper, brightly patterned linoleum, and yards of lace and fabric trimmings."[27]

Again, the correlation of cleanliness and tidiness with the good, white, middle-class house was not new to the postwar period. Nineteenth-century home economists published books and manuals extolling the clean/tidy house as virtuous and middle-class versus the dirty/messy house as ungodly, immoral, and lower-class.[28] Late nineteenth-century and early twentieth-century photographs of urban America depicted the

A child plays on a sterile outdoor patio while his mother works in the sterile kitchen. From *Window Planning Principles*, Small Homes Council Circular Series Index Number F11.0, *University of Illinois Bulletin* 52, no. 8 (September 1954), University of Illinois Archives.

trash-strewn, crowded, and ramshackle spaces of black and immigrant life—the spaces of the poor in cities such as Washington, D.C., and New York. Turn-of-the-century real estate agents in Chicago used stereotypical correlations to influence house sales in specific neighborhoods—essentially blockbusting—by encouraging and even paying African Americans recently arrived

from the South to occupy dwellings in white neighborhoods and to embody and perform racist stereotypes in white neighborhoods where the agents hoped to provoke whites to sell. Among the "objectionable" behaviors performed by these paid occupants and noted in the Chicago newspapers were sitting on front porches, congregating noisily on sidewalks, and keeping overcrowded and untidy dwellings.[29] And the famous Farm Security Administration photographs produced between 1935 and 1942 further cemented—especially through their mass circulation in magazines such as *Life* and *Look*—the notion that dirt, crowding, trash, lack of privacy, and untidy spaces signaled poverty and insecure racial identities.[30] In contrast, clutter-free and clean environments were construed as belonging to middle-class, white occupants (although if a room contained elements of high-style modernism or too many books, it could be identified as belonging to Jewish occupants, as detailed in a later chapter).

Many recent immigrants—whether moving from outside the United States or from within and moving from South to North—understood this domestic sanitary imperative in terms of "respectability," and they carried it with them from locations around the globe, but especially those where colonialist occupation prevailed. As Stuart Hall has written about his parents' efforts to create a recognizably middle-class home in Kingston, Jamaica, "The staging of respectability was a matter governed by many unwritten rules" that included "right moral conduct," proper attire, and careful selection and arrangement of objects in the front room of the house. It was also based on a household aesthetic promoted by Unilever, a British imperial corporation whose advertisements, Hall notes, were "designed to persuade the colonies to purchase the means to achieve standards of cleanliness appropriate to the metropoli-

tan world: 'Soap is Civilized.' "[31] And for blacks living on Chicago's South Side between 1910 and 1935, significations of respectability crystallized around what Davarian Baldwin has identified as "markers of refinement" that indicated degrees of "bourgeois status," such as "economic thrift, bodily restraint, and functional modesty in personal and community presentation." Baldwin notes that churches in Chicago's Black Belt worked to reform the behaviors of southern migrants by presenting programs "structured by heightened orderliness and bodily restraint," and they frowned upon loud/noisy behaviors such as "singing, shouting, and talking."[32]

Even a 1954 short film produced by the National Clean Up–Paint Up–Fix Up Bureau with the Federal Civil Defense Administration deployed these ideas to connect cleanliness and household order to middle-class whiteness and respectability, albeit somewhat abstractly. The film, titled *The House in the Middle*, was produced on the Nevada nuclear test site. In the film, three small, one-room "houses" sit side by side on the site. The house in the middle is neatly coated in white paint and exhibits a tidy interior and exterior. The houses on either side, in contrast, exhibit signs of neglect; they are unpainted or have peeling paint and have trash-strewn exteriors and untidy, overcrowded, and cluttered interiors. As an atomic bomb is detonated in the distance, the film's narrator explains that the clean, well-maintained, tidy, and white house in the middle suffers the least amount of damage in the heat wave from the blast, while the dark-colored and messy houses on either side ignite, burst into flame, and are destroyed. Absurd (and frightening) as this short film appears to us today, it serves as further evidence of the deep connections that existed between these signifiers for whiteness and middle-class identity, and their deep connections to ideas about homeownership and even to patriotism and American citizenship.[33]

An article from a 1950s *Better Homes and Gardens Gardening Guide* reinforces the point. Essentially a twelve-point lesson in home maintenance, the feature was intended to help suburban homeowners keep the proper appearance of cleanliness and order.[34] In an aerial perspective, the illustration showed the kind of chaos and clutter that can result from an ill-kept yard: overgrown shrubs, trash receptacles on display, lawn maintenance and gardening equipment lying about, lawn chairs tipped over, children's toys distributed randomly, and laundry drying on the line for all to see. The article asked, "Does your lot and setting make a nice picture for you?" and emphasized that a well-kept, tidy home reflects the "spirit of wholesome family life and reflects . . . the people in it. Others [homes that are not well kept] tell us that within and around there is insensitiveness and indifference." The article and its illustration made the point that litter and untidiness signal unwholesome, and therefore lower-class, living. Trash and its containers are to be hidden, along with laundry lines and many other signs of everyday, active family life. By

asking readers to consider the "picture" made by their lots, the authors signaled an increased emphasis on the development of what might be imagined as a postwar suburban picturesque, one that was notably framed by a "picture window," a term that connoted both visual consumption and artful presentation. Through such images, postwar Americans were presented with representations of domestic life that appeared ubiquitously through their publication in magazines and newspapers, in films, and on television. And those pictures invited readers to project themselves, their lives, and their families' lives into an imagined realm, a mirror against which they were asked to compare and construct themselves.

Readers certainly noticed the contrast that often existed between their lived experience and the incredibly tidy homes depicted in the magazines. In 1949, a woman named Ann Griffith wrote about the obsession with cleanliness in American women's magazines, noting that nothing ever seemed to be clean enough. Everything was supposed to be "white-like-new," and, she noted, "there is no end in sight, no hint that there is an optimum whiteness to which you can bring your clothes and then relax."[35] The postwar house was promoted as a remedy to the dirty conditions of inner-city cold-water flats, but concerns for its cleanliness endured. The images also brought attention to questions about the optimum whiteness of the owners. To follow the magazines' instructions in home decorating, entertaining,

Ever really <u>look</u> at your place?

Sure you have—but lately? Have things gotten a bit out of line? Take an appraising look as you swing into your drive tomorrow

and lifestyle was to hedge against troubling questions about belonging and identity.

The pervasiveness of this association between white middle-class identities and cleanliness in the popular literature attests to its significance. A 1956 article in *Ebony* featured a black developer in Gary, Indiana, who noted that he "envisioned someday building blocks of homes that could not be identified as Negro by the familiar signs of shoddy construction and cramped homesites."[36] So widely recognized was the iconography of race that even *Ebony*'s writers and readers acknowledged and affirmed it: shoddy, untidy, and cramped living spaces were universally recognized as spatial and visual signs of nonwhite occupancy. In another 1956 *Ebony* article, titled "I Live in a Negro Neighborhood," the white author, Leon Paul, assured readers: "Ours is a happy, vibrant neighborhood. Any outsider would be impressed with the neatness of the gardens and the attractive appearance of the houses. Our block looks good because the people who live there are always working in their gardens and on their lawns, improving the look of their houses and driveways and generally keeping their homes in good shape."[37] Paul clearly understood that these were the visual clues to ethnic or racial identity that resided in the domestic sphere—neatness chief among them—and he wanted to assure his readers that his black neighbors could make their neighborhood appear as clean and bright, and therefore as white, as any other, despite the contrary prevailing stereotypes.

Mary and Russel Wright's *Guide to Easier Living*, first published in 1951, provides an example of the postwar obsession with cleanliness in the domestic sphere and its links to race and class distinction. Although scholars have examined it primarily as a design handbook, the *Guide to Easier Living*, which was widely read and published in multiple editions, equally served to educate first-time homeowners about how to live as white middle-majority members. It provided detailed instructions for housewives about how to clean their houses as white-collar professionals and how to distinguish themselves from their lower-class or ethnic servants. In fact, the book was dedicated to the Wrights' former housekeeper, Dorcas Hollingsworth, and, as the Wrights noted, to "the whole present generation, who will never have a Dorcas Hollingsworth." As a guide intended to help families learn to cope in the postwar world of homeownership without servants, the book contained chapters on "the housewife-engineer" that included time-and-motion studies, as well as appendices and charts on cleaning routines and products, providing lessons on how to appear solidly middle-class by keeping the house spotlessly clean. Again, the Wrights drew on a range of well-known precedents, but as leading participants in the production of the all-white majority culture that constituted midcentury homeownership, they responded to the implicit concerns of their audience.

The *Guide to Easier Living* focused to a large extent on eliminating household disorder, and the Wrights

FACING
"Ever really *look* at your place?" *Better Homes and Gardens Gardening Guide,* circa 1950s. Douglas and Maggie Baylis Collection [1999-4], Environmental Design Archives, University of California, Berkeley.

wrote that bedrooms should be kept functional to avoid the following scene in

the cold light of morning: Bedcovers cascade to the floor, and lamp shades hang askew; the housewife must stumble over assorted shoes, slippers, and oddments of clothing that litter the carpet. Drawers and closets are open-mouthed, mute witness of the frantic hunt just made within their disordered depths. The elegant dressing table lewdly bares its skinny legs, and lint is a dingy film over everything. From coast to coast, in rich homes and poor, the American bedroom at 8:00 AM looks the same . . . like an Okie camp.[38]

Design for a well-organized closet from Mary and Russel Wright's *Guide to Easier Living* (1951). Reproduced with permission of Gibbs Smith, publisher.

The message was clear: if you don't keep an uncluttered house, you look like an "Okie," a Depression-era image of itinerant poverty most Americans sought to escape or avoid.[39] Indeed, Okies were imagined as not quite "white," in the same way that those described as "white trash" are configured as possessing a tainted form of whiteness.[40] The book therefore provided a wealth of diagrams for appropriately designed rooms, closets, and storage spaces.

The Wrights' time-and-motion studies of household efficiency were designed, like the well-known precedents on which they drew, to make housework and gardening white-collar endeavors for the generation that had no hired help. Like the trend in postwar kitchen design that dictated inclusion of a kitchen desk, so that housewives could comport themselves like white-collar executives or engineers controlling their households (analyzed in further detail in chapter 6), the Wrights advised women to "sit down to work whenever possible. . . . Have chairs or stools of the right height for your various tasks."[41] When scraping and polishing absolutely had to be done, they recommended hiring someone to do the job.[42] Likewise, if maids no longer helped inside the house, hired gardeners, also typically nonwhite and from the lower economic classes, were no longer a common part of the outdoor middle-class suburban scene. Instead, suburban homeowner-gardeners used new and expensive power tools to provide the required maintenance—a topic explored in greater detail in chapter 8.

Keeping dust and dirt out, preventing them from infiltrating the home, and maintaining order were also about preventing contamination, both real and racial/social. Many nonwhite and lower-economic-class Americans did not have equal access to home and personal sanitation in this period, and the stereotype of the dirty nonwhite was pervasively held.[43] To be white and middle-class was to be clean, clean, clean. Even in the garden, the Wrights' primary rule for design or selection of things for the outdoors was "to ask yourself whether you can wash them with a hose."[44] Outdoor floors were to be hard-surfaced and supplied with drains, wall coverings were to be washable with a garden hose, and furniture was to be protected by rubberized "raincoats," with "whisk brooms tied to the furniture for a quick brush-off."[45] For especially fastidious Americans, a 1953 issue of *Life* magazine recommended the implementation of washable rooms that could be hosed down on cleaning day, thereby minimizing the housewife's labor.[46]

If tidiness was a key sign of middle-class, white identity, the illusion of spaciousness was equally important. Just as cramped and crowded living conditions signaled ethnic origins and reminded Americans of a Depression-era past, cramped and crowded suburban houses and gardens appeared undesirable. Landscape architects grappled with the problem of small housing lots in a variety of ways. For example, one of the period's most successful landscape architects, Thomas Church,

WASHABLE ROOMS

Paul McCobb, new best seller in modern furniture design, devises vacation house whose iron, canvas, rubber furnishings can all be cleaned with soap and water

recommended moving plantings to the lot lines, away from the foundation of the house, a design trick that, as he stated, "greatly expands the apparent spaciousness by pulling the eye away from the house to see the distant view."[47] In the drawings, the aerial perspective could be manipulated to great advantage, giving an impression of a large lot instead of the more diminutive reality, whether or not the designer followed a formula like Church's. No matter what their actual dimensions, all the houses and gardens in the drawings seemed ample, stretching out on the page, unconfined by the realities of lot lines or budgets.

Although the designs may appear somewhat formulaic to us today, architects and draftsmen took care to produce designs that appeared distinctive within the framework of acceptable homogeneity. The drawing and appearance of the garden were especially important as means for creating distinguished environments in otherwise monotonous suburbs. Readers of magazines such as *Popular Mechanics* and *Life* understood that the images portrayed in the magazines were of houses whose plans could be purchased or easily replicated, so that one's own house could be identical to that owned by thousands of other Americans. To have a house that looked exactly like the neighbors' house could be comforting for its assurance of belonging, but look-alike houses were also stigmatized, especially by the high-style design critics and magazine editors who

"Washable rooms" from *Life* magazine, May 18, 1953, 74.

PREVAILING WEST WINDS

"American Style in a Pace-Setter House." The boundaries of this house appear to extend almost infinitely into the landscape, an impression made possible through the use of aerial perspective. The title of the illustration connects the unbounded space of the white, middle-class house with American identity. *House Beautiful*, September 1950, 108.

associated look-alike houses with lower-class or ethnic occupants. A telling illustration of this association between house form and racial stereotypes of conformity appears in Elizabeth Mock's 1946 publication *If You Want To Build a House*. Mock wrote that "the real basis for house planning should be the individual, not the group," and she illustrated her assertion with a cartoon captioned "Undifferentiated Indians entering an undifferentiated tepee."[48] For Mock, the tepee was a vernacular and therefore lower form of architecture, one tepee indistinguishable from the next, and, therefore, a perfect illustration of the lower-economic-class housing her readers hoped to avoid by designing or selecting houses and gardens that were inflected with individual character. Despite their formulaic approaches to representation generally, the renderings of gardens aimed to help banish subdivision monotony through the depiction of modernistic settings containing families

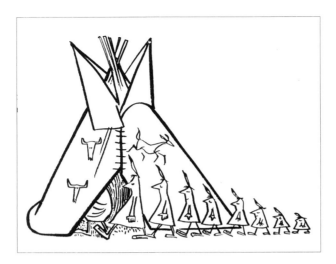

depicted as "hayseeds," hicks who spray each other or the dog with the garden hose and loudly announce their presence. Kartwold even depicted rain clouds over some of his architecturally appealing domestic worlds. Little is known so far about Arne Kartwold's career, but these renderings are remarkable for their wonderful comic deviance from drafting conventions. The very deviance of Kartwold's drawings points to the rigidity of architectural drawings generally, and of postwar house depictions specifically. Kartwold's drawings do not really differ greatly from the norm, but even subtle moves away from convention attract our attention because they are so rare.

engaged in leisure activities that conveyed distinguishing identities.

The uniformity of these clean images is most starkly illuminated by a look at an exception: Arne Kartwold's eccentric drawings. A Bay Area architect and draftsman who worked in the firm of Wurster, Bernardi and Emmons from 1944 to 1946 and served as illustrator for at least one popular publication on home buying and construction, Kartwold produced renderings that include vegetation that seems to have been irradiated to grow to enormous and threatening proportions.[49] Homeowners lounge around reading newspapers that they carelessly cast aside and scatter about, their peculiar possessions crowd the space and clamor for attention, and their dog seems constantly to be doing something strange and almost subversive. The owners, oddly enough, are

Despite the eccentricity of Kartwold's garden inhabitants, it is important to note that they doze in the garden rather than work and play with the garden hose rather than toil in the soil. A class issue emerges here, for if immigrant and blue-collar Americans were in gardens before 1945, they were likely working in them instead of lounging—making productive vegetable gardens of their own, working in "victory gardens," or weeding, hoeing, pruning, fertilizing, mowing, and clipping for someone else. Even those Americans who planted victory gardens during the war wanted them gone or hidden once the war was over, because they symbolized an era of scarcity, apartment living, and pre-middle-majority lifestyle.[50] For lower-income people of color, garden work often recalled unpleasant past associations and was considered something to be left behind as

Arne Kartwold, *Design for a Suburban House.* Arne and Lois Kartwold Collection [2000-11], Environmental Design Archives, University of California, Berkeley.

quickly as possible. Therefore, any images that implied physical labor were banished entirely from postwar garden renderings, located at the peripheries or hidden, tucked away discreetly in the corners of the designed spaces. I examine this further in chapter 8, but what matters here is the convention that continually produced exterior home environments as sites of leisure rather than of labor, thus adding to the representational system for portraying white domesticity.

Because the garden was to be strictly for leisure, and to obscure further any associations of labor with garden spaces, many of the drawings made the garden appear to be an extension of the living room of the house—an additional room, albeit outdoors, for lounging, reading the paper, or sipping martinis. If women were at work in the home, men were depicted at leisure in the garden. Images of backyard barbecues and of relaxed living predominated in the renderings; people were shown swimming, chatting, and lounging while wives served drinks on trays and husbands tended to steaks on the grill. In a *Popular Mechanics* article of 1959 titled "Unusual and Modern Ideas for Living

Outdoors," the author provided ideas for "converting your back yard into an open-air 'room' where you can bask, dine, and spend the summer in true lazy-man style."[51] An illustration for the piece appropriately depicted a barbecue in progress, with a grinning "dad" holding his cooking implement aloft and a scene of active entertainment in the background. The outdoor furniture industry prospered under this conception of the garden, and furniture outdoors—especially the ubiquitous chaise lounge—became a potent symbol of the leisure class. To be in a garden designed exclusively for ease and comfort was a white and upper-class concept and image (one with a long history), as was the very idea of outdoor living, which was so persuasively

Arne Kartwold, *Design for a Suburban House.* Arne and Lois Kartwold Collection [2000-11], Environmental Design Archives, University of California, Berkeley.

publicized in the postwar era. But it was outdoor living for the backyard only, as far away as possible from the front-stoop culture of inner-city ethnic neighborhoods. It was also a shift away from the front-porch culture of earlier suburban and of rural settings. Children might play games such as hopscotch or basketball in the front yard, and parents might wash a car in the driveway or kibitz with a neighbor on the way into the house, but adult leisure and family group activities were best located and depicted in the privacy afforded by the backyard.

When they looked to the popular magazines while they were shopping for the small houses they might one day afford, postwar Americans saw plans that fulfilled dreams. But as they read the housing features, with their enticing drawings, they equally looked to the house to confirm identities, images of the self, and, perhaps more subtly, racial and class assignment and affirmation (albeit undoubtedly troubling for some) of the dominance of heterosexual nuclear families. The man pausing by his car in one image, or working in the garden as a leisure or hobby activity in another, or an efficient and contented mother serving beverages in the garden from a tray, or the family swimming in the backyard pool—all were part of this system of representing a classed, raced, and heteronormative world. The drawings contained images of whiteness that became enshrined in the magazines and in popular media but also, therefore, within the house. As such, the draw-

ings "were in actuality part of a multifaceted cultural matrix that was diagramming and urging conformity to a white ideal."[52] The representations of houses and gardens joined a constellation of images in midcentury visual culture that served as markers of class and racial distinction. By employing an iconography of whiteness, combined with the viewing mechanism of the architectural drawing, popular publications in the 1940s and especially the 1950s attempted to capture the broadest possible consumer audience through the development of "eye appeal" that targeted the mass, middle-majority readership to the exclusion of nonwhite viewers, who were of little interest to advertisers. The drawings therefore did not merely reflect the virtual absence of a black middle class in the midcentury residential world, but they also contributed to the construction of that condition through continual reinforcement.

Although historians have focused on architectural modernism's innovations in this period, we have to remember that for all their emphasis on formal and spatial novelty, most architects persisted in imagining within the social box—one that implicitly accepted racially restricting covenants and the social armature of the pre–civil rights era. Given the visual codes described herein and their persistence in popular representations of the home, the tastemaking and design literature from the postwar era onward must be viewed in an entirely new light—one that considers race and class as embedded subjects in discourses on the built environment.

4

PRIVATE WORLDS
The Spatial Contours of Exclusion and Privilege

My grandparents' house sat on a corner lot in Van Nuys, California. The house and detached garage occupied a substantial portion of the lot, but the sides and back of the lot were completely sealed off from the street by a high, stockade-style fence. Sometime in the last decade or so of his life, my grandfather cut a small circular portal into the fence along the driveway, so their dog could have a window on the world but no one could look in. A long, narrow space for drying clothes sat along one side of the house, concealed from the backyard by a separate gate, so that even visitors admitted to the garden would not see drying laundry or the work involved in making the clothes clean and dry. With a fence enclosing the entire rear perimeter of the lot, their yard became a zone of safety and privacy. An electric garage door opener permitted entry of their car and closed the door behind them with the push of a button. With the intercom, peepholes in the doors, and burglar alarm systems my grandfather installed, the house seemed impenetrable to intruders, a San Fernando Valley residential fortress. Relatively small windows covered with blinds or drapes faced the street; large sliding glass doors opened to the enclosed backyard. My grandparents' world was a private one, a domestic realm both sealed and concealed from all but family and invited guests, and in keeping with the white, middle-class norms prescribed, as they had been for decades, by architects, designers, tastemakers, and progressive reformers.

———

FACING
A postwar model house
with exterior privacy wall
(*detail, see p. 137*).

The 3 Big Ideas of 1950

Climate Control

Privacy

The American Style

House Beautiful merges them all in

three $25,000 Pace-Setter Houses

In 1950, a feature article in the popular magazine *House Beautiful* proclaimed that the three big ideas for house design were climate control, privacy, and "the American style."[1] The latter was a description coined by the magazine's editor, Elizabeth Gordon, but all three concepts appeared repeatedly, intertwined, in articles published in numerous magazines between 1945 and 1960. They formed a trinity of design imperatives that were meant to be mutually reinforcing and that were linked to nationalistic and social ideals. Through her design editorials, Gordon ultimately became a renowned Cold War propagandist, and, like some others of her time, she viewed house form and design as crucial tools in the effort to establish the cultural supremacy of capitalism, democracy, and American national identity.[2]

Climate control became a central feature because it involved the possibility of mitigating harsh weather conditions through proper design and achieved through implementation of consumer durables and technologies that were essential to the U.S. postwar economy, but *House Beautiful*'s climate control research project was also heavily linked to the use of large areas of glass in postwar homes. The increased amount of glazing that appeared in houses during this period signaled aesthetic modernity, and therefore class distinction. But glass came with attendant problems: rapid heat loss and gain that resulted in thermal discomfort and high energy costs, and a lack of internal privacy, especially if the

"The 3 Big Ideas of 1950."
House Beautiful, June 1950, 85.

glazing appeared on facades that faced public streets. Over and over again, the concern that one might "live like a goldfish in a bowl," with all of the family's activities observable by strangers and neighbors, appears as a plaintive refrain in the literature of the time. If the picture window became an icon of postwar domesticity and lightweight aluminum-frame sliding glass doors the ideal solution for enhanced indoor/outdoor living, they nevertheless prompted debates about the need for privacy in the home. Concerns for privacy extended far beyond concerns about increased glazing, however. Privacy—a concern addressed in American home design and its attendant literature for decades—increasingly became a way of thinking about postwar residential life that was linked to identity construction in terms of race, class, and citizenship. Indeed, privacy became a primary concern for the designers and builders of small, affordable houses in the period between 1945 and 1960.

This chapter examines personal and family privacy as a determining factor in the design of domestic interior and exterior spaces in the postwar period, as well as privacy's links to the formation of personal and family identities. Privacy, like race, is historically contingent and culturally constructed.[3] It is not universally privileged, nor is it monolithically constituted over time and space. But in the United States after 1945, concerns regarding the maintenance of privacy in the domestic realm became an increasingly pervasive theme in the literature on house design and construction. Books and magazine articles, whether aimed at the middle majority or at audiences who could afford custom houses designed by architects, repeatedly emphasized the need for the exclusion of the outsider's gaze and the reduction of interior familial frictions through proper design for privacy that would simultaneously maintain architectural modernism's various aesthetic and stylistic imperatives. Indeed, it would be difficult to find a single book or article on general house planning and design from the period that ignored the topic—most featured privacy as a focus.[4] Certainly, privacy constitutes an unremarkable, even quotidian planning concern, one that any pragmatist can understand. But the intensity of focus this issue received in the design literature and in shelter and popular magazines signals a deeper significance. Like images of whiteness and its connection to sanitary, sparely decorated, quiet, and tidy environments, as analyzed in the previous chapter, privacy—both as a term and as a spatial imperative—became a rhetorical device, a strategy for articulating and asserting specific values that were linked to racial, class, and sexual identities.

Why was the idea of privacy so pervasively represented in the postwar media related to house design and domesticity? What did privacy symbolize, and how was it to be achieved? How did the strong desire to attain a private residential world change the design and construction of some ordinary postwar houses? And how was residential privacy represented to a national audience for whom it was clearly intended or imagined to be a compelling concern? In this chapter, I will demonstrate that ownership of a single-family detached house with its own private, fenced garden (analyzed in the book's final chapter) and carefully designed interior spaces that allowed for spatial, acoustical, and psychological privacy symbolized not just security from outsiders who might threaten home and family but also, and equally, the security of respectability through confirmed membership in the white, middle-class American majority. The absence of residential privacy was seen as a key feature of prewar, immigrant, ethnic, and lower-class lifestyles—something many Americans wanted to leave behind as they fled to new developments in the suburbs.[5] Furthermore, as William H. Whyte noted in 1956, the uniform appearance of the early suburbs made many middle-class inhabitants uncomfortable because they feared the look of the lower-class housing projects or developments they had lived in on their way up the economic ladder.[6] But no matter how small the new suburban house, no matter how similar its appearance to that of the neighbors' houses, it was still a house of one's own, on an individual and distinctively defined lot, separated from the noises, smells, and activities of family members, neighbors, and street life that recalled inner-city, prewar lifestyles.

In the early years of the twenty-first century, concerns for privacy are ever present, especially with the global spread of digital technologies. Satellites can track our cellular phone calls, hackers can steal our financial identities and empty our bank accounts, and e-mail correspondence, we are frequently reminded, is subject to surveillance by authorities. Gated communities in wealthy neighborhoods restrict the movements of outsiders, and home security systems protect families and their privacy within the home. Yet Americans increasingly embrace voyeuristic media that allow degrees of visual access to the intimate lives of others. Social media platforms such as Facebook and so-called reality television shows, both of which are popular and highly rated, claim to allow viewers to watch the detailed movements, intimate moments, and intricate relationships of participants day and night, often within their homes, and even in their bedrooms and bathrooms. But the tension these embody—between the desire to maintain personal privacy and the desire to know the intimate details of the interior lives of others—is not new to this decade. As the sociologist Alan Ehrenhalt observed in 1995: "The worship of privacy is, like the worship of choice and the fear of authority, rooted so deeply in our end-of-century value system that it has been virtually immune to serious debate, let alone reconsideration. But it is time to reconsider it nonetheless, and to confront the possibility that all of these self-evident contemporary 'truths' are doing far more harm than good as they persist in the closing years of the century."[7] Moreover, privacy has long been privileged in the discourse of domesticity, though its meanings and spatial manifestations have changed over time.

In his magisterial history of architecture and suburbia from the late seventeenth century to 2000, John Archer demonstrates that privacy has existed as a concern articulated by architectural writers for centuries. He notes, for example, that the fifteenth-century Florentine architect and treatise writer Leon Battista Alberti focused on the gradations of the experience of privacy that were possible in a "Country house for a Gentleman," a dwelling that was of considerable size and that allowed private rooms for various members of the family and separation of the family in the dwelling from the public portions of the house.[8] But it is in England in the eighteenth century that Archer finds a more profound turning point in the articulation of residential privacy emerging alongside the privatization of land that resulted from the enclosure movement and the abandonment of community. As he puts it, "The house became the axis of the privatized domain."[9] Enlightenment philosophies of self-determination and the cultivation of personal and family identity demanded the cultivation of the self that could be attained only in a private residential sphere that excluded the outside world and its demands. As a result, eighteenth-century British architects such as Robert Castell and Robert Morris created designs that facilitated greater degrees of domestic separation, the home as a site of retreat and of personal fulfillment. In the seventeenth century,

"privacy still would have been experienced in terms of a scale of degrees or gradations; as one passed from one room to the next, hall to antechamber to chamber to cabinet . . . one arrived at places that were increasingly restricted but by modern standards never perfectly 'private.'" But in the eighteenth century, new designs for staircases and corridors afforded greater levels of privacy by allowing circulation that circumvented private rooms. Concurrently, new ideas about the body and its functions resulted in the increased privacy of privies and bedchambers.[10] As Archer summarizes, "The dwelling, in other words, had become a crucial apparatus for the material implementation of Enlightenment notions of privacy and autonomous personhood, and for their naturalization into a belief system that persists as 'normal' to the present day."[11]

Nineteenth-century American architects and builders both imported and translated these ideas, which then appeared in architectural pattern books. By the 1860s and 1870s in the United States, as Margaret Marsh has noted, "the typical design for a freestanding middle-class house . . . both protected family privacy and encouraged intrafamilial separation." It did so by creating a private second-story zone of bedrooms that were increasingly unavailable to guests and by enlarging and opening the hall and parlor, "presented as the public face of the family." Two-story houses seldom included first-floor bedrooms, so that "private areas had become more private."[12] At the same time, retreat to suburbia and away from urban environments created an additional layer of separation for some middle-class families who sought exclusion—privacy of a different type and at a different scale—from a range of perceived urban ills. John Stilgoe refers to this as the development of a "borderland aesthetic . . . grounded in a growing love of domestic privacy." I will focus in chapter 8 on the importance of hedges and fences for the creation of outdoor residential privacy, but here it is important to note that turn-of-the-century retreat to urban edges and to suburbs constituted a retreat from urban crowding—from the cramped living quarters experienced in the city by all but the upper classes and from the masses on the streets. Even in this early part of the century, popular periodicals addressed the importance of residential privacy for the creation of healthy families, and the private house on its own lot was already being promoted as the site for personal individuation.[13]

For those addressing the living conditions of U.S. tenement dwellers between 1890 and the 1920s, residential overcrowding became a particular point of concern and a stimulus to the promotion of residential privacy. Economists and social reformers believed that the lack of privacy in tenements correlated directly with the propagation of immorality and public health problems, though these were frequently elided in their arguments. That lodgers also sometimes lived with families in overcrowded tenements heightened the reformers' concerns. As one Chicago settlement worker wrote, "The overcrowding of small family apartments with lodgers also breaks down all family privacy and often leads to gross immorality."[14] The subject of family privacy appeared frequently in the writings of housing reformers around the turn of the century; many categorized the loss of privacy as an "evil" that could lead to juvenile delinquency and adult immorality and criminality. Although these reformers never specifically articulated a definition of residential privacy, they spoke out against the accommodation of both lodgers and domestic servants within the home; Jane Addams referred to the latter as "alien[s] within the household."[15]

The open plan, which architectural historians have so closely associated with the advent of architectural modernism, is also not strictly a twentieth-century invention. So-called open plans are generally less costly to build because they require construction of fewer interior partition walls, and they can be found in houses and apartments dating from the nineteenth century.[16] But like the evolution of privacy as a residential concept, the term *open plan* is a relative one. Nineteenth-century American houses may have opened the living room and parlor to a greater degree, and used sliding pocket doors to create opportunities for more plan flexibility, but they did not approach the open-plan ideal implemented by twentieth-century architects such as Mies van der Rohe. Still, twentieth-century technological advances in heating and lighting also changed ideas about privacy within the home, because the advent and installation of electric light meant that family members could retreat to their own spaces in the evening rather than clustering around communal areas lit by fire, candle, or gas lamp. The installation of central heating systems and furnaces likewise allowed family members to move away from the warmth of the hearth and toward the far corners of the house or to individual bedrooms.[17] As the parlor and living room opened and became less private, bedrooms and bathrooms became more private.

By the postwar era, most Americans were living more privately than ever before, with more seclusion among family members and more seclusion from neighbors than had been experienced by previous generations, despite the popularity and implementation of at least limited open-plan concepts. By the 1950s, this level of privacy had become the standard expectation, linked to notions of middle-class prosperity. Postwar Americans had more privacy than ever before, yet privacy remained a high-profile topic in the design, shelter, and popular media concerned with design of the home.

Certainly, an individual, privately owned home may be valued for its ability to exclude outsiders and for the control it permits the resident. A private home allows complete retreat if desired, so that the home becomes a privileged realm for its occupants.[18] Although some historians have defined the decade of the 1950s as belonging to a culture of conformity, houses that allowed high levels of privacy for occupants also ensured that non-conforming lifestyles could be accommodated. In fact, domestic privacy was extremely important for anyone whose sexual orientation defied accepted heterosexual norms, whose political beliefs and activities were suspect, who practiced a religion outside the accepted Judeo-Christian norm, or whose racial or ethnic identity might be seen as unsuited to the neighborhood.[19] Any behavior or set of behaviors that an individual had to hide from public view in order to ensure social acceptance in the broader world demanded a private space for its performance. Yet the requirement for domestic privacy is also compelling because of its link to self-fashioning. As was true in the eighteenth century, privacy in the postwar residential realm continued to be described as necessary for the fashioning of the self and for the cultivation of individuality. Even late twentieth- and early twenty-first-century scholars continued to examine the interplay of the house and its design/decoration and occupants as a continually reflexive and mutually reinforcing process that is largely dependent on specific forms of domestic privacy and that allows the creation and enactment of shifting personal, family, and even national identities.[20]

Moreover, privacy is a highly nuanced concept, the definition of which varies widely according to time, place, and the individual. Although it is sometimes created through the establishment of rigid boundaries, it can also be created more fluidly. Truly, the "public world does not begin and end at the door," just as the private world does not begin and end in the bedroom and bath-room.[21] And as Lynn Spigel has noted, the ideology of privacy in the postwar era "was not experienced simply as a retreat from the public sphere; it also gave people a sense of belonging to the community"; by joining the numerous community organizations available to them, postwar homeowners "secured a position of meaning in the *public* sphere through their new-found social identi-ties as *private* land owners. In paradoxical terms, then, privacy was something which could be enjoyed only in the company of others."[22]

Public and private can be imagined realms that are constructed equally by the psyche and by the home builder, and a house designed for family privacy can still afford a life that feels linked to a community. But for those who wrote prescriptive design literature and for those who designed and built postwar houses, privacy was defined in fairly precise terms that dictated the specific forms detailed below. Because those authors and designers imagined a largely monolithic audience, a public generically conceived as white, middle-class, and organized around a heterosexual set of parents and their children, who behaved according to the norms established by accepted social and sexual conventions, their ideas about privacy were perhaps less fluid than those held by some members of the public who pur-chased such homes.

As it was considered by postwar authors, designers, and builders then, and as it appeared as a rhetorical strategy, design for privacy was design for exclusion—it was about the prohibition of others, whether family members, neighbors, or strangers. As a term with polite and practical overtones, *privacy* also usefully served as a code word that symbolically indicated a specific type of house, meant for a specific class and sort of person or family. The use of coded language was not unique to the period, but as Paul Boyer has pointed out, powerful cul-tural constraints prevented or inhibited the production of discourse that ran counter to dominant narratives in Cold War culture, such that "much of postwar Ameri-can social commentary, cultural production, and artis-tic expression is best read as a kind of hidden code."[23] The discourse of privacy in the visual and textual field attendant to house and garden design is an exclusionary discourse, and in that sense privacy largely connotes spatial purification. The geographer David Sibley iden-tifies this discourse as part of an exclusionary drive that leads to "never-ending invitations to consume further the privatization of the family, which is closed off from the outside world. Life beyond the home enters the private sphere through stereotyped images, conveyed by videos, television commercials and similar media messages."[24]

The desire for privacy is connected to the idea of a pure self, a pure identity (at least as projected to the outside world and as constructed by those prescribing, designing, and building), a pure family, unsoiled by the influence of outsiders.[25] Domestic privacy likewise symbolized respectability, and, as such, privacy carried specific connotations for social and economic class status as well.[26] Despite the fact that many newly constructed postwar suburbs housed populations that were largely homogeneous in terms of race and class (though not necessarily ethnic identity or religion), the specter of the "outsider"—an imagined figure who intended harm through invasion (scopic or actual), influence, or contamination via proximity—loomed large. Examined within the context of the whiteness of postwar suburban housing, privacy is easily connected to a desire to remain pure by excluding anything or anyone identified as "other." The boundaries that define the home also serve to delineate "the area which lies beyond cleanliness."[27] Fears of privacy loss, then, are also a "fear of pollution" that comes from the actions of others. The varied mechanisms for attaining and maintaining privacy do indeed "define the limits and boundaries of the self," and thus they are key to understanding identity formation within the home.[28]

In the first chapters of this book, I asserted that constructions of whiteness demand an imagined view of its opposite in order for whiteness to attain its salience. Hence, if residential privacy served as a partial cipher for white, middle-class identities, we must also consider how representations of "unprivacy" have signaled the opposite. What representations circulated in popular culture and were widely available to white Americans who might have measured their own lives and identities against images of unprivate residential circumstances? Again, photographs of tenements and overcrowded shacks located in inner-city ghettos circulated in the national press. But many Americans might equally have imagined the impoverished, overcrowded, and unprivate house as a nonwhite space because of depictions in popular films such as *Song of the South* (1946), *A Raisin in the Sun* (1961, based on the 1959 play by Lorraine Hansberry, which takes its title from a line in a 1951 poem by Langston Hughes), and *Porgy and Bess* (1959, based on the 1935 opera by George and Ira Gershwin and DuBose Heyward), which depicted black houses as small, ramshackle, and dilapidated.[29]

That privacy is a racializing concept becomes yet more clear when one considers that the inalienable right to ownership and control of private property in the United States has historically been a privilege reserved largely for whites. As a concept, then, privacy begins at the property boundary, related to the deed of ownership and to an entire ideology that it encapsulates. The legal dictates of private property rights comprise a language of exclusion that is based in entrenched notions of privilege and individualism that continuously ingrain inequity into questions about property rights and access.[30] The strong links that have existed in the United States between private property ownership and race, and between home ownership and American identity, indicate that the discourse about domestic privacy is equally about symbolic membership in the nation. To

have a privately owned home that was equally designed to ensure the privacy of the occupants was to affirm one's race, class, and citizenship.[31]

FORMING PRIVACY

Although most Americans never fully embraced the radically open plan that reached its fullest expression in examples such as Mies van der Rohe's Farnsworth House in Plano, Illinois (1945–51) or Philip Johnson's Glass House in New Canaan, Connecticut (1949), the majority of high-style tastemakers in the postwar era insisted on the superiority of the open plan. All the design literature that recommended custom-designed houses and the use of a licensed architect advocated the open plan as stylish, liberating, spacious, efficient, light-filled, airy, and modern—words that helped to form the lexical parameters for the accepted domestic tastes of the white, American middle-majority class. Many modest postwar houses opened kitchen and eating areas to the living room, so that the public spaces of the home were opened to each other to some degree.[32]

In its most conservative expression, an open-plan arrangement could simply mean implementation of a pass-through from the kitchen to the dining or living area, and it generally embraced at least a strong visual connection between interior and rear exterior spaces. But in the literature that was truly geared toward working-class and middle-class Americans—those who were just entering the house-buying ranks and for whom tiny houses on tiny lots were an everyday reality—it was acknowledged that the open plan could constitute a source of family friction. As detailed below, the conflicts that resulted from the clash between the ideals of high-style tastemakers and the realities of average homeowners were played out in the pages of magazines and a variety of mass media, revealing the tensions inherent in postwar beliefs about family life and national identity.

According to numerous scholars, *McCall's* magazine coined the slogan "family togetherness" in 1954, and, as Andrew Hurley notes, the phrase "embodied the ideal of domestic social relations and priorities to which responsible Americans aspired."[33] Although much has been made of the postwar period as the era of family togetherness, the concept actually first received increased attention from early twentieth-century male authors who offered women advice about the domestic sphere. Instead of the Victorian era's rigidly defined separate spheres for men and women and segregated spaces for family members to retreat from each other, family unity became a popular feature of domestic advice literature around the turn of the century, promoted as a means to achieve a healthy urban family by discouraging children from finding potentially dangerous or immoral entertainments outside the home. The idea found even further expression as increasing numbers of white, middle-class families moved to suburban residences in the early twentieth century. As Margaret Marsh has noted, both Frank Lloyd Wright's and Gustav Stickley's designs promoted open plans that facilitated togetherness and family activities rather than spaces for individual retreat. The living room, especially, became symbolic of this ideal of family togetherness, the place where family members could gather to talk, play games, and relax.[34] By the 1950s, the notion of family togetherness was so closely linked to ideas about privacy in home design that American identity and the notion of the family unit became conceptually collapsed in the discourse during this period. To design the private domestic sphere was to design the family, and to design the family was to assimilate and affirm American identity. The ability to own an individual, private house on its own privately owned lot, and to fashion family identity according to the contours of that acquired space, had never been so widely available to so many as it was in the postwar United States. The rhetoric of domestic privacy was thus available to a very wide national audience of potentially interested readers and viewers.

Typical, ordinary postwar houses were neither big enough nor intended to accommodate extended family members such as the in-laws or grandparents, who might have shared housing as first-generation immigrants in prewar periods or in families whose ethnic traditions included multigenerational patterns of living. Yet despite this newfound single-family privacy, and despite the prevalent postwar rhetoric of family harmony and togetherness, Americans sought refuge and privacy from their family members both within and outside the home. Familial closeness—although prevalent as a domestic theme in earlier periods, as noted above—became an ethic, one that Hurley has asserted gained cult status in the postwar era and became the focus of marketing campaigns thereafter.[35] He rightly sees *family* (as I see *privacy* here) as a code word that was used as part of a critical marketing strategy throughout the 1950s in which "the nuclear family was the vehicle through which Americans climbed the rungs of the social ladder," and he argues that marketers banked on the idea that "domestic bliss and social stability could be commodified and purchased." Hurley refers to a "family fetishism" that "reached the heights of absurdity after the war."[36]

The factitious ideal of the classless American democracy of distinct individuals who were nonetheless unified by the fabrication of the familial myth was closely linked to domesticity and its architectural framework, the private house.[37] Although critics and architects heaped accolades on the modern open plan as the ultimate expression of family togetherness, those who inhabited open-plan spaces also sometimes experienced tensions that arose from the forced congeniality they experienced daily. The fiction of family togetherness confronted the reality of shared family life—a topic examined below. Those tensions could escalate when families grew but their houses did not. Privacy became a fraught concept, one that was equally crucial to the maintenance of family togetherness and to the cultivation of a distinctive and separate individual identity. Whatever the tensions that may have existed within homes, privacy served as an extremely effective rhetorical strategy, carrying a range of meanings that extended beyond the purely practical necessities of domestic life.

TECHNOLOGY AND UNPRIVACY

New technologies that had been created and implemented during the war were put to use in postwar domestic residential contexts, resulting in a rise in media coverage about the risks to domestic privacy posed by surveillance mechanisms. For the first time, Americans were aware that their intimate lives could be exposed without their knowledge through the use of invisible, albeit mechanical, eyes and ears. Prevalent in law enforcement and in private investigation in the 1940s, surveillance technologies did not enter the public consciousness until after 1955, when a growing public concern related to the endangerment of personal and public privacy emerged.[38] To understand such issues as they translated to the domestic realm, one need only recall John Cheever's 1947 short story "The Enormous Radio," the tale of a mechanically malfunctioning receiver that inexplicably reveals the intimate lives of the residents of an entire New York apartment house

to the building's voyeuristic owner.[39] The invention of parabolic microphones, small wireless resonator radio transmitters, and cameras—sometimes referred to as "television eyes"—that were small enough to be hidden in heating ducts or lighting fixtures, stimulated broad civic discussion about wiretapping from 1953 through 1955. The 1953 Hearings on Wire-Tapping for National Security, carried out by a subcommittee of the House Judiciary Committee, were accompanied by coverage in the popular press that featured "the arrival of 'Buck

The novelty of a hidden tape recorder at a party in 1950. Courtesy of *Popular Mechanics*; originally published in the March 1950 issue.

Rogers' technology," so that public reaction was typically contradictory, embracing space-age science while rejecting its implications for the maintenance of individuals' private lives.[40]

If Americans began to fear mechanical intrusions into their lives, media critics and sociologists also suggested that they concern themselves about the use of subliminal suggestion delivered through various media, but specifically through television, particularly after about 1957, when all the major news services carried stories about the topic. Significantly, Vance Packard's *The Hidden Persuaders* also appeared in 1957; the book warned readers about a range of techniques that could be used to penetrate their psyches, including hypnosis, which the author claimed was being used by corporations to explore the minds of model consumers.[41] The topic of subliminal suggestion—"the projection of messages by light or sound so quickly and faintly that they are received below the level of consciousness"— became linked to national debates about ethics and the social impact of advertising.[42] An article in the *New Yorker* stated that Americans "had reached the sad age when minds and not just houses could be broken and entered," and that "nothing is more difficult in the modern world than to protect the privacy of the human soul."[43] That the instruments of this manipulation were in the home—radio, television, newspapers, and magazines—indicated not only that one's private world was less than secure but also that the house itself contained potential dangers that masqueraded as modern and desirable elements.

Publications such as Packard's clarified that one could trust neither the media nor one's own mind, which was evidently subject to invasion through subconscious means. Furthermore, security could no longer be guaranteed, even within the closed walls of a privately owned, single-family dwelling. Perhaps the ultimate invasion of privacy, then, was this intrusion into the individual's brain, and Packard's chapters included titles such as "The Psycho-Seduction of Children," "The Packaged Soul?," "Marketing Eight Hidden Needs," and "Cures for Our Hidden Aversions." Then, as now, advertisers naturally pitched their products toward the hopes and dreams, just as they also preyed on the fears, of potential consumers, so that Packard's thesis was at least theoretically accurate if not always substantively so. Concerns about privacy loss therefore affected every aspect and scale of life, from the outdoors to the indoors and even into the mind of the individual.

If television could be imagined as a mechanism for spying and for brainwashing, it also blurred the boundaries between public and private space by making a "window" to the outside world within the home—one that knew no temporal boundaries. With the advent of late-night television, for example, television and its commercial messages penetrated the home both day and night—"the option of privacy was being challenged around the clock."[44]

Cold War campaigns against communists, both within and outside national borders, were central to the discourse about domestic privacy. But it could be difficult to recognize Cold War enemies, since communists (like others who "passed") bore no specific physical attributes. Threatening people or activities, or even contaminating germs, one might imagine, could be surrounding one's family at any moment. Excluding such people and perceived threats and segregating them from everyday life to the greatest extent possible became a central concept underpinning the advocacy of domestic privacy.[45]

INDIVIDUALITY AND PRIVACY

Readers of the postwar popular press and shelter magazines encountered an abundance of text and images that promoted an ideal of insular togetherness as connected to the creation and maintenance of a happy family and of healthy individuals. It was important, they were told, to be privately together. Many Americans may have kept a close eye on and measured themselves against their neighbors, but achieving a degree of individuality through private introspection and leisure was, they were instructed, essential to the construction of the self, which was in turn important for the maintenance of democracy. A number of sociological studies from the period recorded their authors' concern about the effects of mass suburban conformity. These so-ciological texts, as Wini Breines has pointed out, were concerned primarily "with the defense of American democracy against the danger of mass movements such as communism and McCarthyism or, some have argued, against the masses themselves."[46]

To be an individual was to be a democratic citizen, a true and independent American, and authors frequently linked these characteristics to the design and appearance of houses. Architects and critics ranging from William Roger Greeley to Walter Gropius to Elizabeth Gordon believed in the importance of fighting against what Greeley called "the dead-level of mediocrity caused by standardization and nationalization. . . . to produce houses by the thousand all the same, like trailers; to have mail-order lampposts and hydrants and street signs; this is not banality—it marks the road to apathy and stultification."[47] The reference to the trailer is key here, because Greeley was linking the conformity of standardized housing to a perceived lower-class form of housing that conjured nonwhite and lower-class identities. In essence, the sociologists' and critics' writings sought antidotes to societal overconformity through the cultivation of individuality, and residential privacy was considered the essential ingredient. But they also linked class and race to individuality and privacy.[48]

In his 1950 work *The Lonely Crowd: A Study of the Changing American Character,* David Riesman likewise emphasized the importance of individuality to national character formation, focusing on a perceived trend toward postwar overconformity. He shared this concern with Lyman Bryson, who considered the cultivation of individualism the duty of every American for the preservation of democracy.[49] Riesman encouraged Americans to "break free of their conformist peer-group aspirations" as he sought possibilities for the development of an autonomous society. Such studies undoubtedly arose from the publication of images from and media coverage of World War II and the then newly recognized horrors of fascism, which certainly disallowed individuality and diversity. But they were also linked to published critiques by sociologists, urban planners, and design critics concerning the perceived growing homogeneity of suburban life. In the closing chapter of his book, titled "Autonomy and Utopia," Riesman extolled the virtues of city planners, whom he called "the guardians of our liberal and progressive political tradition," and advocated a view of the city "as a setting for leisure and amenity as well as work."[50] Riesman considered recreation and leisure vital components in the fight against the mass conformity fostered by the workplace and the homogeneous postwar suburban tract.

According to the critics, distinctively designed houses were far more desirable because they could affirm the individuality of the occupants' identities, but it is important to recognize that the stereotype of the homogeneous suburban house (the houses "made of ticky-tacky" all in a row) was, to an extent, just that. Developers may have mass-produced houses that had little variation in plan arrangements and materials, but homeowners nevertheless became expert at creating subtle variations and distinctions that could be read by neighbors and friends.[51] Choices in home decor, including carpets, window coverings, paint colors, furnishings, and the display of art objects and personal artifacts, created a fine-grained sense of differences within development homes. Children were perhaps most aware of these variations, since they commonly had access to the bedrooms in a neighborhood's homes, whereas visiting adult neighbors would usually have been confined to the more public kitchen or living areas.[52] As detailed in chapter 6, those subtle differences—the choices and placement of furniture, decisions about which artifacts and art to display and how—all amounted to indications of degrees of conformity and the display or erasure of ethnic, religious, racial, and class identities. Nevertheless, the stereotype of the conformist development house was a powerful one, and its currency was reflected in the insistence on the creation of the private, individual home.

To attain individuality, one had to have privacy as well, since privacy was understood to foster self-expression and inward contemplation, both of which facilitated free thinking. But such free thinking was ultimately linked to democracy, to the American way of life. As Riesman wrote: "People may, in what is left of their private lives, be nurturing newly critical and creative standards. If these people are not strait-jacketed before they get started . . . people may some day learn to buy not only packages of groceries or books but the larger package of a neighborhood, a society, and a way of life."[53] Houses and gardens, then, became a key to individualization, a means to autonomy, and ultimately, it was hoped, to the strengthening of democracy. The key was to increase the amount of leisure time available to homeowners and to help Americans, especially the new middle majority, achieve a degree of distinction that did not make them appear eccentric or radically different. The balance was crucial: one's house and garden should reflect one's outlook and personality, but they should also conform to a level of embellishment in keeping with that established in the neighborhood and following the guidelines set out in tastemaking books and journals.[54] As Russell Lynes noted in *The Tastemakers*: "A home of one's own meant a house different from one's neighbors. . . . [A house that had] a semblance of individuality without a trace of eccentricity. . . . Taste was a quality to be carefully strained, and the court of appeal on all such matters was first a peek into your neighbor's window and then a careful study of the women's magazines."[55]

Lynes underscored the fundamental tension that existed between the desire for the maintenance of privacy and the desire for the cultivation of distinction through emulation. Postwar homeowners were supposed to look inward to develop their individual lives, but if they did not take at least a peek outward into their neighbors' picture windows to see what was on display, or into the women's magazines to see what everyone else was admiring and, perhaps, purchasing, they could not be certain of either their emulative success or their achievement of even subtle degrees of one-upmanship. To keep the curtains drawn or to allow the neighbors that moment of voyeurism required by parties on both sides of the glass became at least a publicized (if not real) dilemma of modern domestic life.[56]

The emphasis that Lynes and others placed on leisure time as prerequisite to the development of individualism was, as Sarah Goldhagen and Réjean Legault have pointed out, linked to the idea that democratic freedom was "constructed as the personal and psychological freedom to play—*homo ludens*—in the face of an increasingly work- and consumption-oriented society."[57] Architecture was to create a playground for *homo ludens*. Proper play and recreational activities could happen only in well-designed homes and gardens, and therefore good design was considered critical for the development of free-thinking and individualistic Americans. Given this notion, it becomes clear that home entertainment and design publications such as Russel and Mary Wright's *Guide to Easier Living* of 1951 were also part of this focus on the cultivation of *homo ludens*, since, as they instructed their readers, it was in play, leisure, and home entertainment that good, free-thinking Americans—who likewise possessed tasteful tableware, linens, furnishings, and homes—were constructed.[58] This idea led to a new emphasis on the inclusion of spaces within the home for hobbies, craft projects, children's play, parental retreat, leisure, and informal entertaining.

Among the well-known publications that made explicit connections between the conformity of suburban residences and the loss of individualism were John Seeley's *Crestwood Heights: A Study of the Culture of Suburban Life* (1956); William Dobriner's *The Suburban Community* (1958), which contained an essay by Philip Ennis titled "Leisure in the Suburbs"; William H. Whyte's *The Organization Man* (1956); and John Keats's classic diatribe against suburban living, *The Crack in the Picture Window* (1956). Forging an explicit connection between leisure and individuality, and addressing the meaning of leisure in a larger societal organization, Ennis wrote: "Leisure activities, therefore, become an important source of self identification. . . . Leisure styles are often the basis of self image and subsequently of group membership criteria."[59] But Keats's arguments against suburban conformity had a much broader impact, and Keats went the furthest toward painting a bleak picture of a suburbia filled with drone housewives and characterized by homogeneous anomie that threatened the democracy. He wrote:

> Mary Drone in Rolling Hills. . . . Dwelt in a vast, communistic, female barracks. This communism, like any other, was made possible by destruction of the individual. In this case, destruction began with obliteration of the individual house and self-sufficient neighborhood, and from there on, the creation of mass-produced human beings followed as the night the day. . . . If we are going to live in bedroom neighborhoods, we must either accent our individualities or all go to hell in the same handbasket, and it's as simple as that. In an homogenous community of look-alike houses peopled with act-alike neighbors of identical age groups, there's not too much we can do to improve our lot except accent such small discrepancies as may exist, and lock our differences within our doors to keep them safe. . . . More insidious and far more dangerous than any other influence, is the housing development's destruction of individuality. . . . The closer we huddle together, the greater this pressure for conformity becomes. . . . The physically monotonous development of mass houses is a leveling influence in itself, breeding swarms of neuter drones.[60]

Keats's swarms of drones invoke a subtext that is far more subtle than his explicitly stated fears for an imperiled democracy. His "act-alike neighbors" in the housing development were equally upsetting because people and things that looked exactly alike were associated with nonwhite, lower-economic-class groups. White, upwardly mobile Americans were thought to be distinctive, their individual characteristics thought to be clearly visible to all, unlike the stereotypical notion that differences among people of color are not discernible, not visible. Middle-class whites possessed the cultural and symbolic capital that allowed at least a small degree of visible personal/corporeal distinction.

Homogeneously designed, look-alike houses were likewise associated with a particular form of lower-economic-class living, the trailer or mobile home. In their 1946 book *Building Your New House,* Mary and George Catlin advocated the purchase and use of stock house plans, but they drew the line at prefabricated trailers or anything that resembled them. They warned their readers that prefabricated or mass-produced houses lacked the individual expression their readers required, referring to the "Wingfoot Home" as "a sort of glorified trailer."[61] The Wingfoot was a prefabricated, compact housing unit that resembled a trailer, but it also offered affordable housing that could be

An example of a Wingfoot prefabricated house.
Photograph by Wingfoot Homes, Inc. From Raymond K. Graff, Rudolph A. Matern, and Henry Lionel Williams, *The Prefabricated House* (Garden City, N.Y.: Doubleday, 1947), 29.

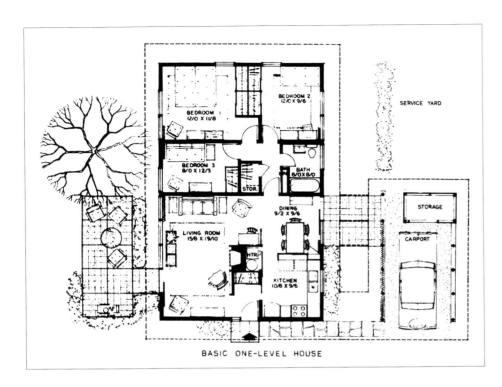

BASIC ONE-LEVEL HOUSE

Writers such as Kate Ellen Rogers equated privacy inside the home with healthy and tasteful family occupants.

From Rogers, *The Modern House, U.S.A: Its Design and Decoration* (1962). Copyright Robert C. Lautman Photography, National Building Museum.

constructed rapidly during a time in which those attributes were desperately needed in the American housing market. Still, the Catlins discouraged their readers from purchasing the Wingfoot or other prefabricated and mass-produced units; they believed that by purchasing and constructing from stock plans, a person could obtain "an individual home."[62] A stock plan could, after all, be manipulated to fit the homeowner's tastes and requirements, thereby providing a degree of distinction that signaled solid membership in the white middle majority. The critiques of suburbia, sociologists' writings, and design prescriptions are therefore significant for what they reveal about the pervasive ideology of upward class mobility and, though frequently unstated, its links to race. It was far easier, and far more acceptable, to admonish suburban dwellers to cultivate distinction and privacy for the sake of democracy than it was to advise them to do so for the sake of safeguarding a social, economic, and political system that was inherently linked to race and to the preservation of all-white suburbs.

In addition, the authors of design literature frequently returned to the promotion of late nineteenth- and early twentieth-century ideals by making explicit the link between the establishment of a private domestic realm and the creation of familial health. Kate Ellen Rogers wrote in *The Modern House, U.S.A.* (1962) that "family atmosphere is conceived as a protective zone in which children can healthily grow to autonomy," and she likewise asserted that "the family with personal values puts the individuality of each member first, stressing personal enjoyment and privacy. This group more than the others valued 'good taste' and were concerned about the design of their homes."[63] Rogers therefore equated families who cared about their health and privacy, as expressed through design of house and garden, with those who possessed a higher standard of taste and, therefore, were of a higher class than those who did not.

According to the shelter magazines, proper design of house and garden constituted the clear antidote to overconformity, and *House Beautiful* in particular repeatedly stated the need for houses to be designed to maximize privacy. Editor Elizabeth Gordon was also deeply concerned about societal conformity, and she used the magazine as a forum to advocate free thinking and individuality expressed through design of the home. Gordon chose the magazine's 1952 "Pace-Setter" home as exemplary of the "American style" she repeatedly advocated—a telling choice of words that indicates again the extent to which domestic design ideals were correlated with national identity in this period. According to Gordon, the house displayed "a relaxed, democratic architecture—a modern house that belongs, yet has an individuality essential to personal culture. Just as it is the essence of Americanism for each of us to develop our differences, so the Pace-Setter, while honoring the general character of the community, arrived

The 1952 Pace-Setter house exemplified what *House Beautiful* editor in chief Elizabeth Gordon called the "American style." *House Beautiful*, November 1952, 212.

at distinction and originality because it freely solved the problems of a unique site and a particular owner."[64] As she promoted it, the house struck the requisite and perfect balance for suburban dwellers and served as an ideal example of the elevated class status of the architect-designed home, which few of Gordon's readers could actually afford. The "American style" modernism that Gordon and her staff repeatedly advocated, then, was a soft or everyday modernism that retained comforting signs of the traditional (hipped roofs, familiar materials such as wood and stone) and that was linked to the editor's belief in the importance of autonomy to the development of democratic national character.[65] Attaining an "American style" home might have held great appeal, particularly for home buyers such as immigrants and/or their children who had only recently received citizenship, a white racial assignment, and a middle-class identity.

Privacy was essential to the achievement of this identifiably American style in house and garden design. Without privacy, there could be no autonomy, no democracy, and these were closely linked to the idea of individuality. As Elizabeth Gordon stated in a speech delivered at the Chicago Furniture Mart in 1953:

The challenge of our time is individualism versus totalitarianism—democracy or dictatorship—and this struggle is on many fronts. Our front, yours and mine, happens to be on the home front. . . . It is a time of profound spiritual crisis. . . . The individual is under assault from many sides. . . . We judge all design for the home in terms of what it offers for the encouragement of individuality, for the development of individual differences, for the provision of privacy and personal creativity, in short, for what it contributes to the humanistic values of a democratic age. . . . The modern American house—the good modern house . . . provides privacy for the family from the community, and privacy for individuals of the family from each other. It inspires democratic living by encouraging a personal life.[66]

Because Gordon equated privacy with the development of individuality and democracy, she devoted more pages of *House Beautiful* to articles related to privacy than to any other aspect of modern design. The emphasis on privacy is somewhat ironic considering that the houses she used to illustrate her point were exposed to millions of readers through a vehicle of mass communication. The stories on showcased houses included the owners' names along with their homes' locations (cities if not full addresses), so that every good example of privacy achieved through design was immediately exposed to the possibility of the throngs of prying eyes Gordon so vehemently admonished her readers to exclude from their own homes. The model homes and research villages that invited thousands of Americans to tour the interior spaces of the displayed houses while simulta-neously touting the exceptional privacy afforded by the houses exposed the same duality of desires for the attainment of a private residential world and the ability to enter and view houses owned by others (even if the owners were corporations or groups of developers). Such examples again reveal the inherent tension existing then as now in American society: privacy is jealously guarded and maintained as the counterpart to a wider societal impulse for voyeurism.

Gordon's garden editor, Joseph Howland, authored a 1950 piece for *House Beautiful* titled "Good Living Is NOT Public Living," which connected privacy to the American Dream of individual homeownership. He wrote:

> We Americans give much lip service to the idea of privacy. We consider it one of the cherished privileges we fought a war to preserve. Freedom to live our own lives, the way we want to live them without being spied on or snooped around, is as American as pancakes and molasses. . . . The very raison d'être of the separate house is to get away from the living habits and cooking smells and inquisitive eyes of other people. . . . if your neighbors can observe what you are serving on your terrace, your home is not really your castle. If you can't walk out in a negligee to pick a flower before breakfast without being seen from the street or by the neighbors, you have not fully developed the possibilities of good living.[67]

In this passage, Howland evoked a number of key phrases that would have resonated powerfully with new suburban residents. He summoned Cold War surveillance paranoia in one sentence, then played on fears of Depression-era conditions (memories of living with noises and cooking smells from neighbors), and referenced prohibitions about exposure of the body and private eroticism (the negligee as an erotic form of lounge- or sleepwear seen and discovered by neighbors, coupled with widely held notions about the white body as a desexualized and therefore concealed body when negligees were sometimes made of transparent fabrics) all in one paragraph, making a compelling argument for proper design for privacy. These were precisely the urban conditions *House Beautiful*'s readership of largely suburban homeowners had fled, and Howland's argument for the private residential world was cleverly constructed to resonate with his readers' interests.

According to some authors, postwar suburbanites experienced a sense of exposure that was far greater than that of city dwellers. In his study of class in suburbia, William Dobriner wrote of the "visibility principle" of suburbia. The city dweller's personal life, he wrote, "can be lost on the busy street and in the transient apartment house. But the suburbs are something else again. They are physically open. Neighbors can see who is having a party, who is cooking in the backyard; they can see the garden, the new car, the Sunday afternoon visitors. I am not suggesting that within the neighborhoods of the city these things are not known—they are, but city-dwellers have to go out of their way to find out. The suburbanite knows these things without trying."[68] Like Joseph Howland, Dobriner saw surveillance as a constant feature of suburban domestic life, and the street exposure he described echoed the focus on internal exposure outlined in magazines such as *House Beautiful*.

PRIVACY FROM THE OUTSIDE WORLD

The primary points of possible visual intrusion into the home were, of course, at the property lines and the windows. According to Sandy Isenstadt, picture windows became popular in the early 1930s when the glass manufacturer Libby-Owens-Corning began advertising "The Picture Window Idea" in home magazines. Isenstadt's study reveals the conflicts that resulted when a form that had its origins in the ribbon windows of high-style modernism became "demonized as emblematic of pretty much everything wrong in architecture, America, or both." As Isenstadt notes, "In architectural circles, picture windows became the apotheosis of commercial vulgarization: the subordination of high ideals to crass consumerism."[69] In its favor, the picture window allowed increased amounts of sunlight into the home and offered the promise, if not the reality, of an ever-changing, suburban pastoral view, one that signified wealth for its links to an Arcadian, romantic past. But as Isenstadt has also pointed out, views came to acquire real cash value in the real estate markets of the 1940s, when "'view' began to appear as a line item on appraisal forms."[70] To be able to claim a view outside one's picture window, then, also signaled wealth in the real terms of market value. Moreover, small windows signaled the past and perhaps even low economic status, since large areas of glazing had long appeared as a symbol of wealth.

Working against the picture window were notions related again to privacy and the maintenance of class values. A critic of the picture window, John Keats called it "a vast and empty eye" that stared across the street at an identical aperture that reflected it and looked vacantly back again. He wrote that his suburban heroine, Mary Drone, "moved by subconscious need . . . lowered the venetian blinds across her picture window to shut out the ghastly view of the mirror of her empty life staring at her across the treeless, unpaved street. Listlessly, she picked up a woman's magazine and began to read."[71] Even more troubling to Keats was the role he believed the picture window played in the loss of individuality. He wrote: "In the American house, the picture eye in the tokonoma reflects the outside world; instead of representing the family, it represents other people's activities. It is specifically designed to turn attention outward, away from home."[72] The picture window thus represented a trespass against the development of inward-looking individualism, and Keats's voice was one among many condemning glazing that exposed the family to outsiders or that directed the family's view toward the street and neighbors instead of inward, toward the family.

Window walls and large amounts of glass also received criticism because they required constant maintenance. As Mary and George Catlin explained, large areas of glass were hard to keep clean, and "the servantless housewife is harassed and oppressed by a job which always seems to need to be done: getting at washing those pesky windows."[73] A dirty picture window could reflect very poorly on a housewife and her family, especially because of the classed and raced iconography associated with dirt. Remembering also the classic declaration of hired, wage-earning housekeepers who "don't do windows!" it is easy to imagine that housewives would have associated window washing with work performed by hired laborers who were likewise generally of color and of the lower economic classes. As such, the picture window created a housekeeping nuisance, just as the Catlins cautioned. Indeed, the architectural and design publications from the period are filled with heated prose concerning the mind-numbing effects of the picture window on suburban inhabitants

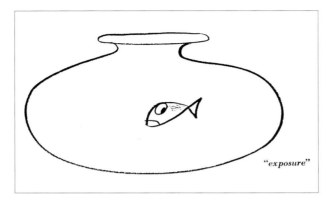

"exposure"

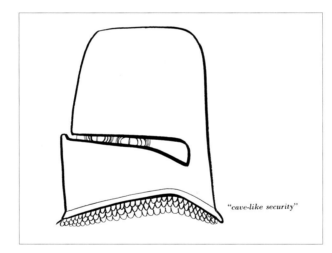

"cave-like security"

TOP "Exposure," cartooned here as a condition to be avoided in the domestic sphere. Cartoon by Robert Osborn from Elizabeth Mock, *If You Want To Build a House*, 40. Reprinted with permission of Eliot and Nic Osborn.

ABOVE "Cave-like security" was considered by many tastemakers the more desirable domestic condition. Cartoon by Robert Osborn from Elizabeth Mock, *If You Want To Build a House*, 40. Reprinted with permission of Eliot and Nic Osborn.

and linking it with crass consumer culture.[74] Nevertheless, thousands of postwar homes included picture windows. The Levitts, for example, designed some version of a picture window into nearly all their houses in their first two developments. How, then, were suburbanites to deal with this feature of their homes?

Far from providing an acceptable remedy, blinds and curtains, though almost always implemented in houses that contained large amounts of glass, were seen as a Band-Aid approach to solving privacy problems. If one had to implement window coverings, why have the glass in the first place? Heavy window coverings and dark interiors might also conjure prewar housing conditions and lower-class living. As a contributing author to *House Beautiful* wrote in 1946: "Unfortunately, in our best residential areas, obsolete restrictions created in times before the Glass Age prevent our putting fences, hedges, or walls close to our property lines and keep us from creating privacy, both indoors and outdoors. As a result, many people who responded to the urge for more sun and light are living behind drawn venetian blinds and thin curtains to escape living like fish in a bowl."[75] To live in the "glass age" was to embrace the bright sparkle of the unimpeded view from the picture window and, therefore, to be among the modern middle majority. But no one wanted to be so thoroughly on display, to be exhibited like a household pet in its cage, and manufacturers and tastemakers cleverly marketed blinds that created "windows that peeping Toms

can't see through" that still allowed a view out and light in.[76]

Exterior privacy walls that shielded the picture window from passersby on the street but allowed a controlled view of a contained atrium garden to the family, and permitted invited guests to peer indoors as they approached the house's front entry, created some degree of reconciliation for the conflicts inherent in the use of the picture window. Houses designed by A. Quincy Jones and Frederick Emmons for the developer Joseph Eichler used this solution, as did many houses of less adventuresome design that appeared in shelter and popular magazines. Still, such features seldom appeared on ordinary house lots, and privacy continued to be a chief design issue throughout the postwar era.

A postwar model house with exterior privacy wall, San Diego, California. Architect unknown, circa 1950s. Photograph by Maynard L. Parker. Courtesy of the Huntington Library, San Marino, California.

PRIVACY WITHIN AND THE STRUCTURAL MODIFICATIONS OF THE OPEN PLAN

Maintaining privacy among family members within the home and between family members and invited guests became a balancing act for merchant builders, developers, and architects, one that was also dictated by the Federal Housing Administration. In its 1952 *Underwriting Manual,* the FHA stated:

> A high degree of privacy, from without as well as from within the dwelling, enhances livability and continuing appeal. It is essential to a high feature rating that the interior arrangement be such as to avoid the impairment of privacy, either by exposing the bedroom-to-bathroom passage or the bathroom to view from the living portion of the dwelling. Other arrangements which impair interior privacy include a bathroom which opens into two adjoining rooms, and one which can be reached from a bedroom only by passing through the living room, dining room, or kitchen.[77]

Privacy, then, had an exchange value. Without proper design for privacy, a house would not obtain the "high feature rating" required for FHA mortgage underwrit-

FACING A gate and low wall serve as an additional barrier to the front door of a Barker Brothers model home. Architect unknown, circa 1950s. Photograph by Maynard L. Parker. Courtesy of the Huntington Library, San Marino, California.

ABOVE The Eichler X-100, designed by A. Quincy Jones, San Mateo, California, 1955. The concrete block wall is a privacy barrier for the house along the street facade. *Concrete Masonry Review,* April 1957, 16–17.

ing, and the property value would therefore be significantly decreased. Given the redlining practices that effectively segregated many postwar suburbs, it is easy to imagine that the exclusionary language of privacy would have resonated with the FHA, which embraced the concept and used it as a measuring device for its underwriters.

While the FHA sought designs that allowed for specific forms of internal privacy, the postwar fashion for open-plan houses worked, at least to some extent, in opposition to that ideal. If the picture window outwardly signaled the modernity of a house's inhabitants, the open plan was its internal and organizational counterpart. Through the elimination of selected partition walls, open plans were intended to increase the physical and visual mobility between spaces, thereby increasing living space and freedom of movement for inhabitants. A general sense of spaciousness characterizes houses with open plans. In conservative examples, living room, dining room, family room, and kitchen spaces flow into each other, while sleeping areas remain enclosed and separated. But in truly open plans, space flows freely, at least to some degree, between the majority of household spaces, with movable screens or partitions substituting for floor-to-ceiling walls. With the increased manufacturing of various kinds of sliding or folding walls and doors, such as the Modernfold doors that appeared in magazine and book illustrations, the open plan became more practical and available in

more rooms of the house, since such partitions could be installed to make, for example, one large bedroom into two smaller ones or vice versa.[78] Even very ordinary houses, such as those constructed in Levittown, Pennsylvania, made use of this technology. Instead of folding doors, the Levitts included bamboo screens that slid on ceiling tracks. The screens were used to conceal closets, but they also separated kitchen from living area in some of their models. In others, a series of sliding panels on a track could be closed to separate a guest room from the living room.[79]

The desirability of the open plan, according to its proponents, was that it facilitated modern living by allowing multipurpose spatial definition and freedom of movement and view. Because the open plan was an important feature of architectural modernism, open-plan houses conferred distinction on those who owned them. Houses divided into warrens of small rooms lacking sunlight recalled tenements and old and crowded apartments. By erasing the architectural barriers between spaces inside the house, architects and merchant builders shifted some of the living conditions for the family members who inhabited those spaces, so that, like the picture window, the open plan became a fraught design component.

If open-plan houses signaled modernity and conferred status on owners, they simultaneously opened the potential for friction among family members. Despite the pervasive persuasion to the open plan in much

of the literature of the time aimed at design professionals, ordinary, middle-class housing built from stock
plans or by most merchant builders (Eichler and some
Levitt houses excepted) seldom implemented open-plan
principles. If a wall was eliminated, it was usually to
incorporate the formerly separate dining space into the
kitchen or to connect the dining space with the living
space by means of a pass-through. Still, privacy problems existed in some homes, despite the traditional
implementation of partition walls.

A 1958 series in *Life* magazine about American housing detailed the complaints of new homeowners, stating that 80 percent felt that their ready-made houses
were not acceptably designed, that they were too small

A sliding wall in the living
room of a house in Levittown,
Pennsylvania. The wall can be
slid closed on a track to create a
private guest room or opened to
include the space in the living
room. Courtesy of Bucks County Free
Library, Levittown Branch.

and cramped, and that they had been badly planned. Indeed, the authors stated, "Most families are unhappy with their homes." According to the survey, compared with families in the past, families in 1958 were living in houses with lower ceilings, smaller rooms, less storage, and smaller grounds. The series included photographs to illustrate a traffic jam in the hallway of a builder house, where "doors, people and toys collide." The authors stated that although it would seem that home life should be great because of families' increased free time and the many new appliances available to them, "behind the cozy facade of many builder houses there lurk rasping nerves, bitterness and frustration. . . . 'Living on top of one another has destroyed our enjoyment of each other as a family. Unless you have privacy, you can't live decently,'" complained one family, who also noted that the TV could be heard all over the house, causing disturbance and a sense of intrusion.[80]

If the owners of traditionally designed postwar houses complained about such problems, it stands to reason that the owners of homes with open plans withstood even greater difficulties. Noise control was certainly a significant issue in open-plan homes, a particularly troublesome one because bothersome noise from neighbors and family members was supposed to be a problem of the past, associated with overcrowded, multigenerational living conditions. But with the postwar

LEFT AND FACING "Little houses, rasping nerves": a *Life* magazine article demonstrated the problems families faced when overcrowded and deprived of proper privacy inside the house versus the relative calm of a properly designed plan. *Life* magazine, September 15, 1958, 60–63. Photographs by Dmitri Kessel/Time & Life Pictures/Getty Images.

baby boom, larger families were actually living in smaller houses (albeit houses of their own on individual lots), and they were sharing their spaces with many more noise-producing appliances and entertainment systems than ever before. Open-plan houses exacerbated the noise problem, as did the hard surfaces increasingly found in newer homes and advocated by modernist tastemakers. In houses without basements, large appliances moved into the first-floor living space, making the noise problem more pronounced. Furnaces, water heaters, and laundry machines were often located in closets or in small spaces adjacent to or in the kitchen, adding the hum of their machinery to the sounds of the motors of smaller appliances, motorized children's toys, radios, stereo systems, and televisions, not to mention the voices of active children.[81]

To deal with this problem, Mary and George Catlin advocated the use of "noise-abating plaster" for the construction of interior walls to achieve what they called "greater emphasis on frictionless living." The plaster they recommended was more porous than the ordinary kind, and they claimed that its air cells would absorb sounds.[82] Whether or not such plaster indeed constituted a solution to noise abatement within the home, by the mid-1950s, gypsum board and other forms of inexpensive, prefabricated wallboard increasingly substituted for plaster, so the Catlins' advice proved quickly outdated. Acoustic ceiling tiles were also marketed as an aid to achieving in-house privacy. In 1957, Gold Bond Building Products, which was a subsidiary of National Gypsum Company, ran an ad in *Popular Mechanics* for "Acoustamatic Ceiling Tiles," stating, "Here's a game room where the kids (and you) can raise a rumpus without rousing the whole house and neighborhood."[83]

To measure the success of the open plan, Thomas Creighton and Katherine Ford asked the owners of thirty-six custom-designed houses to evaluate them in terms of five criteria or planning concepts: open planning, relationship to the outdoors, flexibility of use of spaces, finishes and materials, and the elimination of architectural ornament in the basic design. Their 1961 book, which contained examples of architect-designed homes, was essentially a tool for the endorsement of the architectural profession, since like other publications of its kind, it defined the role of the architect and built a case for hiring one rather than selecting the "builder house" or development house. Keeping in mind that nearly all of the profiled clients had enough money to purchase substantial homes, and that all were predisposed to stylistically modernist aesthetics and design principles, it is surprising how many of them complained about the problems of living in an open-plan arrangement. One of the most humorous responses came from Mr. and Mrs. Thomas F. Slattery, whose house was designed by architect Roger Lee in Berkeley, California. Of their open-plan house, the Slatterys wrote: "The house makes for great intimacy in living. In fact, no real privacy is possible. When we entertain on any scale, we park our son elsewhere for the night. Since one of us detests the accordion, it is safe for the other to practice only when he is alone in the house. Our son cannot very well have his friends in at the same time we have ours. However, we enjoy an intimate home life and the limitations are not important."[84] The Slatterys' facetious response was not an isolated one. In fact, twelve of the thirty-six homeowners profiled in the book complained about inconveniences resulting from the open plan, specifically calling attention to noises, odors, and lack of personal privacy from family members or guests.

Despite the fact that one-third of their sample expressed dissatisfaction, Creighton and Ford contended in their summary that the open plan is worth the problems inherent in its implementation and that it should be used even if some adjustments are needed to take care of noise abatement, odor control, and accommodation of the desire for privacy within the home.[85] For these professional advocates, the modernity of the open-plan house and the distinction it conferred on its owners were worth the difficulties, and even worth the risk of familial friction it imposed on their lives.

An example of an open plan that, according to the owners, afforded no family privacy on the interior. House of Mr. and Mrs. Thomas Slattery; Roger Lee, architect. From Thomas Creighton and Katherine M. Ford, *Contemporary Houses Evaluated by Their Owners* (1961).

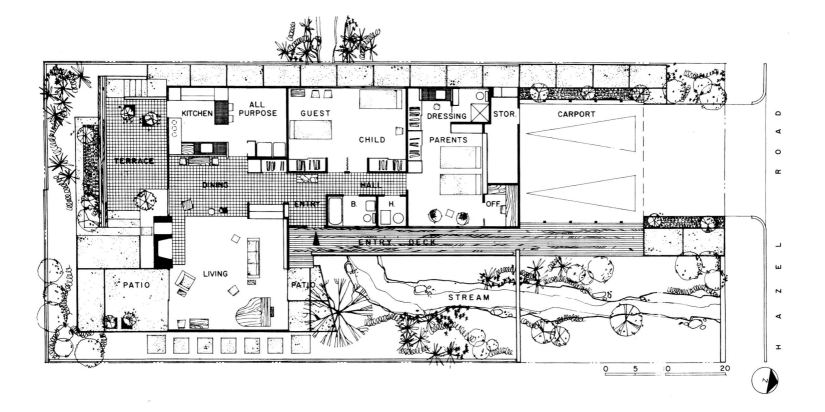

To propose an antidote to the problems of the open-plan house, John Burchard published "The Better Dream House" in a 1958 issue of *Life*. In keeping with the prevailing published rhetoric, Burchard emphasized privacy as a key issue in house design; he asserted that privacy was essential to cultivating individuality and that a house had to be spacious and imaginative in plan. He noted the problem of contested space in the open plan: "moments when one must pound the piano while another needs to nap, when some should play while others nurse headaches or study, when the television amuses some and repels others. To achieve privacy while retaining some sense of space and freedom is the glory of a good plan."[86] Burchard linked these planning characteristics to what he called "spiritual values," articulating again the connection between a well-designed home and the facilitation of spirituality and happiness.

In Roger Woods Kennedy's 1953 book *The House and the Art of Its Design*—a book intended for both architects and members of the house-buying public—privacy appeared as a recurring theme around which Kennedy framed his analysis and recommendations. Illustrating his points about privacy and its relationship to space planning through numerous diagrams, Kennedy described the need for privacy among family members but also the need for privacy from and for servants (for his upper-class readers) and guests. For him, residential planning pivoted around what he called "three neces-

sities of family life; to wit, conflict, privacy, and communication"; he wrote, "Privacy and sympathetic personal contact are regenerative, and help consolidate our knowledge." Kennedy described the breakdown of privacy within the home, ascribing it to sociological and cultural changes, noting that "the radio, for example, is now tolerated as a companion of study, particularly by children. And in a subtler form the telephone allows even more drastic invasions of privacy."[87] With regard to innovations in the open plan, he asked, "Where does too little privacy begin to have bad effects on the individual and on the family's self esteem as a whole?"[88] He followed this question with a detailed explanation of degrees of privacy required in the home based on a variety of functions and daily life needs. Privacy was certainly his primary consideration in planning the house, and he developed a system for zoning according to program, age, gender, and the need for sexual privacy. Kennedy notably emphasized the need for privacy in the bedroom as an outgrowth of what he called "the new sexual freedom," and, unlike most authors of the period, he explicitly instructed that in the bedroom, "it goes without saying that privacy from without and within, freedom from interruption, are also essential" in order for good sexual relations to occur in the modern home.[89]

Kennedy's explicit call for freedom from bedroom intrusions linked to sexual activity was unusual for the period. Most authors simply referred euphemistically

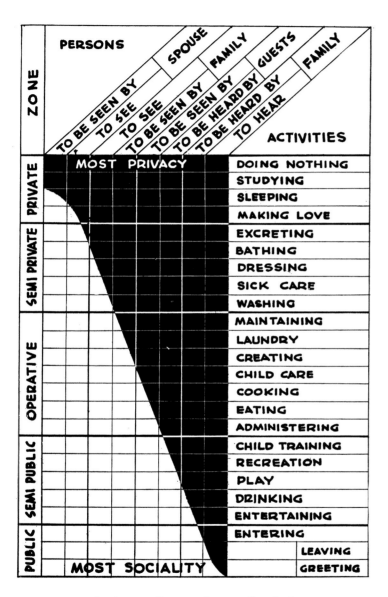

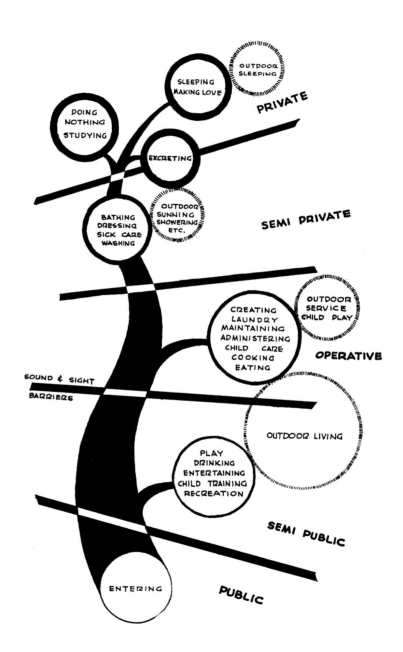

ABOVE This diagram illustrates the centrality of privacy to the development of a good house plan. From Robert Woods Kennedy, *The House and the Art of Its Design* (1953), 109. ABOVE RIGHT From Roger Woods Kennedy, *The House and the Art of Its Design*, 112.

A garden fence creates generational zoning by separating children from parents in a backyard. *Better Homes and Gardens,* April 1950. Douglas and Maggie Baylis Collection [1999-4], Environmental Design Archives, University of California, Berkeley.

to acoustical privacy requirements for bedrooms and bathrooms. The planning Kennedy advocated, however, which removed children as far as possible from the parents' bedroom, was not unusual and constituted a kind of generational zoning pattern that became commonly prescribed, especially in larger, architect-designed houses. Separating children from their parents increasingly became an ideal, one that was frequently seen in media representations of homes that tended to "render children a polluting presence"; David Sibley has connected the exclusion of children inside the home to the exclusion of "a larger cast of 'others' outside the home."[90] Moreover, children could be viewed as the literal and symbolic bearers of dirt from outside. They carelessly carried the mud on their shoes and the dirt on their hands into the home, disrupting the house's order and potentially sullying the adult occupants within.[91] As Denis Wood and Robert Beck have noted, children represent a form of barbarous alterity in the home—they are outsiders who both dirty and disorder the home. As such, they must be trained to observe domestic rituals and made to observe the patterns of privacy within a home. The creation of separate zones for children and parents meant the ability to control disorder, to contain the dirt associated with childhood activities, and to contain the symbolic "other" that is the child.[92]

Domestic accord is predicated upon agreements about the control of space. In families, that control typically belongs to parents, who can more easily assert

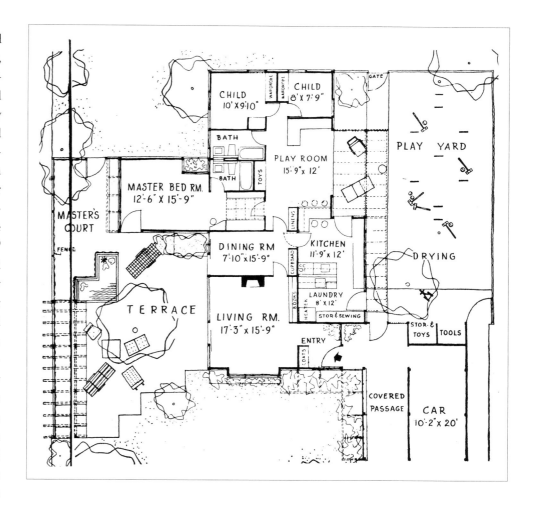

Richard Pratt, "Equal Rights . . . for Parents and Children": a garden plan that allowed parents privacy from their children by providing a play yard and adult terrace that are separated by the house itself. Originally published in the November 1945 issue of *Ladies' Home Journal* magazine. All rights reserved.

their dominance when spatial boundaries—rules about who controls which spaces—are explicit.[93] As a result, published house plans began to appear for still affordable (if somewhat more expensive) houses with separate wings for parents and children, with adults' and children's bedrooms located on opposite sides of the public areas (living room, dining room, kitchen) of the houses. Some even included separate outdoor areas for parents and children, with a private patio appearing off the master bedroom, delineated by a fence separating it from the rest of the backyard.

Like Robert Kennedy, Elizabeth Mock cast privacy and individualism in house design as what she called the "battle between the generations."[94] But Mock's gen-

Children play in their separate wing of the house. "Pushbutton Paradise in California," *House & Garden*, April 1953, 110. Copyright J. Paul Getty Trust. Reprinted with permission. Julius Shulman Photography Archive, Research Library at the Getty Research Institute (2004.R.10).

erations, like Kennedy's, were all from a single-family unit. Neither Mock nor Kennedy referred to conflicts between parents and in-laws or extended family members living under the same roof, as once was so common for many immigrant and lower-economic-class Americans. Rather than the frictions between multiple generations, Mock, Kennedy, and many others sought to resolve the frictions that developed between parents and their minor children and between siblings—in short, they tried to mitigate the tensions (real or imagined) caused by the forced congeniality of the open plan and the very small house.[95] More frequently than not, the offered solution was separate wings for parents and children, so that the myth of familial bliss was made possible through a division of household spaces that offered forms of privacy through separation.

Experts such as Dr. Benjamin Spock also advised that healthy families resulted when parents were able to maintain privacy from their children.[96] Children were to be able to play without obvious interruption from adults, but some degree of supervision was required. The public nature of family rooms or dens and living rooms certainly made it possible for parents to maintain their bedrooms as private realms. When families could afford them, intercoms likewise allowed the separation of parents' and children's bedrooms into separate wings of the house—at least for somewhat larger houses—because they enabled parents to maintain acoustical supervision of their children. The magazines also included advertisements and designs that featured folding walls and collapsible accordion-fold room dividers that served as popular solutions to problems of visual privacy between rooms of the house. Indeed, as Lynn Spigel has observed, collapsible room dividers "were the perfect negotiation between ideals of unity and division. They allowed parents to be apart from their children, but the 'fold-back' walls also provided easy access to family togetherness."[97] As more families accumulated televisions and stereo systems, concerns for acoustical privacy likewise increased. Folding doors did little to prevent sound traveling, but *Popular Mechanics* suggested that readers consider the use of a room divider/shelving system such as one designed by Motorola that was intended to mitigate competing family uses of broadcasting technologies so that television and stereo or radio could be used simultaneously.[98]

In many respects, then, visual and textual representations of the postwar house indicated a space that was constantly being negotiated by family members. Indeed, a *Ladies' Home Journal* article of 1945 described the plan of a modern house as a "division of territories" between spaces for adults and spaces for children. As was common for the period, the division of territories was carried out both inside and outside the house. The featured design included separate patio spaces for parents and children and separate bedroom wings at opposite ends of the plan, divided from each other by the living room, kitchen, and dining area. Two outdoor

This is a rear view of the playground seen directly below (upper right-hand corner of the house). Mother working in the kitchen or laundry can see everything her children are doing all the time. Glass partition back of the lounging chairs swings lightly up to the ceiling in fair weather, merging the indoor playroom with the outdoors at a touch of the hand.

View of children's segregated play area.
The plan for this house appears on page 149.

terraces served the adults: a larger area with a small pool extended off the living and dining areas, and a smaller patio was located adjacent to their bedroom. The children's patio on the other side of the house connected to the laundry room, kitchen, and playroom. This particular house featured flexible modern panel construction that allowed the indoor arrangement to be altered to suit the family's needs. The article's author stated: "The result of the whole arrangement is a pleasantly intimate family life, where at the same time complete privacy can be enjoyed. Off by itself, the parents' bedroom, with dressing room and bath adjoining, still opens right onto the playroom and has a sound-device connection with the children's bedrooms which can be turned on at night whenever you wish to keep in earshot."[99] The intercom, then, made separate territories possible while still allowing parental supervision, and if parents worried about technology impinging on their domestic privacy, they were nonetheless encouraged to use it to monitor their children's activities.

A promotional brochure for the experimental Eichler X-100 house in San Mateo, California, stated this interior zoning philosophy and its links to privacy most clearly:

> The design philosophy of Eichler living has always been that the home should fulfill one's inner desire for happy, lighthearted everyday freedom. Everyday freedom is a matter of space . . . unconfined space

As you walk through the Eichler Homes X-100 you will discover a dynamic new design for living.

The plan of the Eichler X-100 included a division of territories for family members. A. Quincy Jones, architect, San Mateo, California, 1955.
From a promotional brochure courtesy of Elaine Sewell Jones.

within the walls blending with convenient, liveable, private outdoor spaciousness. . . . You will see that the research laboratory X-100 not only provides the serenity of unconfined spaciousness—it also gives the peace and repose of privacy. The sleeping wing of the Home is completely separated from the living wing by a compact plumbing core containing kitchen, laundry, utility room and baths. Further, the children's play area opening from their bedrooms is away from adult living patios and is enclosed by a wall of Basalite concrete blocks.[100]

The architect for the X-100, A. Quincy Jones, believed, as did other designers of the era, that families needed age-determined spatial separation within the home for generational privacy, despite his equally firm conviction that privacy was primarily to be maintained from outsiders.[101] Indeed, Jones would perfect this planning principle with his designs for Joseph Eichler and then later apply it to more elaborate, custom homes, such as his Smalley residence of 1973, which featured the parents' wing separated from the children's by the core of the house. Despite the fact that Eichler homes were among the few mass-produced models to feature open plans, by 1955 the living rooms in Eichler houses were once again being divided from the kitchen and family room so that the all-purpose open space began to separate children's spaces from adults' spaces.[102] One can only imagine that Eichler, a successful merchant builder, was sensitive enough to market trends to recognize the need to reconfigure his later plans in this slightly more traditional manner. But he may also have shifted his designs to accord more closely to the rhetoric of privacy that prevailed throughout the postwar period and that he likely understood to be shaping consumer notions of residential requirements.

The separation of adults and children for both sleeping and recreation became commonly promoted for postwar house plans. It was typically achieved through the articulation of separate sleeping wings or through the placement of adults' and children's bedrooms on separate floors. Ten of the thirty-six houses featured in Creighton and Ford's study implemented such schemes

for division of territories, but considering that some of the houses in the study were designed for childless clients, the proportion is higher than the numbers strictly indicate.[103] Even in smaller homes, children's recreation became relegated to the remodeled basement, or "rumpus room," when it existed. The modest experimental home designs created by the University of Illinois Small Homes Council and advertised in its circulars and in publications such as *Popular Mechanics* contained separate outdoor areas for children and parents, for example, dividing an "adult terrace" from an area for "child's play" by a wall or some other form of vertical separation.[104] The basement could also be a place for fathers to escape. One *House and Home* article stated that "men seem to want a place to putter around in even if it's only to get away from the kids or television," and recommended creating "an area apart" for children and TV watching.[105]

When outdoors, children and their play equipment were to be segregated from adult zones of leisure. In *House Beautiful*, landscape architects Marie and Arthur Berger recommended that homeowners implement steps in the garden to form "a strong psychological barrier" between wheeled toys and adults; they also advised the inclusion of storage space to hide the clutter of toys. Likewise, landscape architect Thomas Church recommended that the home playground be seen but separated from adult areas, noting that play spaces must be well designed for fun to encourage children to stay

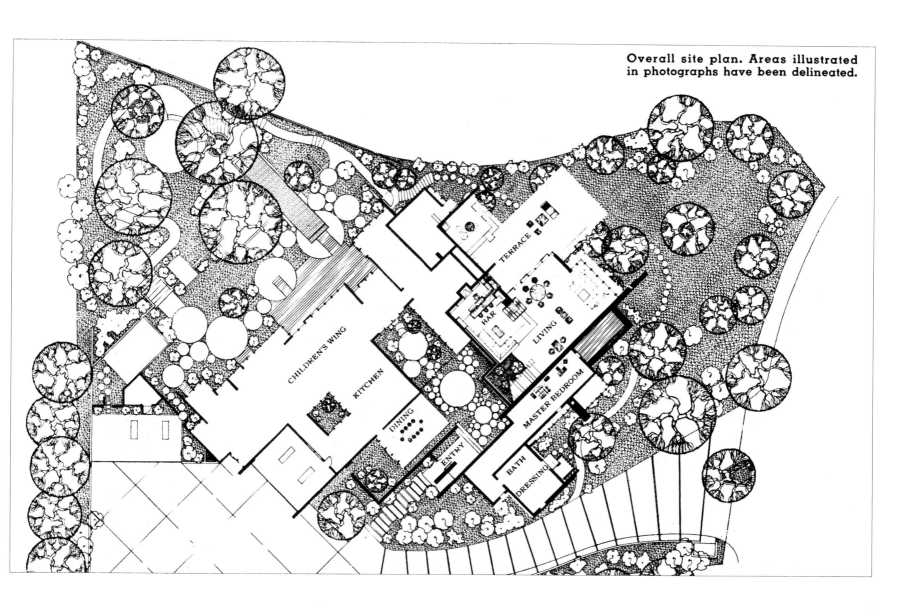

Overall site plan. Areas illustrated in photographs have been delineated.

CHILDREN'S WING

KITCHEN

DINING

ENTRY

TERRACE

BAR

LIVING

MASTER BEDROOM

BATH

DRESSING

within those spaces.[106] In the age of "family togetherness," then, the design and shelter magazines advocated the achievement of spatial separation between family members whenever it could possibly be achieved.

In the third installment of its 1958 housing feature, *Life* magazine included a house designed by Harwell Hamilton Harris for a Texas doctor and his family. The article positioned this custom house as an example of good planning based on the fact that it met the doctor's requirement for privacy from his noisy children after his long hours of work. Harris divided the house so that common spaces (dining room, playroom, kitchen) were located in the center, creating separate bedroom wings for the adults and children. The children's wing was essentially a large dormitory with its own bath and entrance. The author of the article noted that the parents' wing, with its bedroom, dressing room, bath, and sitting room, were "as far away as possible, in the right arm" of the house.[107] The children's playroom was equipped with acoustical ceiling tiles to absorb sound, so that the children could essentially disappear from the life of the household. Other houses in the series were likewise considered notable for aspects such as a "serene master bedroom suite . . . kept separate from the rest of the house."[108] The fourth and final part of the *Life* series featured a house with a study that had doors that closed to "make a retreat for grownups" and showcased houses with "tot spots," or outdoor play spaces for young children, generally situated just outside a kitchen

window so that the mother could observe them while they played "without getting underfoot."[109] To examine these feature articles is to get the distinct impression that postwar family members were very much in each other's way, tripping over one another as they moved through the house, seeking zones that would accommodate their desire for escape, not just from the outside world but also from each other. In a somewhat extreme example, a house designed by Pietro Belluschi located the parents' bedroom on a level above the main living area and hidden from the rest of the house by a door. With its own dressing room and bathroom, and an intercom that was "used to talk to the other levels," the parents could hide in their bedroom for extended periods of time, meeting the family face-to-face for meals and little else if they preferred.[110] What emerges from an examination of the pervasive postwar privacy rhetoric is a mandate—created from words and pictures—for the sorting of family members and activities within the home, established along a hierarchy of needs for privacy according to generation. The first priority was the exclusion of strangers and outsiders from family activity, followed by internal privacy for parents, and then privacy from children.

CONCLUSION

Overall, the published discourse about pe
family privacy achieved through manipula

design of house and garden was connected to the desire for a private world, secluded from the conforming masses and the potentially threatening outside world. According to mass-media sources, one's home and garden were best designed when they allowed one to turn one's back on the world so that one could achieve individuality and carefully measured degrees of distinction. Although the social vision of postwar housing was seldom broad or oriented toward community development, one could argue that it worked on behalf of the individual and the single-family unit by promoting the idea of the private, single-family dwelling as an ideal icon of American life. The do-it-yourself blueprints that could be purchased from magazines and through advertisements promoted an ideal of housing that emphasized the privacy and primacy of the individual in American culture.

The images of domesticity displayed in the normative design literature of the period, with their texts that repeatedly emphasized the need for creation of private domestic realms, sold rapidly to an audience eager to read stories and to see images that affirmed their economic status, racial assignment, and claims to national identity through specific associations with particular modes of residential life. Privacy was one of these modes, especially as it linked to the creation of an individual and distinctive identity. Amid the apparent sameness of suburban domestic life, it could be difficult for outsiders to distinguish the subtle differentiations of class and ethnicity that existed despite the relative homogeneity of postwar demographics in many new and restricted suburban developments. Magazine editors and staff writers, critics, architects, sociologists, and tastemakers advocated an American style of housing that was therefore closely connected to this rhetoric of privacy, creating persuasive publications for readers who might be eager to create their own American self-image and a self-contained universe independent of the outside world. The texts and images about privacy invited readers to locate themselves and their aspirations within an idealized formula that emphasized the exclusivity of the residential realm at a range of scales. With food stored in the new deep freeze, a Bendix washing machine and clothes dryer, home entertainment such as high-fidelity sound systems and television, and a garden that met the requirements of a country club, there was no need to venture outside the safe and controlled environment of one's private residential world. As *House Beautiful* warned its readers, "You must give your personal expression, your taste, free play—or you will emerge like an end-product on an assembly line of canned culture."[111]

5

HOUSEHOLD GOODS
Purchasing and Consuming Identity

My grandparents' house was always immaculately clean, orderly, and filled with a sense of the new as displayed in their possessions, decor, and furnishings. Their house was not like my friends' houses, or my friends' grandparents' houses. There were no doilies, no lace, no carved furniture, no rocking chairs, no rag rugs or early Americana knickknacks. Instead, my grandparents favored the modernism of Charles and Ray Eames and George Nelson. As a young man in Germany, my grandfather had been captivated by the works he saw that were produced at the Bauhaus. For him, as for many of his generation, modernist designs symbolized a modern lifestyle, an escape from the burdens of tradition and of the past.

Following my grandparents' move to Los Angeles, my grandfather had the good fortune to become friends with a fellow audiophile who worked as a Herman Miller sales representative and from whom he was able to purchase the furniture he loved. As a small child, I was frequently attracted to the frilly and common furnishings seen in department stores, to garish costume jewelry displays, or to bright clothing. My grandmother and mother carefully explained to me that these things were *ungehpotchkey*—a Yiddish word meaning garish and overly elaborate, or tacky and vulgar. From them, I learned that taste, class, and identity went hand in hand, and that something serious was at stake in the making of such aesthetic distinctions.

FACING
Photograph of an advertisement for S&H Green Stamps (*detail, see p. 180*).

Nearly every home is filled with objects. Some are ordinary and useful, even necessary to the reproduction of everyday life. Others contribute to the creation of bodily and/or psychological comfort. In this chapter and the next, I examine the cultural work performed by domestic artifacts and their representations, with a particular interest in understanding the ways in which ownership of and proximity to certain objects contribute to the construction of raced and classed identities. I concern myself with the ways in which consuming familiar objects may be perceived simultaneously as a quotidian feature of domesticity and as a symbolic practice that contributes to the construction of personal and family identities, examined here again primarily in terms of race and class.

Scholars who study material culture have long understood the links between the consumption of goods and projects of self-definition. In the postwar period as now, consuming was key to the fashioning of individual identity, which was in turn considered crucial to the continued success of freedom and democracy in the United States. To buy was, in effect, to be American. Lizabeth Cohen provides a thorough account of the extent to which mass consumption defined American citizenship in the postwar era, documenting the emergence of "a consumers' republic." That republic was characterized by an ethos in which shopping and, more important, purchasing were equated with patriot-ism. Suburbia, Cohen notes, "became the distinctive residential landscape of the Consumers' Republic," and "the suburban home itself became the Consumers' Republic's quintessential mass consumer commodity, capable of fueling the fires of the postwar economy while also improving the standard of living of the mass of Americans."[1] Moreover, as Greg Castillo has demonstrated, consumption of homes and of products related to the home was considered a key component of Cold War policies that were intended to demonstrate American superiority and power. The suburban home became the ultimate symbol of capital accumulation—perhaps especially so because so many small homes were available to the new and growing middle majority—and an effective material demonstration of a capitalist democracy's success.[2] Connections between the consumption of material goods and the construction of a patriotic American middle-class identity accelerated after 1945, along with the purchasing power of many Americans.[3] Things alone may not have defined or created the postwar middle majority, but they certainly became an increasingly important factor and must be considered as part of the larger economic shift that restructured postwar housing.[4]

Although the connections among purchasing, domesticity, and patriotism accelerated dramatically after 1945, the links between consuming, homeownership, and class identity were not new to the postwar era. The nineteenth-century American home was equally a site in which notions about what it meant to be middle-class and to be a family were continuously refined and updated through the acquisition and display of possessions.[5] As noted in previous chapters, reformers in the late nineteenth and early twentieth centuries also worked to educate immigrants about the links between the acquisition and display of furnishings they found tasteful and the construction of a white, middle-class American identity. For some Americans, particularly for recent immigrants and their children or for those who might not be easily identified as white, one particular dilemma involved securing an unequivocal sense of racial identity. For these Americans, purchasing and the artifacts purchased helped define racial—and particularly white—identities.[6] Whiteness is fundamentally associated with the ability to purchase commodities and the promises they embody of affluence, ease, safety, and sanitization. The ability to literally buy (or attempt to buy) happiness through the purchase of products has largely been a white phenomenon because of the historic links that have existed between race and class as American modalities.

As noted in previous chapters, whiteness is often constructed in relation to or against that which it is not. Sara Ahmed makes this point when she describes how the home of her mixed-race family combined objects from England and Pakistan in ways that created a constantly fluctuating set of family and personal identities and that intersected with decisions about what language was spoken in the home and a range of other domestic practices: "The whiteness of my home is perhaps revealed by the very way in which Pakistan was experienced as color. In many ways it was a white home, where its whiteness was shaped by the proximity of certain objects and how those objects gathered over time and in space to create a point for dwelling." Pakistani objects represented "color"; English objects represented whiteness, and these became more white because of their proximity to objects that (no matter what their material form or actual chromatic disposition) were imagined as colored.[7] Similarly, a lexicon of white consumption emerged in the postwar United States that could also sometimes exist in contrast to the possession of inherited objects from ethnic pasts, though this depended very much on the objects themselves and the status and racial or ethnic identities of the individuals who possessed them. But in addition to objects' existing against opposites that could be discerned through examination of the objects' appearance or form, the very act of consuming new goods could itself constitute white and middle-class identities. Active and full participation in the postwar economy was the right of those who possessed societal power more generally: white Americans whose privileges allowed them access to the jobs and spatial mobility that afforded purchasing power. Examinations of the representational field—especially in a range of publications derived from the national, white press—indicates that to shop was, in some respects, to be white.

Valerie Babb has also examined the "merchandising of whiteness" to recent American immigrants in the first decades of the twentieth century through its manifestation in settlement houses such as Chicago's Hull-House, where "everything from home furnishings to the content of the various clubs . . . reaffirmed a standard of white privilege." Art, furniture, cooking—everything within the domestic sphere was intended to affirm a white American identity and to erase ethnic identities. All the artifacts in the house "subtly dictated what constituted authentic and sanctioned American values. They implicitly rearticulated an ideology that those who contributed to American history and cultural development came from one idealized racial, cultural, and class group having western European origins."[8] Although reformers tried to persuade Jewish immigrants to purchase furniture with clean lines, such as mission-style furnishings, most Jewish immigrants preferred the more ornate, heavy, and colorful aspects of traditional styles.[9] By midcentury, however, and as explained below, the simple lines of modernist furnishings became associated, to some extent, with Jewish identity. The example is important because it demonstrates at least a degree of the complex iconographic fluidity of consumed artifacts and the ways in which their signifying capabilities shift according to time and place.

The rise in purchasing and consumption by Americans in the 1950s also reflected a desire to leave behind the hardships of the Great Depression. Certainly, foremost for many was the desire to buy houses. They wanted, as Alan Ehrenhalt has noted, to leave behind "landlords, cooking smells, neighbors one flight above or uncomfortably close next door, physical surroundings that carried indelible reminders of hard times years ago."[10] These aspirations had as much to do with their anxieties over racial and class assignment as with their concerns for increased comfort and upward mobility, given that renting, uncontained domestic odors, and uncomfortably close neighbors all signaled non-white and lower-class living. Attaining a home of one's own, on an individual lot, was the apparent solution, and the house—frequently located in a suburban development—offered the possibility of a private remedy to any broader societal malaise (whether real or imagined) and insurance against a return to past and perhaps more impoverished conditions.[11] To purchase a house and the commodities to fill it was, in effect, to purchase safety and security. Consuming became an American pastime, a new mode of recreation, and, for some, an antidote to a selection of life's dilemmas.[12]

Buying "correctly" has mattered for as long as consumption has been linked to status. The wise shopper purchases both the object (desired for its use value) and a specific sense of security that ownership of the object confers through confirmation of identity for both self and family.[13] In fact, scholars who study the material culture of domesticity largely agree that consumption is "a social process whereby people relate to goods and artifacts in complex ways, transforming their meaning as they incorporate them into their lives through successive cycles of use and reuse." Individuals construct and reveal their identities through artifacts purchased for and displayed in the home in an ongoing process that changes as individuals and families try out different notions of the self that are nonetheless contained within specific parameters of race, class, and gender.[14] Possessing the right items also helped to ameliorate the homogeneous monotony of homes in some postwar suburban developments—a homogeneity that could be associated with images of the nonwhite lower classes. Consumer goods were a crucial measure of distinction among those who were newly upwardly mobile, newly affluent, perhaps even newly "white." Material goods, then, helped affirm class and race and became especially important to those whose identities were in flux as they moved from dwellings shared with immigrant parents into homes of their own and, in the process, forged new identities.

As the American economy regained vigor after the cessation of war in 1945, returned GIs resumed their lives, eventually finding employment that produced steady income and allowed increased amounts of leisure time. Although the number of families whose incomes could define them as middle-class grew steadily, such that the middle class assumed a majority position,

incomes could not keep pace with desire in an economy based on the rapid production of new consumer and luxury goods that were likewise cleverly marketed. Although credit systems that allow consumers to buy now and pay later (usually with accumulated interest) are centuries old, the credit card first emerged in the 1950s, facilitating an ease of purchasing that encouraged Americans to acquire rapidly and beyond their means.[15] With each purchase, postwar consumers stimulated a market that increasingly targeted middle-majority buyers, creating rapidly spiraling economic cycles of supply and demand. Indeed, postmodern theorists such as Fredric Jameson point to the immediate postwar period as the key moment for the development of an American culture of mass consumption based primarily on the dictates of exterior styles and appearances.[16]

In the immediate aftermath of the war, housing topped the shopping lists of many Americans, followed by large durables such as refrigerators, freezers, washing machines, ranges, and vacuum cleaners. Such purchases were, not coincidentally, exactly the items that magazine advertisers had promoted to their readers as postwar rewards. Advertisements that appeared in the *Ladies' Home Journal* just before the end of the war consistently promised readers that as soon as the war ended and materials were released, they would be able to buy better refrigerators with more storage, electric irons that would never scorch, automatic toasters that would "revolutionize toast making," and so on. As optimism and consumer confidence rose—which they did rapidly—spending also increased, such that consumption from 1945 through 1950 increased 60 percent overall and 240 percent for household furnishings and appliances.[17]

THE HOUSE AS CONSUMER PRODUCT

More than any other item, a house was—as it remains today—the most important purchase Americans made in the postwar period. A 1955 article in *Life* magazine stated:

> In the first half of 1955, the 409,000 workers of G[eneral] M[otors] made an average of $103 per week . . . a lot of long green for the American workingman. Not only at GM, but everywhere, his income has been comfortably rising. His sights as a consumer are inevitably rising too. What should he spend his new income on? One good candidate is better housing.[18]

Such articles urged working-class Americans not only to purchase homes but also to try to improve their current living situations. If they already owned homes, they were encouraged to find better, larger, more modern houses, outfitted with all the latest appliances and designed in the most up-to-date forms. The house was the preeminent symbol of class for many Americans,

but it was also the single most important purchase one could make to establish or confirm identity of any sort. Purchasing a house had important consequences for economic, class, and racial mobility; life opportunities could be increased or diminished depending on the location, size, and form of the house. The right choice of house in the correct location could make all the difference in the determination of a family's future.

If Americans were uncertain about the importance of their house purchases for the establishment of their economic, social, and racial status, the editors of *Life* magazine made the relationship clear. As early as 1949, the magazine published the research of a University of Chicago sociologist, W. Lloyd Warner, that ranked Americans in terms of six social classes: lower-lower, upper-lower, lower-middle, upper-middle, lower-upper, and upper-upper. Assigning points for specific attributes, the magazine used Warner's methods to allow readers to score their own social standing according to four factors: house type, dwelling area or neighborhood, occupation, and source of income. Focusing on six subjects living in and around Rockford, Illinois, the *Life* article provided a vivid lesson in distinction. The lowest class was represented by a man who lived in a trailer with his wife and dog. His race and occupation mattered little, since trailers were already associated with and symbolic of the undesirable, nonwhite, lowest-class citizen.[19] The subject rated second lowest was an Italian immigrant who lived in "a neighborhood across the tracks from Rockford's main residential district [with] Negro families . . . on both sides" of the seven-room house. This lower-class man, then, was not only nonwhite because of his Italian background but also because of his proximity to black neighbors, which further destabilized his class and racial assignment.[20] The lower-middle-class subject was a grocery store owner, and, as the magazine assured its readers, his social prestige had risen since he acquired his own store. As such, he represented the blue-collar worker who was, like so many of *Life*'s readers, upwardly mobile. However, the fact that the grocer was "living for the time being in a six-room apartment over his store rates him a notch lower (by 3 points) than Armato [the Italian immigrant] as far as 'house type' is concerned. But his dwelling area (8 points) makes up for that."[21] Surprising in their frankness as such mainstream articles may now seem, they clarify postwar calibrations of class and status and their links to racial assignment and American identity, all of which were centrally linked to house form, style, and location.[22] By simply looking at a house belonging to one's friends and neighbors, an entire narrative could be revealed, or at least imagined, about the owner's identity.

Surprisingly, neither the upper-middle-class nor the lower-upper-class subject of the *Life* article was associated with a specific house type, but the authors duly noted the latter's membership in an exclusive country club. Likewise, the upper-upper-class subject's house

was not specified, perhaps because the mere mention that his was among Rockford's oldest families automatically signaled his social and economic placement and white racial identity. Family lineage, then, could certainly substitute for, and even outrank, the house as a crucial signifier of status. But many Americans could not claim such lineage. The attainment of distinctive, personalized living through the purchase of a custom, architect-designed home was the surest way to confirm class and privilege. The real rub for middle-majority Americans came from their lack of access to such distinctive accommodations. The equation of homogeneity in house form and style with a primitive, vernacular, and foreign past was a factor to be overcome for the vast majority who could afford only the standardized, rapidly produced, and aesthetically repetitious small houses found or imagined to exist in many new suburban developments.

Architectural writers of the period, such as Kate Ellen Rogers, took the matter as their subject. According to Rogers, as Americans fled to the suburbs, "the monotony of the city sidewalk merely gives way to the monotony of the developer's bulldozer and the tedious repetition of look-alike houses, ill planned and shoddily built, likely potentials for new slums. . . . One of the great objections to the builder's house from an aesthetic standpoint is uniformity—the dreadful monotony of a poor house design, endlessly repeated." She specifically called attention to "the poorly designed, endlessly repeated, lock-step sort of neighborhood [that] is infinitely deadening and can only be deplored."[23] Her critique is not surprising considering that Rogers was herself an architect and interior designer and therefore an advocate for architect-designed houses. Like many other architectural critics, such as Elizabeth Mock, she therefore cast vernacular architecture, which frequently appears superficially homogeneous and typically follows norms established by cultural or regional traditions, as acceptable in "remote villages in Europe and Asia," but these remained "other," identified primarily with non-Western and economically regressive cultures.[24] Moreover, her use of the term "lock-step" to describe homogeneous housing evoked the militaristic marching of troops—an image that could have multiple possible negative connotations for postwar homeowners. Rogers thus emphasized the need for and the importance of individuality, custom-designed housing, and distinctive living as hallmarks of American democracy and freedom, again linking individuality to national identity.

Recent studies of individual U.S. suburbs have revealed an architecture that is far less homogeneous than that both feared and reported by the midcentury critics. In fact, some merchant builders made substantial efforts to vary the architecture in new housing developments, specifically to avoid criticism and to appeal to buyers who were sensitive to those critiques and did not want to live in look-alike houses. Yet even when the houses were substantially varied, as was the case in Levittown, Pennsylvania, for example, individual neighborhoods tended to contain the same house types, because streamlined mass-construction techniques demanded a single house type per block in order to maintain cost-efficient assembly. In such cases, neighborhoods within developments became specific indexes of class, since home costs were generally well-known and house size could be read easily from the street.[25] Still, the stereotype of the homogeneous suburban house was not derived from nothing, and the many published images of Levittown, Long Island (in which only two house types were constructed), and Lakewood, California, for example, confirmed the myth in the minds of many, whether or not the images matched reality.

The close relationship between questions of domestic distinction, identity formation, and consumption could be read in the national press as well as in the work of academic sociologists. *Harper's* magazine editor Russell Lynes addressed the issues related to distinction that arose in an era in which so many had access to so much, but in which the commodities available for purchase were often very similar to one another. In a satirical essay, he wrote that Americans could "have rather more than the usual number of books, some drawings and probably a painting or two . . . and possibly a mobile." And as Barbara Ehrenreich adds in her sociological analysis of class in the 1950s, those same consumers might also "ostentatiously display the *New Yorker* on the coffee table, move the TV from the living room to the

Living room of Chicago sociologist James A. Davis, circa 1958. From James A. Davis, "Cultural Factors in Perception of Status Symbols," *Midwest Sociologist* 21, no. 1 (December 1958): 3. Reproduced with permission of John Wiley & Sons, Inc.

den, serve wine with meals, join the Book-of-the-Month Club."[26] But the possibilities for status and identity differentiation were limited, so that fine, even minute, gradations became critically important.

A revealing 1958 sociological study focused on the decoration of living rooms and the display of material goods as a key to the definition of status and class. University of Chicago sociologist James A. Davis showed twenty-four photographs of four living rooms to 134 housewives in Cambridge, Massachusetts. The women, selected to represent a range of economic and social backgrounds, were asked to comment on the living rooms seen in the photographs and to rank them according to the class of the owner. The first living room was the one in Davis's apartment. It was the most aesthetically modern of the group, with bookshelves, "butterfly" or "sling" chairs, and a low wood coffee table with a *New Yorker* magazine displayed on it. The participants in the study found this living room very spare and clean, and they associated its modern aesthetic with the subculture of the young intellectual. They also equated modern with "bohemian," low-income inhabitants, since the furniture was known to be inexpensive. One woman even said, "It looks like a Jewish person's house," while others thought it looked like an office and not homey.[27] The respondents did not associate the room's modernism with family life or togetherness, and they did not recognize intellectualism—as represented by the books on the bookshelf—as symbolic of a family-centered life. Instead, the absence of family artifacts in the room (no photos, no bric-a-brac) signaled for them a lack of femininity and a dearth of familial values.[28] Modernism, then, was perceived as an elite, Jewish, cold, and nonfamilial style. Its class associations were ambiguous, but it was not a style that neatly equated with white identities.

The second living room depicted in the photographs in Davis's study was one found in a demonstration apartment in a public housing unit; its actual location remained unknown to the survey participants. Despite

Demonstration living room in public housing unit, circa 1958.
From Davis, "Cultural Factors in Perception of Status Symbols," 3. Reproduced with permission of John Wiley & Sons, Inc.

this living room's traditional furnishings, the women found it very sterile, commenting specifically on the obvious newness of the furniture, which was stiffly grouped around the perimeter of the room, the walls of which were adorned with cheap floral paintings. The women identified this room as "not fashionable," and they guessed that it was a hotel lobby that was conventional and that indicated a lack of imagination. Some also guessed that it was a room for a low-salaried family, since they found it cold and empty. Mere tidiness and traditional forms, then, did not guarantee the conveyance of the desired class identity, and it is clear that these women possessed very keen abilities to discern fine-grained and subtle distinctions.

The third living room was small and cluttered, with lace doilies on the furnishings, floral fabrics, a lamp with an elaborate shade, and a number of small decorative objects displayed on shelves. The subjects identified this room as belonging to someone of ethnic descent, of low status, yet warm and colorful.[29] The room was neat but, according to Davis, "betrays the continuation of European taste traditions. Perhaps the clearest single

An Italian American living room, circa 1958. From Davis, "Cultural Factors in Perception of Status Symbols," 4. Reproduced with permission of John Wiley & Sons, Inc.

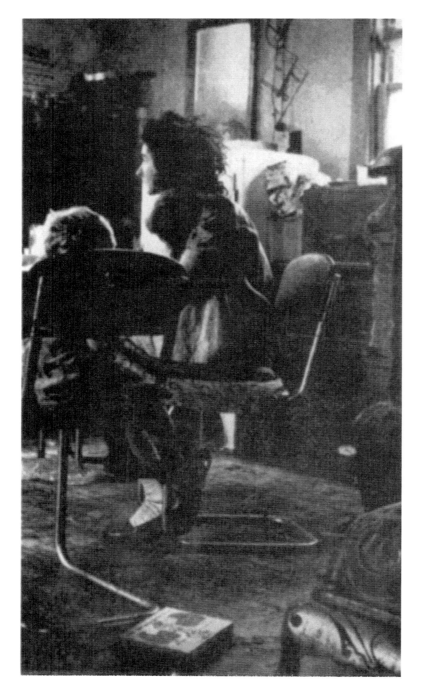

index is the presence of a very ornate lamp shade en-cased in cellophane."[30] Although the room contained treasured and traditionally configured items, the sub-tlety of their arrangement and the size of the room be-trayed a nonwhite, non-American identity to the survey participants.

The final set of photographs portrayed a white woman and child in a tiny kitchen/living room that was in a state of disarray. These photographs—the only ones to include human subjects—immediately evoked responses about the obvious low status of the family portrayed, who were seen variously as tragic, ap-palling, dirty, sloppy, cluttered, and uneducated about spending. As one respondent noted, "There would be too much trouble with these to let them into the neigh-borhood."[31] Dirty, disorganized, cluttered, small, and cramped living spaces clearly signaled poverty and low economic and social status. That the appearance of the subjects in the photographs caused one viewer to call for the prohibition of their entry to her neighborhood situates the subjects as nonwhite, despite their actual skin color, since the only de facto means of restricting access to housing was on the basis of racial and ethnic identity. The stakes in postwar home decorating deci-sions were significant, then, and nearly every woman in the United States had at least some degree of instinctive ability to make the distinctions on which status were based.[32]

A disheveled room and its occupants, circa 1958.
From Davis, "Cultural Factors in Perception of Status Symbols," 4.
Reproduced with permission of John Wiley & Sons, Inc.

As early as 1949, Russell Lynes published his now-famous essay making distinctions among highbrow, middlebrow, and lowbrow tastes. The illustrated chart on which he collaborated and that appeared in *Life* magazine helped Americans discern their status through their selections of art, furnishings, music, and even salad dressing.[33] The popularity of the article and chart were such that, as Lynes himself later noted, both began to be used as the basis for parlor games at parties in which friends and neighbors aimed to fix their own class status through Lynes's fine-grained, if satirical, differentiations in taste. The chart became so popular that it became the basis for a Broadway show. As Lynes later stated, its embrace nationwide indicated the extent to which people were self-conscious about their taste and class status and the widespread desire to understand and decode the iconography of consumption.[34]

Other sociologists and cultural critics made similar observations. Although critics have rightfully noted that Vance Packard's famed 1959 book *The Status Seekers* used a blunt approach to explaining class and status differentiation and offered little in the way of new information, Packard made a number of trenchant observations in the book whose wide reception makes them noteworthy, so I cite them here at some length. Packard created a five-tiered system of classes in which the top-tier "diploma elite" included the "real upper class" and the "semi-upper class"; his lower-tier "supporting classes" included the "limited success class,"

the "working class," and the "real lower class." Intellectuals, whom Packard called "genuine eggheads," did not fit into these categories, since they are "the working intellectuals who create culture . . . or who disseminate and interpret culture." These eggheads, he noted, were among those most likely to live in "contemporary" homes, since they had "the self-assurance to defy convention, and they often cherish the simplicity of open layout." Without mentioning the developer's name, he alluded to the popularity of Eichler homes near Stanford University as appealing to eggheads, who appreciated what he called the "severely contemporary and terribly avant-garde" style of the homes. Eggheads, after all, were more likely to favor "the primly severe," while the lower classes favored "the frankly garish." Packard asserted, for example, that "the lower-class people preferred a sofa with tassels hanging from the arms and fringe around the bottom. The high-status people preferred a sofa with simple, severe, right-angled lines." He cited the work of a social research firm in Chicago: "The Wage-Town wife thinks in terms of 'decoration' rather than 'décor.' She uses bright colors and bold pattern, and side-by-side mixtures of both. Muted tones and severe lines are apt to be too 'cold' for her taste. What might seem garish to the white-collar wife is 'warm' or 'cheerful' to the Wage Earner wife." Backing up his assertions with the published results of market analyses, he informed his readers that Italian Americans wanted "lots of goop" in their houses;

	CLOTHES		FURNITURE	USEFUL OBJECTS	ENTERTAINMENT	SALADS
HIGH-BROW	TOWN Fuzzy Harris tweed suit, no hat	COUNTRY Fuzzy Harris tweed suit, no hat	Eames chair, Kurt Versen lamp	Decanter and ash tray from chemical supply company	Ballet	Greens, olive oil, wine vinegar, ground salt, ground pepper, garlic, unwashed salad bowl
UPPER MIDDLE-BROW	TOWN Brooks suit, regimental tie, felt hat	COUNTRY Quiet tweed jacket, knitted tie	Empire chair, converted sculpture lamp	Silver cigaret box with wedding ushers' signatures	Theater	Same as high-brow but with tomatoes, avocado, Roquefort cheese added
LOWER MIDDLE-BROW	TOWN Splashy necktie, double-breasted suit	COUNTRY Sport shirt, colored slacks	Grand Rapids Chippendale chair, bridge lamp	His and Hers towels	Musical extravaganza films	Quartered iceberg lettuce and store dressing
LOW-BROW	TOWN Loafer jacket, woven shoes	COUNTRY Old Army clothes	Mail order overstuffed chair, fringed lamp	Balsam-stuffed pillow	Western movies	Coleslaw

	DRINKS	READING	SCULPTURE	RECORDS	GAMES	CAUSES
HIGH-BROW	A glass of "adequate little" red wine	"Little magazines," criticism of criticism, avant garde literature	Calder	Bach and before, Ives and after	Go	Art
UPPER MIDDLE-BROW	A very dry Martini with lemon peel	Solid nonfiction, the better novels, quality magazines	Maillol	Symphonies, concertos, operas	The Game	Planned parenthood
LOWER MIDDLE-BROW	Bourbon and ginger ale	Book club selections, mass circulation magazines	Front yard sculpture	Light opera, popular favorites	Bridge	P. T. A.
LOW-BROW	Beer	Pulps, comic books	Parlor sculpture	Jukebox	Craps	The Lodge

Polish Americans preferred houses that were "very garish, with loud, screaming colors"; "Jewish people . . . don't care about having a back yard," and they are "horrified at the thought of owning a place with large grounds" since "relatively few Jews ever earn their livelihood at manual work, and so are not handy at such things." He added that Jews "more than any other group" were "receptive to 'contemporary' architecture with its openness and modernity."[35]

As essentializing as Packard's study appears today, his findings are largely corroborated by more recent studies of class, ethnicity, and material culture. As Shelley Nickles has demonstrated, midcentury consumer research found that the upper-middle-class preferences held by designers and by the producers of design culture for the reduced forms and quiet hues of modernist simplicity stood in contrast to the tastes and preferences of working-class consumers, who preferred bulk, embellishment, shiny surfaces, and bright colors. These varied preferences, Nickles asserts, were widely held and understood, so that everyday purchases came to signify important indications of race and ethnicity.[36]

If the house could serve as the primary marker of distinction, then, and if many of the most affordable houses lacked distinctive design attributes, home buyers and homeowners had to make their choices carefully. The house itself had to be chosen wisely, and the objects purchased to fill it were of paramount significance. The architect A. Quincy Jones, whose career

was characterized by a true desire to bring revolutionary house form to the masses, understood this well. As Jones stated during a 1959 seminar sponsored by Arcadia Metal Products, "Whether you like to think of it this way or not, the house as executed today is a 'consumer product.'" He discussed the role of marketing analysts' surveys and market research in house design and construction in helping architects, like other manufacturers, discover what consumers most desired. Jones even used terms such as *consumer appeal* to refer to the attributes of various house types.[37] Perhaps his involvement with merchant builders such as Joseph Eichler helped Jones understand, better than most architects, that the ordinary house—and not just the high-style custom home—was a consumable object connected to desire as well as to the pragmatics of dwelling. The house had certainly been considered this way before. The writers of architectural pattern books had for centuries catered to a consumerist view that positioned the house as yet another catalog item. Postwar houses, like their antecedents, held an essential function within the framework of desire, one that increasingly served the requirements of specifically determined modes of racial and class distinction.

FURNISHING THE HOUSE

The house was clearly among the most important purchases to which postwar Americans aspired. But once the house was obtained, what items were to fill it? What were Americans buying? How were they using their purchasing power to fashion and to confirm their personal and family identities? Regular museum exhibitions and publications such as those sponsored by the Museum of Modern Art in New York and by the Walker Art Center in Minneapolis tried to sell "good design" to the masses. They attempted to create a mass market for high-style design and products, as did magazine articles such as "Good Design for 1949" and similar essays.[38] In reality, relatively few Americans purchased these high-style items—many were never made widely available and others were priced outside the means of the average family budget. In addition, they were frequently less comfortingly familiar than more mainstream items.[39] Moreover, the same magazines that published such essays filled their pages with advertisements for traditional home furnishings, realizing that many of their readers did not prefer the so-called modern design. Even Russel Wright, whose designs were less surprisingly modern stylistically and whose products were distributed nationally through department stores, struggled to keep his most innovatively styled product lines on the market.[40] Many new homeowners viewed aesthetic/stylistic modernism—that represented by Scandinavian furnishings of the postwar era or by furnishings designed by Isamu Noguchi, Charles and Ray Eames, or George Nelson, for example—as feminine, European, elitist, and Jewish, and therefore

as vaguely destabilizing. As a stylistic category for home furnishings, modernism was somewhat suspect, "outsider," and eccentric rather than populist and "normal." It could therefore be troubling for anyone concerned with establishing a distinctively American identity.[41]

What, then, were ordinary Americans actually purchasing? Certainly they bought cars and houses. But what items did they buy to fill their houses? As early as 1953, the editors of *Fortune* magazine proclaimed that it was the suburbanite whom economists should watch to understand fashion and purchasing trends, for it was the suburban dweller who started the fashions for "hard-tops, culottes, dungarees, vodka martinis, outdoor barbecues, functional furniture, picture windows, and costume jewelry."[42] The editors noted that the average suburban family's annual income was then $6,500, a sum that was 70 percent higher than that of the rest of the nation, and that, indeed, suburbia was "the cream of the market. . . . Anybody who wants to sell anything to Americans, from appliances to zithers, must look closely at Suburbia."[43] *Fortune*'s economic analysis indicated that American families were spending $15 billion annually to furnish and equip their homes: $3.5 billion for appliances, $2.2 billion for radio and TV, $4.4 billion for furniture and floor coverings, and $4.8 billion for other house furnishings.[44] In 1953, sales of room air-conditioning units and televisions were booming, as were those for electric broilers and deep-fat fryers; sales of dishwashers and deep freezes lagged somewhat.

In home furnishings, the contour chair was much in demand, with $50 million in sales that year, and, according to *Fortune,* for those Americans replacing their furniture, "comfortable Modern" was the preference—a label that was liberally and variously interpreted but that often simply meant "new."[45]

We can gain some understanding of the desires and purchasing patterns of Americans in the 1950s by examining the redemption records of trading stamp programs. Trading stamps were ubiquitous in postwar domestic life in the United States; the colorful gumbacked and perforated strips littered the countertops and utility drawers of households across the nation. The tremendous popularity of the stamp programs in the 1950s provides evidence of the pervasive desire to acquire beyond one's economic limits, since the stamps were marketed as means by which families could obtain goods that their budgets would not normally allow. Trading stamp histories provide us with one index, however incomplete, of consumerism and of the acquisitive impulses of postwar Americans.

To acquire trading stamps, consumers merely had to shop at participating retailers, which dispensed one stamp for every 10 cents in purchases. The consumers then pasted the stamps into saver books that could be redeemed later for merchandise at conveniently located redemption centers. According to a report by Sperry and Hutchinson, which operated the S&H Green Stamps program (the largest trading stamp program

A sheet of S&H Green Stamps.

in the United States, with sixty thousand retailers participating in 1956), two out of three American families saved trading stamps in the 1950s.[46] By 1956, seven hundred stamp programs existed in the continental United States, and they collectively issued five million dollars in stamps that same year.[47] The trading stamp companies targeted women as their primary audience, since women did the majority of household shopping; as one member of the 1956 Consumer Council to the

ONLY 1200 STAMPS
FILL THIS

S&H GREEN STAMPS

QUICK SAVER BOOK

THE SPERRY AND HUTCHINSON COMPANY

An S&H Green Stamps Quick Saver Book with a white family on the cover, circa 1950s.

national media generally pointed toward whites as the primary targets for the housing market. The widespread images of women shopping produced and reproduced a cultural field in which the normative expectation was that heterosexual women shopped for domestic goods (and the act of shopping configured them as white heterosexual women) just as white heterosexual families were portrayed as the expected occupants of postwar houses and their occupancy of those houses made them white and heterosexual. The act of shopping itself and the representations of shopping worked recursively to fix identities.

The trading stamp companies noted that American women wanted more than their husbands' incomes could purchase for them, and if they did not, the redemption catalogs helped to cultivate that desire by presenting a wide range of appealing merchandise—along with the appeal of enacting lives/identities like those of the women portrayed in the catalogs' glossy pages or in the trading stamp companies' supplements to Sunday newspapers.[50] The stamps, according to the companies that operated the programs, allowed women to save for luxury goods, gifts, and (usually) nonessential household items. Curtis Carlson, the owner of Gold Bond Trading Stamps, explained that "when a housewife brought home a shiny new toaster or a pretty new set of pillowcases, that gift was something that enhanced her home, impressed her neighbors, and told her family and friends that she was a smart and value-conscious

Governor for the State of New York noted, "We are speaking substantially of housewives when we speak of consumers."[48] The council's study found that 80–85 percent of housewives saved stamps, and the council argued that the stamp industry was raising the American standard of living by making goods available that families otherwise could not afford or save for.[49]

The trading stamp companies pointed toward the gendered nature of consumption (women as the purchasers of domestic goods) in the same ways that the

shopper."[51] Others noted that women particularly liked trading stamps because they were like "mad money which they can use for luxury purchases with no need to account to their husbands," and that "stamp saving helps most women to satisfy two conflicting yearnings simultaneously. It brings them the luxuries they desire while still letting them feel that they are thrifty budget managers," concluding finally that "this stamp practice is based upon an emotional, psychological appeal to women."[52] Trading stamps, then, gave many postwar-era women free access to consumer goods they might otherwise have found too costly or felt too guilty to purchase from their limited household accounts. The stamps provided a small degree of discretionary capital for women who had no earned income of their own, a kind of female currency for many postwar housewives. Still, savvy women realized that not all redemption values were a bargain, since the stamp values were often not much better than ordinary retail prices, and sometimes the cost of accumulating the stamps was higher than the retail value of the item.

Despite this fact, a 1966 survey showed that 54.1 percent of housewives had purchased a product illustrated in a stamp catalog, though not necessarily with redeemed trading stamps.[53] The catalogs, like the advertisements for products in the mass media, cultivated desire, both for the objects illustrated in them and for the act of purchasing those objects through stamp redemption. Women purchased a wide range of items

She's smart! She's thrifty! She saves…
America's most valuable stamps.

Good Housekeeping Guarantees Performance of America's Only Nationwide Stamp Plan

JOIN THE 27,000,000 SMART, THRIFTY WOMEN WHO EARN THE BEST VALUES WITH S&H GREEN STAMPS

An advertisement for S&H Green Stamps that features a white mother and children, circa 1950s.

MRS. DAVID V. DUNKLEE in the living room of her home in Denver which contains many lovely gifts obtained with S&H Green Stamps. With her are daughters Kathy, Obie Sue and Virginia. Mrs. Dunklee is Executive Secretary of The United Nations Committee of Colorado and a Board Member of Kent School. Mr. Dunklee is an attorney.

"I'm dollars ahead—thanks to S&H. Green Stamps" says MRS. DAVID V. DUNKLEE, Denver housewife

—AND OVER 27,000,000 SMART, THRIFTY WOMEN AGREE...

As Mrs. Dunklee says about her own experiences with S&H, "Whenever I shop at King Soopers and other fine stores that give S&H Green Stamps I know I'm dollars ahead. First, I'm dollars ahead because these stores give fine values. And I'm dollars ahead again when I redeem S&H Green Stamps for lovely gifts." S&H, you know, is America's oldest, most reliable stamp plan. It's the overwhelming favorite because women learned long ago that with S&H Green Stamps you get what you want when you want it. Your choice of over 1500 gifts made by the finest companies in America.

Good Housekeeping Guarantees Performance of America's Only Nationwide Stamp Plan

SINCE 1896 S&H GREEN STAMPS

You can be dollars ahead too! Shop where you get S&H. Green Stamps.

COPYRIGHT 1960—THE SPERRY AND HUTCHINSON CO.

from the catalogs, for themselves and for their families. The catalogs—often called "wish books"—typically displayed between one thousand and two thousand items.[54] A 1963 survey found that the items most frequently purchased with redeemed trading stamps were bed linens, tables and/or chairs, lamps, toys, clocks, blankets, and bedspreads. Following these were ovenware, towels, cameras and projectors, silverware, bathroom scales, irons, watches, luggage, heating pads, hair dryers, electric blankets, fryers, outdoor furniture, electric can openers, and waffle irons. Linens constituted 28 percent of all purchases; furniture and lamps, 10 percent; and electrical appliances, 20 percent.[55] Surprisingly, in an era in which the front lawn was a requisite element of suburban life, just 2 percent of stamp redemptions were for lawn supplies.[56]

The majority of the goods purchased with trading stamps were hardly luxury items by today's standards, but they were not strictly necessities either. They were largely items that made household life easier and/ or electrified, a point that stands in opposition to the stamp companies' statements about women's use of the stamps to obtain luxuries. That so many were electrical appliances is significant: they helped domestic life appear modernized, up-to-date, apace with the life lived by (or imagined to be lived by) the neighbors. They also

LEFT A white family in their living room surrounded by the purchases made with their trading stamps, circa 1950s. FACING This advertisement for S&H Green Stamps includes a background image of a redemption store showing the items available to consumers.

"Such wonderful gifts"
says MRS. NANCY M. KIRK

"S&H Green Stamp Redemption Stores like this have so many wonderful gifts of all kinds—over 1500 items to choose from! Of course, lots of them are ideal Christmas gifts. So I always put aside some of my S&H Green Stamps to use at Christmas time."

"At Christmas and all year through I'm Dollars Ahead with S&H Green Stamps"

MRS. KIRK is typical of more than 27,000,000 smart, thrifty women from coast to coast who save S&H Green Stamps. Like Mrs. Kirk, they not only get wonderful things all year long for their homes and families, but they also redeem some of their stamps for Christmas gifts as well. They're dollars ahead with S&H Green Stamps.

P.S. *Of course right now you're spending more with Christmas just ahead. So be thrifty like Mrs. Kirk. Do all your shopping at the many fine stores and service stations where you get the extra savings of S&H Green Stamps.*

COPYRIGHT 1959, THE SPERRY AND HUTCHINSON CO.

"I'm dollars ahead in two ways on my food bills," says Mrs. Kirk, "thanks to S&H Green Stamps. First, with low prices at supermarkets giving S&H. And dollars ahead again with S&H gifts."

"At Christmas I turn my extra spending into extra savings by shopping for gifts at department stores and other stores that give S&H Green Stamps. You should see how fast books fill up."

"It's just good sense—and good saving too—to buy everything where you get S&H Green Stamps. My service station, drugstore and dry cleaner are wonderful sources all year 'round."

GREEN STAMPS

SINCE 1896—AMERICA'S ONLY NATIONWIDE STAMP PLAN

gave labor the appearance of leisure that was so important to the attainment of white, middle-class identities.
One could certainly open cans with the time-tested
manual opener, but an electric can opener made the
job appear a bit upscale, the elegant and easy work of
a solidly middle-class white housewife rather than the
manual labor (no matter how slight) of a lower-class
cook or maid. Moreover, redemption catalogs offered
standard merchandise from major manufacturers such
as General Electric and Westinghouse, companies with
recognizable brand names that carried their own status
and in which Americans had faith and that represented
the safety and promise of the good life. They did not
offer products by designers such as George Nelson or
Charles and Ray Eames—the high-style products displayed in the museums as "good design" that would cultivate good living. Instead, they featured traditionally
designed objects and goods that were of known and recognized value and therefore were significant as markers
of status. As one author noted, the "catalogs merchan-
dised good living. According to the 1963 National Appliance Survey sponsored by *Look* magazine, the stamp
industry purchased some 29% of all electric clocks, 10%
of all automatic coffee makers, 13% of all toasters, and
8% of the steam irons shipped by American manufacturers. In addition, stamp houses feature lamps, has-
socks, silverware, and bedspreads. In full view and
frequent use around the home, the premiums remind

An advertisement for S&H Green Stamps features
Arlene Francis surrounded by goods that could be
obtained through redemption of the stamps.

and motivate the consumer to continue saving."[57] They also allowed a form of consumption that was simultaneously—even paradoxically—about the value of thrift, since saving and collecting were essential aspects of stamp redemption.

The trading stamp industry truly understood American desires and values, and it carefully marketed its products to appeal to middle-majority tastes and their associations. As Harold Fox wrote in 1968:

> The stamp company envisions an "average" home owner whose tastes are middle-of-the-road. Universality and versatility are the main criteria for selection from eligible merchandise. Buyers seek something functionally superior to what the "average" housewife might get for cash but they shun cost-boosting attachments. The listings must conform to a catalog's theme, such as "Modern Living" or "Traditional America." Some items in higher-priced lines or for specialized taste may be included if they do not disturb the sense of unity. . . . Buyers scan shelter magazines and trade journals, observe fashion trends and analyze manufacturers' opinions, visit trade shows and factories [to find items for the redemption catalogs].[58]

Trading stamp merchandise, then, did follow the trends established in a range of mainstream media outlets, and such merchandise was an important component of the culture of consumption that characterized the era. Redemption catalogs, like shelter and women's magazines, provided images of a correct and attainable lifestyle, a secure and palatable future and identity that could be purchased for a collection of stamps pasted in a book. And like the nineteenth-century mail-order catalogs that preceded them, the redemption books provided readers with something to which they could aspire, images of what constituted an acceptable American life and lifestyle, portraying role models and patterns for social and economic mobility.[59] But they also contributed to the large corpus of representations that configured American middle-class domesticity as white, heteronormative, and specifically gendered. They were about purchasing more than just objects for the home—they were equally about purchasing specific identities.

In addition to trading stamp redemption catalogs, ordinary magazines, even those not dedicated exclusively to the home and domestic life, promoted consumers' desires for a wide range of products. *Popular Mechanics* published a series that appeared regularly from 1945 onward titled "Inside Stuff for Your Home" and "What's New for Your Home." These one- or two-page features were typically illustrated with six to twelve items each, with captions that detailed the products' capabilities and design qualities. The products

included vacuum cleaners, dishwashers that doubled as clothes washers, lamps, irons, refrigerators, freezers, clotheslines, space-saving devices for hanging and storing, curtains, phonographs, electric fans, inflatable furniture, high-frequency cooking units, ashtrays, glowing switches, outlet covers, lawn mowers, sprinkling devices, and intercom systems. The dazzling array of consumer goods ranged from the quotidian to the kind of futuristic gadgetry that made the magazine so appealing, but even the most forward-looking products remained within the realm of the traditional in their outward appearance. Magazine features such as those in *Popular Mechanics* are another indication that middle-class postwar Americans were interested in products that promised an easier, more mechanized and convenient way of life, which in turn signaled a leisured life of middle-class whiteness, even if few of the items could be classified as luxuries.

Finally, with more leisure time than ever before, postwar Americans were buying hobby equipment, and it too required storage. According to *Fortune*'s 1953 analysis, the leisure market was one of the most lucrative in the American economy, bringing in that year $30.6 billion—half again as much as Americans spent on clothing or shelter and twice what they spent on new cars or household goods.[60] A *House and Home* article proclaimed in 1954: "Weekend carpenters spent over

A set depicting a typically cluttered garage in a postwar house. Without basements and attics and with limited closet space, many postwar houses easily became crowded with their owners' material possessions. *Life* magazine, September 15, 1958, 66. Photograph by Dmitri Kessel/ Time & Life Pictures/Getty Images.

$3 billion on home carpentry in 1953. Over 11 million have their own workshops. And that's only part of the story of the new leisure Americans are enjoying. With literally thousands more leisure hours per year than their grandparents had, and hundreds more than their parents, people are spending millions on hobby gear. . . . If hobbies are not putting a strain on the family budget, they are at least putting a strain on the space in which to do them."[61] Not only did family members need space to sew, paint (often by numbers), garden, and work on carpentry and craft projects, they also needed space to store the requisite equipment for those activities. As families filled their time, they also filled their living spaces with the accoutrements of leisure, straining the holding capacity of their small postwar houses, which seemed suddenly to be bursting at the seams.

As Americans made purchase after purchase for their homes they simultaneously made numerous careful decisions about the affordability and value of items, about the imagined necessity or usefulness of each, and perhaps about the novelty or delight each might confer. But they also calculated—whether consciously or not, and whether articulated or not—the degree to which those items solidified desired identities that were frequently considered in terms of race, class, and sexual orientation. And as the sociological studies detailed here reveal, Americans were highly attuned to the fine-grained distinctions conveyed by domestic objects and furnishings. If they were not initially so attuned, articles and images that appeared in the tastemaking literature and in the popular press helped them become so. As detailed in the next chapter, finding the appropriate means to store and display their new possessions would become yet another "consuming" concern.

6

BUILT-INS AND CLOSETS
Status, Storage, and Display

Although my grandparents did not maintain a kosher household, my grandmother kept an extra set of dishes and cookware for use when kosher-observant relatives came to visit. However, storage of these items posed a problem because her house was not designed for observant Jews and their arrays of kosher dishware. Like most houses, it was designed for a generic public presumed to be white and Christian. My grandmother did manage to find some space for her dishes in the small utility room that housed their washing machine and dryer, but still, the absence of more abundant storage space for extra sets of dishes likely reminded her that the house's builders did not imagine Jewish occupants. Because their house included no basement or attic, my grandparents found that storage demanded careful consideration. Always tidy, their closets were regularly pruned and organized to accommodate their belongings without disorder.

Aside from a few family heirlooms displayed in a glass cabinet, my grandparents had few luxuries save one major exception: my grandfather owned an impressive and regularly updated set of high-quality high-fidelity sound-system components and excellent speakers. The speakers sat in the living room, their spacing and location carefully calibrated for optimum sound quality. To house the components, he turned a hall closet (the kind normally used for coats in most houses) into a magnificent walk-in, hidden chamber for his hi-fi components and for his collection of reel-to-reel tapes, tape recorders, and vinyl records. One adult or two

FACING
View through the exterior window to the kitchen in developer Fritz Burns's Postwar House (*detail, see p. 202*).

small children could step inside the closet and observe the tuners, recorders, turntables, and related electronic paraphernalia, which had been carefully organized to produce an exceptional system. If one entered the closet and closed the door while the system was in use, one experienced a marvelous glow from the components in the darkened space as they hummed with the possibilities implied by an electronic present and future. Despite his sound system's beauty and impressive expense, my grandfather nearly always kept the door closed, the components concealed. Only the living room speaker system revealed the hidden presence of these high-tech devices of status and recreation; only family members and some guests were allowed into the closet. It was closely guarded (unaccompanied grandchildren were generally not admitted); it glowed in the dark; it excited the imagination. The Seder plate may have hung on the wall above the fireplace mantel, but the stereo closet seemed to me to have equal importance that was likewise nearly spiritual, and it said as much to me about my grandparents' identity as the plate ever did or could.

In 1958 and 1960, *Popular Mechanics* published features with similar titles: "A House Full of Built-Ins" (November 1958) and "*PM* House of Built-Ins" (October 1960). The 1960 article led the magazine's eighth annual home section and featured full-color illustrations and plans, while the 1958 article was more modestly produced, in-cluding only black-and-white illustrations and no house plan. Both, however, focused on a theme of critical importance in the postwar era: storage and its counterpart, display. By the time these articles appeared, with their elegant solutions for concealing specific material artifacts within the home, dozens, if not hundreds, of pages had already been devoted to this topic in publications from the preceding twelve to fifteen years. The *Popular Mechanics* articles offered design solutions, but the problem itself had also been the focus of discussion in other venues of popular media attending to domesticity. The number of these publications and the persistent repetition of the topic in the national popular and design press clarifies that, as this chapter demonstrates, specific modes of displaying domestic artifacts and the careful design and orchestration of storage for things that could not or should not be on display in the home became central to the construction of white, middle-class American identities in the postwar period.

Perhaps the most famous (or infamous) confirmation of postwar Americans' consumerist identity came in 1959, in Vice President Richard Nixon's remarks to Nikita Khrushchev, premier of the Soviet Union, during the exchanges that became known as the "kitchen debate." Nixon asserted the superiority of American domestic life by explicitly correlating material consumption with the creation of American domesticity: "There are 44 million families in the United States. . . . Thirty one million families own their own homes and the land on which they are built. America's 44 million families own a total of 56 million cars, 50 million television sets and 143 million radio sets. And they buy an average of nine dresses and suits and 14 pairs of shoes per family per year."[1] Although this quote appears frequently in postwar histories, especially in studies that focus on popular culture and/or the Cold War, few scholars have considered the impacts of all those goods on the form of the new, small houses many Americans had so recently purchased.[2] Where would all the new things go, especially in houses with very limited storage space, many of which had no basement or attic? Should they be displayed? If so, how? And where? Elite tastemakers and architectural writers expressed concerns for style, but the problems of storage and display had equally significant impacts on the design and configuration of ordinary postwar houses, and thus on the configuration of homeowner identity.

The articles in *Popular Mechanics* and the many similar publications from the period indicate that Nixon was right (at least at that particular historical moment and about the rate of consumer purchasing in the United States). Americans owned increasing amounts of "stuff," often more than their small houses could accommodate. Certainly the need for storage is a quotidian concern, but it manifested somewhat differently after 1945. As interior decorator Elizabeth Halsey wrote in 1954, "The well planned home has a place for everything, and everything covers a wide range of belongings."[3] The emphasis was on proper planning; Halsey and other design professionals and writers believed that efficient design could solve the problem. With the high rate of consuming that began to characterize the postwar era, storage—as it was described, evaluated, and promoted in the national press and as it was increasingly constructed and promoted in new homes targeted at middle-class consumers—became defined primarily as the need for the well-ordered accommodation of commodity excess. Storage also became characterized and built as a carefully calculated matter that balanced what had to be concealed with what best served the family through being revealed. Cabinetry assumed new significance, since a closed cabinet implies capacity and occupation by goods that are simultaneously well managed. (This, as we will see, is a key to understanding the "House of Built-Ins" referred to above and analyzed in more detail near the end of this chapter.) Moreover, storage became a factor in the determination of property values, and the FHA noted that "provision for storage is a most important element in determining the desirability of the property to prospective purchasers."[4] The lack of proper storage thus diminished the value of a house, and (as remains true of homeowners today) nothing captured the attention of postwar homeowners like questions related to changes in property values.

It may seem strange to study cabinetry and storage systems as a way to understand race and class, but as the preceding chapters have demonstrated, familiar domestic objects contributed in important ways to the fabrication and strengthening of particular notions of the self. In this chapter I examine the cultural work performed by the storage systems themselves and by the rhetoric about storage and display that appeared quite pervasively in shelter and popular magazines and in the design press nationwide. A house full of built-ins was novel to be sure, but more was built into the walls of postwar houses than hidden shelves, cabinets, desks, and beds. Equally important (perhaps more so for the purposes of this book) was the way in which such storage systems permitted notions of class, race, gender, and sexuality to be metaphorically built into the house as well, symbolically constructed through the many careful choices midcentury families made about storage and display. Questions about display extended as well to women, whose daily tasks and efforts within the house shifted along with the reduction in live-in or day-laboring household servants. As an abundance of household appliances became affordable, and as women of color became increasingly rare as workers in middle-class households, postwar housewives were themselves objects of display, their comportment and visibility newly questioned and configured to establish and reinforce notions of femininity, heteronormativity, and whiteness.

STATUS IN THE LIVING ROOM

As the discussion in chapter 5 demonstrated, it is not possible to gather precise information about the numerous things that postwar Americans owned, but it is clear that many owned more than their parents had. This growth in consumption gave rise to concerns about how to store and display all these new possessions. Authors such as Kate Ellen Rogers gave advice on how to purchase and display accessories in the home, including artwork (paintings and sculptures), picture frames, completed craft projects, planters, vases, fireplace equipment, screens and curtains, fabrics, "smoking equipment" (ashtrays and lighters), pillows, books, lamps, and clocks. Rogers advised her readers:

> Select accessories in the light of the best understanding that you have—accessories that *you* really like, not that someone else likes. Be ready to throw them away when they are outgrown—and be ready to grow! The matter of arrangement may also become a matter of storage. All the lovely things that one possesses do not have to be shown at the same time. Show a few and display them well; store the rest until changes are desired. Select and use those accessories that add to the charm and distinction of the home, not those which detract from it.[5]

Likewise, in the November 1945 issue of *Arts and Architecture* magazine, the architect S. Robert Anshen wrote, "We live in an age of potential plenty, wherein we need not display our wealth to reassure ourselves against scarcity."[6] Anshen, like many other architects and critics, worried that Americans would descend into a state of decadence in the burgeoning consumer world that economists were then forecasting, and his statement revealed a widespread concern for the ostentatious tendencies that could accompany the increasingly robust purchasing power available to the growing middle majority. Rogers and Anshen instructed readers to cultivate taste that was distinguished by its selectivity, recommending spare, carefully selected furnishings and decor because a refined and relatively minimal selection of displayed objects indicated higher social and economic status. Their recommendations simultaneously pointed to the importance of adequate storage to facilitate the rotating exhibit that they and others advocated for the achievement of a properly evolving domestic life and for family distinction.

Rogers also made specific recommendations about the display of books and magazines, which, she wrote, formed "accent areas" in a room: "It is well to plan the placement of current magazines not only for the convenience of the family but also for their bright color. The coffee table or side table is the usual place for magazines,

A photograph from Kate Ellen Rogers's *The Modern House, U.S.A.: Its Design and Decoration* demonstrates the tasteful display of household objects for middle-class occupants circa 1962. Design by Edward J Wormley. Courtesy of Dunbar Furniture, LLC.

but recently some home owners have begun using modified magazine wall racks similar to those found in drug stores."[7] As noted in chapter 1, the shelter and women's magazines were important not only for their content and for the instruction they provided their readers in taste, but also, as Rogers clarified, for their mere appearance in the house, since they conveyed a degree of cultural capital on their owners and signaled a higher level of personal and family status. The postwar coffee table, with its books and magazines, became a locus of information regarding the homeowner's knowledge and, by extension, status.

Tastemakers and magazine writers did not necessarily see an extensive book collection as an attribute in the average home, but the coffee table allowed the requisite display of books or magazines without overemphasizing the intellectual (or "eggheaded," to use Vance Packard's term) aspects of the owners. An entire publishing genre flourished in response to this requirement: the coffee-table book, focused on a suitably cultured subject but emphasizing lavish illustrations and heft over intellectual substance. The coffee-table display had certainly existed for centuries; estate owners had long displayed rare and expensive books on tables in their salons and drawing rooms. But in the postwar period, masses of Americans had their own living rooms with coffee tables for the first time, and the elite tradition was transformed to suit the requirements of a new era and its spaces.

Even the design literature that was directed entirely toward ordinary middle-majority homeowners, if written by architects, contained tastemaking messages that likewise held relevance for the construction of class identities. The Small Homes Council of the University of Illinois published a circular in both 1946 and 1950 that focused on interior decoration and essentially served as a manual for the attainment of middle-class taste. The circular promoted interior decoration that would "satisfy the broader standards of good design," and though it did not explicitly define good design, it prescribed a moderate version of the precepts that were simultaneously established in the design literature of the period.[8] The circular provided readers with guidance about furnishings, scale, form, color, and the arrangement of furnishings and objects. It revealed an underlying modernist sensibility that favored the clean-lined aesthetic then popular in design schools nationwide, but it offered advice couched in a practicality intended to appeal to the circular's middle-class and midwestern audience, advocating simple forms for easier housekeeping and maintenance and for ease of arrangement. Without relying on references to architectural theory, the circular advocated a "less is more" style for home interiors, claiming that "some bare spots in your home are desirable. A room with too little furniture is better than a room which is cluttered. Simplicity enhances beauty. . . . Don't mistake 'fancy' elaboration or the sentimental for beauty in furniture, pictures, and accessories. . . . Don't buy several cheap statues or vases. Buy one good piece instead."[9] The circular also instructed readers that if they used traditional furniture, they should include only "authentic reproduction[s] or antiques" and that combining modern and traditional furnishings "helps create that lived-in atmosphere."[10]

The Small Homes Council recognized that few readers of its circulars could afford complete sets of new furniture, but it was important that readers be properly informed so that their home interiors would not appear tacky and, therefore, lower-class. This circular's reference to the creation of a "lived-in atmosphere" signaled to readers the necessity of appearing solidly middle-class, an appearance that they could achieve by creating an established look, as opposed to the contrived-looking and perhaps stiffly arranged decor (think plastic coverings on chairs, sofas, and lamp shades) of a family less comfortably familiar with their middle-class status. Similarly, "informality" and "informal lifestyles," both notions widely cultivated in the design press, indicated an ease of living that was associated not with the crass informality known to the poor, to members of the working class, immigrants, or racial minorities, but rather with the new leisure of the white middle majority or even of the upper classes.[11] And by recommending that readers "eliminate bric-a-brac" and "strive for spaciousness," the circular helped new homeowners learn an aesthetic code that was partly about modernism but was equally an aid to the attainment of class and racial

BEFORE

AFTER

A lesson on tasteful interior decorating provided by the University of Illinois Small Homes Council urged readers toward a "less is more" aesthetic. J. R. Shipley, *Interior Design*, Small Homes Council Circular Series Index Number H1.0, *University of Illinois Bulletin* 47, no. 72 (June 1950): 7, University of Illinois Archives.

identity, since clutter was associated with lower-class, ethnic identities.[12]

Problems of taste and decorating were magnified by the influx of new materials for home decorating. The introduction on the mass market of wall-to-wall carpeting, new linoleum products, and a range of window treatments resulted in so many choices that first-time homeowners could become overwhelmed. Concerns regarding everyday choices that may seem of little consequence today became the focus of entire publications. Numerous books such as Walter Murray's *Interior Decoration for Today and Tomorrow* aimed to help Americans cultivate good, middle-class, white taste in their decorating choices. Murray's book, for example, offered sections titled "Guidepost for Successful Rug or Carpet Buying," "Linoleum Is Smart," and "Why Draperies Should Be Lined."[13]

Surfaces such as countertops, appliance casings, floor coverings, wall treatments, and furniture finishes assume particular importance as tools for domestic differentiation when the forms or spaces of the house itself remain conservative or conventional, as they so often did in ordinary postwar houses. Newer, smoother, cleaner (or easier to clean), and brighter surfaces became important, not just for the imagined hygienic benefits they offered but also because they were part of an aesthetic emphasis on surface appearances, on the way things look, and on the "skin" of all things as a determining factor in status and in identification. The white-wall aesthetic of high architectural modernism seldom appeared in ordinary postwar houses, where brightly colored products and interiors conveyed a specific kind of middle-class modernity. Andrew Hurley has called the liberal application of bright coloring to postwar products "a direct appeal to working-class sensibilities," since brighter colors were associated with upwardly mobile blue-collar families who were seeking to "distance themselves from the bleak and grimy inner-city tenements they came from by surrounding themselves with brightly decorated products that exuded attributes of cleanliness and modernity."[14] But the authors of the period's tastemaking literature devoted significant attention to the selection of the correct color, a task that varied according to frequent fluctuations in fashion.

Paying attention to and decorating in accordance with trends in color fashion likewise held symbolic importance. Between 1948 and 1968, *House & Garden* published a series of annual "Color Reports" that were intended to help readers make correct and stylish home decorating choices. Based on nationwide preference surveys, the results of which were then coordinated with information from four hundred manufacturers, the "Color Reports" were, as William Braham has noted, about being able to discern "exceptionally fine distinctions between different tints, tones, and shades."[15] If readers could recognize the difference between, say, "tortoise-shell hues" and "driftwood" or "sandalwood," they obviously had attained a degree of distinction reserved for the educated, those with the necessary degree of cultural capital to be solidly middle-class.

Furthermore, color choices helped convey individuality, which was connected to notions of American identity and to overcoming the homogeneity associated with nonwhite culture. In 1957, the "Color Report" stated, "We are determined to emanate an aura of gaiety" with respect to color choices, and the report's authors reminded readers that telephones were being produced in "colors to suit your mood (who would choose white?)"[16] Choosing a color to suit one's mood meant that although the item itself might be just like the neighbor's, the color was distinctive, revealing aspects of the owner's refinement, personality, and identity.

Floor coverings, which were also included in the "Color Reports," could be particularly troubling to new homeowners whose previous, apartment-dwelling experiences excluded such choices. But the careful selection of floor coverings also mattered because the "new informality" increasingly made the floor an acceptable site for sitting. To be sure, family members had sat on the floors in their houses in various eras and for various activities, but middle-class family members—particularly women, whose skirts, dresses, and undergarments were not well suited to it—would have avoided floor sitting in earlier decades, when it would have signaled a lack of decorum if not poverty.[17] But postwar manuals and books that instructed housewives on entertaining began to describe and illustrate the lighthearted and

casual fun to be had when the floor was used for party games and even for informal dining—Russel Wright instructed, for example, that "the picnic is the prototype for all informal entertaining," and he staged indoor picnics on living room floors in photographs that featured his designs for linens and tableware.[18] In these cases, the floor's surface mattered differently than it had in the past, its material more available for inspection and evaluation by friends and neighbors.

Like so many of the shelter and popular articles and books published nationwide, the "Color Reports" offered lessons in sophistication to a generation of readers who, like their parents, may never before have experienced home decoration projects that included painting walls and choosing floor coverings, since they were often new to homeownership. Whether correct or not, publishers and authors imagined a readership eager to discern whether their choices were considered garish or elegant, cheerful or naive, sophisticated or tawdry, fashionable or *retardataire*.

The bright colors of postwar interior surfaces and products also resulted from a desire to convey novelty, since color changes can readily signify changes in fashion and the updated model of any product, even if its form or design has not been altered. To possess the newest-color telephone, refrigerator, carpet, or dishware was to possess a recognizable emblem of distinction and to claim the authority of fashion and the capital conveyed by knowledge of its most recent trends.[19]

STATUS, STORAGE, AND DISPLAY IN THE KITCHEN

The kitchen underwent more design change in the postwar era than perhaps any other room in the house.[20] For the women who spent the largest amount of time occupying those houses, kitchens were the primary centers of work. A significant number of the new gadgets and appliances developed after the war were intended to support or to enhance women's work in the kitchen. The new kitchen appliances were especially important because, as their advertisements so often declared, they were intended to help liberate women from household drudgery—a form of work that had formerly been associated almost exclusively with hired, immigrant, nonwhite servants or with lower-class women. As the numerous scholars who have examined women's work in the domestic sphere have shown, the appliances did not free women from work, but the machines did make the labor appear to be white and white-collar through the status conveyed by ownership of the equipment itself, which was generally costly.[21] As Karen Brodkin has noted, "To be white is to direct but not perform the dirty work of cleaning, which marks its doers as racially inferior women."[22] Brodkin asserts further that "the performance of work that was at once important to the economy of the nation and that was defined as menial and unskilled, was key to their [Jews, other non-

Protestants, southern and eastern Europeans, blacks, and so on] nonwhite racial assignment." That "southern European immigrants did dirty jobs" was seen as "proof enough that they too were dirty."[23] To be white was to avoid the appearance of doing dirty, menial, unskilled work. If women owned specialized appliances to help them with housework, they also appeared to become part of a more skilled group, one whose husbands could afford to purchase such goods. In the white, middle-majority house, the servants became electrical, not lower-class or dark-skinned people; in 1946, Mary and George Catlin, like many others of their time, referred to electrical appliances as "electrical servants."[24] Modern appliances were intended as much to remove the stigma from the performance of housework as to reduce the actual work itself, which may be one reason that women were always pictured performing housework with appliances while impeccably dressed, coiffed, and bejeweled.[25] Such representations clarified that these housewives were far from hired servants, since they were dressed instead as the proverbial, nonworking "ladies who lunch," or who might even be imagined as working professionals.

The science of housework had been the subject of domestic and architectural literature for centuries. Catharine Beecher and Harriet Beecher Stowe's nineteenth-century directives on kitchen design constitute just one well-known example of recommendations for

FACING
A professionally attired housewife in her postwar kitchen exemplified the standardized representation of white women as working professionals.
Photograph by Maynard L. Parker. Courtesy of the Huntington Library, San Marino, California.

Mary and Russel Wright instructed women to sit down to work whenever possible.
From Mary and Russel Wright's *Guide to Easier Living*. Reproduced with permission of Gibbs Smith, publisher.

labor-saving kitchen layouts intended to conserve the energy of domestic workers, whether hired or not.[26] In the postwar era, however, prescriptions for streamlining housework were intended to elevate the tasks performed by housewives to an acceptably middle-class and white-collar status. Mary and Russel Wright's *Guide to Easier Living*, with its instructions on the correct and labor-saving methods for making beds and for entertaining, offered recipes for effortless domesticity that would make housework and any other women's work into a middle- or upper-middle-class phenomenon rather than lower-class drudgery.[27] The Wrights' numerous diagrams for household efficiency include illustrations of the correct postures (standing upright or seated, never bent or on hands and knees) women should assume when performing housework. With his spun-aluminum products and mass-produced furnishings, Russel Wright domesticated industrial materials in his designs just as postwar homeowners domesticated their own industrial and ethnic working pasts.

The kitchen, then, not only became a miniature warehouse to store and exhibit new appliances, but it also had to be designed differently to accommodate a worker who was to be seen always as a family member rather than as a hired hand. Kate Ellen Rogers noted that the disappearance of the career servant—whose privacy had to be respected while she worked and whose presence therefore dictated the enclosed kitchen, so that the family could likewise have privacy from the servant—necessitated an opening of the kitchen to integrate it more fully into the house. Rogers observed:

> In place of the old-fashioned servant we now have the occasional worker, whose specialty may be gardening, laundering, cleaning, or catering. These workers may come in during the day or for several days a week or on special occasions only. Their services are available to the homemaker when she needs them, and she is absolved of the paternalistic responsibility usually associated with the old-fashioned servant. . . . It is quite evident, as we look over the kitchen designed by experts—architects and home economists—that the kitchen in today's house is planned for a member of the family, not for a servant.[28]

The kitchen thus became a laboratory, a workshop, and an office, a site designed for a woman who might once have been a wage earner herself and for whom the kitchen's design became symbolic of her worth within the family's daily operations.[29]

To that end, the housewife was also to be integrated spatially into the home, so that she did not appear to be a hired hand and so that she could carry out her supervisory role when she did employ help. The opening of the kitchen to the living areas of the house through the elimination of partition walls or through the construc-tion of pass-throughs served as part of the visual and spatial lexicon that marked the worker as mother and wife rather than as servant. It also allowed the display of her newly acquired appliances and gadgetry to any visitors who might move through the living spaces of the house, indicating her status as a middle-class, white family member. For example, houses built in Levittown, Pennsylvania, between 1951 and 1958 included bamboo screens that slid on ceiling tracks to hide or reveal the kitchen from the living room, depending on the daily preference of the housewife.[30] By 1960, *Sunset* featured the kitchen of landscape architects Doug and Maggie Baylis as exemplary because it was open to the dining area, "so that Mrs. Baylis of San Francisco can participate in business lunch discussions."[31] Doug and Maggie Baylis were partners in their own firm, but the article underscored the notion that the wife and mother, working in the kitchen, was a white-collar worker to be included in the daily operations of the household. The open plan in ordinary houses, then, was an aesthetic choice but also a practical one based on the sociology of postwar domestic life.[32]

Perhaps the clearest formal indication of the changed status of postwar housework was the gradual introduction into the kitchen of a desk or other work space devoted to paperwork—essentially the emergence of the housewife's home office. As the editors of *Fortune* magazine proclaimed, "The sturdy drudge of woman's magazine fame, eternally beleaguered on the cleaning, washing, ironing, cooking, and shopping fronts, is giving way to the competent household executive (also of woman's magazine fame) in charge of a considerable capital investment."[33] Just as husbands were moving away from their parents' blue-collar past into a white-collar world of would-be and actual executives, so too the hopeful executive's wife had to appear as though

from the same economic class and social standing. A desk in the kitchen conveyed the proper atmosphere of executive, white-collar authority while simultaneously providing a designated work space for the tidy and well-managed storage of recipes, bills, receipts, "to do" lists, shopping lists, menu plans, and, of course, trading stamps. In a 1945 Small Homes Council circular titled

A kitchen with a bamboo screen that slides along a track in the ceiling. In this photograph, the screen is pushed open and can be seen on the far left. Levittown, Pennsylvania, 1952. Courtesy of Bucks County Free Library, Levittown Branch.

Planning the Kitchen, the authors recommended the implementation, whenever possible, of a fourth work center in the kitchen, which they called the "planning center" (the other three standard work centers were devoted to cleaning, preparation, and cooking). They wrote: "It would be useful, if possible, to set aside space for a small desk with drawers for recipe files and books, grocery accounts and records relating to kitchen management. A telephone and radio are desirable additions to this planning center." Readers were advised that the planning table or desk, if on wheels, could also be used "to facilitate such tasks as mixing, preparing vegetables at the sink, sorting groceries near the service door, or serving beverages and snacks." If such a space could not be allocated for this purpose, the kitchen table could be used for planning, but, the authors cautioned, "some definite provision . . . should be made for a space to plan housekeeping activities. The homemaker will find that meals can then be planned more easily and efficiently."[34] The desk was a command center, but it was also a place where the numerous papers associated with household management could be effectively organized and stored to avoid clutter.

The kitchen desk did not commonly appear in ordinary suburban homes until the 1970s, but the roots of this element, now widely seen in newly constructed houses, lie in the 1950s notion of the housewife as

A kitchen desk is featured in this plan from Paul R. Williams's *The Small Home of Tomorrow* (Hollywood, Calif.: Murray & Gee, 1945). The desk appears both in plan and in perspective on the right.

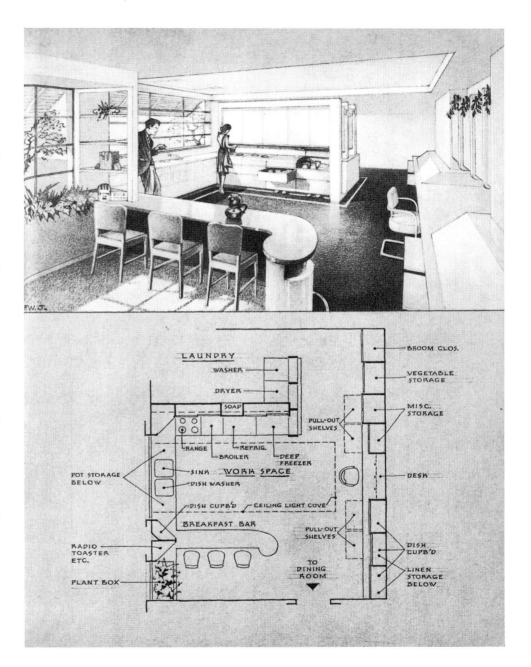

white-collar worker. With her own desk and paperwork in the kitchen, the housewife could have the complete appearance of a domestic white-collar professional, clearly distinguished from lower-class, immigrant workers who might be hired to perform menial labor. The postwar housewife's job required a small office in the center of her working domain, the kitchen. Although many women perceived the entire house to be their special domain because they occupied its various spaces throughout the day as they performed everyday tasks, they also seldom had a space to call their own. Men laid claim to and controlled dens, garages, and hobby spaces; living rooms and adult bedrooms were shared; children's territories included their bedrooms, playrooms if they existed, and yards. Women controlled the kitchen, though they also shared it with the entire family. The desk, then, provided a small zone within the kitchen that women could claim for themselves and that they could point to as evidence of their own managerial status. It was also a place where their bodies could be displayed to family members and visitors in ways that contributed to the class and racial categories the family desired and to which they aspired.

In his 1946 Los Angeles model home known simply as the "Postwar House," developer Fritz Burns took care to include all of these kitchen attributes. In addi-

A kitchen desk in Fritz Burns's Postwar House included a telephone as well as controls for an intercom system, an outdoor sprinkler system, and an automatic garage door. Wurdeman-Becket, architects, Los Angeles, California, 1946. Photograph by Maynard L. Parker. Courtesy of the Huntington Library, San Marino, California.

tion to the house's up-to-the-minute appliances (four-burner range, garbage disposal, automatic dishwasher, a counter-height console refrigerator, freezer cabinet, built-in pressure cooker, and electric mixer), the kitchen included everything a housewife might need in order to commandeer the efficient management of the household and to keep it, like the bathroom, spotlessly clean and organized. As *House Beautiful* proclaimed of Burns's kitchen (designed by architect Weldon Becket): "It's a laundry. It's a sewing room. It's an office. . . . You can eat in it. It freezes food. It's air and sound-conditioned. It has sterilized storage space. It has a radio and its own communication system with the rest of the house."[35] The kitchen's generous amount of cabinetry could be closed with vertical sliding doors that concealed all the contents, lending the room the appearance of a clean and highly efficient laboratory. The vertical sliding doors eliminated the problem of heads bumping on open cabinet doors, but they also may have held particular appeal for middle-class women because they minimized the appearance of work by literally hiding the working machines and the artifacts with which they reproduced daily life for the family. Working-class women took pride in displaying their new appliances, whereas middle-class women preferred to conceal them. Burns's architects struck a careful balance between the two

A kitchen pantry with a view toward a kitchen desk. Architect unknown, circa 1950s. Photograph by Maynard L. Parker. Courtesy of the Huntington Library, San Marino, California.

This view through the exterior window to the kitchen in developer Fritz Burns's Postwar House shows the sliding cabinets that concealed and stored kitchen goods and appliances. Wurdeman-Becket, architects, Los Angeles, California, 1946. Photograph by Maynard L. Parker. Courtesy of the Huntington Library, San Marino, California.

aesthetic drives.[36] A sewing machine could be neatly folded away out of sight under the snack table, and most of the laundry equipment (which included an automatic washer, dryer, mangle, and ironing board) could be hidden also.

Here, too, the kitchen included a housewife's desk (or planning desk), "the nerve center of the house," which contained controls for the outdoor sprinkler system, the intercom system, and the automatic garage door. As a *House Beautiful* writer noted: "A good desk is an inducement to efficient household management. A good housewife, like a good executive, needs a good office, and the kitchen is the logical place for it. Here a whole office is wrapped up in one planning desk," which also included space for filing recipes and household bills and for displaying recently canned goods and cookbooks.[37] The desk served as the ultimate symbol of the professional managerial class, here feminized through its placement in the kitchen, the housewife's domain. In the kitchen desk, white-collar labor performed by men outside the home had its women's equivalent inside the home. With a command center installed in the desk that included controls for the sprinkler system, intercom, and garage door, the housewife managed her domain using the most up-to-date technologies available.

The kitchen desk, along with the new appliances and storage, contributed to the appearance that women's housework was professional labor and that it was distinctly white labor. As Annmarie Adams has demonstrated for the kitchens in Eichler development houses, postwar kitchens manifested characteristics

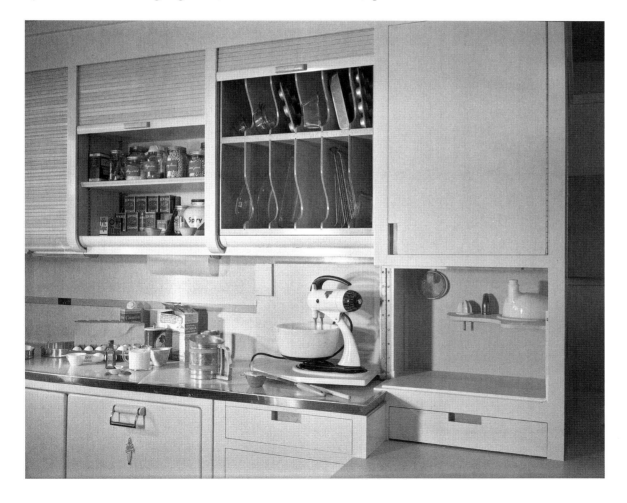

A carefully measured display of goods and appliances in the Postwar House, 1946. Wurdeman-Becket, architects, Los Angeles, California, 1946.
Photograph by Maynard L. Parker.
Courtesy of the Huntington Library, San Marino, California.

that derived from turn-of-the-century ideas about the "progressive house," a concept that was linked to the professionalization of women's labor and the elevation of the status of housewives. If Eichler kitchens did not aim, as Adams notes, to "revalue household labor, but simply to make it more pleasant and less disruptive to the other duties of domestic life," Eichler kitchens and the many commodities that filled them were, like many postwar kitchens and their contents, nonetheless designed to impart a sense that the women laboring within comported themselves and were regarded as middle- to upper-class white women.[38] They were not to be mistaken for immigrant, nonwhite, blue-collar servants. The clean, shiny, bright, well-organized, and electrified kitchen was among the most potent symbols in the house for confirming the identities of all family members, but particularly those of women.

Along with a desk for household management, a 1954 *House Beautiful* article featured a "sit-down sink"— essentially a desk designed for peeling vegetables and washing dishes, complete with a "posture-correct chair" —designed by architect Alfred Parker.[39] The illustration for the article featured a well-dressed woman who could as easily have been a secretary at work in a white-collar, corporate office. Pictured thus—displayed thus—the housewife was clearly figured as an important worker whose ergonomic needs were worthy of consideration. White women were not to be seen stooping, bending, or sweating while at work in the home,

and the sit-down sink or vegetable desk confirmed this status-conforming image.

In the postwar era, kitchens in upper-middle-class and architect-designed homes became more radically altered in size, configuration, and equipment than did those in the new ordinary small houses of 1,000 to 1,500 square feet. In the typical small house the kitchen often remained a small room, albeit one with greater demands for storage and use than ever before. The Small Homes Council circular from 1945 titled *Planning the Kitchen* essentially provided an instruction manual for readers with these small kitchen spaces on how to attain a middle-class, white kitchen. A good plan, the authors stated, should "include space for informal dining in the kitchen . . . a utility room planned together with the kitchen area to contain laundry facilities, a sewing machine, a work shop, a home freezer, a heating plant, etc."[40] Because the house was without a basement, the large pieces of equipment that provided the basic utilities for the house had to be accommodated near or in the kitchen as well. With laundry equipment located in a kitchen alcove, "the worker" could more easily multitask, so that "the woman's strength is conserved with no steps to climb."[41] Referring to the housewife as the "modern day Priscilla [who can] wash, cook, bake, and rock the cradle simultaneously," Walter Murray, along with other tastemaking and home economics authors, turned her into an efficient "worker," a superwoman whose life was made complete by modernity's

FACING
Concealed appliances and built-in storage lined the walls of the kitchen in developer Fritz Burns's Postwar House. Wurdeman-Becket, architects, Los Angeles, California, 1946. Photograph by Maynard L. Parker. Courtesy of the Huntington Library, San Marino, California.

The new ELKAY *Pace-Setter* Sit-Down Sink

Drawing shows ease with which sink work may be done while sitting down. The shallow bowl allows knees to slide under—provides handy depth for vegetable preparation plus many other tasks. The *Sit-Down Sink* evolved from years of research by America's leading college Home Economic Departments. This ELKAY design is the scientific way to end sink fatigue—relieve back strain.

HOUSE BEAUTIFUL magazine features this *Sit-Down Sink* in the fabulous 1954 Pace-Setter house designed by architect Alfred Parker. Shown below is the standard two-bowl version of this sensational sink.

The first really new kitchen sink development since stainless steel

"Why didn't they think of this before?" Once in a great while something new . . . *really new* . . . is introduced in the home equipment field. Like the automatic dishwasher or automatic laundry, it completely revolutionizes the routine of American housewives—makes her life easier, more enjoyable. Now it's the revolutionary SIT-DOWN SINK by ELKAY! Made of stainless steel, *of course* . . . this peninsula model has *three* sink bowls, the customary ones for washing dishes, and a shallow one for easy, *sit-down* preparation of salads, vegetables and the like. You can also enjoy the same *sit-down* convenience with a conventional cabinet type sink. Comes in standard sizes to replace your present "stand up" sink and made with one shallow bowl with plenty of knee room below. Ask your Kitchen Cabinet Dealer or local Plumbing Contractor for more information. If your dealer doesn't yet have this sensational sink, write for full details.

ELKAY LUSTERTONE—THE FIRST AND THE FINEST!
The Pace-Setter SIT-DOWN SINK is another example of ELKAY leadership in sink design and manufacture. Whether you wish a standard sink (conventional or *sit-down* style), or a custom-built sink and counter top to fit your individual plans —choose ELKAY as a long-term investment in loveliness, practicality and permanence. Proud owners love Lustertone for its *carefree cleanliness*, and its *breathtaking beauty* that blends with any color scheme. A *Lustertone* sink never wears out, never needs replacing because it's made of solid stainless steel. It can't rust or chip, never needs scouring or bleaching—it is truly America's finest kitchen sink.
THE ONLY SINK GUARANTEED TO OUTLAST YOUR HOME!

ELKAY MANUFACTURING COMPANY
1876 SOUTH 54TH AVENUE, CHICAGO 50 • *The World's Oldest Manufacturer of Stainless Steel Sinks . . . since 1920*

---

accoutrements, which were all neatly and efficiently put to use and then stored.[42] By referring to women as "modern day Priscillas" and thereby aligning them with the New Testament figure of Priscilla, Murray also emphasized the importance of women who worked at home as emphatically Christian figures who were also unquestionably married, since Priscilla's name appears in the Christian Bible in tandem with that of her mate, Aquila.

In order to keep the kitchen clean and tidy, the homemaker had to keep the goods and their by-products within it—including equipment, noises, and smells—well contained. Proper storage and clean, sanitary surfaces in the kitchen were crucial for the maintenance of family status and white identity, and these were achieved through practices and design considerations that facilitated sterile, tidy, and well-organized environments. An ordinary postwar kitchen contained numerous items that required storage—many more than kitchens in the past—yet storage space in ordinary houses (unlike in the model produced by Fritz Burns) seemed always to be lacking, as evidenced by the numerous detailed storage studies from the period that responded to homeowner dissatisfaction. For example, a 1949 Small Homes Council circular that focused on factory-built kitchen cabinets presented two useful lists that enable us to get a rough sense of the numbers of

House Beautiful promoted architect Alfred Parker's design for a "sit-down sink" intended to keep the housewife off her feet and in a chair that was "posture-correct." Elkay advertisement from *House Beautiful*, March 1954.

items requiring storage in a small home's kitchen in the immediate postwar era. The first, a limited list, contained 100 items of packaged food; 6 fresh, nonrefrigerator items; 84 utensils; and 9 types of cleaning supplies. The second, a liberal list, contained 156 packaged food items; 9 fresh, nonrefrigerator items; 114 utensils; and 12 types of cleaning supplies. The only appliance the circular's author located on the counter was an electric mixer, although the small amount of cabinet space in most kitchens dictated a cluttered appearance for most counter surfaces. All other small appliances in the study, including the electric toaster, waffle iron, and coffeemaker, were to be stored away.[43] It was probably desirable, however, to display some appliances, both because of their status as novelties and as costly and therefore status-conferring items and because cabinet storage space was limited.

Despite the author's efforts, this early study completely underestimated the copious numbers of appliances that would become available and homeowners' desires to keep them handy and displayed on countertops. By 1963, when the Small Homes Council conducted another study on household storage, it found that the Federal Housing Administration's minimum property standard for kitchen storage of "50 square feet of shelf space, with at least 20 square feet in wall and cabinets and at least 20 square feet in base cabinets" was

Items requiring storage in a typical kitchen in 1949. Helen E. McCullough, *Cabinet Space for the Kitchen,* Small Homes Council Circular Series Index Number C5.31, *University of Illinois Bulletin* 46, no. 43 (February 1949): 3, University of Illinois Archives.

Liberal Supplies = Limited Supplies   +   These Items

The lists include packaged, canned and bottled foods, and also some fresh foods for which refrigeration is not necessary, such as bread, cake, potatoes, bananas. They do not include baby foods, pet foods, readily perishable foods ordinarily stored in the refrigerator, or more than a week's supply of canned foods.

Liberal Supplies = Limited Supplies   +   These Items

The utensil lists include small items such as cutlery, as well as pots and pans. They do not include specialized equipment, such as that used only for the preparation of baby food or for canning.

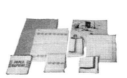

Basic List of Linens

One basic list was used for linens (including paper supplies) since the number of identical items can be varied within the same drawer by stacking them higher.

Cleansers

Only cleaning supplies stored at the sink are included.

Dinnerware for 6 Persons   Dinnerware for 12 Persons

Dinnerware includes all items needed (glassware, silverware as well as china) to serve 4, 6, 8 or 12 persons.

insufficient because the use of packaged foods and purchases of newly available small appliances had increased significantly. The council likewise found that standards for countertop areas were deficient and recommended that countertop space minimums be increased from 11 to 15 square feet; depending on the arrangement, the council recommended as much as 20 square feet of countertop space for ordinary kitchens.[44] Because of the need to maximize kitchen storage space, cabinet shelves were often above the reach of the average housewife. One kitchen designer suggested overcoming this problem by implementing pull-out drawers below the countertop that could be used as steps to make high shelves accessible.[45] In the fourteen years between the two Small Homes Council reports on kitchen storage, the need for counter space nearly doubled as a result of changing patterns of consumption and behavior. The postwar period was thus by necessity a time of clever innovation for kitchen storage design in response to the changing patterns of American material consumption.

Even the designs of some appliances changed to conform to new ideas about the work performed in kitchens and in response to new storage requirements. Although refrigerator/freezer and range/oven combinations were common, some designers advocated sepa-

The cover of a Small Homes Council circular dedicated to household storage units. The photograph inserted over the drawing on the cover shows the reality of jumbled household goods for many postwar homeowners, while the drawing illustrates a rarely attained ideal.

rating these appliances into their constituent parts for ease of labor. Separate ovens that were not part of range units began to appear in the mid-1950s. They could be installed in walls at a height more convenient for home-makers, so that women would not have to bend over to move food in and out, thus preserving the upright pos-ture considered appropriate to the white-collar house-wife. This arrangement, it was also argued, allowed more cabinet storage under the range top and easier cleaning for the range if the burners could be built di-rectly into the counter.[46] Again, the appeal of a cleaner kitchen helped sell new appliances, but equally, the im-age of a housewife cooking on what appeared to be a simple countertop had an appealing look of futuristic modernity and of executive efficiency. In a number of his experimental houses, A. Quincy Jones moved the burners to a compartment in the dining table, so that the mother could prepare food directly in front of the family. Jones went further than any other architect to bring the ordinary middle-class housewife out of the kitchen and away from the image of the hired, lower-class servant.

Aside from increasing the need for storage space, the many new appliances in the kitchen required additional wiring. The authors of the Small Homes Council circu-lar *Planning the Kitchen* took care to note that "electric appliances used in the kitchen require adequate wiring on a separate circuit for safety and efficient operation. There should be at least one duplex convenience outlet

The separate oven can be placed at a conven-ient working height.

Separating ovens from stoves meant that women no longer had to bend to put items in or take them out of the oven. Helen E. McCullough and Martha S. Schoeppel, *Separate Ovens*, Small Homes Council Circular Series Index Number C5.33, *University of Illinois Bulletin* 53, no. 36 (January 1956): 2, University of Illinois Archives.

for each 4 feet of work counter and one at the refrig-erator. . . . Convenience outlets must be provided for an electric clock, fan, or dishwasher."[47] Not only did the kitchen change to accommodate and display new goods, but its walls also thickened to accommodate the new circuitry and wiring necessary for the new appli-ances. As it turned out, nearly all the walls in the post-war house would thicken as homeowners sought means to store and display what they had acquired.

STORAGE

The aesthetic of the clean and antiseptic postwar home, as it was portrayed in nearly every image of the period, was inherently linked to ideas about whiteness and economic strength. But with so many new items in the home, the problem of storage became critical. In the typical 1,000-square-foot house, closet space was at a premium. As Andrew Hurley notes, the home was "supposed to be a showcase for the material possessions, the modern appliances, toys and amenities that signified attainment of the good life and one's arrival in the wonderful world of consumer abundance. But where to place the hi-fi system, the television set, and the washing machine in a small home?"[48]

The hi-fi, television, and washing machine were certainly large, new fixtures that had to be located appropriately within the house. But what about all the ordinary, everyday things families accumulated? The Small Homes Council established a representative list of items that families generally needed to store. A typical living room closet might house coats, books, magazines, card table and folding chairs, musical instruments, business papers, desk supplies, radio, record player, records, table linens, and dinnerware. Bedroom closets contained clothing, bedding, bathroom supplies, and toilet articles. The main work area of the house contained cleaning equipment and supplies, work clothes, and children's play clothes. A range of additional arti-

cles, such as indoor toys, folding beds, luggage, infants' equipment, sports and hobby equipment, and sewing equipment, likewise required storage but had no definite room assignment. Although most postwar houses had small, single-car garages or carports, the author of the Small Homes Council study recommended storage outdoors for items such as canning utensils, empty food containers, flower containers, gardening supplies and tools, old papers and magazines, paints and painting equipment, out-of-season items such as electric fans and Christmas decorations, lawn mower, garden hose, and bicycles. The author acknowledged, however, that most houses could not adequately meet the demand for storage of these items.[49]

One response to the problem of the lack of space in small houses was the design of compact and portable furnishings that allowed more objects to occupy less space. An article in *Life* magazine stated that manufacturers were able to produce reduced-scale and lightweight furniture using newly available plywood and plastics. If designed and selected properly, these compact and portable furnishings could allow one room to "do the work of four," the article claimed. Featured in the article were a miniature piano that weighed just twenty pounds and occupied only 4.5 square feet and a fireplace mantel, made of plastic, with pivoting compartments containing chairs, table, silver, glassware, linens, and dishes, as well as two electrical outlets. An entire kitchen was contained in one cabinet, a vertical floor fan doubled as a hassock, and a living room screen contained panels that swung open to make a bar.[50] Although the piece presented the glamorization of gadgetry made possible through new technologies and materials, its exaggerated solutions provide further evidence of the ubiquitous nature of space and storage problems in postwar houses.

How much did storage requirements actually change in the postwar era? A study conducted for the Federal Housing Administration found that between 1944 and 1951, the need for storage of clothes in a master bedroom increased from 80 rod inches to an average of 94 rod inches. The absolute minimum was a usable rod length of 72 inches. Linen closets, the study found, were too small as well. Overall, the study's author recommended a minimum total volume (interior and exterior) for storage of 150 cubic feet plus 75 cubic feet per bedroom. For closets, at least 6 inches should be added to the width of storage openings in houses to make them more accessible and, therefore, more fully functional. Though seldom found, full-access doors with openings equal to at least two-thirds of the closet width were described as ideal.[51] Again, folding screens substituted for doors in some houses to increase closet space while minimizing the amount of space occupied by the doors themselves.[52] But the walk-in closet, once the privileged storage space of the upper classes, became a desirable, if seldom obtained, space for the masses during this time,

and the Small Homes Council report recommended the walk-in closet as an especially good storage model. Like the kitchen desk, it seldom appeared in the smallest and most affordable postwar houses, but it quickly became a middle-class aspiration and a symbol of economic success.

More specifically, the Small Homes Council recommended that 3 feet of additional rod be placed in the master bedroom closet, requiring a closet addition 3 feet wide, 2 feet deep, and 8 feet high (48 cubic feet). The general storage requirement for small houses would be 375 cubic feet (indoor and outdoor), adding 10 cubic feet to the previous minimum requirement. Exterior storage was to contain a lawn mower, hoe, rake, lawn broom, lawn clippers, garden hose, lawn chairs, grill, large thermos, picnic equipment, recreation equipment, electric fan, paint and removers, storm windows, storm doors, screen doors, window screens, and Christmas decorations, totaling 182 cubic feet. Even this increase, the author noted, would make for tight storage, adding that "more than half the families" interviewed in the study felt their storage was inadequate, especially for children's equipment. The report summary stated that of the six families studied, all "left some articles outdoors for lack of proper storage," an image that connoted disorder and trailer park living, and that was, therefore, highly undesirable.[53]

BUILT-INS

Among the most commonly advocated solutions to storage problems were built-in storage units and storage walls, and a number of designs surfaced that allowed a variety of space-saving configurations. Built-in storage was not a postwar invention; turn-of-the-century American houses, particularly small bungalows, included storage units that were built into the architecture to reduce domestic clutter.[54] But as a 1954 *House and Home* article proclaimed: "Home buyers want organized storage. How much storage do they want? Answer: a basement or attic equivalent."[55] The built-ins found in earlier housing were no longer sufficient. The article was illustrated with a range of solutions, including outdoor plywood "cabins" and bins, storage cabinets attached to exterior walls that doubled as additional home insulation, and interior closet walls. Again, the Small Homes Council was an important innovator in storage design for ordinary houses, and it advised through its circulars that new houses, whenever possible, should be constructed with roof truss systems that allowed non-load-bearing walls.[56] The innovation of roof truss construction allowed for the installation of studless wall panels that could then be used for storage partitions. The studless panels were not only cheaper to construct than the usual wood-frame walls, but they also increased the usable square footage of the house

Storage built into the hallway of a residence. Date and architect unknown. Photograph by Maynard L. Parker. Courtesy of the Huntington Library, San Marino, California.

by reducing the need for cabinet units placed on the floor and against the wall. Once again, such partitions increased the thickness of the walls, but Small Homes Council studies showed that overall savings occurred in terms of livable square footage.[57] Although the amount of space under consideration may seem negligible, postwar homeowners wished to recapture any space they could in their tiny homes, which were filled with their growing families and their accumulation of material goods.

According to Mildred Friedman: "George Nelson and Henry Wright introduced the 'storage wall' . . . [demonstrating] that by thickening an interior wall from the 4-to-6-inch norm to 12 inches, storage for the family's sporting equipment, tools, picnic baskets, and off-season clothing could be created without sacrificing the space—scarce in small-scale postwar housing—required for traditional storage units. Constructed between rooms, the storage wall could be accessible from both sides."[58] Sometimes called an "activity wall," the storage wall was the precursor to the entertainment center found in many homes today. Instead of a freestanding cabinet, however, the storage wall was incorporated into the architectural fabric of the house itself. With the increased availability of fir plywood on the market, homeowners could easily construct their own inexpensive storage walls and units if they were not already installed in the houses they purchased. The

In January 1945, *Life* magazine featured a storage wall that could be used anywhere in the house to contain the abundant goods crowding most American homes.
Life magazine, January 22, 1945. Photograph by Herbert Gehr/ Time & Life Pictures/Getty Images.

storage wall became a widely recommended solution to the problem of storage space in postwar houses, and it was frequently implemented as well. Indeed, Sandy Isenstadt has referred to such built-ins as the "unrecognized space of modern architecture."[59] They not only allowed convenient storage without reducing square footage, but, by thickening the walls of the house, they also added much-needed sound and thermal insulation.

THE HOUSE FULL OF BUILT-INS

In November 1958, *Popular Mechanics* ran an article titled "A House Full of Built-Ins" that opened with the question, "How can you change a modest home into a showplace?" The magazine's readers may have been surprised to be told that the secret to creating a showplace lay in concealing their goods in built-in storage walls and units. Using photographs of a Glen Cove, Long Island, home that cost $9,000, the magazine highlighted the built-ins created for every room and for nearly every wall of the house, including a 16-foot wall unit in the family room that concealed a radio, TV, hi-fi, sewing center, and fold-up bed. Records could be stored in a cabinet below the television. The house also included a hidden work center for the housewife with a fold-out work table, ironing board, and storage for one hundred

Built-in plywood closets featured in "A House Full of Built-Ins." Courtesy of *Popular Mechanics*; originally published in the November 1958 issue.

spools of thread. The wall-bed included shelves and cabinets built into its compartments. The boys' bedroom had an extra bed concealed in a drawer in the bottom of the bunk beds, and a chalkboard folded down from the wall to form a platform for a model train set. A cabinet in the living room contained a home movie projector and screen. Storage walls were also built around the washer and dryer in the laundry room, and floor-to-ceiling cabinets had been installed in the basement, along with a hideaway refreshment bar. The built-ins were all made from plywood with the United States Plywood Corporation's new Weldwood panel facing, which simulated a variety of woods.[60]

Although it may seem contradictory to imagine concealed storage systems as part of the transformation of a house into a showplace, the storage wall embodies the same tensions as those associated with the picture window: the desire for display that facilitates status mobility and identity confirmation versus the desire for concealment that allows for privacy and the requisite uncluttered aesthetic. The activity or storage wall provided an ideal solution to this conflict, because when closed, the drop leafs, swinging panels, and doors still revealed their subtle outlines, hinting to visitors and occupants of the wall's abundant and sometimes expensive contents without precisely revealing the nature of the goods within. Moreover, when properly designed, built-in storage units blended with their surrounding

surfaces, creating a moment of drama and a sense of delight when sprung open to reveal the exciting technologies of the moment or a wealth of entertaining games and toys. Ordinary things may even have seemed slightly more exciting when concealed in hidden storage walls, which also contributed to a slick, no-frills, modern aesthetic.

Built-in plywood bunks, drawers, and a trundle bed. From "A House Full of Built-Ins," *Popular Mechanics*, November 1958. Courtesy of *Popular Mechanics*.

A plywood storage wall contains drawers, shelves, a fold-down ironing board, a sewing machine, and one hundred spools of thread.
From "A House Full of Built-Ins," *Popular Mechanics*, November 1958. Courtesy of *Popular Mechanics*.

Eichler houses, which bridged the gap between custom-designed and ordinary postwar houses, were filled with built-ins, and these features were used as part of the marketing of the houses. Although they were slightly more expensive than ordinary houses and less widely available, Eichler houses serve to illustrate the shifts in size and wall thickness that occurred as postwar architects and builders struggled to accommodate the new appliances and other belongings of their clients and market. A 1955 *House and Home* article titled "Built-In Merchandising Lifts California" focused on Eichler's adjustments to his house plans from 1947 to 1955 and on his implementation of built-in merchandise to sell his houses. In 1947, Eichler houses had small carports. Three years later, the 1950 Eichler houses were constructed with single-car garages that were oversized to include space for a washing machine and dryer. By 1954, the houses increasingly included double carports, and by 1955, all the new Eichlers had double garages, with the laundry appliances moved out but the deep freeze moved in, along with trunks, furniture, the house furnace and water heater, and a "do-it-yourself" workshop. The washing machine and dryer moved indoors, since the appliances made it possible to do laundry several times a week and it was desirable for the machines to be handily located. Eichler's architects put the washing machine and clothes dryer in the bathroom/bedroom wing and included a folding area, hamper, and linen closet.

A comparison of house plans from Eichler's 1950 and 1955 houses reveals a remarkable increase in storage space, along with a general increase in overall house size and the addition of a fourth bedroom. While the 1954 and earlier Eichler houses had freestanding kitchen appliances, by 1955 the houses had built-in appliances in the kitchen and up to 18 linear feet of countertop, with 10 linear feet of cabinets. Eichler houses evolved to have bathrooms that were divided for privacy, so that a so-called makeup center or vanity was moved into the master bedroom, separated from the bathing and toilet facilities. In ordinary houses, the "stretching" of what was often a single bathroom by splitting it into two compartments with a sliding door was the single most distinctive change in bathroom design of the period.[61] The corridors of Eichler houses essentially became one continuous storage wall. Built-in furnishings originally projected into the rooms of Eichler houses, but over time these were refined and built into closet walls.[62] The evolution of Eichler's houses is paradigmatic of the swelling, thickening postwar house, even if these houses were a limited ideal rather than strictly ordinary.

By 1960, when *Popular Mechanics* published its "*PM* House of Built-Ins" as the lead design in the magazine's eighth annual home section, concerns for efficient storage took their place of prominence alongside concerns for privacy and indoor/outdoor living as the primary concerns for postwar house design. The editors implored readers:

Imagine a home where: The kids can make up their beds and slide them into the wall, leaving uncluttered play space. Each member of the family has a complete wardrobe wall, tailor-made to his own needs. The built-ins throughout the home require only a minimum investment in furniture. Stereo, hi-fi, an intercom system and rotating TV are built into the wall. Further imagine that this home has an inner garden court and glass walls to bring the outdoors inside, yet offers privacy from every angle. Imagine, finally, that the house has a broad, sweeping exterior that hugs the ground; a beautiful home you'd be proud to own. That's the *PM* House of Built-Ins. More than a year ago the editors of *Popular Mechanics* made a broad survey of the trends in housing and concluded that built-ins were the biggest news in the home-building field. A house full of built-ins, including built-in privacy, was obviously the kind of house most families wanted.[63]

The full-color feature (somewhat unusual for the magazine) included fold-out views from an elevated perspective of the house's street elevation and interior front courtyard, a rendering of the rear elevation with swimming pool and patio, an itemized color plan, and selected photographs of the interior spaces. Designed by architect Milton Schwartz of Barrington, Illinois, the 1,964-square-foot house with a 538-square-foot garage was significantly larger than most of the houses

OVERLEAF LEFT
A rendering of the *Popular Mechanics* "House of Built-Ins."
Courtesy of *Popular Mechanics*; originally published in the October 1960 issue.

OVERLEAF RIGHT
Plan for the *Popular Mechanics* "House of Built-Ins."
Courtesy of *Popular Mechanics*; originally published in the October 1960 issue.

FROM THE FRONT:
The house offers a long, low silhouette with a landscaped entry court hidden behind a masonry wall and a decorative gate. Privacy is built in everywhere, yet the home brings the outdoors inside.

FROM THE BACK:
The family patio is an ideal location for a pool. Glass walls of the family room and living room permit supervision of the patio-play area. Behind the exterior wall is a second patio that is open only to the master bedroom.

Architect: Milton Schwartz, Barrington, Ill.
Builder: Jim Nuckolls, Royal Homes, Tulsa, Okla.
Decoration: Helen Rambo, Tulsa, Okla.
Furniture: Bull's Furniture Company, Tulsa, Okla.

Photography: Joe Fletcher
Text: Clifford B. Hicks

FOR PLANS:
Complete plans, including specifications, for the **PM** House of Built-Ins are available. Three versions have been prepared: the version shown here (1964 square feet plus garage area of 538 square feet); an expanded version (2281 square feet plus garage area of 538 square feet); and a smaller version (1878 square feet plus garage area of 538 square feet). The cost of each plan is $35.00. Please specify whether you wish the standard, expanded or smaller version. Order from: Plans Department, **Popular Mechanics**, 200 E. Ontario St., Chicago 11, Ill.

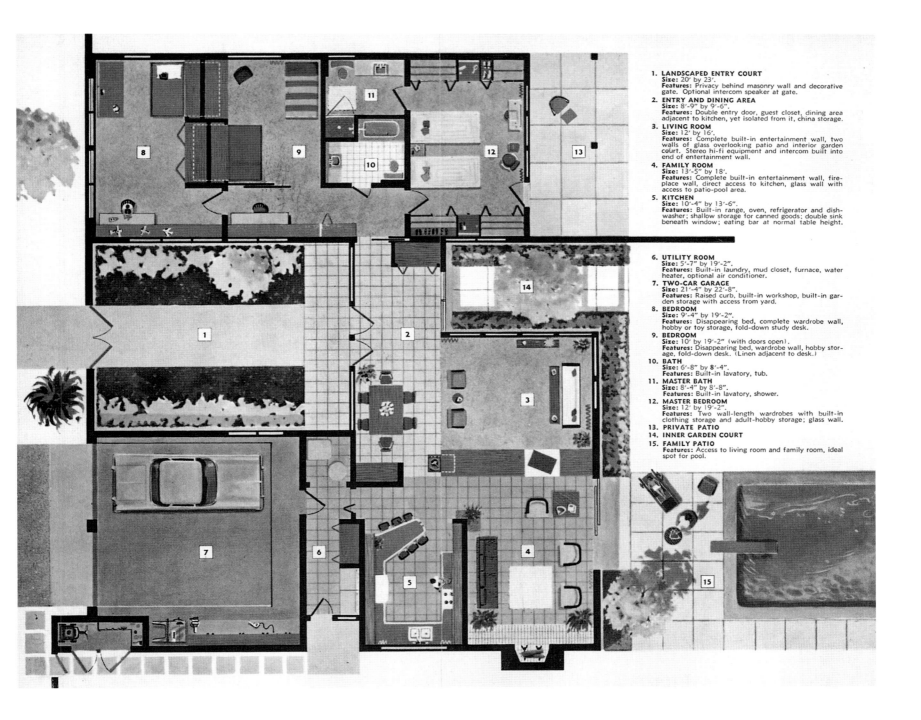

1. **LANDSCAPED ENTRY COURT**
   Size: 20′ by 23′.
   Features: Privacy behind masonry wall and decorative gate. Optional intercom speaker at gate.

2. **ENTRY AND DINING AREA**
   Size: 8′-9″ by 9′-6″.
   Features: Double entry door, guest closet, dining area adjacent to kitchen, yet isolated from it, china storage.

3. **LIVING ROOM**
   Size: 12′ by 16′.
   Features: Complete built-in entertainment wall, two walls of glass overlooking patio and interior garden court. Stereo hi-fi equipment and intercom built into end of entertainment wall.

4. **FAMILY ROOM**
   Size: 13′-5″ by 18′.
   Features: Complete built-in entertainment wall, fireplace wall, direct access to kitchen, glass wall with access to patio-pool area.

5. **KITCHEN**
   Size: 10′-4″ by 13′-6″.
   Features: Built-in range, oven, refrigerator and dishwasher; shallow storage for canned goods; double sink beneath window; eating bar at normal table height.

6. **UTILITY ROOM**
   Size: 5′-7″ by 19′-2″.
   Features: Built-in laundry, mud closet, furnace, water heater, optional air conditioner.

7. **TWO-CAR GARAGE**
   Size: 21′-4″ by 22′-8″.
   Features: Raised curb, built-in workshop, built-in garden storage with access from yard.

8. **BEDROOM**
   Size: 9′-4″ by 19′-2″.
   Features: Disappearing bed, complete wardrobe wall, hobby or toy storage, fold-down study desk.

9. **BEDROOM**
   Size: 10′ by 19′-2″ (with doors open).
   Features: Disappearing bed, wardrobe wall, hobby storage, fold-down desk. (Linen adjacent to desk.)

10. **BATH**
    Size: 6′-8″ by 8′-4″.
    Features: Built-in lavatory, tub.

11. **MASTER BATH**
    Size: 8′-4″ by 8′-8″.
    Features: Built-in lavatory, shower.

12. **MASTER BEDROOM**
    Size: 12′ by 19′-2″.
    Features: Two wall-length wardrobes with built-in clothing storage and adult-hobby storage; glass wall.

13. **PRIVATE PATIO**

14. **INNER GARDEN COURT**

15. **FAMILY PATIO**
    Features: Access to living room and family room, ideal spot for pool.

featured in the magazine and larger than the homes of many of its readers. Yet the home's exterior appearance remained familiar and was not unlike the aesthetic common to the Eichler houses designed by A. Quincy Jones and Fred Emmons. Designed around an entry court that was concealed by a masonry wall, the house featured even privacy as a "built-in." At the rear, a wall extending from the center of the house created a private patio off the master bedroom, separated from the family patio, with its pool, that extended off the family room. The centrally situated living room and adjacent inner garden court sat on axis with the front door and entry court. Bedrooms and baths (private spaces) were located to one side of that axis, and dining room, kitchen, utility room, and two-car garage (public spaces) were on the other. Carefully examined, the plan reveals numerous wall thickenings that served as the spaces for built-ins. The entry and dining area included built-in china storage; the living and family rooms included a shared built-in entertainment wall for concealing a television, stereo, hi-fi, and intercom with a pull-down desk on the family room side; built-in appliances and shallow canned-good storage that eliminated the need to bend and reach appeared in the kitchen, along with a built-in charcoal barbecue and separated wall oven and countertop range; the children's bedrooms featured "disappearing" beds, wardrobe walls, hobby or toy storage, and fold-down study desks; the master bedroom likewise contained two wall-length wardrobes

and adult-hobby storage. The garage included a built-in workshop with garden storage.

The novelty of a house that included a turntable that flipped up to be concealed into the end of an entertainment wall and children's beds that glided into the wall and disappeared must have charmed readers, and some also had the opportunity to experience the house, because it had already been constructed as a model in twelve locations.[64] Nearly all the models had been built in suburbs at the edges of expanding metropolitan areas, some of which were largely restricted to white occupants. As such, the house, on paper and in its constructed form, provided both a representation and a realized ideal, a model for the containment of postwar abundance, for the fetishization of the tidy and well-ordered and carefully measured appearance of a lifestyle of leisure, of too much rather than not enough. It was a house that contained nearly all the features considered important for postwar domesticity, and thus it served as an ideal plan for the fashioning of identities that were predicated on consumption and a very particularized notion of display. Built into the House of Built-Ins was not only an agreed-upon notion of the ideal house form for 1960 but also an unspoken consensus about what it meant to be the occupants of such a house. After all, only people who can afford china need china cabinets, and only those who can afford hi-fi components need stereo cabinets. The built-ins signaled this affluence, just as they signaled the status and therefore identities of those who might occupy such houses. The storage systems served a practical purpose, but they simultaneously conveyed clear if very subtle messages about the rightful owners of postwar houses.

Again, a look at Fritz Burns's 1946 Postwar House is instructive. Designed for an imagined family of four—two adults and two adolescent boys—the two-bedroom, two-bathroom house was developed both to model do-mestic dreams and to instill such dreams in visitors. It included an open-plan arrangement for the living and dining rooms, a kitchen, laundry room, utility room, all-purpose room, service yard, and detached carport/helicopter storage area with its own workshop, greenhouse, and storage. The Postwar House's imaginary occupants were necessarily more affluent than the average consumer of an ordinary postwar house, since the

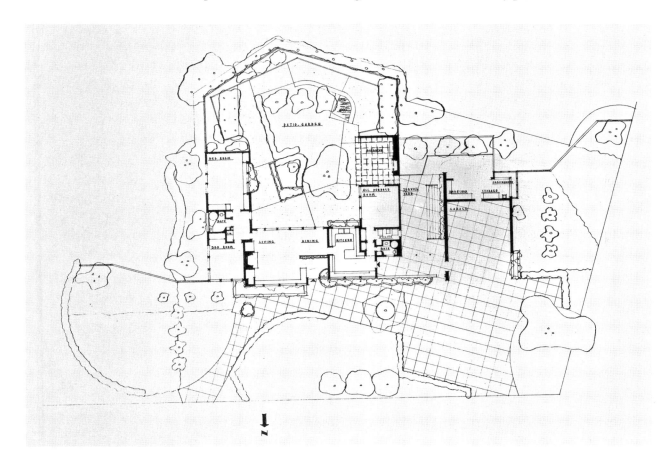

Plan of Fritz Burns's Postwar House, Los Angeles, California, 1945. Wurdeman-Becket, architects; Garrett Eckbo, landscape architect. Photograph by Maynard L. Parker. Courtesy of the Huntington Library, San Marino, California.

technologies and materials included in the house were far beyond the reach of anyone who was not at least upper-middle-class. That the occupants were imagined as white went without saying, but should any question exist, models photographed inside the house both fit the required profile and reinforced visitors' and/or magazine readers' ideas about the intended occupants of such houses. With its U-shaped plan, the house wrapped around a stylish enclosed patio garden that included a paved barbecue patio and raised beds for growing flowers, vegetables, and ornamental shrubs. One wing contained the bedrooms, which were separated from the kitchen/service wing by the living and dining rooms. The all-purpose room was intended as a study, office,

The middling modernism of the exterior of Fritz Burns's Postwar House belied the innovations found inside. Los Angeles, California, 1946. Fritz Burns, developer. Wurdeman-Becket, architects; Garrett Eckbo, landscape architect. Photograph by Maynard L. Parker. Courtesy of the Huntington Library, San Marino, California.

maid's room, guest room, den, or "retreat for parents fleeing their children."[65] As such, the plan was part of the larger trend toward the creation of separate wings for parents and children that increasingly appeared in architect-designed houses after 1955 and as detailed in chapter 4.[66]

The home's stone, glass, and varnished California redwood plywood exterior was attractive if unremarkable—an *Architectural Forum* author labeled the exterior "a high level of average taste"—and nothing about the house's exterior appearance signaled the innovative technologies located within.[67] Like the cabinets that concealed the exciting new consumer products found in the home's interior, the house's facade hid the technological and design innovations that awaited the many thousands of visitors who toured the home. Nearly every inch of this house included some novel bit of mechanical or design ingenuity that was intended to convey a specific and optimistic message about the future of homeownership in the postwar United States. The house's title, after all, indicated the builder's intention: the Postwar House served as a symbolic site, embodying a specific promise in which homeownership, capitalism, and ingenuity combined to reveal a life of affluent, tidy, and nearly laborless leisure. Tidiness, facilitated through the implementation of space-saving and cleverly designed built-in storage units, served as a secondary motif throughout the home, emphasizing

the iconography of whiteness and middle-class sterility throughout. With its over-the-top inclusion of gadgetry and its helicopter parked in the carport, the house did not represent an attainable ideal. But its title made it seem as though it did, as though the house stood for all other houses constructed after the war, as though it was the ideal to which all Americans should aspire.

Every room of Burns's model home included concealed radio, hi-fi, and intercom speakers to ensure reception throughout the house; a television, radio, recording equipment, and record player sat behind the plastic tambour doors of the cabinets flanking the fireplace in the living room. In addition, the hobby room, all-purpose room, and main bathroom contained their own radios. There was, of course, a playful aspect to these hidden goods, and a sense of wonder derived when cabinet doors swung open to reveal the marvels of electrical engineering and their organization. But concealed technology appeared desirable not only because it conformed with aesthetic conventions that demanded tidiness, but also because hiding equipment allowed owners to participate in a visual economy that permitted controlled access to their most precious possessions and that likewise conferred the greatest degree of status. Concealing or partially concealing expensive electronic equipment indicated refinement. Displaying all one's possessions on open shelves could appear crass. What is sometimes called "representing"—the notion

that one should proudly display one's wealth on the body through attire and in the home through possessions—has never been an accepted part of upper-class white culture. At least partially concealing electronics and other possessions was therefore a key ingredient in the recipe for making white houses.

Moreover, receivers that brought the outside world into the home—whether television, radio, stereo, or telephone—could be imagined as occupying a liminal zone between the outside world and the domestic interior. As the conduits through which news and sounds of the public domain entered into the private realm, these technologies held the potential to delight, entertain, and inform, but they could also pollute and disturb the sacred and carefully maintained privacy of the home. By enclosing these technologies in cabinets and hiding them from view, the inhabitants could literally shut out the outside world. And if, as has been widely hypothesized, the television replaced the hearth as the sacred center of the home, its containing and concealing cabinet became a sacred space, a kind of twentieth-century equivalent of the ancient Roman lararium, one that provided the enclosure of a sacral object that could be fetishized and worshipped.[68] Although concealing such

LEFT Stereo equipment and its storage and display system in the Postwar House. Photograph by Maynard L. Parker. Courtesy of the Huntington Library, San Marino, California.
FACING Built-in storage cabinets conceal stereo components and vinyl records in a postwar living room. Architect unknown, circa 1950s. Photograph by Maynard L. Parker. Courtesy of the Huntington Library, San Marino, California.

high-end electronics held wide appeal for architects and elite tastemakers, class status influenced acceptance of the ideal. As with kitchen appliances, working-class and many middle-class families were much more likely to display their televisions, radios, and stereos as treasured and hard-earned items of status. In these cases, entertainment electronics appeared prominently displayed in living and family rooms.[69]

CONCLUSION

Certainly, the ramifications of consumption were made visible in all parts of the house, including the garage and garden (discussed in chapter 8). Rather than detail every newly acquired item and its impact on the home, my intention here has been to illustrate the incremental impact of the new consumerism on selected aspects of the architecture of ordinary postwar houses by considering the storage and display of domestic artifacts. Although architectural histories of the postwar era typically portray the dramatic, bold designs of a progressive period, ordinary houses of the time reflect changes that are far more subtle yet no less compelling, and perhaps more revealing. While ordinary, small houses were less aesthetically charged, the alterations in wall thickness, room dimensions, storage space, and form reveal

A built-in storage wall provides spaces to contain and display stereo and hi-fi components. Date and architect unknown. Photograph by Maynard L. Parker. Courtesy of the Huntington Library, San Marino, California.

a great deal—certainly more than any design changes in their high-style counterparts—about the desires, anxieties, and cultural complexities of the postwar lifestyles of the American middle majority. The coffee table, the kitchen desk, the countertop space we take for granted every day—all are the material residue of a remarkable period of economic growth and cultural transition. If the accumulation of consumer goods affirmed membership in the white middle majority, the house and its storage and display systems became the framework and the text, writ large, for reading that membership. The story of postwar architecture, then, lies less in the glossy photographs of architect-designed houses and great architectural careers than in the contours of ordinary houses with roughly 1,000 square feet of dwelling space that was bursting at the seams with all of the newest, brightest goods that money could buy. The story becomes even richer when we examine the ways in which display—whether of the body in domestic spaces or of material goods—served as an index and as a register for the formation and recognition of racial and class identities. Whether or not Americans adopted the conventions promoted by national publications, the rhetoric of careful storage and tasteful display contributed to the production of a cultural field in the United States that reinforced again the imagined and intended exclusivity of postwar housing.

7

THE HOME SHOW

Televising the Postwar House

Oppressed by ennui, development people turn to the mass-communications media to find new ideas. . . . The communications media, realizing that tremendous numbers of their readers, watchers, and listeners live in developments, have begun to angle their productions for the development public. All this results in less and less variation in taste, and the feeling of ennui is reinforced.[1]

JOHN KEATS, *The Crack in the Picture Window*, 1957

The master bedroom of my grandparents' house contained a television that my grandfather had mounted inside a cabinet high above my grandmother's clothes closet. The cabinet door had been removed so that the tube stared out from its lofty perch near the ceiling, perhaps six or seven feet above the floor. It seemed a part of the wall, an integral part of the room. Lying on my grandparents' king-size bed, I could watch TV and change the channels with the most space-age device known to me at that time: a remote control. At the push of a button, Mr. Ed (the talking horse) would appear. Push another button and the Flintstones were on. Nothing could have felt more luxurious. Because of my grandfather's profession, he had easy access to wholesale electronics, and their house nearly always contained more electronic devices than would typically have been found in such a modest house. By the mid-1960s, my grandparents owned four televisions: color sets in the kitchen and den, the master bedroom set in the wall, and a tiny black-and-white

FACING
NBC's "House That *Home* Built" 1957 (*detail, see p. 254*).

set in the guest room, its miniaturization enchanting. Television was everywhere in their house, a symbol of affluence but also of modernity, of connection to a world outside, a device for seeing postwar America and the world beyond.

As he prepared to bring a version of his famous play *Death of a Salesman* to television for the first time in 1985, Arthur Miller noted a problem he encountered when trying to translate the immediacy of a stage performance to film or television: "In the theater, while you recognized that you were looking at a house, it was a house in quotation marks. On screen, the quotation marks tend to be blotted out by the camera."[2] Miller followed this statement by explaining that he found it more difficult to provide a sense of sustained reality for the viewer when creating a movie or television show because both film and camera removed the viewer from immersion in the immediacy of the action that could be accomplished through live performance. Although he used "a house" in his statement to stand for an imagined theatrical subject, and "quotation marks" to indicate a view of that subject as directly taken (cited) from reality without any translating or mediating (paraphrasing) device, we might consider the playwright's statement a bit more literally here. If, as Miller indicated, television renders imperceptible some kinds of realities and/or visualities through various devices and techniques,

it simultaneously creates others. In this chapter, I ask how television—particularly early television programs about the house and domestic practices—contributed to the production of the ideological and rhetorical fields related to the social realities of race, class, gender, and postwar domesticity. How did the small screen that was increasingly becoming a part of living rooms across the United States "blot out" some domestic social realities while amplifying others? How did that same screen daily invite audiences to consume visually a set of performed practices that reinforced prevailing notions about homeownership and the identities of homeowners? And what role did television, as a mechanism for the relay of symbolic practices and rhetorical strategies, play as a producer in the knowledge industry surrounding domesticity and residential practices in the postwar United States? I will not examine theatrical television productions here, because situation comedies and dramas about domestic life have already received considerable scholarly analysis elsewhere. Instead, my focus is on the journalistic, news-format, and talk-show television programming that took domestic/household life as its primary subject matter for the first time in the 1950s.

The connection between television viewing and postwar living has become a commonplace subject for analysis in many suburban histories. Scholars such as Lynn Spigel and Karal Ann Marling (among others) have amply demonstrated the fascination that television held for Americans in the decades following the end of World War II.[3] Other scholars have examined the ways in which situation comedies intersected with suburban domestic life.[4] To be sure, television programs modeled specific norms of behavior for all members of the family, and the receiver itself changed patterns of living and use within the home. Moreover, television changed patterns of consumption throughout the United States as advertisers quickly grew to understand the medium's substantial economic impact nationwide. But television—along with its mass-media predecessor the popular magazine—also influenced the building trades and ordinary house construction in particular ways that have yet to be closely examined. Although the notion that communications media create (and do not merely reflect) culture dates at least to Raymond Williams's 1974 study *Television: Technology and Cultural Form*, little scholarship has yet examined the connection between television and the built environment.[5] Both are seen here as active agents in the formation of postwar culture in the United States. Moreover, and as Lynn Spigel has recently demonstrated, television contributed to the development and acceptance of specific brands of aesthetic modernism. Spigel focuses on the ways in which graphic design, modern art, set design, and more contributed to an acceptance of a particular aesthetic but also to the success of television itself. As Spigel observes: "The rise of television occurred simultaneously with America's growing influence as an international center for modern graphic and architec-

tural design, both of which influenced virtually all aspects of commodity culture. Indeed, this postwar 'arts explosion' and the rise of television were not a mere historical coincidence; instead, art and television were deeply intertwined and dependent on one another for their mutual ascendance in U.S. cultural life."[6] I add to her argument in this chapter by examining the work television did for the home-building industries in the postwar era. But I also and perhaps primarily seek to understand how that work contributed to a politics of representation that reinforced specific forms of social knowledge and that linked domesticity and identity in that same period.

Regular network television broadcasts in the United States began in the mid- to late 1940s, but the number of households owning televisions was low in the earliest days. In 1950, only 9 percent of U.S. households owned television sets; by 1954 that number had leapt to 55.7 percent.[7] The 1950s then became an era of discovery for network executives, producers, directors, actors, and other performers, who experimented with formats and content to find the optimal uses for the medium that was reaching more homes with every passing year.[8] As network producers faced the challenges and excitement of working in television, they simultaneously struggled to articulate the ways in which the newer medium could function differently from radio or magazines, to consider the various ways audiences watched the new programs, and to understand the impacts of television programming on domestic life. As this chapter shows, some mid-1950s programming relied heavily on the earlier models of radio and print media in particular ways while breaking new ground in others.

As television and print media became increasingly accessible to and affordable for the general public, and as national magazines (and their circulation rates) and TV programs proliferated, builders, designers, product manufacturers, and related trade organizations began to realize the potential for mass commercial sales made possible through advertising in various and multiple media outlets that could be employed more or less simultaneously. Certainly radio had been a boon to advertisers in the interwar years, and both popular and shelter magazines had enticed the public with images of the latest styles and products for centuries. But television held new promise, especially for the promotion of all things visual. The apparently live motion of television allowed an immediacy, vitality, and dimensionality of communication—especially for subjects that involved a three-dimensional, spatial component—that had not previously been possible. Although it would take television producers some time to understand the full potential of the new medium and to take complete advantage of its particular communication attributes in ways that were distinctive from those employed in mass-circulation magazines, the understanding that the medium could communicate in new ways was present from the start.

In the robust postwar consumer culture, advertisements of all sorts sold commodities—houses, cars, appliances, furnishings, clothing, recreational goods, and more. Then as now, they also aimed to sell lifestyles, images associated with class placement and racial identity. In the millions of pictures that were published and broadcast between 1945 and 1960, residents of the United States—both those recently arrived and long-established citizens—monitored a repeated series of indexes for the creation of a culturally sanctioned identity that could be formulated and solidified through the accumulation of specific possessions and the spatialized enactments of specific life patterns. If the advertisements in magazines and on television were selling products, they were equally selling a monolithically constructed image of midcentury life in the United States. The imagined/predicted consumers targeted by the media fell into a carefully studied demographic group: whites or those who appeared white, the portion of the population believed to have the greatest access to surplus capital. But the images likewise reinforced the notion that the United States—with its desirable American-made products—was a place primarily designed for middle-class and upper-middle-class whites. As David Morley has pointed out: "If the national media constitute the public sphere which is most central in the mediation of the nation-state to the general public, then whatever is excluded from those media is in effect excluded from the symbolic culture of the nation.

When the culture of that public sphere (and thus of the nation) is in effect 'racialised' by the naturalisation of one (largely unmarked and undeclared) form of ethnicity, then only some citizens of the nation find it a homely and welcoming place."[9]

In this chapter, I examine the role that specific kinds of television programming played in defining and persuading the viewing public about the parameters that constituted a model domestic realm—one with white, middle-class inhabitants—that was to be emulated, constructed, and desired. The media in this period helped cement a specific culture of viewing, one that emphasized the importance of looking in at other people's lives, whether in print publications, on TV, or at model homes. As such, they (through the work of television producers, magazine editors and publishers, and advertisers) formed the counterpart to the postwar obsession with personal and family privacy in the domestic realm, creating voyeurs who were nonetheless concerned about being themselves observed. The desire to see into another family's living room and into the daily lives of the family members to see the ways they cooked, cleaned, decorated, dressed, and behaved, and even to examine the contours of the house itself, was linked to the desire for self-definition and distinction within a highly prescribed degree of conformity.

That magazines could provide this opportunity for a specifically produced brand of domestic voyeurism was not new, as noted in chapter 1. But in the immediate postwar era, with the dramatic increase in housing need and construction starts, home builders and those in related trades acquired a growing awareness of the importance of promotion and publicity that could be generated through a range of media outlets. For example, in 1954 the National Association of Home Builders published its *Plan for a Homebuilder's Public Relations*. This pamphlet advised builders to participate in the numerous national home-building contests being held during this period, largely sponsored by manufacturers, because participants could gain national prominence if they became competition winners. The pamphlet included a list of competitions and a "Press Relations" section that instructed builders on how to make contacts with newspaper people and how to bring building projects to their attention for publication. The section on "Radio and Television" recommended that builders contact the directors of women's programs, since women were thought to be especially interested in model homes and new developments. Moreover, women made up the most likely daytime audience, since most men, it was presumed, were at work away from the home during the day. Calling television both "your newest opportunity "and "radio shows that people can see," the publication stressed the importance of builders' using visual aids such as maps, charts, floor plans, drawings, photographs, and scale models in order to take full advantage of the new medium's potential.[10]

The idea that television was simply radio with an

added visual component is important because it demonstrates the extent to which advertisers and those in the home industry—and even some in the television industry itself—struggled to imagine the medium's potential in the immediate postwar period, particularly when it came to producing programs that were not dramas, comedies, or musical entertainment shows. A challenge existed in trying to discover how talk radio differed from talk television. What, specifically, could the newer medium offer in programs with a conversational format and that were intended to deliver content that was already well suited to magazines and radio?

Subjects of a spatialized nature were a natural fit for television. For the first time, the construction trades were solidly linked to a plethora of advertising, commercial, and media outlets aimed at helping them market their products and homes. Builders, developers, and product manufacturers joined a new world composed of advertising agencies, corporate sales personnel, merchandisers, editorial teams, and (newly minted) network executives who embraced them in a symbiotic exchange of product sales for advertising/segment minutes or page space. If the printed page had allowed earlier architects and builders to promote their skills in treatises, pattern books, and magazines, television joined popular and shelter magazines as the primary locus of publicity for developers and merchant builders in the postwar era. Because television was so new, its potential was embraced somewhat slowly. Advertisers were confident that televised broadcasts would reach a large audience, but it must be remembered that at least one-third of the nation's homes had no television sets in 1955.[11] In TV's first decade, then, and until the full potential of the medium could be realized, television executives relied on a combination of print and televised tools to support their network endeavors as they began to explore the possibilities for television's intersecting with house design, construction, and sales.

In 1974, Raymond Williams wrote of television as a mechanism for achieving "mobile privatization," bringing events, people, and images from the outside world into the safety of the private domain and facilitating armchair travel for those who did not wish to leave the safety and comfort of home. He noted that suburbia "has depended on developments in media technologies, preeminently radio, television and the telephone, to compensate for loneliness and distance, as well as to make mobilization possible." Television can bring a sense of danger into the home through sometimes disturbing images of turbulent and/or violent events, distant and near, but it also offers comfort through the continuous replay of familiar programs and images.[12] Television programs and the images in popular and shelter magazines serve as one-way windows on the world, providing far better apertures for viewing than the picture window of the house because they preclude the outsider's gaze; they allow the possibility of seeing without being seen, and all viewers are tacitly invited voyeurs. The "tiny box with the picture window" (as John Keats referred to it) thus allows the viewer to imagine a high degree of visual control and authority, despite the fact that the images presented are themselves rigidly controlled through selection by media executives, who are in turn controlled by corporate sponsors.[13] But television also allows viewers to experience a simulated or vicarious form of spatial movement, since the camera can convey depth and dimension—and the body's movements in space—in ways not possible in print. A photograph of a house or its interior remains framed, static, and fixed; a televised tour of a house, building site, or architectural model is dynamic, showing changes in scale, light, and depth that provide a somewhat greater sense of reality (and this despite the fact that television cameras equally frame and screen views).

In the 1950s, television provided a powerful tool for presenting the home, for instructing viewers in its proper design, decoration, and arrangement. Television could bring the newest officially approved ideas directly into viewers' homes with an immediacy and relative spatial realism that magazines could not imitate. Viewers could sit in their living rooms and watch as architects, designers, tastemakers, and celebrities instructed them "live" and essentially "on-site," achieving a degree of propinquity and intimacy—and therefore power—that had not been possible through print media alone.

It hardly needs stating that product manufacturers were quick to realize the sales potential of television, and products related to the building trades and home design appeared in programming segments with increasing frequency through the 1950s. Although television programs that focus on house design, home decorating, and homemaking are common today, no model existed for such programs in the earliest years. As the local and national networks worked at filling out their programming schedules, several innovative segments appeared that brought the latest images of postwar homeownership to audiences of unprecedented scale.

In the earliest years of television, local networks often experienced insufficient programming to fill daily schedules. In response, the National Association of Manufacturers began producing thirteen-minute film clips titled *Industry on Parade.* Each clip included four segments that portrayed different aspects of American manufacturing and industry. The series was considered novel enough to win the Peabody Award for public service, the Freedom Foundation Award, and an award from the Venice Film Festival. During the course of the 1950s, the association produced 428 film clips that collectively constitute a portrait of commodity production in the immediate postwar era. These clips were distributed weekly to TV stations across the country, which used them to fill gaps in their program schedules. Each clip opened with an image of a waving American flag, cementing the connections among consumption, patriotism, and national identity. Between the segments, propagandistic messages appeared that focused on the threat of communism (with American industry positioned as the antidote), inflation/the U.S. economy, and the glories of freedom and democracy. In large part, the aim of the National Association of Manufacturers in creating the series was to define aspirational goals for viewers by projecting appealing images that the imagined target audience might wish to emulate; the message was that the viewers could attain such goals if only they purchased the commodities being promoted.[14]

Several early segments featured new suburban houses as among the most desirable new commodities on the market. They also featured some of the emerging changes in home design and construction. A 1951 segment titled "Creators of Communities!" featured William Levitt and the Long Island Levittown. Produced on-site at the development and focusing on Levitt's mass-production and industrial-derived construction techniques, the segment called attention to features such as the use of a plumbing core for the kitchen and bath, the implementation of radiant heat coils in the house's foundation slab, and the use of power-driven tools that made construction easier and faster. The narrator emphasized that Levitt houses were not prefabricated—a term that connoted the negative qualities of cheapness and overconformity that might signal nonwhite and lower-class inhabitants—since construction crews moved to materials and constructed each house from unassembled parts at each site. The piece aimed to highlight the diversity of the houses (although in reality the lack of diversity among both the house types and the development's residential population remained starkly visible) and called Levittown "a community of young people," conjuring associations with forward-looking, visionary consumers who were the wave of the future.[15]

A 1952 segment on Park Forest, Illinois, likewise emphasized the youthful aspect of the suburb, which was largely populated with returning veterans. It featured a well-dressed white family of four touring the development and walking through a model home, creating for viewers the vicarious ability to move through the development's spaces without ever leaving their own homes, and perhaps the opportunity for them to make immediate comparisons between the spaces they saw on the screen and those in which they sat while viewing the segment. Calling Park Forest an experimental community that is "far more than just another housing project," with ten families per acre, the producers called the development "a town with the look, feel and sound of youth."[16] With its family including two small children—one of each gender—the segment modeled and forecast the desired inhabitants for the development and reinforced expectations about the family's composition. Although Park Forest was among the first postwar suburbs to prohibit racially restrictive covenants, allowing Jews and blacks to purchase homes in its earliest years, the film nonetheless depicted a white family alone.[17] The image of a youthful, white suburb must have had double the impact when broadcast over a new and youth-oriented device such as the television. Few things contrasted more starkly with the dwellings of earlier decades than a new house, in a new development, where everything portrayed was fresh and bright, clean, white, and itself "young." By focusing on the youthful nature of the suburbs' inhabitants, Levittown's and Park Forest's developers capitalized on the emerging youth culture and tied it to a consumer culture that was broadcast through the youngest medium of all: television.

If the segments reproduced their authority through the medium by which they were broadcast, the messages were not always consistent. Advertisers were free to purchase segments whether or not their messages stood in opposition to the surrounding features. For example, a 1952 segment titled "Pre-fabs in Production!" focused on the manufacture and construction of prefabricated houses, touting them—as Levitt had not—as a boon to consumers during a time of housing shortage. Sponsored by the Harnischfeger Corporation of Milwaukee, this segment emphasized some of the same systems implemented in Levittown: the use of power nailers, a moving production or assembly line based on methods derived from the automobile and aircraft industries, precut lumber, and so on. But in this case, the corporation emphasized the speed of house assembly combined with the savings that could be passed on

to consumers, hoping to convince viewers that prefabrication was a popular alternative for home buyers of moderate means and that it did not imply lower-class living.[18]

Whether or not viewers were attuned to the contradictory nature of these messages, they proved to be important precedents for the use of television to promote house sales. The segments provided compelling images of a particular and widely appealing version of the new American postwar life, serving as normative visions that instructed new and aspiring homeowners about the most desirable appearance for house and yard. Moreover, they were viewed not in movie theaters but in the intimacy and privacy of the domestic realm, so that viewers could immediately contrast their own circumstances with those portrayed on the small screen. The televised scenes aimed at forging a visual promise with viewers, showing them what their lives could be if they looked a certain way, purchased the right products, and lived in the right houses. Even more important, interspersed as the segments were with Cold War anticommunist propaganda, they asserted the direct connection between national identity and consumption, lifestyle and American individualism, connecting home ownership with citizenship and privilege with whiteness.

By the middle years of the 1950s, house design, its promotion, and television had become more frequent associates. For example, a fifteen-part series titled

Blueprint for Modern Living appeared on Chicago's educational TV network, WTTW, in 1956. Broadcast from the Illinois Institute of Technology, the series was intended to educate the public about current philosophies in architecture and their sociological implications. Titles for the series' episodes included "Choose Your Home," "The Architect Builds You a House," "Homes Ready Made," "The Subdivision and How It Is Made," "Remodeling," "Apartments," "City–Suburb–Country," and "How Do You Want to Live?" Programs 2, 3, and 4 were all devoted to architect-designed homes, intended to educate the public about the need to hire architects and the "compelling reasons for . . . the custom-made home."[19] A moderator discussed the merits of each house, along with an architect and the inhabitants of the house. The program on subdivisions discussed financing, addressed the ramifications of unionized labor for home construction, and offered an introduction to subdivision planning. Other programs provided advice on how to buy a house in a development and on how to evaluate prefabricated designs. The panel appearing in "City–Suburb–Country" included a sociologist and a planner along with an architect for a discussion of modern living.[20] The conversational or talk-show format of the series was well suited to television's action and immediacy, and the architects frequently used models to bring three-dimensional realism to their presentations. Although it held the potential to be more persuasive than magazine promotions, *Blueprint for Modern Living* reached only a local audience and so had a limited impact.

Similar local productions appeared with some frequency throughout the decade of the 1950s. For example, KABC in Los Angeles broadcast "The House You'll Live In" as part of its 1957 *Discovery* program, which aired on Sunday evenings. Participants included (again) architect A. Quincy Jones, William Winter (KABC news analyst), and Percy Solotoy (president of the Brown-Saltman furniture company). Herman Miller furniture decorated the set, and the program focused on the problems of manpower and materials shortages in housing, examining possible solutions. It featured Jones's design for the Eichler X-100 steel house in San Mateo, California, along with the "All Plastic House" developed by the Monsanto Chemical Corporation and a geodesic dome. Sponsored by Bethlehem Pacific Steel, Arcadia Metal Products, and Herman Miller, the program included illustrations of their products in newly designed and built houses, and it instructed viewers to write to Arcadia Metal Products for a free book titled *Planning the Home*, which included chapters on how to choose an architect, how to plan your future home, and details about mortgage and loan information.[21] Like *Blueprint for Modern Living*, the program's intent was public education, not in this case for the altruistic purposes of the dispersion of knowledge, but for the more instrumental purposes of increased sales and professional promotion to an audience potentially as large as the Los Angeles basin.

AT HOME WITH *HOME*

As locally produced and broadcast programs proliferated during the decade of the 1950s, one program had a particularly pronounced focus on the design and construction of ordinary houses: NBC's *Home*, which aired to a nationwide audience between 1954 and 1957. Hosted by Arlene Francis and Hugh Downs, the show was broadcast each weekday from 11:00 A.M. until noon, a time slot chosen so that, as network executive producer Richard Pinkham wrote, "Daddy and the small fry are out of the way at work and at school and Mama can sit down and watch us."[22] Inasmuch as television broadcast schedules "construct a domesticated public life in common for the whole population, allowing them to then feel at home in this mediated public sphere,"[23] *Home* defined a sense of security and perhaps even community and the terms by which these could be attained for the thousands of women who sat down to watch it; they were alone together and unified by their shared reception of the broadcast messages about femininity, heterosexual family life, middle-classness, and white domesticity.

In fact, *Home* was specifically aimed at an audience of women, and as such, it was intentionally modeled on women's magazines, with segments on gardening, child psychology, manners/etiquette, food, fashion, health, and home decorating. Following the structure of a magazine, Francis's title was "editor in chief" while Downs

was "associate editor." The placement of the woman in the superior role was an unusual arrangement for that time, but it was one ideally suited to an audience of women, who would put greater trust in domestic advice dispensed by one of their own gender. Francis and Downs were joined by a team of additional "editors": Poppy Cannon served as food editor (she was also simultaneously employed as a writer for *House Beautiful* and *Living* and author of the *Bride's Cookbook* and *The Canopener Cookbook*), Eve Hunter served as fashion

An advertisement featuring NBC's *Home* show hostess and "editor in chief" Arlene Francis. Note that the ad calls the program "the electronic magazine for women." *Coronet*, July 1954, 10–11.

editor, Estelle Parsons was "new brides editor" and roving reporter, and Will Peigelbeck was gardening and home improvements editor. The earliest sponsors included Alcoa, Polaroid, Dow Chemical, Dow Corning, American Greeting Card, DuPont, Heinz, and Sunbeam. The network cleverly cross-advertised these corporations' products by featuring and endorsing them on the show and then displaying them with the show's stamp of approval and endorsement in magazines.[24] With this constellation of corporate sponsors, home as a subject once again became conflated with consumption, and technology with an idealized domesticity.

Modern architecture held a place of prominence in the minds of network corporate executives, just as the International Style had become the model for corporate architecture generally by the postwar era. As Lynn Spigel has shown, both NBC and CBS "invested in modern architecture as a means to bolster their corporate image."[25] CBS did this by constructing its own "Television City" in Los Angeles, designed by William Pereira and Charles Luckman after 1948.[26] NBC did it through the *Home* show and its "House That *Home* Built" series, described below. Moreover, arts institutions of the era believed that women were the primary guardians of aesthetic culture and, as such, their target audience for marketing ventures.[27] *Home* thus served as an ideal platform for marketing modernist, postwar ideals, since it was likewise aimed at an audience of women.

Because this was a novel form of television production—indeed, nothing of the kind had appeared on national television before—the producers of *Home* relied quite heavily on the shelter and women's magazines as a model, and they continuously wove television and magazine formats together in their publicity campaigns. Magazine publishers and network executives alike grappled with the qualities that made these media distinctive, just as they sought to understand the ways in which television and magazines might enjoy a symbiotic relationship that would result in amplified communications power. In 1955, the president of Crowell-Collier publishing wrote that television was a growing fact of life and that magazines that were properly managed and edited would use television to their advantage.[28] So, too, television executives would use magazines, with their known and carefully studied formats, to their advantage. The producers of *Home* imagined television as a better form of magazine advertisement, but one that could persuade differently because of the ways in which it was viewed. The medium of television may indeed have been embedded in the message, and NBC's executives understood the potential power of live television programming, but they had not yet imagined Marshall McLuhan's now-famous adage, nor did they yet fully understand the ways in which the television production of talk shows could be conceptualized according to the medium's own particular strengths. It may be true, then, that different forms of media affect the contents of the messages being conveyed, but

FACING
Home endorsed specific products in shelter and trade magazines, such as these sponsorships for American-Standard products in the builders' magazine *House and Home* in February 1956.

Home's producers had yet to discover that particular aspect of their endeavor.

As a result, NBC advertised the show as "a woman's magazine that comes alive" using "TV's sight-sound-movement magic," and as "NBC's Electronic Magazine of the Air." The network initially had some trouble selling the concept, however, because advertisers believed that the impact of print ads resided in their relative permanence—that is, the purchasers of magazines kept them and used them repeatedly as reference tools.[29] Television just seemed too ephemeral in its earliest days, especially when many productions—*Home* among them—were broadcast as live performances.[30] As a proactive measure intended to raise advertisers' confidence, NBC mailed memos to sales staff at advertising agencies across the nation and to potential corporate clients, assuring them that "the American advertising dollar is spent better on Television" through the format of the magazine program.[31]

To reassure advertising executives, and as a supplement to the show, NBC publicized *Home* in women's magazines and created a companion magazine for the show called *How to Do It*. The magazine was to be a monthly, with a projected circulation of three million.[32] *Home*'s producers also established a long-term relationship with *Sunset* magazine that included a regular segment on the program called "*Home* in the West," which featured *Sunset* staff members presenting various ideas

and projects. Some of the topics covered in the segments were playground equipment, western landscaping, serving hot brunch on the patio, patio paving, and the proper selection of ground covers.[33] Over the course of *Home*'s four-year life span, the producers developed cooperative promotional arrangements with various print magazines. For example, in 1956 and 1957, *Home*'s staff collaborated with the publishers of *House and Home* and *Better Homes and Gardens* to sponsor a promotional event called "Homes for Better Living." An awards program that was presented at the annual convention of the American Institute of Architects (AIA), the event also became an important point of contact between NBC and the heads of major home-building product corporations, who were *Home*'s primary advertisers. As one network executive noted, participation in this event placed NBC "on an equal status with the other two shelter books in this major event in the 'shelter' field. It is a 'first' in competing media to do this."[34]

At the same time, the magazine publishers began to realize they could capitalize on TV programs such as *Home* to promote themselves. For example, Dale Olmstead, vice president of the Joseph Hicks Organization and publisher of *Popular Mechanics*, wrote to NBC to ask if the network would promote his magazine's October 1954 housing issue on *Home*.[35] This kind of reciprocity took some time to formulate, and it eventually became moot as network executives began to realize the supreme power of their medium, which only increased as the decade closed and the majority of American homes included at least one television set. Still, the first two years of *Home* were modeled on print magazines, such that the producers considered including an annual "*Home* Spectacular" that would appear on Sunday afternoons to broaden the audience to include men. This Sunday supplement to the weekday program would be, as the executives stated, "comparable to the special issues shelter magazines put out from time to time."[36]

Home became known, in part, for its groundbreaking live broadcasts from various venues and remote locations, including Chicago's Merchandise Mart and the American Furniture Mart in Chicago in 1954 and 1955. As an author in *Retailing Daily* noted, "The home furnishings industry will get what is considered its biggest promotional push in television when the *Home* show covers the market for several days."[37] In time, the show became known in some circles as NBC's "$6,000-a-minute television show," a title that referred to the advertising fees it commanded, and its producers were among the first to understand that an entire program can be, essentially, an advertisement for various products.[38] With an innovative set constructed to resemble a giant turntable that rotated to facilitate the presentation of segments on various topics and that could be captured for viewers by an overhead camera (another innovation), the producers called the stage a "machine

for selling," and they made effective use of that machine to market a wide range of products.[39] But they were equally marketing a specific lifestyle construed in terms of race, class, and gender.

As Inger Stole notes, "*Home*'s producers were explicitly determined to attract an upper-class audience, and to appeal to those who aspired to that class, stating in an early memo that they wanted to 'reach class rather than mass. . . . We don't want to alienate lower education levels. We want to keep them but attract higher types of dames in addition.'"[40] In order to set the proper terms of class aspirations, the producers selected Arlene Francis as their carefully considered ideal hostess because she possessed what they considered to be a high-class appearance combined with down-to-earth attitudes. The show had to maintain a fine balance between educating and engaging women and lecturing them, dispensing off-putting experts' advice that made stay-at-home women feel inadequate. Francis generally handled this skillfully, although her big-city ways sometimes betrayed her. For example, Francis wrote of the social hazards she sometimes encountered when she traveled for *Home,* describing a visit to a suburban community: "I tried to be what I thought was proper and wore white gloves. After the show, an apologetic but nonetheless forthright matron informed me that her town was a casual place. She explained . . . 'we never wear white gloves in the morning!'"[41] The faux

The producers of *Home* called their circular, rotating set "a machine for selling." Here is the set on March 1, 1954.
Photograph by Ralph Morse/ Time & Life Pictures/Getty Images.

pas seems slight by today's standards, but it reveals the scrutiny Francis withstood daily from her viewers. Women examined every aspect of her dress and comportment, transferring their acceptance of the hostess to acceptance of the products and ideas she endorsed. A pair of gloves, worn in the morning or not, revealed much about a woman's status and identity, and the net-

work executives keenly understood this point. *Home* therefore equally articulated the contours of middle-class, white femininity along with the promotion of its featured products. Because class and race were so closely intertwined, the program's constant display of upper-class conventions and lifestyles meant that—advertently or not—it defined gender, status, privilege, and whiteness as part of the promotion of the products the corporate sponsors paid NBC to feature.

That *Home* daily displayed a white "family" in Francis, Downs, and the rest of the staff did not mean that race was an invisible issue at the network. Several NBC programs of the period featured topics related to racism and race relations in the United States, including various episodes of *The Open Mind*, a talk show hosted by Richard Heffner.[42] And when food editor Poppy Cannon attracted some negative attention because of her interracial marriage to NAACP leader Walter Francis White, network executive Dick Weaver stood by Cannon, deciding to "risk" negative letters from the public.[43] However, her career at *Home* was short-lived. Cannon resigned in March 1954, stating that she "never felt quite at home at *Home*" and wished to return full-time to her job at *House Beautiful*.[44] Whether Cannon resigned because of racial tensions or not, *Home* remained

Arlene Francis studies a script for *Home*, March 1, 1954. Francis embodied a gender-specific ideal for the show's producers, who aimed for a hostess with a high-class appearance and down-to-earth attitudes.
Photograph by Ralph Morse/ Time & Life Pictures/Getty Images.

this is
the lady of
the house that
H■ME
built...

...and, in one day, she welcomed 180,000 people into her home.

On September 23rd the welcome mat was out early in the morning at the houses that HOME had built in 30 cities across the nation. By the end of the day 180,000 people had accepted Arlene Francis' invitation to visit and the dazed builders were sitting back counting their orders and getting ready for the next day. Since the opening there have been an estimated half million visitors—and the lines haven't stopped yet. This was the climax to HOME's year-long project that Variety called "television's most fabulous promotion"...and another tribute to the drawing power of HOME's hostess, Arlene Francis. But the builders themselves tell the story best. Here are some comments: "12,000 people viewed the home...an almost unbelievable record." Washington, D. C. "I am flabbergasted at the response...needed police direction for traffic...constant line throughout the day." Canton, Ohio. "Reaction was tremendous...the most talked about home in the area." Grand Rapids, Mich. Participating advertisers, too, are overjoyed because these houses, featuring their products, have become the number one housing attraction wherever they've been built. With renewals starting to come in for 1957, find out now, how Arlene Francis and The House That HOME Built can fit in with your plans. Your NBC Television Network sales representative will be happy to give you the full story. **NBC TELEVISION**

a show designed for a rather narrow vision of American domestic life. The pervasive whiteness of the housing market, and in all things concerned with consumer culture, meant that *Home* remained a show developed by whites for an assumed and expected generically white audience. And like the shelter magazines on which it was modeled, *Home* tried to match the expectations of that audience by articulating the terms by which viewers could realize their desires.

THE HOUSE THAT *HOME* BUILT

If *Home*'s producers and stars effectively encouraged viewers to purchase products that would improve their domestic lives and elevate their status through imaginatively constructed sets and segments, nothing compared to the marketing genius of the "House That *Home* Built." This annual project, conceived in collaboration with the NAHB and utilizing the housing expertise of C. W. Smith, who served as a consultant and was director of the Southwest Research Institute's Housing Research Foundation, ultimately involved the design of one model home each year that was to be constructed by local builders in at least fifty cities (it was originally hoped) in the United States. Since model houses would be built in most of the network's affiliate markets, the stations, as executive producer Pinkham noted, "stand to pick up local business from building trade and department stores by phasing into our plans."[45] Advertis-

ers stood to profit significantly from such a project, as did the network.

The idea for the project originated in March 1954, when a network executive, Joe Culligan, proposed that the network launch a home-building program in response to the national demand for new housing. As Culligan noted, print magazines had profited considerably from their sketch plan and building plan services, and the television show could take that idea even further. His initial conception followed the magazine model closely, such that one architect each month would develop a house plan that could be purchased by the public for 25 cents per copy, and builder's plans could be purchased for $100 per set. He imagined that a house or two would be built from the plans and the network would give the houses away as prizes in a *Home* show contest. When enough homes had been built, he envisioned a publication called *The 50 Best Homes from NBC* that would sell at $5 to $10 per copy. He even imagined collaborating with a developer, such as William Levitt, to construct an entire development of NBC homes. As a former *Good Housekeeping* staffer, Culligan had seen the success of that model—the magazine published a new house plan every month, and sales of sketch plans averaged between 27,000 and 50,000 per issue.[46]

"House That *Home* Built" (HTHB) houses could be (and were) constructed by any builder who paid the nominal fee for plans, which also entitled the builder to take advantage of the promotional activities *Home*

FACING
An advertisement featuring Arlene Francis promoted the first "House That *Home* Built" series in 1956.
Variety, October 17, 1956, 30–31.

Arlene Francis is joined by R. J. Canavan (National Association of Home Builders), C. W. Smith (*Home*'s housing authority and director of the Housing Research Foundation of the Southwest Research Institute), and architect A. Quincy Jones to present a model of Jones and Emmons's design for the 1955 "House That *Home* Built" to NBC's viewers. *Pacific Architect and Builder,* April 1955.

provided. Builders invested their own money in their projects and paid for them in their entirety as speculative enterprises. They had to agree only to use products produced by *Home*'s commercial sponsors, unless given advance permission otherwise, and to advertise and promote the houses according to NBC standards.[47] The NAHB's role was to commission the architects for the project; to make complete house plans available to builders who wished to participate; to screen applications from builders to ensure that "only those who will work to the highest standards will be participating in this project; to provide advice and council to *Home*; and to provide *Home* with the promotion and publicity facilities of the NAHB." Thus the NAHB functioned essentially as a liaison between network and builder.[48] In 1955 the NAHB selected the Los Angeles firm of A. Quincy Jones and Frederick Emmons (Jones and Emmons) as the first HTHB architects. New York architect Eldridge Snyder served as the 1956 architect, and Bruce McCarty of the Knoxville, Tennessee, firm of Painter, Weeks, and McCarty became the final architect in the series in 1957.

The Case Study Houses sponsored by *Arts and Architecture* magazine were, of course, an important parallel to the "House That *Home* Built." The Case Study House projects similarly bound house design and construction to the media and to manufacturers, likewise using the houses themselves as tools for multimedia publicity.[49]

But unlike the Case Study Houses, which remained largely singular experiments that never reached a mass audience, the HTHB houses were relatively more numerously constructed (if still quite limited in number) and made available to the middle-class public. Unlike the homes produced under the aegis of *Arts and Architecture* magazine, they were not conceived as isolated "case studies" but were instead truly intended for mass consumption, even if that was not the eventual reality.

For the first house, Jones and Emmons designed a three-bedroom, two-bathroom house with seven rooms in 1,600 square feet of space. Priced between $17,500 and $20,000, the house was both larger and more expensive than most ordinary middle-class buyers could afford in 1955.[50] But *Home*'s target audience was a cut above the ordinary, so the design matched the producers' hoped-for demographic. Still, promotional articles claimed that the house was designed to meet the needs of the average American family. An open living room/kitchen area in the center of the plan divided the bedrooms from an all-purpose room and the garage. Floorplan "innovations" included a central kitchen work island and dining table, Arcadia aluminum-framed sliding glass doors and glass walls in the kitchen, placement of the laundry between two of the bedrooms, a

Arlene Francis with the model for the house designed by A. Quincy Jones and Fred Emmons for the 1955 "House That *Home* Built." This view of the model reveals the house's connections to outdoor spaces and its structural system. *NAHB Correlator,* October 1955. Copyright 1955 by the National Association of Home Builders of the United States. All rights reserved. Reprinted by permission.

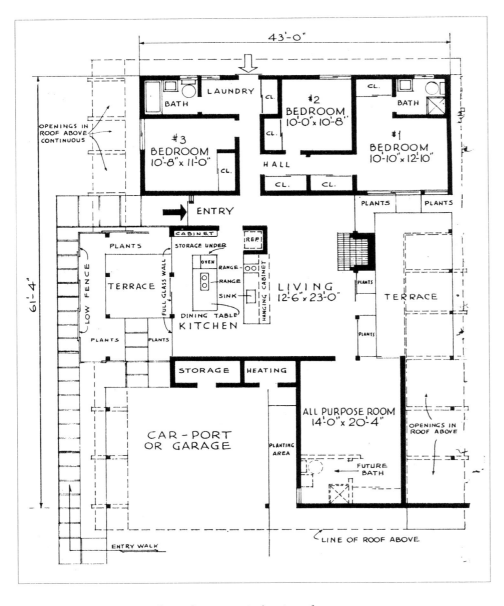

43'-0"

61'-4"

OPENINGS IN
ROOF ABOVE
CONTINUOUS

LAUNDRY

BATH

#3
BEDROOM
10'-8" x 11'-0"

CL.

CL.

#2
BEDROOM
10'-0" x 10'-8"

CL.

CL.

HALL

CL.

CL.

BATH

#1
BEDROOM
10'-10" x 12'-10"

ENTRY

PLANTS

PLANTS

PLANTS

CABINET

STORAGE UNDER

REF.

PLANTS

TERRACE

OVEN

RANGE

RANGE

SINK

FULL GLASS WALL

HANGING CABINET

LIVING
12'-6" x 23'-0"

TERRACE

LOW FENCE

DINING TABLE
KITCHEN

PLANTS

PLANTS

STORAGE

HEATING

CAR-PORT
OR GARAGE

PLANTING
AREA

ALL PURPOSE ROOM
14'-0" x 20'-4"

OPENINGS IN
ROOF ABOVE

FUTURE
BATH

ENTRY WALK

LINE OF ROOF ABOVE

ABOVE AND FACING Plan and axonometric drawings of
the Jones and Emmons house designed for NBC's 1955
"House That *Home* Built." *Pacific Architect and Builder*, April 1955.

Holly forced-air gas furnace, and a Western-Holly automatic gas built-in range and oven in the kitchen island. The house was frankly modern in appearance, which was typical for the Jones and Emmons idiom, with a low-pitched roof, vertical redwood exterior facing, and a carport.[51] Trellis-covered terraces lined the two long sides of the house, visually increasing the appearance of the home and suggesting space for outdoor living. Jones and Emmons included an all-purpose room at the opposite end of the plan from the bedrooms and separated from them by the living room, thereby providing a space with the potential to become a fourth bedroom or a children's play space separated from the adults' bedroom area. To accommodate regional climate variations, the architects explained, the roof overhang could be shortened or lengthened to provide more or less shade.

As a *House and Home* article indicated, "Mail received from some of the estimated 3½ million housewives who watch *Home* each day varies from 'A nice seaside shack' to 'I can't wait until June to see it.'" By April 1955, twelve builders had requested plans to build the house in Kansas City, Denver, Chicago, Oklahoma City, San Antonio, New York, San Francisco, Detroit, Buffalo, Knoxville, Los Angeles, and Milwaukee.[52] However, only nine houses had been built by the originally set deadline of June 4, 1955, a delay caused in part by the slow process of receiving FHA and VA approval for insurance on loans. Moreover, some architects hesi-

tated to build the project because they considered it too contemporary in style, even though, as Jones noted, there was nothing in the design that had not been implemented for at least ten years, and the house was far less radical in its design than the houses the team produced for developer Joseph Eichler in California. Still, by July 1955 architect Donald Drummond had sold his Kansas City model and planned to build more; architect Irvin Blietz had sold two in the Chicago area and had four more under construction. NBC planned to have at least twenty-nine of the houses built in time for the September 10 initiation of that year's National Home Week.[53]

In 1956, Eldridge Snyder designed three models for the HTHB, two of which were grander than the 1955 model. No plans for these models are available for our examination, but small renderings of the exteriors appeared in *House and Home*'s June 1956 issue. In keeping

with overall housing trends, Snyder's designs were somewhat more conservative than the Jones and Emmons model from the previous year. It is possible that NBC executives wanted to present a variety of design styles to their audience, but in choosing more traditional-appearing houses, they may also have been aiming to avoid the kinds of delays they experienced with the more aesthetically progressive Jones and Emmons design. Despite their horizontality and generous glazing, Snyder's houses did appear somewhat more conventional, perhaps also responding to the slowdown in the housing market after 1954, which sparked a trend toward conservatism in some new housing developments. The smallest, known as the "Celebrity," featured three bedrooms and two baths in 1,385 square feet. This model was designed to fit on a 60-foot lot. The "Aristocrat" contained the same number of bedrooms and bathrooms, but included a fireplace and family room in 1,695 square feet of space. The "Spacesetter"— the name perhaps a deliberate play on *House Beautiful*'s well-known annual "Pace Setter" houses—was a split-level with five bedrooms, three bathrooms, and a laundry room in 2,085 square feet. Again, this was far larger than most ordinary houses at the time. Snyder's plans included large areas of glazing in the living room that opened to rear gardens and terraces; "luminous plastic ceilings to give extra daylight in the kitchen, baths,

Photographs of built examples of the "House That *Home* Built" designed by A. Quincy Jones and Fred Emmons. *NAHB Correlator*, October 1955. Copyright 1955 by the National Association of Home Builders of the United States. All rights reserved. Reprinted by permission.

and entry hall; sound absorbent partitions isolating sleeping rooms. Equipment included indoor and outdoor barbecues adjacent to the fireplace; recessed and revolving TV installations; and built-in Hi-Fi chambers with loudspeakers throughout the house." For this second project, however, the network changed one policy: it decided not to announce the prices for the houses on the air, so that builders would not be committed to those prices in advance. By the time the project was announced, thirty-six builders had already received approval to construct models around the country.[54]

The HTHB for 1957, designed by Bruce McCarty, consisted of two models. "Plan A" occupied 1,460 square feet, and "Plan B" was somewhat larger at 1,600 square feet. Both represented a return to relative modesty after 1956's largest model. Each plan could be constructed with various alternatives. A builder could choose to construct the house with or without a basement, with a garage or with a carport, and using cost-saving components construction or standard framing techniques. The builder could also select from alternate window arrangements and a variety of exterior cladding materials and choose from among various arrangements on the lot. In both plans, the eat-in kitchen backed up to either one full or two half bathrooms that formed the core of the house and divided public from private spaces. Three bedrooms occupied one side of both plans, while a living

Architect Eldridge Snyder created three alternative models for the 1956 "House That *Home* Built": the "Aristocrat," the "Celebrity," and the "Spacesetter." *House and Home,* June 1956, 114.

An illustration of the house designed by Bruce McCarty for NBC's "House That *Home* Built," 1957. Courtesy of the Wisconsin Historical Society Archives, WHi-25951.

room and family room occupied the other. Enclosed outdoor garden/terrace areas separated the house from a detached two-car garage. In "Plan A" the garage included space for a heater and storage; in "Plan B" a work space occupied the back portion of the garage. "Plan B" also included a second story that sat over the back portion of the house (over the bedrooms) and included a large recreation room, storage area, and space for the heating unit. Both plans included extensive outdoor terrace areas, including an optional "bedroom porch" off the bedrooms in "Plan A" and an enclosed entrance courtyard in "Plan B." Both plans included a children's sandbox at the rear of the terrace, located off the kitchen and accessed through sliding glass doors. Deep overhangs projected from the roof over the rear terrace to provide shade, and a covered walkway connected the house to the garage.

The exterior rendering portrays a house not dissimi-

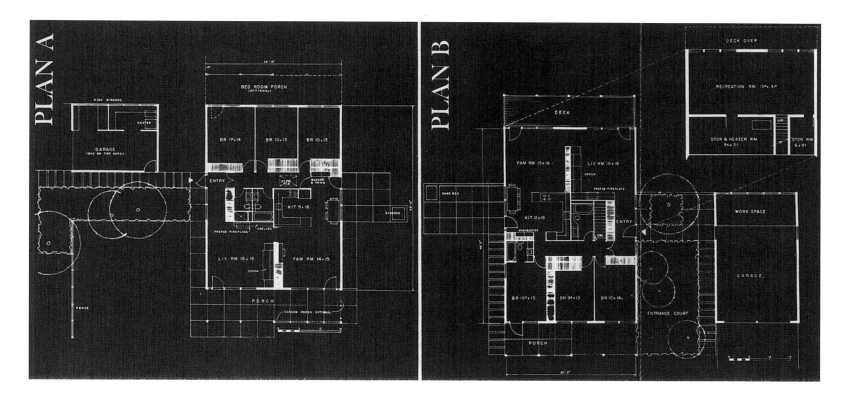

Two plan alternatives for the house designed by Bruce McCarty for NBC's "House That *Home* Built," 1957. Courtesy of the Wisconsin Historical Society Archives, WHi-25950.

lar to those designed by Jones and Emmons for Joseph Eichler, indicating a return to a slightly more modern design with this project. The brochure for the house proclaimed that the design's features "correspond to the home planning principles agreed to at the Women's Congress on Housing"—an important point considering the demographics of *Home*'s audience. The brochure listed features that were actually common to most architect-designed houses of the period and included all the virtues prescribed in the shelter magazines and tastemaking literature: separation of the house into activity zones using a utility core system, generous distribution of storage space that would also provide sound abatement, insurance of privacy at the entry and orientation of the house away from the street, sequestering of bedrooms away from primary areas of activity, a kitchen placed to allow supervision of play yard and outdoor areas, a family room conveniently placed near the kitchen and with access to the outdoors, and central plumbing and ventilation. But it also included "extras," such as landscape plans by Robert Zion, and decorating layouts and color plans supplied at no extra cost to builders.[55]

As these descriptions of the houses indicate, there was actually nothing particularly innovative about the HTHB houses—their designs were no more novel than those found reproduced in the popular and shelter magazines. In fact, they adhered quite strictly to the ideas and images that were simultaneously being widely promoted in the printed sources—they essentially conformed to what we might see as a canon of design for such houses. Each house included features deemed essential to postwar domestic life: privacy for family members from outsiders and from each other within the house, the promotion of an indoor/outdoor lifestyle, low-maintenance design, spaces that promote leisure and recreation, plenty of storage space, and so on. What made the houses seem special was the medium through which they were represented and displayed to the public. Television, for the first time, brought the house design and construction process to life for an estimated 3.5 million viewers, all watching at the same time.

The earliest promotional spots included the architects displaying a half-inch scale model of the house. Remote telecasts from the construction sites made it easy for viewers to monitor the progress of the HTHB, a technique that was used with greater frequency for the 1956 model constructed on Long Island.[56] As the HTHB projects became established, *Home* included regular monthly features or "editorials" on the projects that focused on design, building, and decorating. For example, in 1957 HTHB features were scheduled from February through the end of September, when the houses were to open across the country. In February, viewers met the architect, Bruce McCarty, who discussed the features of the house. In April, the landscape design was previewed, using rear projection of the house in the background of the studio set. In May, *Home* visited the AIA convention and used the HTHB as an example of good building practice. Later that month, the landscape architect Robert Zion appeared to discuss the landscape plan in greater detail. Throughout the summer months, *Home* focused on the HTHB with segments on teamwork between design professionals, design of the house for both adults' and children's needs, entertaining in the home, the convenience and comfort of the bedrooms and bathrooms, cooking in the HTHB, good manners at home (a segment that featured HTHB room dimensions sketched onto the studio floor so that various scenarios could be enacted within them), storage, the convertible room, and, finally, the much anticipated "open house" across the country, with segments produced at several houses in different locations. Between these segments, daily plugs for the HTHB included builders' names, which were repeated again at the final open house segment.[57]

When the houses were finally scheduled to open, segments appeared more frequently, especially during the week leading up to the Saturday open house event. Each of *Home*'s spots during that final week allowed local stations to cut away on cue to announce the location of the local HTHB and to give credits to product manufacturers.[58] *Home* continued coverage of the HTHB for the ten days following the Saturday national open house, which was the duration for which builders agreed to keep their houses open to the public. Since the network could not control what individual builders put inside the houses, it encouraged all the builders to cooperate with local department stores that could provide interior design and furnishings, with the promise that the stores would receive local promotion as well.[59]

HTHB home openings were also planned to coincide with NAHB and AIA events. In 1957, for example, HTHB homes opened around the country at the beginning of the NAHB's National Home Week, and the network sent staff members to the NAHB convention in Chicago in 1957 in order to promote that year's HTHB.[60] One of the show's top sponsors, American-Standard, maker of plumbing fixtures, had a booth at that convention promoting the HTHB as part of its strategy to try to get more builders to participate in the project.[61] Such promotional campaigns were deemed necessary after

the first project failed to meet expectations. The editors of *House and Home* initially expected that seventy-five builders would construct the 1955 HTHB,[62] but by July they reported that only nine houses had been built in nine cities by the opening-day deadline of June 4. The slowdown was in part caused by delays in FHA and VA loan approvals, but it was also a result of some builders' resistance to the "contemporary aspect of the plans."[63] However, three of the houses had been sold—two in the Chicago area and one in Kansas City. Network records indicate that twenty-one builders had committed to constructing the 1955 house, in locations that spanned the country.[64] Although, again, no records indicate the precise number of HTHB houses that were constructed, the network apparently deemed the project successful enough to warrant continued support; it remained a part of *Home* until the program was canceled in 1957.[65]

Indeed, the network clearly saw the HTHB as a point of pride. As network executive Pat Weaver wrote:

The "House that *Home* Built" is an example of a project designed to push television beyond its normal dimensions of information and entertainment. The "House that *Home* Built" is an example of a woman's service program actually making a definite creative contribution to better living in America. . . . During the past year when the "House that *Home* Built" of 1955 was presented to the public, builders actually told us that its reception by the public changed their thinking toward what homebuilders wanted in their local areas. Thus, the "House that Home Built" is an excellent illustration of why service programs on television today represent a brand-new force for good in this country.[66]

As another network staffer noted, "To build a house for television is as radical an innovation as the Home set was a year ago."[67]

Still, increased advertising revenue remained the primary goal. To that end, NBC developed a lengthy list of prospective clients for involvement with HTHB projects. The list included U.S. Plywood, Reynolds Metal Company, Pittsburgh Plate Glass, Libbey-Owens-Corning, Portland Cement, U.S. Gypsum, Armstrong Cork Company, Congoleum, Goodyear Tire and Rubber, Bakelite, DuPont, Republic Steel Corporation, American Radiator and Sanitary, Stanley Tools, Delta Tools, Masonite Corporation, and many more.[68] Ideally, advertisers could be signed up for a full year, their products featured regularly as the house was being developed and constructed.[69] The 1955 HTHB campaign had been successful enough that network staffer Murray Heilweil could write in 1956, "From where I sit, the 'House that Home Built' promotion, 1956, is red hot," and the program's success was spilling over to boost advertising sales for the *Today* and *Tonight* shows.[70] In fact,

the "House That *Home* Built" attracted $2.5 million in advertising revenues from manufacturers of home equipment, building materials, and appliances.[71]

The April 17, 1957, episode of *Home* featured Hugh Downs presenting the HTHB for that year as "one of the most exciting and efficient developments in modern living." It represented "the answer to the needs of the average sized family by combining comfort, quality, and convenience," and Downs promised viewers that they would be able to experience the houses "firsthand" when they either watched the program or visited one of the houses in their local communities.[72] With 3.5 million housewives watching each day, and with television's live action and compelling images, *Home* could portray the HTHB as the right house for viewers, convincing them that it represented core American values in its appearance, forms, and products, and that it was the most exciting house of its kind in the nation.

Television has largely been intended and imagined as a relatively equal-opportunity sales device, its messages available to anyone in range of a receiver. But the HTHB, like all the houses presented in shelter and popular magazines, became yet another component in the constellation of images of whiteness and privilege connected to domesticity and homeownership, another representation of American identity rooted in class and, at least notionally, skin color. There is no evidence, of course, that *Home*'s producers, actors, and sponsors, or the builders and architects who designed and constructed the HTHB projects, consciously considered that middle- and upper-middle-class whites alone would qualify for loans for the HTHB houses. Nor is there recorded evidence that they ever considered anything but a generically conceived mode of living; to the contrary, they actively reproduced a standard and a norm that viewers already expected to see. *Home* provided a daily opportunity for a televised prompt to the recursive practice of identity formation that viewers could interpret through lessons in taste, home decorating, gardening, cooking, and even manners. In many respects, the program was no different from the print rivals it sought to emulate so closely, imagined as their "electronic" alternative. However, magazines could be picked up or put down, traded or lost, saved or discarded. They could be flipped through at random or studied in detail. In short, the mode of viewing magazines remained unpredictable in terms of time, duration, and circumstance. *Home,* in contrast, could be viewed only when it was broadcast, its presentation—and therefore, to an extent, its reception—more tightly controlled. The program's audience sat primarily at home, watching a better, tightly controlled, scripted, and more desirable world constructed before their eyes in what appeared to be real time. That the viewers could observe the process of house construction made this world all the more palatable, since they could imagine themselves conducting

the work that was presented in easily digestible stages by reliable workmen in sanitized conditions. In short, the apparent "reality" of the presentation exponentially increased the power of the multilayered messages being conveyed—something NBC's producers came to realize and on which they surely capitalized. *Home* was thus both like and unlike its print predecessors, and it serves as a fascinating example of the ways in which the producers of live television programs came to understand the power and potential of the medium and the talk-show or conversational format in the first half of the 1950s. If the medium was the message, it took NBC's producers a few years to understand the ramifications of that axiom for this particular genre.

Despite *Home*'s relatively short life span, the show's success can be measured by the numbers of similar programs that followed and that exist on cable television today. Formats have changed, but the essential concept for such programs remains the same. With an audience measured in millions of viewers, *Home* provided solutions to private domestic problems for a large segment of the television-watching public. As John Hartley has written of such programs, they "treated mundane subjects seriously, ordinary life with respect . . . all with authentic, show and tell simplicity." Each segment focused on improving everyday life, displaying a "mystical belief in the ability of (capital intensive) technological inventions to solve social problems." As a product that was explicitly invented as a domestic medium, television became the ideal tool for promoting, defining, articulating, and disseminating the terms of domesticity that satisfied the known aspirational goals of an audience, a medium that encouraged viewers to "invest in homes as sites of privatized consumption." This "capitalization of the home" was a recursive phenomenon in which television became ever more essential to specific forms of domesticity, just as homeownership became increasingly important for television's expansion.[73]

If strong correlations existed between print and television in the formulation of *Home*, and if the messages conveyed about domesticity and identity were consistent between the two forms of media, then why examine *Home* at all? What can we learn by studying *Home*'s representations of housing and domesticity that we cannot learn by examining other visual and textual representations of domesticity and housing in the national print media alone? Since a primary objective of this study is to understand the ways in which cultural iconographies are and have been formed in the United States, and to examine the impacts of such iconographies on American cultural formations, what matters here—and what I hope this chapter helps to demonstrate—is the accretive impact of multiple media forms operating simultaneously, even if their modes of operation differ in ways that may appear either great or somewhat slight. If we want to understand (as I do here) a

politics of representation and the mechanisms by and through which Americans recognized, embodied, and lived specific notions of the self in space and then recursively re-created those notions through countless repeated engagements with the media they both influenced and viewed, we must understand the multiple means by which those mechanisms operated. Television producers, like magazine editors and advertisers, projected broadcasts at the audiences they understood to be most likely to have the economic capacity to purchase whatever was being sold, and audiences largely understood that they participated in a culture of drastically uneven social and economic opportunity. Then as now, they knew, and yet they watched; they knew, and yet they emulated; they knew, and yet they purchased. And in performing these acts of watching and emulating and buying, viewers participated again in the reflexive process of creating and re-creating the social structures projected on the screen. If my analysis here seems to level the differences between print and television media, it is because those producing various forms of social knowledge imagined their project from a largely shared set of beliefs about the deeply intertwined connections among race, class, gender, and housing in the postwar United States.

Television helped to define and sustain racial identities that were bound to space and place; through its various programs it helped perpetuate ideas about who belonged in suburbia and for whom postwar houses were intended. Persons who were not identified as white were mostly absent from early television programming, just as they were largely absent from representations of house and home.[74] *Home* and the "House That *Home* Built" were therefore two additional entries into the constellation of representations that situated the postwar house as belonging to white American citizens positioned within the middle or upper-middle class. With its emphasis on a gendered mode of consumption and its presentation of houses that fit the requirements for a specific brand of postwar domesticity, *Home* became an ideal vehicle for the reinforcement of ideas about the rightful occupants of postwar houses and, by extension, the rightful owners of a specific brand of privilege.

8

DESIGNING THE YARD

Gardens, Property, and Landscape

When they first purchased their Van Nuys home in 1955, Rudy and Eva Weingarten must have found the design and maintenance of the garden surrounding their house somewhat puzzling. As European immigrants who had previously lived either in shared housing with relatives or in rentals, the prospect of taking care of front and back yards was both exciting (this is ours, we can grow whatever we want) and troubling (we know very little about gardening or horticulture, we are very busy with our own business and don't have much time or extra money to devote to gardening, we want to observe neighborhood gardening conventions). Their corner lot afforded the usual front yard and backyard, and they also had a side yard to contend with. Like many other immigrants and first-time homeowners, they were concerned with appearances, and this made them astute observers of the surrounding landscape. A lawn accompanied by foundation plantings of shrubs near the house with a few carefully placed ornamental trees was the model they observed in their surrounding neighborhood. A high wooden fence enclosed the backyard, which was broken into three portions: a large area of concrete patio that sat between the house and the detached garage, a smaller area of lawn bordered by trees and shrubs, and a long narrow space along the side of the house that served as a laundry-drying area and was closed off with its own separate gate so that it could not be observed from either street or garden. Eva and Rudy had only a few desires for their garden: Eva liked the smell of

FACING
Front lawns in Levittown, Pennsylvania (*detail, see p. 296*).

gardenias and she wanted citrus trees; Rudy claimed an allergy to geraniums and professed affection for cactus. Because both Rudy and Eva worked outside the home six days a week at Weingarten Electronics and had little time for yard maintenance, they hired a gardener to take care of their yard as soon as they could afford to do so, a man who came to clip, clean, mow, mulch, and tend every other week or so. As with the interior of their home, nothing in their yard was out of place. The lawns were always mowed, the edges trimmed so that an inch or so of soil appeared between the lawn and the adjacent concrete paving or sidewalk. All plants and trees were clipped or pruned so that some space appeared between most shrubs and trees in the yard. Their garden also exhibited all the major characteristics of postwar residential gardens: it was nonproductive (except for the orange tree), fenced for privacy, required little maintenance, contained a paved terrace or patio located off sliding glass doors that allowed for a degree of indoor/outdoor living, included spaces for children's play, and emphasized the division of spaces instead of horticultural variety. In many respects, it was a quintessential postwar garden.

At their new suburban Long Island residence in 1952, Sam and Eve Goldenberg noticed that "every time a family moved in, the neighbors gathered to celebrate and help out. A new homeowner would drag a little shrub out into the sandy dirt and begin to dig, and all of a sudden a crowd would gather, laughing and congratulating, offering tips and assistance." They described their yard as follows: "If there was any incongruity in a weathered corral-style fence set so close to a fancy wrought-iron railing, itself only a few feet from the neighborhood's first cast-iron rendition of a beaming, black-faced, high-booted jockey with a lantern in his hand, then none of the other Harbor Isle settlers chose to point it out." By 1958, the Goldenbergs noted that—like Rudy and Eva Weingarten—the neighbors had enough financial security to hire gardeners to do this work for them.[1]

The Goldenbergs' experiences were shared by millions of first-time homeowners in the postwar era. Their collective lack of knowledge about the design, implementation, care, and maintenance of home grounds spawned entire industries that included advice columns in newspapers and magazines, television segments, the nursery trades, retail garden centers, and, of course, the residential design–build landscaping industry.[2] These industries arose from market forces that catered to the same culture of consumption and display outlined in previous chapters. But outdoor spaces took on special importance because the front yard served as a significant component (along with the house facade) of the public face of the private family, and the backyard became—like the house interior—a private realm for the use of invited guests and family members.

That the Goldenbergs recalled both the corral-style

and fancy wrought-iron fences and the cast-iron, black-faced jockey ornament is not surprising. Lawns, along with the plantings, fences, and ornaments owners chose for their yards, served as symbols of status and identity. Could one imagine objects that more potently conveyed the symbolic power of white property ownership than a corral fence, with its connotations of a tamed and colonized frontier, and the lawn jockey, with its references to black slavery?

Just as an examination of cabinetry and storage systems served in an earlier chapter to elucidate the ways in which the accumulation and display of domestic goods and artifacts participated in the production of the ideological field related to notions of postwar homeownership and occupancy, in this chapter I aim to address the ways in which residential landscapes and their visual and textual representations participated differently but contributed in equal measure to the production of that field. By examining the ideals for postwar residential gardens that were promoted in various media outlets, and by looking at what homeowners typically implemented, this chapter will demonstrate the particular ways in which ideas about garden design and gardens themselves contributed to the formation of the multiply constituted cultural iconography of domesticity. In short, this chapter examines the forms of cultural work performed by residential landscapes and their representations. An exploration of the significance of specific design elements—the lawn and its material culture

artifacts, postwar garden technologies, indoor/outdoor design, and fences—reveals another facet of the complexly formulated iconographic field that continually and mutually reinforces an image of domesticity that is overtly classed and raced.

It is important to add an examination of gardens to this study for at least two reasons: First, residential gardens are a ubiquitous element of ordinary residential environments, and they occupy a significant amount of developed land. To study the single-family postwar house on its own lot without studying the parts of that lot not occupied by the house itself (the portion I will call the *garden* or *yard* in this chapter) would be to ignore a significant portion of the residential domain. Second, and as I and others have written elsewhere, landscape is among the most potent conveyors of ideological content, because its long association with ideas about nature and the natural render its appearance as seeming inherently benign, vacant of meaning, and (contrary to everything good landscape histories now tells us) completely without political import. Landscape appears and is largely understood by the general public to be little more than verdant background, as "softening" for the hard edges of architecture, or as a zone for recreational activities that, increasingly in recent decades, includes the creation of productive gardens. As such, landscapes and gardens are powerful conveyors of ideological content if we consider ideology according to conventional ways of understanding its operations.

If, as I noted in this book's introduction, Žižek's notion of ideological cynicism suits my analysis because (simply put) it allows us to see the ways in which ideology can be apparent and works anyway, landscape may prove the exception to Žižek's theory. Magazine readers and television viewers have always understood, to varying degrees, the persuasive intentions inherent to those media; that is to say, and using today's terminology, readers and viewers have always possessed at least some degree of media literacy. They knew what the magazines and television programs were doing, and even if they may have often read passively and unquestioningly, they nevertheless understood that both media forms operated in a rhetorical field intended to sell and to persuade about both products and ideas. They also, as I have asserted, largely understood the content of the messages being conveyed (that is, they consumed and understood the ideology). Household inhabitants, on the other hand—and those who aspired to be homeowners—tended then as now toward much lower levels of spatial literacy than media literacy, because the spaces that surround us daily can so easily lose their foreground qualities as they become the backdrops to other activities (such as reading and watching). The notion that either house or garden spaces, and ideas about those spaces, might contribute to widely held conceptions about the identities of homeowners and rights to homeownership is neither popularly under-stood nor commonly discussed and evaluated. Houses shelter us while we sleep, eat, drink, laugh, love, rest, and learn, but they also convey clear messages that are enmeshed in ideologies about capitalism (for example) as their sizes and styles (again, for example) express status. Gardens provide space for relaxation, fresh air, sunshine, and recreational and leisure activities. Yet even when they are especially well manicured, gardens and their representations can be difficult for untrained eyes to imagine as anything more significant, anything more than pleasingly aestheticized spaces—especially as forces that contributed to the production of a postwar landscape that was rife with unequal housing opportunity—so the argument can seem strange even if it also resonates with our cultural knowledge in ways that make it starkly familiar. By looking here at lawns, fences, garden ornaments, and ideas about outdoor leisure and indoor/outdoor lifestyles, I hope to bring the garden into focus as another component in the politics of representation that contributed to the history of postwar housing in the United States.

It is important to note that not all postwar homeowners were without experience when it came to single-family dwelling and gardening, and some came to their postwar houses with considerable previous experience. For example, Becky Nicolaides has demonstrated that prewar residents in the immigrant, working-class community of South Gate, near Los Angeles, possessed homes that "were humble, yards were productive, streets were dusty, and families made do." The gardens of these 1920s and 1930s homes could be conceptualized in terms of their value as productive spaces. Ordinary postwar houses, however, with their largely ornamental yards, were imagined primarily as leisure spaces that were not depended upon for contributions to the family's meals. Chickens and vegetable patches disappeared, and the status of domestic animals changed "from meat to pets." As Nicolaides states: "Yards had become sites of rest and relaxation, barbecues and lawns, cala lilies and hydrangeas. They took on the middle-class suburban function of a decorative barrier to the outside world, denoting suburban respectability." Working yards became ornamental gardens and, like the houses they surrounded, became a variably valued commodity in the real estate market. This shift, Nicolaides asserts, came about as the result of homeowners' need for "sheer survival to protect their rising affluence and identity as white homeowners. . . . Ultimately, a new concern with race emerged to dominate local political commitments."[3]

The shift from imagining the residential yard in terms of its productive value to regarding it as property valued largely for its ornamental qualities—as decorated land that served in part as a signal for the decorated interior of the home it surrounded—is key here. Historically, the removal of land from production in favor of its aesthetic arrangement—usually in the form of an ornamental garden—has been a sign of wealth and status. That King Louis XIV, for example, or the owner of a large, enclosed, eighteenth-century English estate such as Stowe removed large tracts of fertile land from production and used them instead for aesthetic and nonproductive ends indicated to all within sight (or all who viewed painted, printed, or delineated views of these gardens) that the owner was indeed powerful and wealthy beyond measure. The eighteenth-century English precedent is the more relevant of the two examples because the Arcadian pastoral of the so-called picturesque landscape, with its false naturalism, sweeping lawns, irregularly placed clumps of trees, and serpentine paths and waterways, ultimately became the large-scale model for American suburban landscapes from the nineteenth-century onward. That this aesthetic has a deep historical connection to England's eighteenth-century enclosure movement is also highly relevant. As the section in this chapter on fences makes clear, the privatization of landscape and the detachment of land from productive purposes has deep connections to the formation of suburban residential space in the postwar United States.

When the model moved to the United States through early suburbs such as Frederick Law Olmsted's Riverside, Illinois, in 1868, the form was not divorced from its symbolic content. The picturesque suburb dominated by manicured, nonproductive lawns simply transplanted the aesthetic of the English estate to a scaled-down set of lots.[4] The lawn surrounding each suburban house became the symbol par excellence of the property value of the residence, even if eventually situated on a 60-by-100-foot lot by the postwar era instead of an immense estate composed of many thousands of acres. Because the new postwar housing market was almost exclusively available to whites, the lawn also became a green symbol of exclusion, a horizontal boundary between sidewalk and home, and a sign of affluence that not only produced nothing but also consumed water, energy in the form of fossil fuels, and labor. The lawn stood further as a cipher for the psychological distance between city and suburb, as the symbolic buffer between those who belonged and those who did not. Again, the Goldenbergs' description of the cast-iron, black-faced lawn jockey is not surprising, since such racist ornaments only reinforced the powerful iconography of the lawn—and the house it surrounded—as a white space. I will discuss both the lawn and such ornaments below, but my point is that connections made between the residential yard and identities formulated in terms of race and class are easily forged and have been for centuries, even if they are seldom discussed. Given the exclusionary practices prevalent in postwar housing markets, those connections became even more charged than they had been in previous decades.

DESIGNING THE YARD

Readers of the landscape design literature that was aimed at design professionals and, to some extent, a more general audience in the postwar era might easily have encountered books and articles that featured residential landscapes created by a group of landscape architects who were interested in forging a modernist style of garden for the postwar era. Books and articles either written by or featuring the work of landscape architects such as Thomas Dolliver Church, Garrett Eckbo, and James Rose reached the public to varying degrees, but the impact of their designs published in the professional design press meant that their ideas reached anyone who studied landscape architecture in the postwar era and therefore even trickled down into the nursery and garden center industries that served suburban homeowners.[5] Thomas Church's 1955 book *Gardens Are for People* sold thousands of copies, its publication in multiple editions a sign of its nationwide popularity over several decades.[6] Readers, it seems, were interested in such gardens; homeowners were likely at least occasionally exposed to them. Yet despite the widespread publication of the modernist designs these landscape architects advocated, the vast majority of postwar homeowners fashioned their residential landscapes almost astylistically, conforming quite rigidly to a fairly narrow set of formal and horticultural parameters. Creating innovative garden forms and spaces appeared to matter little to postwar homeowners, while a range of other concerns mattered far more: tidiness, order, the creation of an appearance of leisure as opposed to labor, conformity, and even the maintenance of a relatively quiet residential surrounding. All of these became residential landscape imperatives because they matched expectations based on what homeowners understood and experienced around them and because their repetition in built form assured participation in the cultural formations surrounding white middle-class homeownership.

When it came to designing the yard, developers and homeowners alike recognized that ornamental gardens could help mitigate the raw, just-built look of many new houses and developments. Planting the lot also, and importantly, reduced the amount of dirt and mud tracked into the home. Although new suburban homeowners understood that the empty space surrounding their homes stood as a silent call to gardening action, and that inaction could arouse the antipathy of neighbors, not everyone enjoyed the activity. Suburban developments across the United States may have hummed with the sound of lawn mowers on Saturday afternoons, but it would be wrong to assume that every homeowner engaged in gardening because of a passion for experience in nearby nature. Instead, evidence suggests that many new homeowners had to be encouraged to work in their gardens and that the primary motivation came from concerns for status maintenance and the maintenance

Color photo and black-and-white inset were taken from same corner of Hedden yard—two years apart

A 60-foot lot can be transformed into a place for outdoor living on a grand scale with

PM's Landscaping Plan for the Small Yard

"*PM's* Landscaping Plan for the Small Yard" in *Popular Mechanics* included all the key components considered necessary for the postwar backyard. It is fenced and requires little maintenance, with an area of hardscape, an uncluttered storage area, and space for children's play.
Courtesy of *Popular Mechanics*; originally published in the April 1957 issue.

of property values. *House Beautiful's* gardening editor, Joseph Howland, recognized this problem, and he equally understood his obligation to the magazine's advertisers: he had to find a way to get readers to buy from the nurseries, landscape architects, and garden suppliers on whose revenue the magazine relied. In 1949, Howland wrote a memo to an executive at the Conrad-Pyle Rose Company in which he stated:

> You wonder about the effectiveness of the national magazines in creating new gardeners. The majority of gardening articles published by the magazines and newspapers do just about nothing toward creating a new garden market. Most are written by ardent gardeners for other equally enthusiastic hobbyists. . . . Most of these people have no interest in becoming ardent gardeners, but they would be willing to spend money to have the yard planted if they were convinced that by so doing they would increase their enjoyment in living, raise their social position with their neighbors.[7]

The memo shows that Howland clearly understood—as did readers—the links between residential gardening practices and status formation and maintenance. By 1951, Howland's appeal had shifted slightly, yet he still recognized that many homeowners were not natural gardeners and that they would instead respond to those very same status interests. In an appeal to garden supply retailers, he wrote that they should try to sell gardening as a fun hobby that likewise reflected well on the gardener's status:

> Sell fun. Sell pride. Sell a hobby. Don't waste selling space and time on pious talk about gardening to save money. Gardening is expensive. Don't get off the subject by talking about gardening to grow better tasting food: with rare exceptions your customer can buy better stuff than he can grow. Sell gardening simply as a way to have a whale of a good time.[8]

Gardening, then, could be marketed to postwar homeowners as both recreational and status enhancing—as an expensive leisure activity (a bit like golf). In both cases, the sales pitch was linked explicitly to the value of the residential lot. The promotion of gardening for food production, which would frame the yard in terms of its use for the family table, was dismissed outright. That Howland noted the wide availability of relatively inexpensive food is not without significance, since food prices dropped noticeably in the postwar years. Still, the quality of supermarket produce declined precipitously and in synchronization with the rise of U.S. agribusiness, so homeowners might have been inclined to grow their own, tastier produce at home had sentiments against the appearance of extensive vegetable patches—and the work required to maintain them—in suburban residential settings not been so pervasive.

Homeowners who did plant vegetable patches did so only in their backyards. If displaying a wartime victory garden conferred patriotic associations on its owner, those status benefits largely disappeared with the end of the war itself. Front yards, like living rooms, were strictly for the maintenance of appearances. Their visibility made them easy targets for the evaluative glances of neighbors, and this very visual prominence conveyed both a power and a symbolic significance to these spaces that backyards never held. In his 1963 book *Class in Suburbia,* sociologist William Dobriner noted:

> The suburbs are open and spacious, in comparison to cities, and because of that life in the suburb is more visible. The visibility principle is a characteristic suburban feature: suburbanites can observe each other's behavior and general life style far more easily than the central city dweller. . . . Gardening is a big thing in the suburbs. Suburban gardening is compulsive, and it has, it seems, all kinds of insidious linkages to the status structure. People may garden because they feel they have to; there is a standard to be lived up to. As one overcommitted suburban housewife finally admitted, "I really hate gardening; we both do." . . . This suburbanite and her husband struggle with their garden work be-

cause they feel they have to—"it is the thing to do." And there is no escaping the omnipresent eye of the community. One may not like to garden, but—since gardening is a characteristic of this suburb—garden you must. A sloppy and inept garden is visible. An untidy and poorly conceived and executed garden can be seen and judged by one's neighbors.[9]

Dobriner's observations reveal more than just a distaste for the panoptic quality of everyday life played out in neighborhoods dominated by the simultaneous and conflicting impulses of a voyeuristic, picture-window culture and one increasingly concerned with residential privacy. In this passage Dobriner neatly delineated the links among social pressures, gardening activity, tidiness, and status identity. Gardening became a social imperative for suburban homeowners, its aesthetic dimensions defined primarily by neatness, lack of disorder, and the containment and concealment of artifacts related to the ongoing operations of family life. Maintaining an uncluttered yard was of paramount importance. Landscape architects such as Stanley White conveyed the importance of designing and maintaining orderly home grounds by instructing postwar homeowners to avoid a cluttered appearance by not using too many different varieties of plants. He advised that they should design their yards to avoid "haphazard" effects, just as he warned about "cheap construction that results in shabbiness." He admonished his readers to keep children's toys out of the way by making sure that children are "provided with a corner where they are permitted to dig and build and keep their stuff."[10] For White, as for many other designers and tastemakers, the most important thing was to avoid anything that could appear polluted, cluttered, fussy, or untidy, because, as detailed in previous chapters, the vocabulary associated with cleanliness served as a crucial aspect of the lexicon of white, middle-class identities.

That the garden was to be as neat and tidy as the domestic interior was not enough. It also had to be quiet. Noise was its own kind of pollution that could likewise connote the chaos of urban lifestyles and overcrowded, multifamily dwellings from which postwar suburbanites had retreated. *House Beautiful*'s Joseph Howland therefore planned a September 1954 feature that focused on the creation of quiet gardens, and he made a list of "irritating experiences that cause mental exhaustion" that should be banished from the garden. These included "unpleasant sounds," "monotony," "intrusion by people, odors, winds, animals," "over-ornamentation," and "busyness."[11] That various kinds of noise emanating from either the private or the public sphere—noises that intruded in unexpected or undesirable ways into the daily lives of domestic occupants—could have implications for social identity in a residential context is also not unique or new to the postwar era. As Dell Upton has shown, for example, various kinds of sounds played particular roles in the identification of personal and family identities in antebellum American cities, helping people think about and understand where they and others belonged (both physically/spatially and socially) in urban life in the new republic. And those understandings were inflected by notions of both race and class such that specific kinds and levels of noise came to be associated with working-class neighborhoods, black neighborhoods, and so on. To distill Upton's complex argument to its essence: cacophony was linked with darkness, savagery, whereas quiet and/or sounds deemed harmonious had associations with the upper classes and whiteness.[12] Similarly, the authors of postwar articles about the domestic sphere insisted that maintaining a quiet residential surrounding was paramount for the preservation of a neighborhood that conveyed the appropriate messages about the status of the occupants.

Clean, quiet, well-maintained, orderly properties held their property value and signaled the identity of the occupants—a significant fact for real estate agents and appraisers as well as for owners. Real estate appraisers' manuals clarify the fact that a residential landscape's appearance affected the sale value of the home, even if (and as explained below) they seldom attached a particular value to landscape improvements or regarded sophisticated forms or spaces as contributing to a property's value. As recently as 1981, one such manual instructed novice appraisers: "The social dimensions of the neighborhood are also noted by the analyst. He or she observes the extent of the similarity in the obvious life-styles of the owner-occupants and renters of the residential neighborhood. The single-family dwellings commonly show by means of the exterior architecture, the landscaping, the upkeep of the lawn, lawn equipment, and the parked cars, and boats in the driveway the socio-economic standing and general life-style of the household members."[13] Landscape, then, served and continues to serve as a crucial cue for establishing the market value of a home, even when the appraisal includes qualitative judgments about such vaguely defined and racially coded notions as lifestyle. If lifestyle could be part of a property value assessment, so could each part of the garden, and appraisers even debated the best way to assign monetary values to trees on a given property.[14]

With the emphasis on an orderly appearance, storage became as important outdoors as it was indoors. Garages and carports served significant roles as containers—for cars, certainly, but also for the numerous items that families formerly stored in the attics and basements many postwar houses lacked. Indeed, the builders' magazine *House and Home* recommended building outdoor bins to store garden furniture, bikes, fishing rods, skis, tools, and play equipment.[15] Storage walls therefore were integrated into the structural frameworks of carports, and enterprising homeowners built deep cabinets into the rear walls of their garages,

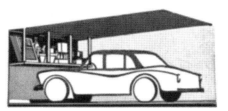

Space over hood of car can be utilized for storage in a minimum garage.

Storage units form one wall of this carport. Raised sidewalk and roof of carport provide a pleasant covered outdoor area.

This double garage is arranged so that there is a raised laundry area along the wall which opens into the kitchen. Storage units are built into the opposite wall. Two 9-foot garage doors are used for convenience.

These illustrations showed homeowners how to make the most of the space afforded by carports and garages. In addition to installing carport storage walls, homeowners were encouraged to create storage space that would fit over the hood of the car. *Garages and Carports,* Small Homes Council Circular Index Number C5.9, *University of Illinois Bulletin* 51, no. 78 (July 1954): 2, University of Illinois Archives.

Instead of a double garage, this house has a carport and a single garage. The carport also serves as a covered outdoor living area. Storage space is provided in one wall of the carport.

taking advantage of the empty space above the hood of the car.

The garage, however, also frequently became the first space colonized during remodeling efforts, since it could easily be converted into an extra room that, if properly designed, could be used for storage, a workshop, a place for an extra freezer, and for recreation.[16] A neat and well-organized storage area therefore became an important design element for the ordinary yard. Garbage cans, clotheslines, garden tools, flowerpots, firewood, children's toys, and outdoor furniture were all to be concealed when not in use.

The use of fences to conceal clotheslines was not new to the postwar period. In the first quarter of the twentieth century, the Olmsted firm advocated the construction of six- or seven-foot-high fences to conceal laundry dried outdoors, as the firm's designers believed it was uncivilized to hang clothes to dry outdoors where neighbors or strangers could see them.[17] Increasingly, the practice of hanging laundry outdoors to dry became associated with lower-class living, especially as ownership of an electric clothes dryer became a sign of affluence in the 1950s. Storage sheds to contain family necessities became a popular solution, as did fences (in some locations) or screens that concealed drying yards and service areas, which, as spaces of domestic labor, had to be concealed.[18]

Impediments to furthering the modernist aesthetic in the landscape went beyond the concerns for confor-mity (having a tidy, clean, orderly yard) noted above. Although rarely considered as a force in the determination of midcentury landscape design, the FHA played an important role in determining the appearance of ordinary residential landscapes. The lending agencies that offered mortgages insured by the FHA provided little incentive for spending on outdoor improvements, especially those that might appear distinctive or nonconforming. The FHA's 1952 *Underwriting Manual* indicated that the outdoor space, or the setting, for a dwelling contributed to the visual appeal of the property as long as it conformed with the neighborhood character and was characterized by "simplicity . . . freedom from complexity, intricacy, and elaborateness . . . the avoidance of excessive embellishment, of features and motifs which compete for attention . . . of immoderate variation and inappropriateness in the use of materials." Gardens, according to the FHA, were to exhibit "refinement, sometimes termed 'good taste,' characterized by freedom from ostentation, and by restraint in design."[19] To this end, the *Underwriting Manual* included general recommendations for driveways, walkways, lawn construction, and planting that were to contribute to the maintenance of "a continually presentable neighborhood appearance."[20]

The FHA continuously updated and revised its recommendations regarding the evaluation of residential landscaping throughout the 1950s, and thus became a largely unnoticed but important force in the determina-

A typical garden in front of
an ordinary postwar house,
Harrisburg, Pennsylvania,
circa 1950s. J. Horace
McFarland Collection, Archives of
American Gardens, Smithsonian
Institution.

tion of trends in residential landscape architecture. By
1956, the FHA recommended that trees be planted on
new housing lots for "screening of objectionable views
and providing adequate shade"; this amounted to at
least one tree per lot, "preferably at the southwest side
of the house." The FHA also preferred yards that included foundation planting—more for tenant-occupied
homes than for owner-occupied—"to soften the line between house and ground." A new recommendation that
year included "finish grading of the entire lot" that was
"suitable for lawns or plant growth or such that it can
be made suitable by the owner without removal of large
quantities of soil or importation of large quantities of
new soil." The FHA further mandated that "topsoil, existing trees, shrubs, and ground cover be preserved during construction whenever possible."[21] But as was true

with its policies for house design, the FHA underwrote the predictable, the traditional, and the conforming. For example, the indoor/outdoor spatial innovations promoted in the national design press and in shelter magazines (examined below) were, like other design innovations, considered a lending risk. Homeowners who planned to install the modern landscape designs promoted in the magazines therefore risked refusal of mortgage insurance from the biggest residential housing underwriting agency of the postwar era.

Moreover, to install an innovatively designed garden was to risk an expenditure that lacked a certain assignment of its contribution to the property value, since such a garden could not be clearly appraised as a home improvement. And the so-called outdoor rooms so frequently touted in the magazines were not included in calculations to determine the square footage of houses, so they fell outside the FHA's minimum house definitions.[22] Although the magazines and design literature promoted modern landscape improvements as cost-effective, real estate appraisers seldom placed significant value on particular landscape enhancements of any kind and made no distinctions among landscape styles in their assignment of value. Although mentions of "miscellaneous land improvements" appear in assessors' real estate manuals from the period, neither the delineation of specific forms nor the integration of inside and outside spaces figured in their calculations. They also worked then, as now, from the so-called principle of conformity, which taught that "where the houses within a neighborhood have a sameness of design (meaning the exterior style, the construction materials, the floor plan, and the equipment within a structure), there will be stabilization of values." Conversely, "where this sameness does not exist, the value of the incongruous dwelling will not be equivalent to its cost, nor at a price level proportionate to the other houses which surround it."[23] The house was to appear as a component in a visually unified, if bland, neighborhood. Carefully measured planting, combined with proper grading and the placement of paved walks, driveways, and patios that were in keeping with the rest of the neighborhood, could add value to a property. Unusual landscape designs were not, therefore, encouraged. Although some appraisers recognized the need for changed methods of evaluation that would accommodate greater variation, particularly regarding the relationship of a house to its site, most agreed that uniformity and conformity ensured retention of value. For homeowners, conformity also ensured continued social acceptance within their neighborhoods and reassured the homeowners and those around them about their participation in the privileges afforded by conformity itself.

Finally, it should be noted that, along with the FHA and real estate appraisers, retail plant nurseries and garden centers influenced the form and design of ordinary postwar gardens. The popularity of gardening in the 1950s and the increased number of people owning houses with gardens led to the rise and proliferation of the now well-known garden center, a retail environment that provided the ease of one-stop shopping for garden needs, generally located in a shopping center with plenty of parking. Then, as now, such centers carried plants, seeds, pesticides, peat, power mowers, plant foods, pots, garden furniture, paving materials, lighting fixtures, and more. Garden centers served as exhibition spaces as well—they were places to get both materials and ideas, and many employed landscape designers who sometimes provided planting plans without charge to customers who purchased the centers' products.[24] But no matter what their garden centers' nurserymen recommended and no matter what they read, most homeowners managed to install only the most rudimentary garden elements: a small concrete patio, lawn, fence, and a few shrubs and trees, creating grounds that conformed with those of their neighbors and that signaled a very precise and carefully controlled set of identity signifiers. As long as residential grounds were kept tidy, well organized, and reasonably quiet (although the happy noises of children at play seems to have been acceptable), and as long as they required minimal maintenance for their upkeep and afforded an image of leisure, the formal contours of the site and the lack of any discernible modernist stylistic characteristics mattered little.

THE INDOOR/OUTDOOR IDEAL

The April 1958 issue of *Popular Mechanics* included a fifteen-page article by Illinois do-it-yourself builder Tom Riley titled "We Built a Family Room Outdoors."[25] In it, Riley proclaimed outdoor living part of "an informal way of life that started on the West Coast" and was sweeping across the entire country, affecting the lives of millions of people through proper design of their homes and yards. According to Riley, the ideal space for outdoor living immediately adjoined the house and afforded pleasure for the whole family, serving as an outdoor family room.[26] To achieve this usable exterior space with its frank associations with a West Coast lifestyle, which was already mythologized through popular film and texts, Riley recommended building a patio roof to allow overhead protection from the elements—his was made of Flexboard, a lightweight corrugated-asbestos cement panel developed during World War II. He also recommended closing the patio at one end for privacy and wind protection, situating the terrace off the dining room, with its sliding glass doors, and constructing built-in patio benches that could be used to support a portable TV or hi-fi. For night use, Riley recommended installation of an outdoor lighting system and construction of a barbecue cabinet made out of plastic-coated plywood.[27]

Likewise, designer Wayne Leckey published his plan in an article titled "Unusual and Modern Ideas for

Jaunty roof of the outdoor room was designed to let in more light; it protects grill, tables, even the TV

Family Room Outdoors

Strategically placed lights glamorize room at night as guests sit around fire in "wishing well" grill

Living Outdoors" in the April 1959 issue of *Popular Mechanics*. The article was part of the magazine's fourth annual outdoor living section, described as "16 pages of ideas for converting your back yard into an open-air 'room' where you can bask, dine and spend the summer in true lazy-man style." Appealing to their readers' patriotism, the editors called living outdoors "America's outdoor way of life." Leckey showed readers the advantages of an enclosed and sheltered patio with a fence constructed from new materials such as lightweight Diamond-Rib aluminum or colorful panels of translucent glass fiber such as Filon and Corrulux, which provided diffused light. "Privacy," he wrote, "is the best reason for having a fence around your patio. Screened from direct view of neighbors or passersby, you will feel less like a fish in a bowl and free to relax in solid comfort." He also assured readers that the fence would serve as both windbreak and decoration if properly designed. Leckey recommended the installation of an outdoor barbecue and patio lighting with bubble units and 75-watt reflector lamps, and he provided instructions for proper wiring and circuitry.[28] His recommendations took advantage of the waterproof bulbs, heavily insulated wires, and low-priced fixtures that were all postwar innovations and that encouraged outdoor living on patios after dark.[29]

Riley's essay and Leckey's design were similar to countless others that appeared in popular and shelter

"Family Room Outdoors." Courtesy of *Popular Mechanics*; originally published in the April 1958 issue.

magazines, build-it-yourself manuals, and the taste-making literature in the United States between 1945 and 1960. They list all the elements considered necessary for a well-designed postwar garden, emphasizing privacy, climate control, indoor/outdoor living, and recreational leisure, all achieved through the use of newly developed materials and technologies.[30] During that period, the popular and design press repeatedly promoted indoor/outdoor spaces and lifestyles, asserting the need for an uninterrupted flow of space, vision, and activity between house and garden.[31] As the editors of *Fortune* magazine wrote in 1955: "The combination of children, limited interior space, and ample outdoor space has driven even the least outdoor-minded suburbanites to integrate their houses with the outdoors. Instead of the old-time porch and terrace and hedged-in lawn, the suburbanite now takes pride in his picture window, open patio, his barbecue equipment."[32] Taste-makers imagined the ideal as a requisite aspect for all new houses of the period, regardless of their geographic location and including the ordinary middle-class dwellings that were not typically designed by architects and that were priced for middle-majority buyers who could afford houses in the $7,000–$14,000 range. Along with the mandate for privacy, indoor/outdoor living became a pervasively publicized design imperative.

Concern for the integration of interior and exterior long predates the postwar era—it can be traced to at least as early as the ancient Roman villa in the Western world, and as a design impulse it can be traced throughout architectural history and around the globe, though it appears to varying degrees and executed in a range of forms. In the second half of the nineteenth century especially, writers ranging from Harriet Beecher Stowe to William Morris in England and Morris's arts and crafts style followers in both his own country and the United States extolled the virtues for mind and body of bringing aspects of the outside in and the inside out. Whether arranging branches and flowers for interior ornament or creating sleeping porches that provided the benefits of fresh air, bringing the healthful aspects of nature inside and encouraging the movement of children and other family members outside into the sunshine became a moral as well as an aesthetic priority.[33]

The primacy of the indoor/outdoor ideal in the literature (both popular and professional) related to design accelerated after the end of World War II. The increased availability of low-cost aluminum-frame sliding glass windows certainly helped facilitate the construction of houses that included an ease of visual and physical access between house and garden, and the availability and installation of such windows in homes in turn created increased demand. Sliding floor-to-ceiling windows could be made to appear as movable transparent walls—a modernist ideal that held particular appeal for design professionals—rather than simply as transparent doors. As Richard Pratt wrote in the *Ladies' Home Journal* in 1945: "Windows after the war will let a house hold the garden closer in its arms. The barrier between indoors and outdoors will be broken down by glass, and you will be able to sit in your living room and look right into the flowers. This will create a very happy and healthful condition."[34] The patio was to be an extension of the indoor living space, separated from it only by a transparent glass wall, and in the best examples, the colors of the garden were to be designed to blend with those of the living room.

We might also understand the push toward indoor/outdoor living as Lynn Spigel has analyzed it, as connected to a growing 1950s culture of televisuality, one that increasingly expected to see the outside world brought into the home through a glass screen that, however small, eradicated distances by bringing the world into the living room. Spigel notes: "Television meshed perfectly with the aesthetics of modern suburban architecture. It brought to the home a grand illusion of space while also fulfilling the 'easy living,' minimal motion principles of functionalist housing design." She observes that 1950s sitcoms often featured domestic settings with large picture windows that incorporated an illusion of a view to outside spaces and that became central to the mise-en-scène:

> It was not just that these domestic interiors imitated the popular architectural ideal; they also fulfilled expectations about television that were voiced in popular discourses at the time. That is, the depic-

tion of domestic space appears to have been based in part upon those utopian predictions that promised that television would provide for its audiences a view of outside spaces. Thus, the representation of the family's private interior world was often merged with a view of public exteriors, a view that was typically a fantasy depiction of high-priced neighborhoods not readily accessible to television's less affluent audiences.[35]

Another dimension of television's importance to this book's argument, then, is that it helped to both create and fulfill expectations about the relationship of interior to exterior domestic space, even when the connections to the outside world afforded views to sites very distant. As noted in chapter 4, it also shaped perceptions and public discourse about domestic privacy, since the desire for a view outside and the immediacy of the images of world events that television provided seem to have created a more pronounced desire for personal privacy—for protection and for the exclusion of intruding forces—within the home.

Part of the appeal of and for postwar outdoor living (and not simply viewing) also derived from the reduced size of newly constructed homes. Living in these homes, which often lacked basements and attics and were designed with minimal storage space, many postwar families complained of the crowding they experienced daily. Space was at a premium in the typical

1,000-square-foot house, and as the shelter and popular magazines suggested, the yard could serve as a much-needed extra room, complete with hardscaped play areas for children, storage facilities, and areas for outdoor dining. As early as 1939, a *Life* magazine article explained that the land around the house should be "useful in the enjoyment of living," a concept the author called "the most important thing that has happened to landscape gardening in the past 20 years. . . . Americans now begin to value the garden as a space for living . . . an extra room which is an integral part of the house."[36]

Perhaps it is not surprising that this ideal appeared repeatedly in the pages of *Sunset,* the magazine of western living that came to define the California lifestyle. Yet magazines promoted the ideal—which was well suited to the California climate—nationwide, despite climatic differences. Almost twenty years after *Life's* feature appeared, landscape architect Harold Klopp told the readers of *Popular Mechanics* that a proper plan for a 60-by-113-foot lot in the Chicago suburbs included a patio for outdoor parties, play space for children, and storage space for bikes, garden tools, and patio furniture. Klopp stated, "The major difference between modern landscaping and the older, formal landscaping

Small houses and large families created the need to use outdoor space as an extra room of the house, as shelter magazines urged their readers to do. In this illustration, indoor/outdoor living is explicitly connected to the creation of a futuristic (and therefore modern) "American" identity. Joseph E. Howland, "The Garden of the Next America Is an Outdoor Room," *House Beautiful,* April 1953, 148.

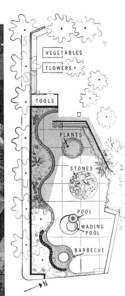

*The Garden
of the Next America
is an*
Outdoor Room

It's furnished with plants, of course, plus stone, wood, concrete, water, texture, and the

By Dr. Joseph E. Howland
House Beautiful's Garden Editor

An example of planting that created an indoor/outdoor connection at the home of architect Cliff May, circa 1950s. Photograph by Maynard L. Parker. Courtesy of the Huntington Library, San Marino, California.

is . . . that modern landscaping integrates the house and yard."[37]

But how were middle-class homeowners to achieve such an integration of house and garden? Was the creation of an outdoor room through the implementation of a semi-enclosed terrace or patio space adequate? The shelter magazines were filled with photographs and drawings that portrayed the strategies architects used to link inside and outside in more expensive homes. In most examples, such an integration could most read-

ily be achieved through the creation of horizontally defined connections, facilitated primarily through the implementation of aluminum-framed sliding glass doors and large areas of glazing that achieved a visual porosity from both within and outside the home. In addition, some of the best known of the architects' strategies included paving or flooring that remained the same inside and out, areas of planting that appeared to be continuous from outside to inside and occurred at grade, ponds that appeared to flow from patio to living room beneath a large sheet of glass (one of Richard Neutra's design devices), and a retaining or exterior wall that became an interior wall, without a new surface treatment or change in material. The extensive use of outdoor lighting, made possible through the postwar innovations of waterproof bulbs and heavily insulated wires as well as increasingly affordable fixtures, facilitated nighttime use and twenty-four-hour views to the garden. The availability of inexpensive, lightweight, portable outdoor furniture that was fade resistant and easily cleaned was one element of outdoor living that nearly everyone could afford. Sales of lawn and porch furniture nearly tripled between 1950 and 1960.[38] Climate-control devices such as heating coils embedded in terrace paving were also intended to allow the extended use of outdoor space.

Ideas about creating indoor/outdoor connections usually focused on the use of transparent walls and of other materials that forged visual connections, as noted above, but in some cases the outdoors literally came inside. The California architect A. Quincy Jones, for example, believed that 25 percent of a house plan should be devoted to landscape spaces dispersed throughout the interior, existing as planting areas at grade. Jones favored such solutions because they offered a way to bring the garden inside and to erase the apparent boundary between exterior and interior, but also because vegetation planted against areas of glazing reduced condensation and served as safety markers that kept occupants and their guests from walking into the glass itself. Jones's idea had its critics, however. For example, a letter writer responding to Jones's published design for *House Beautiful*'s "House of the Year" in 1950, which also received the AIA's award for the best small house for that year, pointed out how difficult it would be for a homeowner to water and otherwise care for the house's numerous small interior garden patches.[39] Although many owners of ordinary houses might have enjoyed such indoor gardening, few would have been willing to relinquish the required square footage, especially when faced with more pressing needs, such as storage. Moreover, bringing soil/dirt into the house went against all the aesthetic norms prescribed for white, middle-class identities, as did the fact that these small interior garden beds increased the amount of maintenance labor required in the home—work that had to be performed

Architect A. Quincy Jones broils porterhouses in the living room of his home. Note the amount of vegetation planted inside the house. *Life* magazine, September 5, 1955, 93. Photograph by Eliot Elisofon/Time & Life Pictures/Getty Images.

on hands and knees rather than comfortably seated at a desk or in a chair. As noted in a previous chapter, such forms of labor were deemed unsuitable for white women, who were, whenever possible, to remain seated or comfortably standing when performing housework.

If more sophisticated houses that appeared in magazines such as *House Beautiful* consistently aimed to persuade readers about the value of indoor/outdoor designs, *Popular Mechanics*, which targeted a do-it-yourself audience of working-class and middle-class homeowners, embraced this ideal as fully as did the more upscale magazines. In the October 1959 issue, for example, the magazine introduced its "*PM* Indoor–Outdoor House" designed by Chicago-area architect Edward D. Dart. The magazine's editors asked Dart to "design a house with no 'indoors' or 'outdoors.' . . . Design a house with

"*PM* Indoor–Outdoor House," Edward D. Dart, architect, 1959. The tree growing through the roof in the entry court and the extensive amount of glazing are the primary elements that created a sense of indoor/outdoor living in this house. The architect called the central room of the house a "porch."
Courtesy of *Popular Mechanics*; originally published in the October 1959 issue.

House itself lends privacy to the pool. On this side of the home there are no visual barriers between the indoors and outdoors, thanks to the huge expanses of glass. Below, front of house has big block of masonry contrasting with low roof no real separation between the two; a house that flows from Dad's easy chair right on out to the patio, diving board or rose garden. At the same time, insure privacy where it's needed." In response, Dart designed a 1,555-square-foot house intended to be built anywhere in the United States—a remarkable response considering the climatic extremes in many parts of the country that render impractical a house without separation of indoors and outdoors. Nonetheless, Dart created an open plan for the public areas of the house using large areas of glazing in every room except the kitchen to eliminate visual barriers. An outdoor atrium with a tree growing through its sheltering roof served as the main entrance to the house and as a signal for the indoor/outdoor concept inside, since the covered atrium space was simultaneously inside and outside.

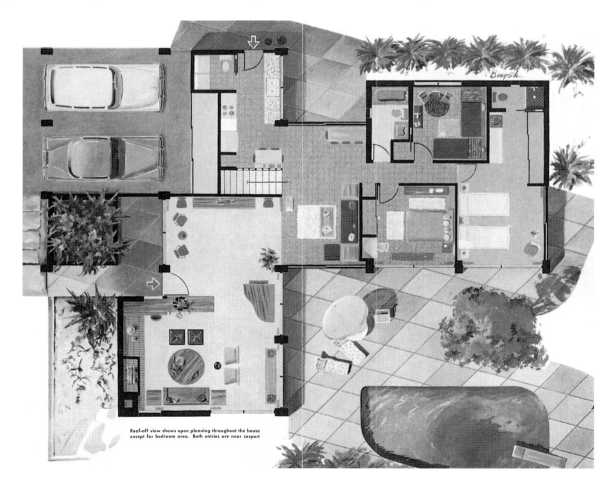

Roof-off view shows open planning throughout the house except for bedroom area. Both entries are near carport

A rendered plan of Dart's "Indoor–Outdoor House" intended to illustrate the plan's porosity. Courtesy of *Popular Mechanics*; originally published in the October 1959 issue.

A family room/porch in the center of the house divided the public from the private areas, and both walls had large sliding glass windows. One of these opened to the front of the house, with its play and service areas off the kitchen; the other door opened to the garden/patio/pool area. With both doors open, what Dart described as a "porch" was formed, a semi-outdoor space through which the family members must pass in the course of their daily routines and that served as a buffer between the home's public and private zones. Such spaces were not particularly uncommon in warmer climates, but they were decidedly rare in Chicago and its suburbs. Moreover, the design was not particularly innovative for 1959; most of the ideas and forms Dart integrated had been promoted in design and shelter magazines for at least a decade. Nevertheless, the editors of *Popular Mechanics* considered the design fashionable enough to place it as the headliner in their annual home section that year; they called Dart's design "a home ideally suited to informal living. And who doesn't want to live informally, inside and out, these days?"[40] Indoor/outdoor planning and idealized notions of informal living are key to understanding the popularity of the ideal across geographic space, because they contributed to an image of leisure that was essential to the maintenance of specific race and class identities—the same ideas about informality and leisure that made picnics on the living room floor seem inexorably linked to white, middle-class identities.

Despite the widespread advocacy of indoor/outdoor design to a range of economic groups, relatively few ordinary houses included such features. And despite Tom Riley's claim that the trend to outdoor living had affected the lives and dwellings of millions of people, the majority of postwar homeowners never attained the frequently published ideal, living instead with something far more conventional. The ordinary middle-class house typically sat squarely on its lot, surrounded by an area of lawn, the site developed to include a walkway and a driveway accompanied by foundation plantings, various shrubs, and occasional fruit and shade trees. That postwar houses largely followed this model is not surprising when one considers that lawn and foundation planting became an established model for U.S. residential landscape design during the second half of the nineteenth century. By the beginning of the twentieth century, it had become the accepted pattern, and it remains so today. As Christopher Grampp has noted, the elevated Victorian homes of the nineteenth century, which were raised above grade to accommodate flooding and central furnaces, displayed a significant amount of foundation to the street, sometimes as much as six feet. Plants became a popular way to conceal these exposed foundations and to beautify front yards. This design solution was then promoted repeatedly in popular and shelter magazines, as well as by writers such as Frank Jesup Scott, whose popular 1870 book *The Art of Beautifying Home Grounds* advocated such foundation plantings. As

Grampp has noted, "The style became so popular that it was difficult to find a garden design book from the 1880s up until World War II (and to a large extent to this day) that did not encourage it tacitly or overtly."[41]

If landscape designers, nurserymen, and authors advocated foundation and lawn planting as the accepted best-practice standard for suburban home grounds, the developers of postwar suburbs helped establish it as a suburban canon, since some suburban developers designed and planted front yards and backyards themselves. For example, in Levittown, Pennsylvania, Abraham Levitt designed a template that he applied to all the yards in his development. As with Levitt house construction, assembly-line techniques and postwar machinery helped workers complete the task of planting the thirty-four pieces of shrubbery on each lot. Each house was provided with a seeded lawn and three fruit trees chosen from among plum, apple, peach, pear, and crab apple. Ford tractors seeded each lawn, and a posthole digger dug holes into which shrubs were placed by hand.[42] By designing and planting each Levittown lot, Abraham Levitt established a norm for the appearance of suburban home grounds in his development of more than seventeen thousand houses. Because the development was widely publicized in shelter and popular magazines, images of this template appeared nationwide. In Levittown, Pennsylvania, which was restricted to whites until August 1957, the Levitt model of landscape

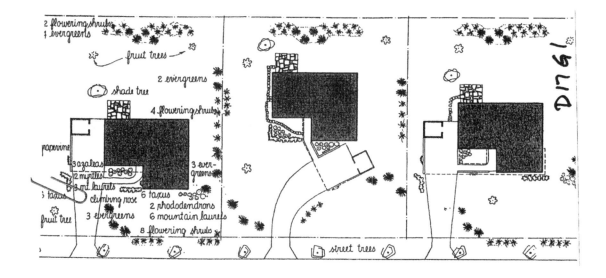

Planting plan for houses in Levittown, Pennsylvania, circa 1953. The plan indicates the typical limits of residential planting found in suburban developments in the postwar period. Courtesy of the State Museum of Pennsylvania.

View of planting in front
of a house in Levittown,
Pennsylvania, circa mid-1950s.
Courtesy of Bucks County Free Library,
Levittown Branch.

design became the accepted image of the white, middle-class domestic landscape. Largely without visual distinction, the placement of lawns, shrubs, and trees in Levittown yards existed within the historical and aesthetic continuum of the picturesque mentioned above, an aesthetic rooted in an iconography of race and class. The Levitts certainly did not invent this aesthetic, but the repetition of their planting design throughout their development and its repeated representation in print media contributed to the formation and acceptance of an entrenched model of acceptable suburban garden design practice that largely persists today.

Thus the high-style models promoted by the magazines and by other tastemakers were overshadowed by the example of the vast American landscape itself and by the practical realities faced by first-time homeowners given the limitations of the houses they could afford to purchase. Because many postwar houses were built on concrete slabs on grade, a flow of movement to the outdoors was easily achieved, since most steps could be eliminated in basementless houses. This automatically provided ready access to a small patio, a portable barbecue, and garden spaces. Even modestly priced houses that attempted a somewhat more "modern" look seldom extended the spatial or design innovations to the outdoors. Certainly the idea of an outdoor room and the integration of indoor/outdoor spaces appealed to many, but a number of practicalities—financial constraints among them—hindered the adoption of these design strategies at the scale of mass housing.

In addition, adoption of the indoor/outdoor ideal suffered, predictably, from geographic specificity. With relatively few regional exceptions, the presence of humidity and insects dramatically curtailed the extensive use of outdoor terraces. In her 1946 book *If You Want to Build a House*, Museum of Modern Art curator Elizabeth Mock wrote optimistically of the potentials of pesticides, noting that "even in mosquito-bitten New Jersey people are beginning to discover that an unscreened terrace is delightful for at least three months of the year, and if the new insecticides fulfill their promise, outdoor dining will become a national institution rather than a sporting event."[43] But she also acknowledged that "unless you build in a specially favored climate, you will also face the nuisance of insect-screens,

a problem which will be decently solved only when the necessity is removed by some such miracle as D.D.T."[44] Writing before the publication of Rachel Carson's pivotal *Silent Spring* (1962) and before the dawning of the environmental movement in the United States, Mock saw only that although screens were a practical solution to the problem, they interrupted the visual flow between house and garden, diminishing the ideal of a

The backyard of a typical slab-on-grade postwar house, accessed via a sliding glass door. Courtesy of *Popular Mechanics*; originally published in the October 1957 issue.

seamless visual and spatial transition, and were therefore not recommended if pesticides could eliminate the problem.

Air-conditioning also likely contributed to the lack of majority enthusiasm for creating spatially developed indoor/outdoor connections. Prior to the widespread implementation of air-conditioning, the outdoor room served as an important means of escaping the smothering heat of interiors. But after about 1954, the situation began to change. In an office memorandum of that year from Joseph Howland, *House Beautiful*'s garden editor, to his editor in chief, Elizabeth Gordon, Howland wrote that "the revolution set off by air conditioning is sweeping away outdoor living just as fast as it caught on after the war. . . . eliminating interest in the big-terrace garden developed before air conditioning became common, which assumed that people will live outdoors as many hours as possible. This just isn't true anymore."[45] A 1954 *House and Home* article likewise emphasized that air-conditioning rendered the outdoor terrace obsolete, describing a home in Dallas in which the outdoor terrace "is seldom used because . . . it's pleasanter inside. . . . Owner Herman Blum soon discovered that air conditioning was so pleasant that he and his wife almost never use their outdoor terrace."[46]

Howland also wrote that the innovative movements in terrace design—seen in highly publicized works by the California landscape architects Thomas Church and Douglas Baylis—had already occurred and stated that "inventiveness is definitely behind us."[47] Despite the rhetoric of the tastemaking literature, Howland believed that the era of the outdoor room, with its large area of paved terrace and easy connection to the interior spaces of the house, was over. As Howland wrote to Gordon in 1954, the "big-terrace-garden" concept would fail for the following reasons:

1. It is a pre–air conditioning concept, so assumes that people want to be outdoors.
2. Its big pavings outside big glass adds dramatically to the air conditioning load.
3. It ignores the lessening interest in being heroic about the worsening mosquito and fly problem—and it is a short step from a screened porch to a close, air-conditioned room.
4. It is too short-lived—because while we talk about "permanent control" we ignore the quick deterioration that starts the very day the big-terrace fences and canvas are installed (there is no growing better with each passing year).
5. It is too monotonous (you see everything in the first glance) when it becomes a picture viewed from a window rather than a place to be lived in.
6. It looks barren and cold (you notice the scarcity of fine plants and flowers) when the color and movement of people are lost.
7. It is too sunny—because trying to introduce sufficient shade trees into a big pavement is

hazardous, expensive, and seldom successful in practice.

8. Its expense doesn't seem as necessary to owners of yards where big trees already exist as it did to the post-war crop of treeless, flat lots where garden design had to be created intellectually rather than from the site conditions—and now more gardens will be remodel jobs, or for new houses going into a sub-divided estate with fine old trees and shrubs already in place.

9. It needs considerable furniture to make it livable—but good terrace furniture is now so expensive that most people buy it mainly for indoor use and won't risk leaving it outdoors.

Instead, the "emerging garden," as Howland called it, would rely more heavily on fine trees and shrubs and on intricate planting than on paving, fencing, and bold compositions. In contradiction to the FHA's underwriting manuals, he emphasized again the enhancements to property value that derived from a well-designed postwar garden: "Gardens are going to be considered again as long-time investments once we use them less intensively as living spaces."[48]

Howland recognized, as many others at the time did not, that the indoor/outdoor ideal was just that—a model largely unrealized by ordinary middle-class homeowners nationwide. Although obviously popular and reasonably prevalent in warmer climates, espe-cially in parts of California, where the idea reached its fullest maturity, the outdoor room was seldom more than a concrete pad outside the back door of many modest postwar dwellings, accessed through an ordinary solid swing door that might also have a screened component. As Howland himself noted in his memo to Gordon, *House Beautiful* need not have feared that it had misled its readers or "missed the boat" on reporting this trend, because "few people even know there is a boat [to miss]."[49] Though the magazine's readers had been exposed to the indoor/outdoor model repeatedly, Howland recognized that few knew it as a lived reality and so would not miss it in the event of its predicted demise.

If the practicalities of postwar homeownership often made the creation of elaborate indoor/outdoor connections impossible, why did the magazines, design publications, and popular media persistently continue to promote such connections over a twenty-year period? Why did tastemakers consider features such as the stylistically modern "outdoor living terrace" so attractive, so important for Americans at midcentury? Professional advocacy was certainly one important factor, since the magazines featured the work of skilled and licensed professionals whose services were generally required to create the more elaborate models. But words such as *informality, casual lifestyle, leisure, individuality,* and *privacy*—all of which were used repeatedly to describe the significance and benefits of indoor/outdoor living—also constituted a lexicon for class distinction

DINING KITCHEN BEDROOM
LIVING HEAT BEDROOM
PATIO BEDROOM
BREEZEWAY
CARPORT GARAGE

Copyright Cliff May · Chris Choate

A design for indoor/outdoor living. Courtesy of
Popular Mechanics; originally published in the April 1956 issue.

and mobility and for the understood contours of whiteness and middle-classness. The implicit assumption of designers, developers, the FHA, and lending agencies—as well as most homeowners and even those who hoped to own homes—was that new houses were for whites of the middle and upper classes, a reality that was both self-reinforcing and ensured by government policies embedded in agencies such as the FHA and the Home Owners' Loan Corporation. Indoor/outdoor living (presented as an ideal rather than a reality) was one component of that rather complexly coded social entity that would later be called *quality of life*—a phrase that now appears frequently in racialized battles over space in suburban contexts.

Indoor/outdoor lifestyles and the so-called outdoor rooms promoted by the tastemaking publications were distinctly white-collar spaces. Instead of a vegetable patch or a victory garden, postwar landscapes were to be hardscape, not horticultural, and as maintenance-free as possible. The horticultural garden of the prewar era required the kind of labor frequently associated with working-class, immigrant, or nonwhite citizens.[50] As Andrew Weise has noted, blacks who lived in unincorporated suburbs such as Chagrin Falls Park outside Cleveland, Ohio, benefited from the lack of municipal restrictions on the uses of their residential yards in that they were able to add provisions to the family table by cultivating vegetable gardens and raising livestock.[51] And, as noted above, the residents of working-class Los

Angeles neighborhoods in the 1920s and 1930s raised vegetables and livestock in their yards.[52] These practices thus came to be associated with immigrant, non-white, and lower-economic-class status.

As landscape architect Stanley White admonished in a circular he authored for the University of Illinois Small Homes Council in 1947: "The private area today is the outdoor living space for the family. It is very different from the 'back yard' of yesteryear." He advised readers, therefore, to "choose good outdoor furniture" and to try to keep children's toys out of the way, avoid clutter, and eliminate rock gardens, flower gardens, and vegetable gardens, to "get rid of work."[53] Maintaining a tidy appearance, inside and out—one that was uncluttered, without visible laundry lines or any outward signs of work that was unassisted by a newly designed and (if possible) electrified tool—was essential. Outdoor labor that was conducted without the assistance of a motorized machine (lawn mower, power tool) could visibly connote lower-class status or nonwhite identities.

In the rhetorical and discursive fields pertaining to garden design, ideas about leisure and leisure activities dominated. The living terrace of the outdoor room was to be designed as a space for both leisure and recreation, and so that its maintenance required as little labor as possible. As noted above, the 1959 *Popular Mechanics* annual outdoor living section proclaimed that

Plans of "traditional" and "modern" houses in *Popular Mechanics* reveal that the "modern" house was characterized by indoor/outdoor connections to garden courts and to numerous outdoor areas. Courtesy of *Popular Mechanics*; originally published in the October 1957 issue.

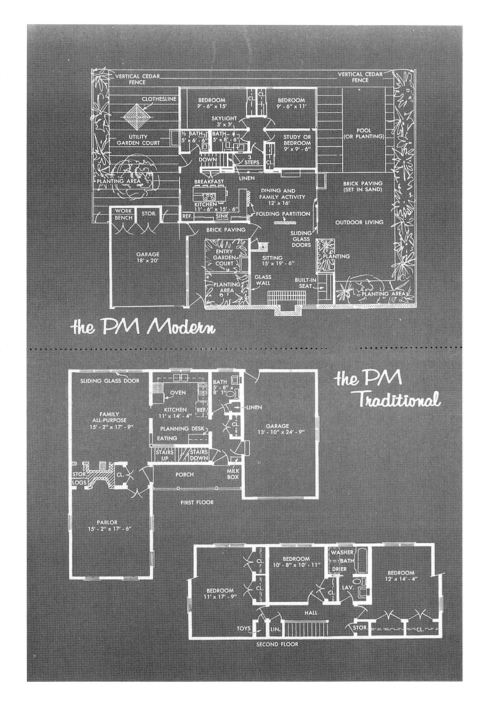

it included "16 pages of ideas for converting your back yard into an open-air 'room' where you can bask, dine and spend the summer in true lazy-man style," and thereby attain what the magazine called "America's outdoor way of life."[54] The "American style" of living that repeatedly appeared in the popular and shelter magazines, centered on the garden as the site for conspicuous relaxation and the living terrace with its close connection to the home's interior, was tied to an ideology of American identity that was as much about class affiliation and whiteness as it was about health or the aesthetics of postwar modernism.

"A modern patio landscape" by landscape architect Harold Klopp. Klopp's landscape was designed to require as little maintenance as possible. Courtesy of *Popular Mechanics*; originally published in the October 1959 issue.

TECHNOLOGY AND THE LAWN

As described above, the aesthetic ideal embodied by a manicured lawn and nonproductive landscape surrounding an individual dwelling served as an important cipher for middle- and upper-middle-class white identities. From at least the eighteenth century, this aesthetic was also predicated on the importance of maintaining an image of leisure for those who possessed the property. Eighteenth-century painters of English country estates took care to portray the leisured lives of property owners in sunlit foregrounds while the agricultural work that supported such lifestyles was relegated to shadowed boundaries or rendered invisible.[55] Andrew Jackson Downing famously suggested that the ideal nineteenth-century estate landscape was one that appeared to be tended by invisible hands at night and where none of the actual work involved in its creation was visible.[56] Given the long history of this ideal, it is not surprising that ordinary postwar gardens were intended primarily as zones of leisure, even though the past tradition was applied to the grounds of upper-class homes. Postwar gardens belonged to working- and middle-class occupants, but as with their eighteenth- and nineteenth-century predecessors, the absence of apparent labor was intended to enhance the status of the homeowner. To achieve such an impression in ordinary midcentury yards, homeowners needed power tools and a range of other mechanized devices that

were newly available for purchase. These tools held the promise of turning labor into leisure, or at least into a reasonably pleasant recreational activity, and they reveal as much about advances in postwar technologies as they do about a wide acknowledgment of the importance of such artifacts of material culture for determining class status and racial identity.

The ideals of indoor/outdoor living and a leisured lifestyle are both portrayed in this illustration from Mary and Russel Wright's *Guide to Easier Living.* Reproduced with permission of Gibbs Smith, publisher.

Front lawns in Levittown,
Pennsylvania, circa 1956.
Photograph courtesy of Temple
University Libraries, Urban
Archives, Philadelphia.
Copyright Associated Press.

Much has been written about the verdant, horizontal, and highly manicured outdoor surface known as the lawn.[57] Rather than rehearse the findings of scholars such as Virginia Jenkins, I aim to examine here specific ways in which lawns and lawn technologies contributed to the establishment of postwar personal and family identities. Without lawns, postwar homes would lose a crucial marker of their status identity, and this was clearly understood by postwar lending agencies and mortgage underwriters, who, like the imagined owners of new development houses, had a deep concern for the maintenance of appearances. Again, the FHA played a role. In its *Underwriting Manual* of 1952, for example, the FHA stated that developers and builders were to "assure that an acceptable setting will be developed on each property," and acceptable settings included manicured lawns. Moreover, the FHA recommended that all properties should be finish graded with adequate topsoil to support lawn growth and that they should be finished with seeded or sod lawns "from the front property line to a line ten to twenty feet beyond the rear wall of the dwelling."[58]

Lawns, then, were not simply the aesthetic preference of suburban homeowners—they were essentially mandated by the FHA, without whose underwriting power most postwar developments would not have existed. That lawns also reinforced an aesthetic of the rural and the picturesque and its associations with landed gentry was an unarticulated part of the rationale behind the FHA's guidelines, though the authors of the *Underwriting Manual* were likely unaware of the explicit associations of the historical precedents. The FHA's redlining practices, however, which were based largely on visual assessment of neighborhoods, reveal that the agency had a keen eye for the iconography of whiteness, and well-kept, healthy lawns served as an essential element in the system of landscape presentation and representation the FHA favored.

Real estate appraisers likewise privileged the lawn in their assessments of property values, assigning it a real value. In an essay titled "The Value of View," the author of a 1951 article on real estate appraisal noted that views from the home constituted a marketable commodity that must be carefully constructed and cultivated to improve property values. He wrote that "at least one of the many views from the home should be a distant view" and that near views should be carefully chosen and created with gardens, flower beds, plants, trees, and shrubs. Views, the author contended, are best created in backyard gardens, because front-yard views in developments might include a neighbor's "shabby" house. He therefore recommended unbroken expanses of lawn in order to achieve the best front view: "View is one of the greatest assets a home can have—and often is the only asset one house may possess which is not common to all other houses in the vicinity. View lends individuality to a property. . . . View keeps the ordinary house out of the potential class of a rental property, helps it retain its self-respect and stability as a residence—a home."[59] Lawns were thus essential, not only for the maintenance of property values but also for their ability to signal private homeownership and therefore citizenship, class status, and whiteness. The recommended view to an unbroken expanse of lawn served as the ideal image—one that could even help overcome a view to a neighbor's "shabby" house.

So firmly established remains the correlation of a manicured lawn with solidly middle-class status that the residents of black suburbs today pay close attention to lawn maintenance as a key measure that distinguishes them from blacks of lower economic classes. In her sociological study of the black middle class in suburbs surrounding Washington, D.C., Karyn Lacy notes that lawn maintenance is one of the standards that establishes a black suburban community as middle-class and therefore distinct from more impoverished surrounding areas. The most upscale of Lacy's three residential subjects, a suburb she calls "Sherwood Park," is distinguished by its picturesque landscape of extensive lawns that are several acres in size and that serve as the only boundaries between the elaborate houses. She notes that "outsiders often are surprised to learn that Sherwood Park is predominantly black" because the neighborhood's landscape aesthetic has for so long been closely associated with white identities.[60]

So essential was the lawn to the proper image of middle-class, white private homeownership in the postwar period that some new developments mandated the installation and maintenance of lawns in the covenants that accompanied deeds of ownership. The *Homeowner's Guide* given to those who purchased houses in all-white Levittown, Pennsylvania, for example—where restrictive racial covenants held sway until a 1957 race riot dissolved their potency—devoted nine of its twenty-three pages to landscaping instructions, and a generous portion of those nine pages was devoted to lawn care.[61] With residential lawns established as an essential component in the loan underwriting and real estate appraisal industries, it is not surprising that the lawn-care industry grew as rapidly as did postwar housing developments themselves. According to Becky Nicolaides, the number of lawn mower companies, nurseries, and other businesses related to the horticulture industry in the United States more than quadrupled in this period.[62]

Just as maids no longer helped inside most post-war houses, hired gardeners, also typically nonwhite and working-class, were no longer a common part of the outdoor middle-class suburban scene. Instead, suburban homeowners used new and expensive power tools to perform the required yard maintenance. As Virginia Jenkins has pointed out, the names of 1950s lawn mowers, such as Dandy Boy, Lawn Boy, and Lazy Boy, appealed to racial stereotypes held by many white Americans, since they may have conjured associations with, for example, a Filipino "houseboy" or an African American "yard boy."[63]

The thirteen-minute televised segments that made up the *Industry on Parade* series, which appeared between scheduled programs in the 1950s (as discussed in chapter 7), frequently included subjects that focused on the new garden-care products that emerged to satisfy the growing demand for labor-saving devices in the garden and also served the boom in these residential landscape-related industries. In addition to features on drywall/gypsum board, new uses for plywood, prefabricated houses, plastics for home use, and electronic garage door openers, the series included segments on lawn sprinklers, lawn furniture, and lawn mowers. For example, "Lawnmowing Made Easy!," sponsored by Remote Control Lawnmower of Portland, Oregon, demonstrated the convenience and modernity of a robotic mower controlled by a radio receiver. The moderator for the segment called the robot "the householder's dream" and noted that owners of the device could look forward to mowing their lawns from distances as much as a quarter of a mile away from their houses.[64] In another segment titled "More Power to the Householder!" and sponsored by the Jacobsen Manufacturing Company of Racine, Wisconsin, snow shovels and power lawn mowers for small yards were featured along with a gasoline-powered rotary snow plow. As the moderator stated, these devices were designed "for people used to labor saving machines at home—not just for parks, cemeteries and estates anymore."[65] Whether or not these machines actually saved labor, they projected an image of affluence for those who owned them, as well as at least the appearance of work made less strenuous.

By 1958, as the demand for new power tools for yard and garden maintenance continued to grow, the industry had become highly competitive. That year, *Industry on Parade* produced a feature that devoted its entire thirteen minutes to the theme of "Power in the Yard." Jointly sponsored by Rowco Manufacturing, Porter Cable Company, Hiller Engineering, Toro, Choremaster, and the Asplundh Tree Expert Company, the segment asked viewers to consider how power tools were changing their pattern of living and then answered that question for them by displaying the sponsors' newest products. A snow blower made the work of snow removal into a "pleasant diversion." "Ingenious sprinklers" freed homeowners from the tedium and time-consuming work of standing with a hose and moving about to water the garden. Each featured product demonstrated a move toward increased comfort and ease for homeowners by eliminating the tedious work of outdoor chores. As viewers watched a homeowner at work in his yard, the segment's moderator exclaimed, "Not a bead of perspiration as he achieves in half an hour more than he used to do in half a day." Even wives and children, viewers were told, could operate the new power tools and lawn mowers. And since new homes were built with electrical outlets outdoors, power tools could easily be plugged in anywhere they were needed. In essence, the segment advertised the increased amounts of leisure time for homeowners made possible by improvements in industrial and manufacturing productivity. The segment closed with the moderator's observation that the featured products made for a new home life that was richer, easier, and happier. The concluding scene of a family enjoying a backyard barbecue cemented the notion that outdoor leisure was desirable and that it could be purchased by savvy consumers who understood and could afford the latest, most up-to-date products produced by the home-gardening industries.[66] Consuming these products thus appeared to make the buyer into a patriotic citizen who supported the domestic economy, just as the purchases simultaneously conferred upon the owner the appearance of a leisured lifestyle and pockets deep enough to afford these new machines.

In addition to mowing, irrigation was a particular point of focus for postwar manufacturers, and the lawn-care industry evolved to include sophisticated watering

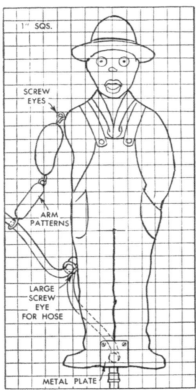

The "Sambo Lawn Sprinkler" appeared in a make-it-yourself article. Courtesy of *Popular Mechanics;* originally published in the May 1949 issue.

nean irrigation systems that could be turned on and off with the twist of a key enjoyed increasing popularity in more arid climates, along with the rise in the availability of relatively inexpensive PVC piping and do-it-yourself lawn centers that appeared in local nurseries and garden centers.[69] Still, many homeowners continued to utilize sprinkler attachments connected to garden hoses, and an array of fanciful and decorative sprinkler attachments, generally fabricated in cast iron but sometimes in plastic, appeared in the 1950s. Animals such as frogs, turtles, seals, squirrels, mallards, and other fanciful figures served as popular and decorative motifs for sprinkler attachments.

However, some lawn sprinklers were far less innocuous. The "Black Sambo" lawn sprinkler featured in the 1949 issue of *Popular Mechanics* clarifies the ways in which lawns and their attendant material culture served as markers of racial identity during the postwar era.[70] The instructions for making the sprinkler were accompanied by an illustration in which white homeowners (a father and son) stood by watching as a mechanized "black" servant watered the yard. The Black Sambo lawn sprinkler allowed its owners to maintain the notion that black servants toiled happily in support of a white life of leisured privilege. As Maurice Manring has shown in his analysis of Aunt Jemima products, the purchase of such artifacts allowed the consumer to appropriate "a life of leisure with racial and sexual harmony, seemingly more free but inherently dependent

systems intended to ease the homeowner's burden.[67] Products like the Green Spot Line helped homeowners learn about the best time of day to water their lawns and the most effective means of doing so.[68] Sprinkler systems were intended to be more efficient than hand watering, and, of course, they became the technological version of Downing's invisible hands, working to make a lush lawn that required little visible labor. Subterra-

on a black laborer." With the growing absence of servants in postwar America, the Black Sambo lawn sprinkler "was sold with the promise that the buyer could appropriate the leisure, beauty, and racial and class status of the plantation South."[71]

The Sambo sprinkler served much the same function as the cast-iron lawn jockeys (sometimes known as "Jocko" sculptures and dating from at least the 1880s) that once served as locations for tethering horses but had become strictly decorative by the postwar era, or the flower planters designed to appear as black figures serving as porters, holding plants in one hand while tipping their hats with the other.[72] As Steven Dubin has suggested, such artifacts recall again Flannery O'Connor's short story "The Artificial Nigger," the title of which refers to the mass-produced lawn statues, and they symbolically reproduce the assumption that blacks should perform servile tasks, particularly when positioned on property owned by whites. Like all such objects, they literally reduce blacks in size (making them diminutive—and therefore controllable—figures in the landscape), symbolically re-creating systems of cultural domination and oppression as they recalled the plantation-era South during the Jim Crow years that remained after World War II. The white homeowners who purchased and placed such artifacts as lawn decoration created a symbolic field of solidarity with other whites by indicating those who were not accepted within their social and physical boundaries. Dubin asserts that the

A lawn jockey of the sort commonly found adorning front yards across the United States in the 1950s. From *Ethnic Notions: Black Images in the White Mind. An Exhibition of Racist Stereotype and Caricature from the Collection of Janette Faulkner, September 10–November 12, 2000* (Berkeley, Calif.: Berkeley Art Center, 2000).

lawn jockeys and similar items "helped to shore up a sense of racial superiority," particularly in the face of threatening social or economic change, which might include the threat of desegregation that faced many new suburban developments, particularly after 1955. These items are also linked to status aspirations, "creating the illusion of having servants for a group who never had them."[73]

Lawns, then, and the artifacts of material culture associated with them, were important components in a system of status and racial differentiation that masqueraded as a benignly verdant surround for postwar houses. With newly devised technologies that made lawn care and maintenance easier than ever before, and with mechanized "servants" performing the tasks formerly completed by nonwhite hired help, postwar homeowners could bask in the leisurely lifestyle required for the status positions they sought and hoped to preserve.

FENCES: DELINEATING BOUNDARIES

Unlike the storage cabinets, lawn mowers, and kitchen desks that have been the subjects of analysis in previous chapters, fences do not appear—have perhaps never appeared—to be benign elements in the built environment. To the contrary, fences imply the delineation of property; of insiders and outsiders, of access restricted; of views screened, impeded, or blocked; of restricted mobility. Fences also keep livestock from disappearing or from trampling particular grounds; fences can keep children and pets from harm by impeding their movement into traffic or into unmonitored backyard swimming pools. But for many Marxist scholars, fences are part of the historical process of enclosure that began in England in the eighteenth century and part of "the classic formulation in Marxist historiography that places the privatization of public property at the crux of the transition to capitalist modernity." Framed as such, the fence (large or small, grand or ordinary, public or private) sits at the center of inquiries into historical changes in the distribution of property and the logic of human geography. Fences, as Amy Chazkel and David Serlin tell us, "are 'good to think' about the social, economic, and legal—not to mention architectural—dimensions of the process of the creation of a propertyless working class" (ever growing in number in the present-day United States). As such, they have powerful implications for thinking about issues related to space and social justice. Although these scholars seek answers to a range of problems related to globalization and the eradication of the commons (among other issues), they astutely point to the connections between "the fencing off of common property in the interest of private gain and liberal (or neoliberal) individual property rights."[74] Whether we examine, as John Streamas has done, "the history of barbed wire in the American West . . . the building of Japanese internment camps during World War II . . . [or] the fixation on 'good fences' and 'good neighbors' manifest in front lawns, backyards and playgrounds in postwar American suburbs" (as I will do here), we are in all cases looking at a way of thinking about landscape that is deeply linked to notions of privatization and capital, which are likewise inexorably linked to ideas about race, class, citizenship, and privilege.[75]

The American fence has a long history, one that is

surely linked to the English ethos of enclosure and its concomitant ties to the rise of industrial capitalism but is also inflected by a historically distinctive context of settler colonialism and a frontier ideal that depended on a fundamental tension between the romantic myth of an open and unclaimed (and therefore unfenced) landscape and the realities of territory claimed through violent acts of imperialism. John Stilgoe has summarily recounted the history of the fence in the U.S. cultural landscape: New England stone walls topped with split wooden rails delineated cleared lands until about 1850, and southern fences made of split rails linking

upright wooden posts (post-and-rail fences) separated properties during the same period. Post-and-rail fences moved westward, but in rock-free and treeless plains, cattle ranchers began using barbed wire attached to metal stakes, and the fencing style became popular enough that it moved both west and back east, where it stimulated the use by farmers of various metal mesh fences, which were then adopted by the railroad companies. From the 1890s onward, suburbanites began to delineate the boundaries of their residential properties with these metal railroad fences, which were made of either woven wire or chain link. In early suburbs where

Borrowing a line from Robert Frost's poem "Mending Wall," *House Beautiful* advised its readers that "good fences make good neighbors." *House Beautiful,* January 1950.

large house lots prevailed and where the lots were distant enough from railroad tracks and thoroughfares, homeowners often left properties unfenced, especially in suburbs (such as Riverside, Illinois) where the landscape was designed to appear as a continuous, rolling estate or parkland, or they sometimes used hedges to delineate some property edges.[76]

To fence or not to fence became the subject of some debate in the second half of the nineteenth century. If many early nineteenth-century Americans viewed fencing as a necessary means of controlling the movements of animals and children, and as a practical means of delineating private from public space, architectural and landscape writers such as Andrew Jackson Downing wrote as early as 1840 that fences gave a mean appearance to the residential landscape, and writers in the 1870s such as Frank J. Scott and Nathaniel H. Egleston also argued against fencing on aesthetic grounds. Downing, Scott, and Egleston all sought creation of the sweeping panoramas of green that could be viewed from the windows of upper-middle-class and upper-class domestic interiors, views that emulated the picturesque settings of the eighteenth-century landed English gentry. Nineteenth-century writers on domesticity even opposed fencing on the grounds that it was "unchristian" to deprive others of one's own view.[77] Still, the editors of shelter magazines from the same period continued to note that fences afforded the privacy necessary to healthy family life, and they also framed their pleas for fences and outdoor privacy—as would their successors for the next five decades—in terms of national character development.[78]

In the 1920s, chain-link fences increasingly appeared as barriers to the private yards of suburban homes, though they were often planted with lilacs or climbing vines to mask the harsh appearance of the metal. Thereafter, the history of suburban fences varies according to region and development. Some postwar suburbs, like some earlier upscale and restricted developments, prohibited fencing in their covenants or deed restrictions because they still sought the creation of the appearance of a continuous greensward throughout their grounds—an image that, like the myth of the frontier, counterposes a fictionalized image of openness with the reality it seeks at least partially to mask, one of rigidly divided and controlled private property ownership. In the case of Levittown, Pennsylvania (constructed between 1951 and 1958), fences were also prohibited because the Levitts believed that homeowners could not be relied upon to construct aesthetically pleasing fences that would not have a low-class appearance. This prohibition against fencing was very like the Levitts' prohibitions of laundry lines hung outside and the parking of more than one car in a home's driveway. All these were calculated to preserve an aesthetic that was clearly white and middle-class.[79]

By the advent of the postwar era, the debate over fencing continued to appear in the design and shelter magazines. If the postwar front yard was at least visually public, editors, design writers, and publishers encouraged their audience to create backyards that were private. The majority of postwar backyards were inherently more private than their predecessors because most development plans of the period did not include service alleys or back lanes running behind the lots, so that the rear garden became less subject to intrusion than ever before.[80] Front yards, though visible to the street, could not retain the public function of urban "stoop culture," or even of nineteenth- and early twentieth-century suburban "porch culture," since a life lived on the street, in front of the house, signaled prewar economic and social conditions and facilitated exactly the kind of public life the postwar sociologists and design critics cautioned against. Front lawns were, and still are, the most common treatment for suburban front yards, but in the postwar period social uses for the lawn decreased, so that it became perhaps most important as a green barrier, a way of proclaiming a defensive zone between house and sidewalk or street. Unspoken rules dictated that strangers not tread upon the lawns of others, and while children sometimes played games on front-yard lawns, they more frequently played in the protected backyards.[81]

The idea of the backyard as a private family zone secluded from outsiders held great appeal in the postwar era for numerous reasons. First, the postwar garden accommodated a range of activities that formerly took place away from home. As one author for *House Beautiful* wrote, "Today all the facilities that used to be scattered around the community we now want to exist on our own little piece of land."[82] The garden became a place for "vitamin-conscious moderns" to relax, a new place for housewives to cook on the outdoor grill, a playground for the children, a recreation center for teens complete with stereo system and swimming pool, and an extension of the living room for adult entertaining. As long as the garden was properly furnished with equipment, furniture, sound system, lighting, and climate-control devices, family members need never leave their property to fulfill their recreational needs.[83] The desire to avoid public recreational facilities and spaces in the immediate postwar period was no doubt connected to recurring polio epidemics as well. But the urge toward insularity appears throughout the period in articles that urged readers to turn their ordinary backyards into "Country-Club Living" and to "make home more exciting than anywhere else, canceling the need for seeking family pleasures in private clubs or public beaches."[84] Although Americans in the 1950s were more mobile than ever before because of the upward surge in automobile ownership, the design literature insisted that home was better than anyplace else, and the goal was to leave it as seldom as possible. Even the controlled and socially restricted setting of the country club was less desirable than the insularity of one's own suburban backyard.

Authors and designers writing for the mass media implemented appeals to family togetherness, coupled with rhetorical strategies that targeted exclusionary impulses, by urging readers to direct their thoughts toward creating privacy from the outside world. The family was to be protected, but the only dangers that could be acknowledged were those external to the home. When photographs of Los Angeles–based architect A. Quincy Jones's own steel house were published in the January 1957 issue of *House and Home*, Jones stated that he implemented an open-plan arrangement with floor-to-ceiling curtains used as the only interior dividers because "*inside* the house you're always with your family or your friends—*outside* is where you want privacy. That's why we tried to provide as much privacy as we could, with screens, walls, fences and planting."[85] For Jones, as for many members of the architectural and design professions, privacy requirements were primarily externally, rather than internally, dictated, and they could be resolved through the use of a range of vertical screening devices.

As countless magazine articles informed readers, the construction of a private world was predicated on good fencing or, at the very least, the implementation of a dense, well-clipped hedge. *House Beautiful*, along with much of the normative residential literature, advocated the design of attractive fences or walls that provided privacy without offending one's neighbors. The magazine's January 1949 issue featured an article stating that the secret of a useful backyard was "privacy from nosy neighbors," which was to be attained through careful design of fences, hedges, and plantings that would "discourage over-the-fence talk," block the view of "would-be second-story gazers," and keep out "prying eyes" and "snoopers."[86] By 1960, editor Elizabeth Gordon found the subject compelling enough to devote an entire issue to "Landscaping and Privacy," asking her readers, "Is privacy your right or a stolen pleasure?"[87] Linking politics and domestic design, Gordon urged her readers to consider their political commitment to individuality and the right to privacy. She wrote: "Does Your Front Lawn Belong to You—Or the Whole Neighborhood? The United States is split into two factions over this question—an ideological split just as real as the Republican–Democratic divide. Where do you stand? . . . The issue really boils down to whether or not others have the right to look at or onto your land." The editor encouraged her readers to stop watching each other and, borrowing a phrase used by the sociologists, asked them to "turn inward."

Because fencing was key to achieving privacy, Gordon advised her readers to organize their communities to eliminate deed restrictions and covenants that restricted or prohibited fence construction. Although she noted that such restrictions frequently extended to "the kind of people to whom you can sell your house," she did not elaborate on the problems of racial discrimination in the residential real estate market. But she did

Privacy from the street

Shut out passers-by with a hedge that reaches over head-height and a tree that cuts off the sight line from the house across the street. Put a low planting next to the sidewalk, as shown, to cover the thin places that often occur at the bottom of a tall hedge.

Privacy from second-story gazers

Trees plus a fence make a sure stop against those who would gaze. The trees shut off the view from the second story, and the fence takes care of the first. Keep the trees on your side of the fence so you can feed and water them easily to encourage leafy growth.

advise readers to take the law into their own hands if conventional organizational efforts failed, writing, "If you can't get around fencing ordinances legally, there are a few ways to avoid them without breaking the letter of the law." She recommended hedges, trellises, and climbing vines as suitable alternatives to fence construction.

House Beautiful was certainly one of the most persistent proponents of the fenced yard, and in one 1949 article the editors emphasized the increased property value of fenced postwar gardens while simultaneously emphasizing the importance of excluding outsiders:

The land on which you build your house represents 10 to 30 percent of your total investment. Are you using it to enlarge your living space, better your

living, and provide winter–summer beauty? Most people are not. But they could. And so can you. . . . The secret of a useful backyard: privacy from nosy neighbors. . . . Everyone needs a place to shut out the rest of the world. Your backyard should be one of these places. You should be able to rest, play, or entertain in your yard without sharing the time with idlers. Privacy doesn't mean isolation, and you don't need to own a big lot. But you do need to cut off the view of those outside your yard. Then you can romp with the children and your family pets, or spend the afternoon asleep in a hammock. That's as it should be. You wouldn't think of building a house that exposed you constantly to public view. Your backyard must be equally private to be usable.

House Beautiful advocated backyard privacy repeatedly in its pages. In this article from January 1949, readers were instructed that they could be friendly neighbors while still attaining privacy from "backyard gossips" and "second-story gazers." The article instructed readers that the "secret to a useful backyard" was privacy from nosy neighbors. "The Backyard—America's Most Mis-used Natural Resource," *House Beautiful*, January 1949, 40–41.

A fence enclosing the backyard of a home in an Eichler development includes various fencing designs and vines climbing up the fence. Eichler Home, Palo Alto, California, Anshen and Allen Architects, no date. Photograph by Maynard L. Parker. Courtesy of the Huntington Library, San Marino, California.

facilitated social connection with neighbors. The reference to "idlers" reveals a deep paranoia embedded in the discourse about family life and leisure, but it also casts anyone outside the home and family as a potential danger, as an "other" who must be excluded from the domestic realm for the sake of preserving safety and status. The article thus instructed readers about how to make a fence to discourage "backyard gossips" and "over-the-fence talk" and to achieve privacy from "second-story gazers" by using "trees plus a fence [to] make a sure stop against those who would gaze."[88] Given these descriptions, one could easily imagine American suburbia as populated with Peeping Toms, rumor-mongers, and potentially dangerous "idlers" waiting to disrupt the tranquil idyll of home and family. Worse, each of these images cast the domestic sphere as a fragile realm, constantly susceptible to the influences of those less upwardly mobile, less secure in their status and identity. A fenced yard was, according to the media rhetoric, the obvious remedy.

Despite its centuries-old association with American homeownership, the "little picket fence" seldom appeared, nor was its implementation advocated, since pickets allowed too much freedom of vision between and over the stakes. Instead, magazines and books provided examples that were constructed of tall wood planks used in various patterns, concrete block, corrugated plastic panels, and densely woven aluminum screens, among others.

The article explicitly connected privacy and leisure while linking both to increased property value. Views obtained through picture windows held real value as appraisal items, but only when the windows permitted a one-way gaze. Views that allowed outsiders to see inside the house or yard could actually devalue a house. Backyards, then, became useful and valuable when they were private, not when they were productive or

Likewise, the experimental X-100 steel house designed by A. Quincy Jones for the merchant builder Joseph Eichler in San Mateo, California, had a concrete block wall along the street frontage that served as a garden enclosure, as a boundary containing the children's play area, and as a wall for the father's workshop.[89] The placement of a fortresslike wall to screen the entry and front windows from the street became common among architect-designed houses of the period, and it also repeatedly appeared as a recommendation for attaining privacy in the literature aimed at middle-class homeowners, such as *Popular Mechanics* and the University of Illinois Small Homes Council circular series. A 1957 article in *House & Garden* titled "Seclusion by Design" illustrated the point best with its subtitle "Behind a Camouflage of Screens and Walls: Blessed Solitude." The house illustrated in the article, designed by the architect Frederick Emmons for his family, is completely closed off from the street by a series of masonry walls, translucent screens, windowless front walls, and a carport along the street facade.

Walls that concealed the front of the house from view were an important dimension in attaining exterior privacy, yet they seldom appeared in houses that were not custom designed. Stock house plans that could be purchased in magazines seldom specified designs for construction beyond the exterior walls of the house,

Corrugated panels used as fencing make a private enclosure surrounding a house. Wayne C. Leckey, "Unusual and Modern Ideas for Living Outdoors." Courtesy of *Popular Mechanics*; originally published in the April 1959 issue.

FENCES AND WINDBREAKS

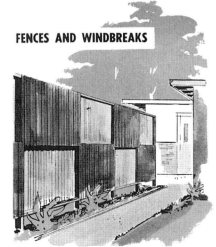

Painted checkerboard style, this eye-stopper fence consists of aluminum panels applied to opposite sides

Attractive masonry wall combines regular 4-in. concrete building blocks with ornamental criss-cross ones
Courtesy National Concrete Masonry Association

Lightweight inserts of corrugated aluminum make a modern patio enclosure that requires no painting

and though readers were urged to employ landscape architects to design their gardens, many could not afford to do so. Many new homeowners, therefore, faced the dilemma posed again by the picture window—an element that signaled modernity through its extensive glazed surface and allowed the requisite display to neighbors, but that was deeply problematic for anyone concerned with privacy.[90] Authors such as Mary and George Catlin, whose works were directed at a truly middle-class audience of home buyers and builders on restricted budgets, instructed their readers to place most of the large windows and major expanses of glass toward the back of the house to avoid problems with prying eyes.[91] As a consequence, ordinary postwar houses increasingly did just that. Fewer and smaller windows appeared on the street facade over time, and increasingly the postwar house opened up to the back of the lot, especially when a large wall did not conceal the house from the street in front. Placing the kitchen window at the rear of the house, it was reasoned, also allowed the mother to supervise the children's activities in the enclosed backyard without leaving her work in the kitchen, although as many kept the kitchen on the street side of the house to allow a greater integration of living areas and outdoor spaces in the backyard.[92]

Although ordinary houses seldom had exterior barriers built in front, the use of fences and screens of many varieties was popular for such houses because they were relatively affordable and could serve multiple purposes. In addition to the standard materials—wood, metal, concrete, and concrete block—a variety of new materials, some developed and tested during the war, made inexpensive and attractive screens. By virtue of their very newness, these could likewise signal modernity and personal distinction. Translucent corrugated plastic, frosted Plexiglas, Cel-O-Glass (plastic-coated wire mesh), Transite fencing, and translucent Alsynite (which looks like corrugated plastic and was used as an overhead filter) all appeared in the pages of magazines as possible screening materials. Emphasizing the need for the separation of children and parents, magazine articles advocated the installation of partial fence panels, often translucent, inside yards to create outdoor zones. Such dividing panels could also be used to screen areas of labor (laundry drying, garbage collection, small vegetable patches) from leisure zones.[93]

The California landscape architect Douglas Baylis designed some particularly innovative solutions to garden enclosure. Once again emphasizing the importance of a private backyard for cultivating family leisure (and therefore the correct identity), Baylis noted that fencing set "the stage for relaxing with privacy screens." "The difference between just another back yard and real outdoor living" wrote Baylis, "starts with *privacy*. You and your family want a spot where you can doze in the sun, read in the shade, or eat an outdoor meal without feeling that you are in a showcase for neighbors and passers-by to view." He recommended using permeable verticals that allowed breezes to pass through them, such as wire fences planted with vines, louver fences, partial walls, and alternate vertical and horizontal panels of 1-inch boards. He also designed a wood fence that included raised plastic sprinklers suspended by brackets along the top to provide "an efficient air-cooling system and a no-hands method for watering plants below. While the evaporating water is keeping you cool, the kids will have a field day with their artificial rain." His enclosure designs also included the use of colorful canvas tied to pipes or wooden posts; a cantilevered frame covered with weatherproof material, such as plastic sheeting, that filtered light and allowed plant growth below; a fence made of alternating squares of plywood and wire mesh; and a louvered fence that allowed views out but not in (thus providing the ideal: simultaneous privacy and voyeurism). For families of limited financial means, Baylis recommended constructing a framework that could be filled in with a variety of materials, depending on what the family budget allowed. One such example utilized a tennis court backstop planted with vines.[94]

Some articles also linked advocacy for the fortress-like appearance created by privacy walls and fences to stories about crime rates and the need (however relatively rare in exclusive, middle-class suburbs composed of neighbors with homogeneous financial circumstances) for personal and family security. As early as 1947, *House Beautiful* featured a home with a noteworthy attraction: "a peephole concealed in the west wall of the kitchen so that visitors ringing the front doorbell [could] be surveyed before they are admitted."[95] Within ten years' time, the magazines had elevated security concerns and were publishing articles that highlighted features such as the radio-operated garage door that "enables Mrs. Lindsley to stay in her automobile until she is safely within the confines of her home" and the built-in intercom system that "permits Mrs. Lindsley to answer the door from the main house."[96] With privacy walls concealing the house from the street, automatic garage doors that ensured closure of the largest opening into the house, and intercoms that monitored visitors, the postwar house as advocated by the media became more fortified against the outside world than ever before.

The media and popular interest in creating individual and family privacy, then, changed the look of some postwar suburban developments in comparison with their precursors, which had been largely unfenced, with large, unbroken stretches of lawn and garden passing between house lots, giving an impression of a common greenway. Though inflected to an extent by regional dictates and by developer mandates, many postwar developments became increasingly fenced, broken by the regular rhythms of partitions that separated lot from lot, neighbor from neighbor, family from the street and its occupants. Although some early postwar suburbs, Levittown among them, initially prohibited

Set the stage for relaxing
with these privacy screens

Here's a new twist in privacy screens. By raising a plastic sprinkler on brackets high up on a wood fence, you can have an efficient air cooling system and a no-hands method for watering the plants below.

While the evaporating water is keeping you cool, the kids will have a field day with their artificial "rain."

You'll have quick comfort when you use canvas. Lash a bold-patterned canvas to pipe or wood posts. You will gain extra privacy and good control of cooling breezes, plus shade in late afternoon when it will count the most.

You may choose any color scheme that you wish with canvas.

Cantilevered screen offers more privacy and shade for its height than do the straight vertical types of screens.

Cover an easy-to-build frame with any weatherproof material you like. Plastic sheeting shown here is good because it filters light and lets you grow plants beneath it.

Leave an opening so air can circulate.

Solid panels are quickest to build. Use plywood and wire mesh to get a privacy screen in a hurry.

Color panels with paint or stain, and outdoor room is all ready for use. Checkerboard design shown here relieves sameness of most conventional fence styles.

You can use tub plants for immediate planting effect, then start low-growing shrubs for more privacy.

the use of fences and walls between house lots, most eventually succumbed to the aesthetic of privatization that demanded a fenced yard and also to the practicalities of enclosing pets and small children.[97] As early as 1954, *Sunset* magazine reported that the perimeter fence had become common in California subdivisions, and numerous fencing articles appeared in the magazine's pages.[98] Indeed, some residential suburbs remain largely unfenced today, but by 1969, when the renowned landscape architect Thomas Church published *Your Private World,* the formula, if not the reality, for creating private, fenced outdoor gardens was firmly and unshakably in place.[99]

But did good fences really make good neighbors, as the magazines and design publications claimed? Why did fencing become so central to the published discourse about postwar residential design? What did exterior fencing that enclosed a private backyard symbolize? Amy Chazkel and David Serlin perhaps answer this most clearly: "Like the crumbling wall that separates neighbor from neighbor in Robert Frost's iconic poem 'Mending Wall,' the architecture of enclosure is vulnerable not only because nature stubbornly resists these artificial impositions on the landscape but also because these fences and walls so nakedly display the legal fictions that bolster social injustice. The man mending the

Landscape architect Douglas Baylis designed fences of canvas and pipe, plastic sheeting, plywood, and mesh panels; he even created a fence with a built-in sprinkler system to entertain children. Douglas and Maggie Baylis Collection [1999-4], Environmental Design Archives, University of California, Berkeley.

dividing wall in Frost's poem needs to utter the phrase 'good fences make good neighbors' repeatedly precisely because it is so unconvincing."[100] And herein lies the deep complexity inherent in but belied by the apparent simplicity of this vertically constructed spatial element. Fences seem to assist in the production of healthy social relations, as Frost's neighbor's mantra indicates, because they appear to prevent conflict of various forms by giving literal delineation to the legal constructs of property. In reality, however, fences simultaneously divide and displace, disconnect and defend. As Peter Linebaugh has written, "Enclosure indicates private property and capital: it seems to promise both individual ownership and social productivity, but in fact the concept of enclosure is inseparable from terror and the destruction of independence and community."[101] While it might be easy to dismiss Linebaugh's analysis as pertaining only to the parliamentary enclosures of England in the eighteenth century, it is difficult to ignore his implications for the midcentury United States and even for the present. Midcentury fences did indicate private property and capital; they did seem to promise individual ownership linked to the social productivity of healthy families thus created by the affordance of domestic privacy. But we also now understand the aggregate result of the masses of fenced property in postwar

housing developments, their destruction of public space and public life and community. The fencing solutions that appeared in articles and books communicated yet another way of thinking about domesticity in very specific terms that contributed to the destruction of a rich and diverse public life insofar as they contributed to a narrowly constituted definition of postwar homeownership. To fence one's property boundaries was to do more than create a convenient means of containing children and pets; fences became another symbolic mechanism for relaying ideas about exclusion and privilege, property rights, and citizenship. The iconography of fencing was not unequivocal, since unbounded lots in suburban settings could also signal affluence in upper-middle-class and more elite settings where houses were located at greater distances from each other. But in settings where status was less certain and where signifiers for distinction and exclusion were therefore more necessary, fences generally became more abundant, and the media appeals held greater currency. If good fences did not necessarily make good neighbors, they did powerfully construct a reality of division and an iconography of residential exclusion, one in which families could create private domestic worlds where they could reassure themselves and their neighbors of their exclusive rights to property ownership.

Epilogue

In recent years the U.S. housing market has experienced a dramatic set of shifts. As the national and global economy plunged into the worst recession since the Great Depression, and as the predatory lending practices of the previous decades came to their eventual and inevitable conclusion, the so-called housing bubble burst and thousands of residences nationwide became foreclosed properties. A new kind of housing crisis emerged, one that saw Americans from diverse backgrounds suddenly without the homes they had worked for, saved for, and imagined as a key part of their own American Dreams. The history of suburbia and suburban housing since 2008 is, in many respects, dramatically different from the one told in this book's pages. If housing outside of central cities in the postwar period was in short sup-ply, it today exists as a surplus commodity in many locations; if home loans were relatively easy to obtain in 1950 and for the five decades that followed for many white families, home loan approval has now become more difficult for the group of Americans who formerly obtained loans most easily. The demographics of many U.S. suburbs have shifted along with increased globalization and trends in immigration patterns that reflect various complex world economic, social, and political circumstances. Where suburbs were once all-white, we can now increasingly point to the existence of transnational suburbs and—since the 1990s—identify the emergence of a "suburban immigrant nation," with suburbs that can be characterized by the richness of their population diversity instead of by their homogeneity.[1]

FACING
The exterior backyard of Fritz Burns's Postwar House (*detail, see p. 222*).

315

Still, it would be a mistake to imagine that the U.S. housing market has now become a fair and open market where discrimination no longer exists, or that spatial segregation no longer exists in the residential realm. Unfair lending practices and real estate steering (among other discriminatory practices) remain, creating problems that are still especially acute for people of color.[2] The United States remains a country with racially segregated cities and many racially segregated suburbs, just as it also remains a country where life chances are tied to housing opportunities because of the connections that exist among housing, safe neighborhoods, and access to good schools, healthy food, and clean/nontoxic environments. The fight for fair housing is not over.

Historians of U.S. housing know quite a bit already about the ways in which segregated housing developed and was enacted in the United States. We understand the role the federal government played in encouraging practices that led to segregation in housing, and we understand the ways that various agencies, industries, and some private individuals in the real estate and development worlds contributed to the segregated housing market. We also have an increasingly sophisticated understanding of the ways racism is constructed and its operations over time and in various geographic locations. So while writing this book, I kept one question at the center of my research and writing: What can a book about ordinary postwar houses contribute to what we already know about these conditions and their histories?

In this book, I have endeavored primarily to add a new dimension to our understanding of the development of the deep inequalities that exist in the U.S. housing market by looking closely at some material dimensions of everyday life that are so ordinary, so common, and so ubiquitous that they have largely escaped analysis. If we already know a great deal about the ways in which institutional structures connected to the economics of housing operated, we have known far less about the dispersed and complex sets of practices that created, reinforced, and established the forms of cultural knowledge that ultimately supported a housing market designed primarily for whites to the exclusion of others. Institutions create operational structures that can become realities, but individuals decide whether or not they will live those realities, whether they will accept or contest those structures, and how they will or will not do so.

My project has therefore been to uncover and examine some of the ways in which those ideas were and are formulated by studying the politics of representation and the formation of cultural knowledge about houses and single-family domesticity in the postwar period. Houses, and the media representations of housing, in the postwar period helped to create a specific dimension of racialized knowledge, one that connected white identities to rights related to property ownership and to a specifically classed lifestyle. National publications, television programs, professional literature, domestic artifacts, and even the designs of houses and their interiors all contributed to a rhetorical field that shaped the organization of knowledge about the social construction of race and the spatial dimensions of inequality in the postwar era, as it continues to do today. That Americans in the pre–civil rights era already lived in segregated realms meant that the rhetorical field of images, text, and objects/artifacts was one that in equal parts matched expectations (and even aspirations) and reinforced expected norms. By studying that field, we learn about the ways in which everyday acts of participation in a dominant culture are formulated, taken for granted, rehearsed, and enacted, and the structures are reinforced. By focusing on these rhetorical strategies and iconographic formations, and on our everyday encounters with them, I hope to have added to our knowledge of the operations and spatial ramifications of race in the United States. In doing so, I hope also to have posited the possible formation of alternate rhetorical fields, of alternate cultural formations. If we can, quite literally, picture a world that is different from the one examined in these pages, we may eventually be able to live in one as well.

Acknowledgments

Any project that takes fifteen years to produce is subject to the influence of many minds and results from much assistance. I gratefully acknowledge those who helped shape *Little White Houses* and provided various forms of support. In some cases, that support included years of discussion; in others, it amounted to a crucial e-mail message or a set of questions or comments delivered at a symposium or conference.

First, I am especially indebted to John Archer, Katherine (Kate) Solomonson, and Abigail (Abby) Van Slyck. Kate's belief in and enthusiasm for the project boosted my own when it seemed the manuscript would never reach completion, and, along with Abby, she offered insightful critiques and useful suggestions at important stages of the project. I can't thank Kate and Abby enough for helping me through the rough patches. John Archer, whose scholarship on suburban history has so influenced my own, generously gave detailed feedback that was immensely helpful as I revised the manuscript. I feel fortunate to have piqued his interest, and I'm grateful for his generous assistance.

It will come as no surprise to readers of this book to learn that David Roediger profoundly influenced its focus. Before I met Dave and read his work, this project was a far more conventional architectural history. Nearly a decade ago, he asked questions over coffee and directed me toward literature that was new to me at a critical juncture in this work's development, and he helped me think differently about the questions I was asking and the ways in which they were framed.

FACING
"A modern patio landscape"
(*detail, see p. 294*).

Serving as director of our campus's Center on Democracy in a Multiracial Society, Dave also hosted and made financially possible the symposium "Constructing Race," which I organized in 2004—an event that inspired important intellectual stimulus for my work. I am profoundly grateful to him for this assistance and for his intellectual generosity during earlier phases of the project.

Many others offered helpful insights or supported me and my work in various ways. I wish to thank Annmarie Adams, Beth Amsbury, James Barrett, Susanna Barrows, Nicholas Brown, Harvey Choldin, Lizabeth Cohen, Annie Gilbert Coleman, Mina Coy, Margaret Crawford, Susan Davis, Erica Doss, Cara Finnegan, Peter Fritzsche, James Hay, Greg Hise, Clarence Lang, Heather Hyde Minor, Vernon Hyde Minor, Sharon Irish, Sandy Isenstadt, Jamie Jacobs, James Loewen, Richard Longstreth, Areli Marina, Anne Merritt, Katherine Oberdeck, Melvyn Skvarla, Lisa Spanierman, Lynn Spigel, Inger Stole, Stephen Tobriner, Marc Treib, Dell Upton, and Gwendolyn Wright. I extend my sincere thanks to the anonymous readers of this manuscript, whose generous feedback proved helpful for final revisions.

The late Elaine Sewell Jones opened her home to me in February 1999 so that I could study her personal archive on the career of her late husband, A. Quincy Jones. Her generosity and deep knowledge of Quincy's career opened fresh perspectives that led to the development of two chapters in this book, and I am very grateful to her. I wish she had lived to see this book's publication. After I consulted Quincy's papers in Elaine's private collection, the bulk of the collection was eventually transferred to the UCLA Charles E. Young Research Library, Department of Special Collections. My references in this book to his documents cite Elaine's collection rather than the materials as archived at UCLA.

I presented aspects of this work at numerous venues, including the Charles Warren Center for Studies in American History at Harvard University; the Vernacular Architecture Forum; the Society of Architectural Historians; the University of California, Berkeley; the Graduate School of Design at Harvard University; Dumbarton Oaks; Auburn University; the Chicago Arts Club; the University of Virginia; the Center for Visual Culture at the University of Wisconsin–Madison; and the American Studies Department at the University of Notre Dame. The audiences at each event asked stimulating questions that aided my progress. I am grateful to the faculty who asked important questions in various locations on the University of Illinois campus: the Center for Advanced Study, the Illinois Program for Research in the Humanities, the Jewish Studies Reading Group, the Modern Art Colloquium, and the Critical Studies of Whiteness Reading Group.

This project could not have been completed without the time away from teaching afforded by fellowships granted by the Center for Advanced Study and the Illinois Program for Research in the Humanities at the University of Illinois. The University of Illinois at Urbana–Champaign Campus Research Board gave me critically needed financial support both for release time from teaching and to hire graduate assistants who tracked down illustrations, assisted with bibliographies, produced reproductions of magazine images, and helped me seek permissions to publish them. I gratefully acknowledge the assistance of those students: Abbilyn (Abby) Harmon, Jennifer Langworthy, Rachel Leibowitz, Sarah Rowe, and Yuthika Sharma. Abby Harmon's assistance with obtaining reproduction rights for many of the illustrations in this book was invaluable. I am grateful to the Graham Foundation for Advanced Studies in the Fine Arts and to the University of Illinois Campus Research Board for funding that supported the publication of this volume. A summer residency fellowship at Ragdale in Lake Forest, Illinois, in 2011 allowed me to set aside the demands of my administrative responsibilities (at least briefly) so that I could revise the manuscript for publication. That experience—the heavenly refuge of Ragdale and the opportunity to converse there with writers and artists—is one I will not soon forget and for which I am enormously thankful.

I thank the archivists and librarians at the National Association of Home Builders; the Museum of Television and Radio, Paley Center for Media, New York; the National Museum of American History Archives Center at the Smithsonian Institution; the Horticultural Services Division of the Archives of American Gardens at the Smithsonian Institution; the Chicago Historical Society and Chicago History Museum; the Wisconsin Historical Society Archives; Waverly Lowell at the College of Environmental Design Archives at the University of California, Berkeley; Jennifer Watts at the Huntington Library Photographic Collection; Mary Daniels at the Francis Loeb Library Special Collections at Harvard University; the archivists at the Sackler Museum Archives; the librarians of the Ryerson and Burnham Archive at the Art Institute of Chicago; and the staffs at the University of Illinois Archives and the Building Research Council (formerly the University of Illinois Small Homes Council).

I have been extremely fortunate to have had at my disposal the outstanding collections and brilliant librarians of the University of Illinois Library. I have grown accustomed to finding at my fingertips even exceptionally rare, ephemeral, and esoteric books, journals, and documents, but I have also grown ever more mindful of my good fortune at being employed at a research university that possesses one of the world's greatest libraries. The University of Illinois librarians were especially helpful, and their expertise often resulted in finding a primary-source needle among their (generally very well cataloged) haystack of twenty-four million items. I'm not sure I would have been able to complete this project at an institution without such resources, and I salute the many generous Illinois librarians for their invaluable assistance and expertise.

I thank Pieter Martin and Kristian Tvedten at the University of Minnesota Press. Pieter's active interest in this book and his persistent and politely nudging communications helped keep me relatively on track, which was no small feat given the demands on my time during the final stages of this project. No one could ask for a more patient or committed editor.

This book could never have been produced without my family, both immediate and extended. Nothing good happens in my life that is not made possible by my husband and daughter, Lawrence and Madeleine Hamlin. Any project that took this long to complete is at least half theirs, and I can't begin to thank them for the many hours of my time and attention they so graciously relinquished. I am forever indebted to my grandparents on both sides, but this book owes a special debt to my maternal grandparents, Rudolf and Eva Weingarten, whose house plays an important role in the book. Indeed, the memory of their house, in which I spent many happy hours during the first thirty years of my life, shapes every page of this book. The memory of my father and his devotion to the crafting—both literally and figuratively—of our homes and their contents played an equally important role. He made house building one of his five life priorities, and the house he was building when he died in 1981 is an eloquent and enduring reminder of his love for his family and a future life he imagined but never realized. My mother's discriminating eye and finely honed sense of style, her passion for midcentury design and material culture, and her conviction that our residential surroundings contributed to our sense of who we were played an absolutely definitive role in shaping my own sense of residence and identity. This book is for my family.

Notes

PREFACE

1. My thanks to Charlotte Johnston for providing confirmation of dates related to Rudolf and Eva Weingarten's history. Because he was living on the West Coast, Rudy, like other "enemy aliens" or "suspect" minorities (most notably Japanese Americans), probably encountered more government intervention in his life than he might have had he lived in the East. As Sarah Deutsch has noted, mythologies of the West and of western regional culture made the West Coast seem more vulnerable and less stable. Therefore, its immigrant and ethnic populations received a greater degree of scrutiny and, in the case of Japanese residents, internment than their East Coast counterparts. See Deutsch, "Landscape of Enclaves: Race Relations in the West, 1865–1990," in *Under an Open Sky: Rethinking America's Western Past,* ed. William Cronon, George Miles, and Jay Gitlin (New York: W. W. Norton, 1992), 125.

2. The story of my grandparents' assimilation is certainly not unique among postwar American Jewry, especially in California. Indeed, as D. Michael Quinn has noted, there were much higher rates of Jewish assimilation in the American West as opposed to the East. Moreover, my grandparents' history and the context for their assimilation are far more complex than can be recounted here. I use their story as one that can stand for the stories of members of many minority groups—some of whom likely considered themselves "white"—in the postwar era. See Quinn, "Religion in the American West," in Cronon et al., *Under an Open Sky,* 152. Richard Polenberg cites evidence of the drive to assimilate and the rapidity with which such assimilation occurred during the immediate postwar period, stating that "new immigrants acquired citizenship in record time. In 1946 it had taken aliens, on the average, more than twenty-three years to become citizens; by 1956 it required only seven years." See Polenberg, *One Nation Divisible: Class, Race, and Ethnicity in the United States since 1938* (New York: Viking Press, 1980), 146.

3. Cara A. Finnegan, *Picturing Poverty: Print Culture and FSA Photographs* (Washington, D.C.: Smithsonian Institution Press, 2003), x.

4. Karen Brodkin, *How Jews Became White Folks and What That*

Says about Race in America (New Brunswick, N.J.: Rutgers University Press, 1998), 24.

5. Richard White, *Remembering Ahanagran: A History of Stories* (Seattle: University of Washington Press, 1998), 4.

INTRODUCTION

1. Robert Hariman and John Louis Lucaites, *No Caption Needed: Iconic Photographs, Public Culture, and Liberal Democracy* (Chicago: University of Chicago Press, 2007), 2.

2. W. J. T. Mitchell, *Picture Theory: Essays on Verbal and Visual Representation* (Chicago: University of Chicago Press, 1994), 184, 327, 420–23.

3. The literature on the history of U.S. residential architecture is vast. Excellent studies of nineteenth-century and early twentieth-century domesticity and American domestic architecture include Gwendolyn Wright, *Moralism and the Model Home: Domestic Architecture and Cultural Conflict in Chicago, 1873–1913* (Chicago: University of Chicago Press, 2008); Gwendolyn Wright, *Building the Dream: A Social History of Housing in America* (New York: Pantheon, 1981); Clifford Edward Clark Jr., *The American Family Home, 1800–1960* (Chapel Hill: University of North Carolina Press, 1986); David Handlin, *The American Home: Architecture and Society, 1815–1915* (Boston: Little, Brown, 1970); Alan Gowans, *The Comfortable House: North American Suburban Architecture, 1890–1930* (Cambridge, Mass.: MIT Press, 1986); Jessica Foy and Thomas Schlereth, *American Home Life, 1880–1930: A Social History of Spaces and Services* (Knoxville: University of Tennessee Press, 1992). John Archer's comprehensive study *Architecture and Suburbia: From English Villa to American Dream House, 1690–2000* (Minneapolis: University of Minnesota Press, 2005) includes this period as well, as does Sandy Isenstadt's more focused study, *The Modern American House: Spaciousness and Middle Class Identity* (New York: Cambridge University Press, 2006).

4. Matthew Frye Jacobson, *Whiteness of a Different Color: European Immigrants and the Alchemy of Race* (Cambridge, Mass.: Harvard University Press, 1999), 6, 9.

5. Ibid., 11.

6. Michael Omi and Howard Winant, *Racial Formation in the United States from the 1960s to the 1990s*, 2nd ed. (New York: Routledge, 1994), vii.

7. The Small Homes Council started in 1944. The president of the University of Illinois established it as a cooperative endeavor budgeted out of the university's College of Fine and Applied Arts. Publicized in *House and Home* magazine, the Small Homes Council sent members to all the home builders' shows in the postwar years, where they dispersed their materials from exhibit booths. They also held short courses that were open to the public. The editor of *Popular Mechanics* asked Rudard Jones, a faculty member in the School of Architecture who was active in the Small Homes Council, to write for the magazine sometime after 1949. The Small Homes Council did not sell blueprints, but it did develop house plans for circulars that could be purchased for as little as a dime. The plans published in *Popular Mechanics* could be purchased through the magazine's planning service in Chicago. Small Homes Council, Technical Notes and Research Publications, 12/6/0/11, Box 1, University of Illinois Archives.

8. For example, the California architect Cliff May was influenced by the Levitt family's published house plans. See Dianne Harris, "'The House I Live In': Architecture, Modernism, and Identity in Levittown," in *Second Suburb: Levittown, Pennsylvania*, ed. Dianne Harris (Pittsburgh: University of Pittsburgh Press, 2010), 389n51.

9. U.S. Bureau of the Census, *Census of Housing: 1950* (taken as part of the Seventeenth Decennial Census of the United States), vol. 1, pt. 1 (Washington, D.C.: U.S. Government Printing Office, 1953), xxxv, Table 16, 1–11; and U.S. Bureau of the Census, "United States Summary," in *U.S. Census of Housing, 1960*, vol. 1, *States and Small Areas* (Washington, D.C.: U.S. Government Printing Office, 1963), xli, xliii.

10. The corpus of literature on North American suburban history is large, and a complete bibliography is not possible here. Key texts, however, include the following: Kenneth T. Jackson, *Crabgrass Frontier: The Suburbanization of the United States*

(New York: Oxford University Press, 1985); Robert Fishman, *Bourgeois Utopias: The Rise and Fall of Suburbia* (New York: Basic Books, 1987); Sam Bass Warner Jr., *Streetcar Suburbs: The Process of Growth in Boston, 1870–1900* (Cambridge, Mass.: Harvard University Press, 1962); Dolores Hayden, *Building Suburbia: Green Fields and Urban Growth, 1820–2000* (New York: Pantheon, 2003); Archer, *Architecture and Suburbia*; John R. Stilgoe, *Borderland: Origins of the American Suburb, 1820–1939* (New Haven, Conn.: Yale University Press, 1988). More recent contributions include edited collections such as Kevin M. Kruse and Thomas J. Sugrue, eds., *The New Suburban History* (Chicago: University of Chicago Press, 2006); and Becky M. Nicolaides and Andrew Wiese, eds., *The Suburb Reader* (New York: Routledge, 2006). There are many others, but these provide an overview of the history of suburban development.

11. Both Anna Andrzejewski and James Jacobs have produced and are in the process of producing scholarship that focuses on the history of postwar houses. Anna Vemer Andrzejewski and Adam C. Childers, "The Builder's Wright: Marshall Erdman's Understanding of Frank Lloyd Wright's Architecture" (unpublished manuscript, August 2011); Anna Vemer Andrzejewski, "One Builder: Marshall Erdman and Postwar Building and Real Estate Development in Madison, Wisconsin" (manuscript in progress); James Jacobs, "Detached America: Consuming New Houses in Postwar Suburbia" (manuscript in progress); James Jacobs, "Beyond Levittown: The Design and Marketing of Belair at Bowie, Maryland," in *Housing Washington: Two Centuries of Residential Development and Planning in the National Capital Area*, ed. Richard Longstreth (Chicago: Center for American Places at Columbia College, 2010), 85–109; James Jacobs, "Social and Spatial Change in the Postwar Family Room," *Perspectives in Vernacular Architecture* 13, no. 1 (2006): 70–85. See also Harris, "'The House I Live In,'" 200–242.

12. See, for example, Larry J. Reynolds and Gordon Hutner, *National Imaginaries, American Identities: The Cultural Work of American Iconography* (Princeton, N.J.: Princeton University

Press, 2000). In their notes to *No Caption Needed*, Hariman and Lucaites provide selected references to the rapidly growing corpus of literature in visual culture analysis; see esp. 308–9.

13. Hariman and Lucaites, *No Caption Needed*, 4–5.

14. Ibid., 8–9.

15. Martin Berger, *Seeing through Race: A Reinterpretation of Civil Rights Photography* (Berkeley: University of California Press, 2011), 51.

16. Slavoj Žižek, *The Sublime Object of Ideology* (London: Verso, 1989), 24–25.

17. Ibid., 25–26. Žižek is here referring to Peter Sloterdijk, *Critique of Cynical Reason* (Minneapolis: University of Minnesota Press, 1988).

18. Žižek, *Sublime Object of Ideology*, 33.

19. As Matthew Frye Jacobson has written: "The European immigrants' experience was decisively shaped by their entering an arena where Europeanness—that is to say, whiteness—was among the most important possessions one could lay claim to. It was their *whiteness*, not any kind of New World magnanimity, that opened the Golden Door." Jacobson, *Whiteness of a Different Color*, 8. This is the idea of potency of whiteness to which I refer, and I extend Jacobson's statement to include the children of European immigrants.

20. See Audrey Kobayashi and Linda Peake, "Racism out of Place: Thoughts on Whiteness and an Antiracist Geography in the New Millennium," *Annals of the Association of American Geographers* 90, no. 2 (2000): 397. Kobayashi and Peake specifically note the use of the term "ordinary American" as it is intended to evoke images of whites in traditional nuclear families, where their race, class, and sexual orientation are presumed and need not be mentioned. Hence, they advance the notion of "significant discursive silence" that indicates the operation of race thinking. Such silences are equivalent to the invisibilities I examine here.

21. Omi and Winant, *Racial Formation in the United States*, 55.

22. David Delaney, "The Space That Race Makes," *Professional Geographer* 54, no. 1 (2002): 6. Some of the key studies in

this field include Alastair Bonnett, "Constructions of 'Race,' Place, and Discipline: Geographies of Racial Identity and Racism," *Ethnic and Racial Studies* 19 (1996): 864–83; Owen Dwyer and John Paul Jones III, "White Sociospatial Epistemology," *Social and Cultural Geography* 1 (2000): 209–21; Kobayashi and Peake, "Racism out of Place," 392–403; Laura Pulido, "Rethinking Environmental Racism: White Privilege and Urban Development in Southern California," *Annals of the Association of American Geographers* 90 (2000): 12–40; Richard Schein, ed., *Landscape and Race in the United States* (New York: Routledge, 2006); James S. Duncan and Nancy G. Duncan, *Landscapes of Privilege: The Politics of the Aesthetic in an American Suburb* (New York: Routledge, 2004); Laura R. Barraclough, *Making the San Fernando Valley: Rural Landscapes, Urban Development, and White Privilege* (Athens: University of Georgia Press, 2011). This is just a sampling of works produced by geographers on this topic in the past fifteen years.

23. James S. Duncan and David Lambert, "Landscapes of Home," in *A Companion to Cultural Geography,* ed. James S. Duncan, Nuala C. Johnson, and Richard H. Schein (Malden, Mass.: Blackwell, 2004), 387. See Archer, *Architecture and Suburbia*; Suzanne Reimer and Deborah Leslie, "Identity, Consumption, and the Home," *Home Cultures* 1, no. 2 (July 2004): 187–208; Pierre Bourdieu, *Distinction: A Social Critique of the Judgement of Taste,* trans. Richard Nice (Cambridge, Mass.: Harvard University Press, 1984); Clare Cooper Marcus, *House as a Mirror of Self: Exploring the Deeper Meaning of Home* (Berkeley, Calif.: Conari Press, 1995); Pauline Hunt, "Gender and the Construction of Home Life," in *The Politics of Domestic Consumption: Critical Readings,* ed. Stevi Jackson and Shaun Moores (London: Prentice Hall, 1995), 301–13; Andrew Gorman-Murray, "Gay and Lesbian Couples at Home: Identity Work in Domestic Space," *Home Cultures* 3, no. 2 (July 2006): 145–67; Linda McDowell, *Gender, Identity, and Place: Understanding Feminist Geographies* (Cambridge: Polity Press, 1999); Doreen Massey, *Space, Place, and Gender* (Cambridge: Polity Press, 1994); J. Macgregor Wise, "Home: Territory and Identity," *Cultural Studies* 14, no. 2 (2000): 295–310; Tony Chapman and Jenny Hockey, eds., *Ideal Homes? Social Change and Domestic Life* (London: Routledge, 1999). All these emphasize that neither identity nor home is fixed; rather, the two are "mutually and ongoingly constituted"; Gorman-Murray, "Gay and Lesbian Couples," 147. On identity formation, see Anthony Giddens, *Modernity and Self-Identity* (Cambridge: Polity Press, 1991); Scott Lash and Jonathan Friedman, eds., *Modernity and Identity* (Oxford: Blackwell, 1992); Alan Pred, "Interfusions: Consumption, Identity, and the Practices and Power Relations of Everyday Life," *Environment and Planning A* 28 (1995): 11–24.

24. David M. P. Freund, *Colored Property: State Policy and White Racial Politics in Suburban America* (Chicago: University of Chicago Press, 2007); Karyn R. Lacy, *Blue-Chip Black: Race, Class, and Status in the New Black Middle Class* (Berkeley: University of California Press, 2007), 156.

25. See David R. Roediger, *Working toward Whiteness: How America's Immigrants Became White* (Cambridge, Mass.: Basic Books, 2005), 158–62; Richard Harris, "Working-Class Home Ownership in the American Metropolis," *Journal of American History* 17 (November 1990): 46–69; Olivier Zunz, *The Changing Face of Inequality: Urbanization, Industrial Development, and Immigrants in Detroit, 1880–1920* (Chicago: University of Chicago Press, 1982); Jackson, *Crabgrass Frontier*, 288–90; Daniel D. Luria, "Wealth, Capital, and Power: The Social Meaning of Homeownership," *Journal of Interdisciplinary History* 7 (Autumn 1976): 261–82.

26. For a vivid account of the defense of homeownership as an exclusively white privilege and a Detroit riot that resulted from that defense in 1923, see Kevin Boyle, *Arc of Justice: A Saga of Race, Civil Rights, and Murder in the Jazz Age* (New York: Henry Holt, 2004). On the Chicago riot of 1919, see William M. Tuttle, *Race Riot: Chicago in the Red Summer of 1919* (Urbana: University of Illinois Press, 1996); and, more generally, Janet L. Abu-Lughod, *Race, Space, and Riots in New York, Chicago, and Los Angeles* (New York: Oxford University Press, 2007).

27. Roediger, *Working toward Whiteness*, 173, 175. On the history of restrictive covenants, see Robert M. Fogelson, *Bourgeois Nightmares: Suburbia, 1870–1930* (New Haven, Conn.: Yale University Press, 2005); Charles Abrams, *Forbidden Neighbors: A Study of Prejudice in Housing* (New York: Harper, 1955).

28. Arthur H. Dix, *General-Magazine Competition* (New York: Conover-Mast, 1957), 16.

29. For example, Park Forest, Illinois, which was known as "the Original G.I. Suburb," was unrestricted. Notably, Jews were included among the development group. However, the first black families in Park Forest were mapped by local authorities, their house locations noted on city documents, ostensibly to protect them from harm. This mapping of nonwhites, however, can equally be interpreted as a means of tracking for surveillance purposes. Conversation with Park Forest town manager Janet Muchnick, September 2002. For a study that examines African American suburbs and developments, see Andrew Wiese, *Places of Their Own: African American Suburbanization in the Twentieth Century* (Chicago: University of Chicago Press, 2004).

30. David Roediger, "I Came for the Art: Exposing Whiteness and Imagining Nonwhite Spaces," in *White: Whiteness and Race in Contemporary Art,* ed. Maurice Berger (Baltimore: Baltimore Museum of Art, 2004).

31. An important text that examines the whitening of American immigrants from the late nineteenth century through the New Deal era is David Roediger's *Working toward Whiteness.* See also Thomas A. Guglielmo, *White on Arrival: Italians, Race, Color, and Power in Chicago, 1890–1945* (New York: Oxford University Press, 2003); and Brodkin, *How Jews Became White Folks.*

32. Omi and Winant, *Racial Formation in the United States,* 12.

33. Matthew Jacobson notes that Nazi Germany and the post-Holocaust reality caused race to be "willfully erased" in favor of notions of ethnicity and racial tolerance. See *Whiteness of a Different Color,* 96.

34. Brodkin, *How Jews Became White Folks,* 9, 10, 11, 23, 25. Brodkin sees the postwar period as a divide in racial construction for some groups, especially Jews: "Instead of dirty and dangerous races that would destroy American democracy, immigrants became ethnic groups whose children had successfully assimilated into the mainstream and risen to the middle class"; 36.

35. See ibid., 144, 155, 166. Societal acceptance of Jews in the postwar era was also related to the complex series of events that followed the Holocaust. Still, Jews, along with many Asian immigrants, have long been considered "model minorities" because of their broadly perceived desire to assimilate.

36. Stuart Hall, "Race, Culture, and Communications: Looking Backward and Forward at Cultural Studies," *Rethinking Marxism* 5, no. 1 (1992): 16.

37. Harry J. Elam Jr., "Reality ✓," in *Critical Theory and Performance,* rev. ed., ed. Janelle G. Reinelt and Joseph R. Roach (Ann Arbor: University of Michigan Press, 2007), 174.

38. Paul Gilroy, *The Black Atlantic: Modernity and Double Consciousness* (Cambridge, Mass.: Harvard University Press, 1993).

39. For more on this, see Toni Morrison, *Playing in the Dark: Whiteness and the Literary Imagination* (Cambridge, Mass.: Harvard University Press, 1992).

40. Freund, *Colored Property,* 17 and passim.

41. William M. Dobriner, *Class in Suburbia* (Englewood Cliffs, N.J.: Prentice Hall, 1963), 15, 37–38.

42. See Gilroy, *The Black Atlantic,* 85.

43. As Michael Eric Dyson has noted, class amplifies race and vice versa. See Dyson, *Come Hell or High Water: Hurricane Katrina and the Color of Disaster* (New York: Basic Civitas Books, 2007), 145, where he writes, "Simply said, race makes class hurt more."

44. Susan Ruddick, "Constructing Difference in Public Spaces: Race, Class, and Gender as Interlocking Systems," *Urban Geography* 17, no. 2 (1996): 138.

45. For more on the social construction of class, see Stuart M. Blumin, *The Emergence of the Middle Class: Social Experience in the American City, 1760–1900* (New York: Cambridge University Press, 1989); David Halle, *America's Working Man:*

Work, Home, and Politics among Blue-Collar Property Owners (Chicago: University of Chicago Press, 1984), esp. xiii, 22, 25; Thomas J. Sugrue, *The Origins of the Urban Crisis: Race and Inequality in Postwar Detroit* (Princeton, N.J.: Princeton University Press, 1996), esp. 203–7, 244–45; James Barrett, "Americanization from the Bottom Up: Immigration and the Remaking of the Working Class in the United States, 1880–1930," *Journal of American History* 79, no. 3 (1992): 996–1020; C. Wright Mills, *White Collar: The American Middle Classes* (New York: Oxford University Press, 1951).

46. See Becky M. Nicolaides, *My Blue Heaven: Life and Politics in the Working-Class Suburbs of Los Angeles, 1920–1965* (Chicago: University of Chicago Press, 2002), 61.

47. Barbara Ehrenreich, *Fear of Falling: The Inner Life of the Middle Class* (New York: Harper Perennial, 1989), 13.

48. Martha Gimenez, "Back to Class: Reflections on the Dialectics of Class and Identity," in *More Unequal: Aspects of Class in the United States,* ed. Michael D. Yates (New York: Monthly Review Press, 2007), 108, 109, 110.

49. Polenberg, *One Nation Divisible,* 139, 141, 145.

1. THE ORDINARY POSTWAR HOUSE

1. Darryl Hattenhauer, "The Rhetoric of Architecture: A Semiotic Approach," *Communication Quarterly* 32, no. 1 (Winter 1984): 71.

2. Pamela Robertson Wojcik, *The Apartment Plot: Urban Living in American Film and Popular Culture, 1945 to 1975* (Durham, N.C.: Duke University Press, 2010), 8.

3. Laura R. Barraclough, *Making the San Fernando Valley,* 63. For her statistics, Barraclough cites Mike Davis, *City of Quartz: Excavating the Future in Los Angeles* (New York: Vintage Books, 1990), 168.

4. George Sanchez, "What's Good for Boyle Heights Is Good for the Jews: Creating Multiracialism on the Eastside during the 1950s," *American Quarterly* 56, no. 3 (September 2004): 638.

5. See, for example, Theodore Allen, *The Invention of the White Race,* vol. 1 (London: Verso, 1994); Alastair Bonnett, "White Studies: The Problems and Projects of a New Research Agenda," *Theory, Culture & Society* 13, no. 3 (1996): 145–55; Mike Hill, ed., *Whiteness: A Critical Reader* (New York: New York University Press, 1997); Richard Dyer, *White* (London: Routledge, 1997); Peter Kolchin, "Whiteness Studies: The New History of Race in America," *Journal of American History* 89, no. 1 (June 2002): 154–73; Aldon Lynn Nielsen, *Reading Race: White American Poets and the Racial Discourse in the Twentieth Century* (Athens: University of Georgia Press, 1988); David R. Roediger, *The Wages of Whiteness: Race and the Making of the American Working Class* (London: Verso, 1991). My thanks to Tim Engles and David Roediger for directing me to these sources.

6. David Roediger, "How Old and New Whiteness Keep Showing Up, but Not by Themselves," in *White: Whiteness and Race in Contemporary Art,* ed. Maurice Berger (Baltimore: Baltimore Museum of Art, 2004), 95.

7. Ibid.

8. Cheryl I. Harris, "Whiteness as Property," *Harvard Law Review* 106, no. 8 (June 1993): 1709–95. See also Martha R. Mahoney, "Segregation, Whiteness, and Transformation," *University of Pennsylvania Law Review* 143, no. 5 (May 1995): 1659–84.

9. See, for example, George Lipsitz, *The Possessive Investment in Whiteness: How White People Profit from Identity Politics* (Philadelphia: Temple University Press, 1998). See also Freund, *Colored Property.*

10. Delaney, "Space That Race Makes," 7.

11. Brodkin, *How Jews Became White Folks,* 153.

12. Jacobson, *Whiteness of a Different Color,* 96.

13. Ibid., 100–110, 174, 188, 197.

14. U.S. Bureau of the Census, *Census of Housing: 1950,* vol. 1, pt. 1, xi, xvi–xvii.

15. Ibid., xxv, xxviii, 1–2. To give a sense of regional variation, census data for Chicago in 1950 indicate that whites owned 646,440 dwellings, compared with 24,079 owned by blacks; in Denver, whites owned 93,541 dwellings, and blacks owned just 1,668; in Detroit, 485,548 whites owned dwellings, and

blacks owned just 26,609. Roughly 750,000 whites owned homes in Los Angeles, but just over 24,000 blacks did so. In the San Francisco/Oakland metropolitan area, 333,225 whites owned homes, compared with 9,409 blacks. In some southern cities the proportional discrepancies were less severe, perhaps because the black populations were larger and more firmly established. For example, in New Orleans, nearly 63,000 whites owned their own homes, compared with 13,000 blacks. See ibid., Table 22, 1–38, 1–41, 1–43, and 1–45.

16. Ibid., Table 7, 1–4; Table 8, 1–6.

17. U.S. Bureau of the Census, "United States Summary," xxvi; Table G, xxvii; xxviii.

18. For an excellent analysis of the federal government's role in the construction of racist housing and lending policies, see Lipsitz, *Possessive Investment in Whiteness.*

19. Ibid., 6.

20. Quoted in Arnold R. Hirsch, "Containment on the Home Front: Race and Federal Housing Policy from the New Deal to the Cold War," *Journal of Urban History* 26 (January 2000): 167.

21. Thomas H. Creighton, ed., *Building for Modern Man: A Symposium* (Princeton, N.J.: Princeton University Press, 1949), 28.

22. Kevin Fox Gotham, *Race, Real Estate, and Uneven Development: The Kansas City Experience, 1900–2000* (Albany: State University of New York Press, 2002), 149.

23. Abrams, *Forbidden Neighbors,* 229.

24. Brodkin, *How Jews Became White Folks,* 47; Gotham, *Race, Real Estate,* 53. As Gotham points out: "Some private appraising manuals in Missouri and Kansas still contained listings of ethnic groups ranked in descending order from those who were the most desirable to those who had the most adverse effect on property values. Whites were ranked at the top while Blacks and Mexican-Americans were ranked at the very bottom"; 141. To view some FHA maps that display redlining and for an explanation of FHA color codes, see "Testbed for the Redlining Archives of California's Exclusionary Spaces" at http://salt.unc.edu/T-RACES, accessed May 29, 2012.

25. See United States Gypsum Co., *Operative Remodeling: The New Profit Frontier for Builders* (Washington, D.C.: United States Gypsum Co. and National Association of Home Builders, 1956). This joint publication venture attempted to persuade builders that they could gain solid profits by remodeling older inner-city housing stock that was in neighborhoods deemed "still worth saving"; 11. Linked to widespread concerns about urban blight, the book glosses over the problems of race and discrimination.

26. Ibid., 29.

27. In 1955, NAHB president Dick Hughes warned that builders had to construct new homes for minority occupancy in order to avoid an industry crisis that he believed would occur if groups such as the NAACP and the National Urban League succeeded in getting the government to block FHA- and VA-backed loans that were not open to minorities. However, as an article in *House and Home* noted, "it chiefly is the profit potential, not social motives, that has beckoned a sizeable number of homebuilders into the minority market already." Despite that magazine's occasional coverage of this issue, restrictive federal financing policies ensured that the overwhelming majority of new housing stock was reserved for whites. See "What Builders Are Doing about Minority Housing and What Problems They Face," *House and Home,* April 1955, 138–51, 194, 198. On the NAHB, see Rosalyn Baxandall and Elizabeth Ewen, *Picture Windows: How the Suburbs Happened* (New York: Basic Books, 2000), 81–82. See also Gotham, *Race, Real Estate,* 41, 80, 91–92.

28. Thomas J. Sugrue, "Affirmative Action from Below: Civil Rights, the Building Trades, and the Politics of Racial Equality in the Urban North, 1945–1969," *Journal of American History* 91, no. 1 (June 2004): 145–73. On the Levitts and their use of nonunion laborers, see the essays in Harris, *Second Suburb.*

29. Gotham, *Race, Real Estate,* 23, 24, 26.

30. Flannery O'Connor, "The Artificial Nigger," in *A Good Man Is Hard to Find, and Other Stories* (Orlando, Fla.: Harcourt, 1955), 119.

31. Gotham, *Race, Real Estate,* 35, 36. These codes were embed-

ded in real estate industry literature, as Gotham shows. The National Association of Real Estate Boards (NAREB) textbook, *Fundamentals of Real Estate Practice,* from 1939 and 1946 made explicit connections between race and property values. The book's authors stated that some immigrant groups more readily assimilate and are therefore less detrimental, such as Germans, who are "clean and thrifty people. They take pride in keeping their property clean and in good condition. . . . Unfortunately, this cannot be said of all the other nations which have sent their immigrants to our country. Some of them have brought standards and customs far below our own levels. . . . Like termites they undermine the structure of any neighborhood in which they creep." Quoted in Gotham, *Race, Real Estate,* 35.

32. Anne McClintock, *Imperial Leather: Race, Gender, and Sexuality in the Colonial Contest* (New York: Routledge, 1995), 31–36; 207–31; as cited in Roediger, *Working toward Whiteness,* 115.

33. On histories of the sanitary and hygienic home, see Ruth Schwartz Cowan, *More Work for Mother: The Ironies of Household Technology from the Open Hearth to the Microwave* (New York: Basic Books, 1983); Jeanne Boydston, *Home and Work: Housework, Wages, and the Ideology of Labor in the Early Republic* (New York: Oxford University Press, 1990); Susan Strasser, *Never Done: A History of American Housework* (1982; repr., New York: Holt, 2000); Wright, *Moralism and the Model Home.*

34. George Catlin and Mary Catlin, *Building Your New House* (New York: Current Books, 1946), 19. On the stigma attached to mobile homes and trailers, see Andrew Hurley, *Diners, Bowling Alleys, and Trailer Parks: Chasing the American Dream in Postwar Consumer Culture* (New York: Basic Books, 2001).

35. Catlin and Catlin, *Building Your New House,* 21.

36. Ibid.

37. Ibid., 28, 31.

38. Ibid., 170. Mary recommended building in restricted districts and in neighborhoods that are in new developments, since all the houses would be the same quality. See ibid., 173. The Catlins thanked the FHA in their acknowledgments for never failing "to supply us promptly with needed facts and figures."

39. Ibid., 174.

40. Ibid.

41. Thomas J. Sugrue, "Reassessing the History of Postwar America," in *Prospects: An Annual of American Cultural Studies,* vol. 20, ed. Jack Salzman (New York: Cambridge University Press, 1995), 500–501.

42. See ibid., 493–509.

43. Housing and Home Finance Agency, *Slum Clearance and Urban Redevelopment: The What and Why of Title I Housing Act of 1949,* Washington, D.C., November 1950, Howard Moïse Collection [1965-1], Project Folder III:2, Housing Publications/Bulletins, circa 1949–51, Environmental Design Archives, University of California, Berkeley.

44. See, for example, "What Builders Are Doing," 138–51, 186, 194, 198. See also "Nonwhite Housing Projects," *House and Home,* January 1954, 47; "Non White Housing Started," *House and Home,* April 1954, 54; "Nonwhite Prefabs," *House and Home,* December 1954, 55; "VHMCP Finances $8,500 Negro Housing Tract," *House and Home,* February 1956, 47; Ann Copperman, "Ghettoes, U.S.A.: The How and Why of Segregation," *Task,* no. 6 (n.d.). Copperman's progressive article refuted claims about property devaluation in segregated communities using carefully researched statistics and passionate moral arguments. Of course, the black press had been publishing on this topic for decades.

45. The four recessions that occurred in the fifteen-year period of this study took place November 1948–October 1949, July 1953–May 1954, August 1957–April 1958, and April 1960–February 1961. See Benjamin Caplan, "A Case Study: The 1948–1949 Recession," in *Policies to Combat Depression,* National Bureau of Economic Research (N.J.: Princeton University Press, 1956); Edward E. Leamer, "Housing and the Business Cycle" (paper delivered at the symposium "Housing, Housing Finance, and Monetary Policy," August 7, 2007), accessed June 27, 2011, at http://cr4re.com/documents/Leamer HousingandBusinessCycle.pdf; Leo Grebler, "The Housing

Expansion of 1953–54: A Classic Response to Easy Credit," in *Housing Issues in Economic Stabilization Policy* (New York: National Bureau of Economic Research, 1960); "Business: Housing Troubles?," *Time*, February 24, 1961.

46. "Best House under $15,000," *Life*, September 10, 1951, 123.

47. For a thorough explanation of the FHA's "minimum house" standards, see Greg Hise, *Magnetic Los Angeles: Planning the Twentieth-Century Metropolis* (Baltimore: Johns Hopkins University Press, 1997), chap. 2. See also Federal Housing Administration, *Principles of Planning Small Houses*, Technical Bulletin 4 (Washington, D.C.: U.S. Government Printing Office, 1936); and David L. Ames and Linda Flint McClelland, "House and Yard," in *Historic Residential Suburbs: Guidelines for Evaluation and Documentation for the National Register of Historic Places* (Washington, D.C.: U.S. Department of the Interior, National Park Service, 2002), accessed May 29, 2012, at http://www.nps.gov/nr/publications/bulletins/suburbs/part3.htm.

48. "Same Rooms, Varied Decor: Clever Interiors Win Prizes in Identical Levitt Houses," *Life*, January 14, 1952, 90.

49. "Four-Bedroom Bargain for $8,695," *Life*, October 12, 1953, 101.

50. Richard E. Gordon, Katherine K. Gordon, and Max Gunther, *The Split-Level Trap* (New York: Bernard Geis Associates/Random House, 1960).

51. Alan Ehrenhalt, *The Lost City: The Forgotten Virtues of Community in America* (New York: Basic Books/HarperCollins, 1995), 204–5.

52. According to a study conducted by the NAHB, "The average home on which an FHA-insured mortgage was placed in 1950 had 922 square feet, a generous amount of space." The average house price in 1952 ranged from $5,500 to $11,950. The average annual income of purchasers of new homes in 1950 was $3,861. National Association of Home Builders, *Housing . . . USA* (Washington, D.C.: National Association of Home Builders, 1953), 6, 8.

53. Wini Breines, *Young, White, and Miserable: Growing Up Female in the Fifties* (Boston: Beacon Press, 1992), 104.

54. U.S. Bureau of the Census, "United States Summary," xxxv.

55. Ibid.

56. Adam Rome notes that "the number of new single-family homes with basements fell from more than 50 percent in 1940 to just 36 percent in 1950." Rome, *The Bulldozer in the Countryside: Suburban Sprawl and the Rise of American Environmentalism* (New York: Cambridge University Press, 2001), 61. Rome's statistics are derived from "Surveying Materials Used in House Construction," *Housing Research* 1 (March 1953): 37.

57. My thanks to Peter Fritzsche for suggesting this notion.

58. "Space Savers: Handy Furniture Stacks, Stores and Spreads Out," *Life*, December 22, 1952, 33.

59. Ibid., 36.

60. "A Portfolio of Ideas for Home Planning," *Life*, May 1945, 69.

61. "Introducing—the PM California House," *Popular Mechanics*, October 1958, 132–39, 248, 250.

62. Philip Nobel, "Who Built Mr. Blandings' Dream House?," in *Architecture and Film*, ed. Mark Lamster (New York: Princeton Architectural Press, 2000), 55.

63. My thanks to Gary Portman, professor emeritus of Jewish studies and religion at the University of Illinois, Urbana–Champaign, for helping me understand this way of thinking about the display of Seder plates in American Jewish homes.

64. Jenna Weissman Joselit, "A Set Table: Jewish Domestic Culture in the New World, 1880–1950," in *Getting Comfortable in New York: The American Jewish Home, 1880–1950*, ed. Susan L. Braunstein and Jenna Weissman Joselit (New York: Jewish Museum, 1990), 48, 49, 59. Joselit cites Harry Gersh, "The Jewish Paintner," *Commentary*, January 1946, 66.

65. Yan Xu, "The Chinese 'American Dream' at the Turn of 21st Century: A Case Study of Chinese-Americans' Homes in Madison, Wisconsin" (MLA thesis, University of Illinois, Urbana–Champaign, 2000).

66. Renee Y. Chow, *Suburban Space: The Fabric of Dwelling* (Berkeley: University of California Press, 2002), chap. 7.

67. Xu, "The Chinese 'American Dream.'" See also Renee Y. Chow, "House Form and Choice," *Traditional Dwellings and Settlement Review* 9, no. 2 (Spring 1998): 51–61; Ellen J.

Pader, "Spatiality and Social Change: Domestic Space Use in Mexico and the United States," *American Ethnologist* 20, no. 1 (February 1993): 114–37.

68. Richard Yates, *Revolutionary Road* (1961; repr., New York: Vintage, 2000), 20, 29, 30.

69. Studies of uneven urban and suburban development are fairly numerous, although those that focus on the issue of race as socially and culturally constructed are less so. See, for example, Joe T. Darden, Richard Child Hill, June Thomas, and Richard Thomas, *Detroit: Race and Uneven Development* (Philadelphia: Temple University Press, 1987); Arnold R. Hirsch, *Making the Second Ghetto: Race and Housing in Chicago, 1940–60* (New York: Cambridge University Press, 1983); and Gotham, *Race, Real Estate.*

70. Gotham, *Race, Real Estate,* 150.

2. MAGAZINE LESSONS

1. Benedict Anderson, *Imagined Communities,* rev. ed. (London: Verso, 2006), 35, 36, 44.

2. Ibid., 22.

3. Valerie Babb, *Whiteness Visible: The Meaning of Whiteness in American Literature and Culture* (New York: New York University Press, 1998), 162, 166.

4. Berger, *Seeing through Race,* 51–52.

5. Babb, *Whiteness Visible,* 140. Moreover, turn-of-the-century writers on Jewish etiquette likened education on comportment to the process of becoming an American. As Joselit has noted, "Between the 1880s and the 1950s, the Jews of New York displayed an intense concern for the rituals and routines of everyday life, investing cleanliness, table manners, diet, decor, appearance, and privacy with profound cultural and social significance" such that "manners and morals [were promoted] as vehicles of acculturation." Indeed, the long preoccupation with etiquette manuals for Jews indicates, as Joselit shows, an anxiety over assimilated identities. Joselit, "A Set Table," 21.

6. Among the classic works on American domestic spaces are Dolores Hayden, *The Grand Domestic Revolution: A History of Feminist Designs for American Homes, Neighborhoods, and Cities* (Cambridge: MIT Press, 1981); Wright, *Moralism and the Model Home*; Wright, *Building the Dream*; Clark, *American Family Home.*

7. See Elaine Tyler May, *Homeward Bound: American Families in the Cold War Era* (New York: Basic Books, 1988), 26, 27.

8. Dell Upton, "The Traditional House and Its Enemies," *Traditional Dwellings and Settlements Review* 1 (1990): 78.

9. Kate Ellen Rogers, *The Modern House, U.S.A.: Its Design and Decoration* (New York: Harper, 1962), 19.

10. Babb, *Whiteness Visible,* 122, 124.

11. Here I borrow George Lipsitz's term. See Lipsitz, *Possessive Investment in Whiteness.*

12. If the magazines promoted whiteness somewhat unconsciously, Kevin Fox Gotham has demonstrated that the real estate industry promotional literature was far more explicit and "aimed at convincing middle-class whites that residential life in a racially segregated neighborhood was a mark of social status, upward mobility, and protection from the chaos and social problems of the city." Gotham, *Race, Real Estate,* 43. Still, this literature lacked the compelling visual rhetoric provided by the magazines.

13. Finnegan, *Picturing Poverty,* 175.

14. Erika Doss, "Introduction," in *Looking at "Life" Magazine,* ed. Erika Doss (Washington, D.C.: Smithsonian Institution Press, 2001), 8. It should also be noted that *Life's* founder, Henry R. Luce, saw himself as an opinion maker. See James L. Baughman, "Who Read *Life*? The Circulation of America's Favorite Magazine," in Doss, *Looking at "Life" Magazine,* 42.

15. Theodore Peterson, *Magazines in the Twentieth Century* (Urbana: University of Illinois Press, 1956), 388.

16. Stuart Ewen and Elizabeth Ewen, *Channels of Desire: Mass Images and the Shaping of American Consciousness* (Minneapolis: University of Minnesota Press, 1992), x.

17. Peterson, *Magazines in the Twentieth Century,* 389.

18. Ibid., 391. Peterson cites Bernard Berelson and Patricia Salter, "Majority and Minority Americans: An Analysis of Maga-

zine Fiction," *Public Opinion Quarterly* 10 (Summer 1946): 169–90.

19. On *Life*'s inclusion of articles about race, see Wendy Kozol, "Gazing at Race in the Pages of *Life*: Picturing Segregation through Theory and History," in Doss, *Looking at "Life" Magazine*, 159.

20. David Morley has noted this same problem in his analysis of the meaning of home in his book *Home Territories: Media, Mobility, and Identity* (London: Routledge, 2000), 8.

21. Richard Ohmann, *Selling Culture: Magazines, Markets, and Class at the Turn of the Century* (London: Verso, 1996), 139. This is also a major theme of John Archer's *Architecture and Suburbia*.

22. Ohmann, *Selling Culture*, 127, 135, 140, 160, 174.

23. Nancy A. Walker, ed., *Women's Magazines, 1940–1960: Gender Roles and the Popular Press* (Boston: Bedford/St. Martin's Press, 1998), 4, 5, 19.

24. Ibid., vi, 1.

25. Ibid., 2.

26. According to information collected by the Association of National Advertisers (ANA) based on statistics provided by the Audit Bureau of Circulations (ABC), the combined circulation per average issue of national magazines doubled between 1939 and 1959. The number of ABC-audited magazines increased during that same period, from 235 to 274. Association of National Advertisers, *Magazine Circulation and Rate Trends, 1940–1959* (New York: Association of National Advertisers, 1960), 5.

27. Curtis Publishing Company, *Some Important Facts about Magazine Circulations*, no. 196 (Philadelphia: Curtis Publishing Company, 1953), 1, 6.

28. I have relied on two sources for magazine subscription and circulation statistics during this period: J. Percy H. Johnson, *N. W. Ayer and Sons Directory of Newspapers and Periodicals* (Philadelphia, 1945, 1950, 1955, 1960); and Association of National Advertisers, *Magazine Circulation and Rate Trends, 1940–1959*. The latter provides separate data for subscription versus newsstand sales, while the former lumps these to-gether. The Ayer directory provides statistics by geographic region; the ANA publication provides circulation figures by magazine type. Their categories include "general monthly," "women's," "home," "men's," and "mechanics and science," among others. Of the "home" journals surveyed, *American Home* and *Better Homes and Gardens* led the industry with 1.3 million subscribers and 1.6 million subscribers, respectively, in 1945. These rose to 3 million and 4 million, respectively, by 1959. According to the ANA publication, the 1945 subscription totals for *House Beautiful* were 157,732; by 1959, the magazine had 449,303 subscribers in the United States. *Popular Mechanics* was mailed to 256,825 homes in 1945, and to 785,440 homes by 1959.

29. Crossley, Inc., *National Study of Magazine Audiences* (New York: Cowles Magazine, 1952), 2. This study was conducted by Crossley, Inc, for *Look* magazine.

30. Baughman, "Who Read *Life*?," 43.

31. Crossley, Inc., *National Study of Magazine Audiences*, 33.

32. Ibid., 45. As Erika Doss has noted, *Life* had "iconic presence and cultural prestige." Doss, "Introduction," 3.

33. Dix, *General-Magazine Competition*, 15.

34. *Printer's Ink*, January 6, 1950, 87.

35. Dix, *General-Magazine Competition*, 16.

36. Selma Robinson, "103 Women Sound Off!," *McCall's*, February 1959, 137.

37. Stephen James, "Magazines and Modernity: The 'Home' Magazines and the Making of the Ranch House, 1945–1950," in *Redefining Suburban Studies: Searching for New Paradigms*, ed. Daniel Rubey (Hempstead, N.Y.: National Center for Suburban Studies, Hofstra University, 2009), 51.

38. In 1955, *Better Homes and Gardens* averaged more than $2,133,000 an issue in advertising revenue. This was also about average for the big magazines, such as *Life*, at that time. This revenue began to drive every aspect of magazine production. Peterson, *Magazines in the Twentieth Century*, 23.

39. Subscription records indicate that the audiences for these journals grew every year (see note 28, above). Moreover, the continued publication of the popular and shelter magazines

I rely on in this book over decades indicates their financial success, which was based largely on circulation.

40. "Architecture in America," *Architectural Forum*, September 1955, 111. On the disparity between the highbrow, elite taste and recommendations of professional designers and elite tastemakers and the taste of the middle- and working-class public, see Shelley Nickles, "More Is Better: Mass Consumption, Gender, and Class Identity in Postwar America," *American Quarterly* 54, no. 4 (December 2002): 581–622.

41. For more on Elizabeth Gordon, see Dianne Harris, "Making Your Private World: Modern Landscape Architecture and *House Beautiful*, 1945–1965," in *The Architecture of Landscape, 1940–1960*, ed. Marc Treib (Philadelphia: University of Pennsylvania Press, 2002).

42. Elizabeth Gordon, "Resume of Elizabeth Gordon," n.d., Elizabeth Gordon Papers, Series 1, Biographical Materials, Box 1, Folder 1, Sackler Archives. The two issues of *House Beautiful* that focused on Japan and on the topic of *shibui* appeared in August and September 1960.

43. Gordon, "Resume."

44. Quoted in Diana J. Sims, "Beyond *House Beautiful*: Editor Relaxes After Rich Career," article in Hagerstown, Maryland, newspaper, September 3, 1987, Elizabeth Gordon Papers, Series 1, Biographical Materials, newspaper clippings, 1987–1988, Box Folder 2, Sackler Archives.

45. Ibid.

46. Robert Woods Kennedy, *The House and the Art of Its Design* (New York: Reinhold, 1953), 334–35.

47. Ibid., 336, 338, 340.

48. "Better Keep Your Eye on the Newsstands . . . Because Your Customers Do," *House and Home*, May 1955, 168, 175, 189. In July 1955, the *House and Home* consumer magazine review stated that consumer magazines of that month featured contemporary materials: "Over six and a half million readers of two top magazines will see plastics in interesting new installations, duplexes with income-producing rental units, all-purpose kitchens, post and beam framing with glass walls and a trend to two story houses." *House and Home*, July 1955,

139. In his study of the New Jersey Levittown, Herbert Gans notes: "Forty percent of the people interviewed said they were reading new magazines since moving to Levittown. . . . Only 9 of the 52 magazines were house-and-garden types such as *American Home* and *Better Homes and Gardens*, but then 88 percent of the people were already reading these, at least in the year they moved to Levittown. Although not a single person said these magazines had helped in the decision to buy a home in Levittown, 57 percent reported that they had gotten ideas from the magazines to try out in their houses, primarily on the use of space, furniture, and shrubbery arrangements, what to do with pictures and drapes, and how to build shelves and patios." Herbert Gans, *The Levittowners: Ways of Life and Politics in a New Suburban Community* (New York: Columbia University Press, 1967), 191.

49. *House and Home*, February 1955, 6–7. See also *House and Home*, November 1954, 4–5, which included a *Life* advertisement asking builders and development corporations to advertise in their magazine because "each week *Life* sells more than 5,400,000 copies."

50. Editors of Fortune, *The Changing American Market* (Garden City, N.Y.: Hanover House, 1955), 26. Many of the shelter and trade magazines were essentially one gigantic advertisement, since the pages were all about selling products. As Marsha Ackerman notes: "Advertising never simply mirrors the social order, but reflects advertisers' inevitably partial understanding of who their audience really is and what they can be persuaded to buy. Although it is almost impossible to quantify their effectiveness, advertising texts reveal the framing assumptions within which public attitudes are formed and consumption decisions take place." Marsha Ackerman, "What Should Women (and Men) Want? Advertising Home Air Conditioning in the Fifties," *Columbia Journal of American Studies* 3, no. 1 (1998): 8.

51. "Twelve Top Merchandising Techniques," *House and Home*, May 1955, 176–82.

52. On the Case Study Houses, see Elizabeth A. T. Smith, ed.,

Blueprints for Modern Living: History and Legacy of the Case Study Houses (Cambridge: MIT Press, 1999).

53. As Thomas Hine has noted, *Arts and Architecture* dealt with a "relatively narrow social and cultural context within which the Case Study program operated." See Thomas Hine, "The Search for the Postwar House," in Smith, *Blueprints for Modern Living,* 167.

54. Ibid., 180.

55. "*Life* Houses: Here Are Eight New Homes Planned and Built for U.S. 1940," *Life,* July 1, 1940, 76.

56. Ibid., 76, 90.

57. *Architectural Forum,* November 1938, 31.

58. Ibid., 38–40.

59. Tom Riley, "I'm Building the PM Plywood Ranch House," *Popular Mechanics,* November 1950, 88–89.

60. Elizabeth Gordon, letter to Maynard Parker, January 25, 1943, Maynard Parker Collection, Huntington Library, San Marino, California.

61. In April 1955, each of the six houses constructed in the U.S. Gypsum Research Village appeared separately in one of the shelter and trade magazines, including *House & Garden, McCall's, American Home, House Beautiful, Better Homes and Gardens, Popular Home,* and *Living for Young Homemakers.* Hedrich Blessing photographs illustrated the features of each house, and the photography firm was involved in the Research Village's conception from its earliest stages, indicating the importance of photography and of mass circulation of photography to the project. The spring 1955 issue of *Popular Home* provided an overview of the entire village. The village included houses designed by Gilbert H. Coddington, Francis Lethbridge, Hugh Stubbins, A. Quincy Jones, Harris Armstrong, and O'Neil Ford. The Hedrich Blessing photographs of the village are in the collections of the Chicago History Museum.

62. Elizabeth Gordon, letter to Maynard Parker, November 26, 1943, Maynard Parker Collection, Huntington Library, San Marino, California.

63. Elizabeth Gordon, telegram to Maynard Parker, December 21, 1943, Maynard Parker Collection, Huntington Library, San Marino, California.

64. Elizabeth Gordon, telegram to Maynard Parker, date not visible, Havens House shoot, Maynard Parker Collection, Huntington Library, San Marino, California.

65. Elizabeth Gordon, letter to John Weston Havens, April 14, 1944, Maynard Parker Collection, Huntington Library, San Marino, California.

66. For an analysis of the Havens house and its relationship to its owner's sexuality, see Annmarie Adams, "Sex and the Single Building: The Weston Havens House, 1941–2001," *Buildings and Landscapes* 17, no. 1 (Spring 2010): 85, where Adams notes that Havens "was never married and never discussed his sexual orientation (purportedly gay)."

67. Walker, *Women's Magazines,* 7.

3. RENDERED WHITENESS

1. Brodkin, *How Jews Became White Folks,* 21.

2. "Florida Sheriff Calls White Family Black," *Ebony,* March 1955, 37.

3. "Where Mixed Couples Live," *Ebony,* May 1955, 61.

4. Brodkin, *How Jews Became White Folks,* 50. For an excellent analysis of the federal government's role in the construction of racist housing and lending policies, see Lipsitz, *Possessive Investment in Whiteness.* See also Hirsch, "Containment on the Home Front."

5. Dyer, *White,* xiii.

6. See, for example, J. B. Harley, "Silences and Secrecy: The Hidden Agenda of Cartography in Early Modern Europe," *Imago Mundi* 40 (1988): 57–56; and Dianne Harris, *The Nature of Authority: Villa Culture, Representation, and Landscape in Eighteenth-Century Lombardy* (State College: Pennsylvania State University Press, 2003), chap. 2.

7. For more on this subject, see Charles Aguar and Berdeana Aguar, *Wrightscapes: Frank Lloyd Wright's Landscape Designs* (New York: McGraw-Hill, 2002); Dianne Harris, *Maybeck's Landscapes: Drawing in Nature* (San Francisco: William Stout,

2004); Debora Wood, ed., *Marion Mahony Griffin: Drawing the Form of Nature* (Evanston, Ill.: Mary and Leigh Block Museum of Art, 2005).

8. For more on this subject, see Greg Castillo, *Cold War on the Home Front: The Soft Power of Midcentury Design* (Minneapolis: University of Minnesota Press, 2010); Archer, *Architecture and Suburbia,* chap. 6.

9. Dorothée Imbert, *Between Garden and City: Jean Canneel-Claes and Landscape Modernism* (Pittsburgh: University of Pittsburgh Press, 2009), 59, 61.

10. Recognizing the difficulty laymen faced when confronted with architectural plans, *Popular Mechanics* published an article titled "How to Read a Blueprint," October 1953, 154.

11. On the iconography of the bird's-eye view or aerial perspectives, and on the relationship between perspective and aerial views and scopic knowledge, see David Harvey, *The Condition of Postmodernity* (Cambridge, Mass.: Blackwell, 1990); Michel de Certeau, *The Practice of Everyday Life,* trans. Steve Randall (Berkeley: University of California Press, 1984), 92–93; Louis Marin, *Portrait of the King,* trans. Martha M. Houle (Minneapolis: University of Minnesota Press, 1988); Lucia Nuti, "The Perspective Plan in the Sixteenth Century: The Invention of a Representational Language," *Art Bulletin* 76, no. 1 (March 1994): 128.

12. On "soft modernism" or "everyday modernism," see Marc Treib, ed., *An Everyday Modernism: The Houses of William Wurster* (Berkeley: University of California Press, 1995). That the FHA made it difficult or impossible for home buyers to obtain FHA-insured mortgages for nontraditional house forms is not widely known, but architects' files indicate that this was the case. For example, although the Los Angeles architect A. Quincy Jones published and sold designs for a modern house that could be built affordably, many of those who purchased his plans were unable to obtain FHA-insured mortgages because the plans were considered too modern, untested, and, therefore, a poor risk. A. Quincy Jones papers, "San Diego House" files, courtesy Elaine Sewell Jones. Some of the documents pertaining to this project are in the cor-

respondence file for Huistendahl. See, for example, Huistendahl, X060.0 482, letter to Henry F. LaVoie, February 4, 1954. Gwendolyn Wright also acknowledged this fact. See Wright, *Building the Dream,* 251. This point is also discussed in some detail in later chapters.

13. Yves-Alain Bois, "Metamorphosis of Axonometry," *Daidalos,* no. 1 (September 1981): 45, 48.

14. On the problem of noise from neighbors and lack of privacy in prewar housing conditions, and on fears about a return to those conditions, see Ehrenhalt, *Lost City.*

15. On the postwar cult of family togetherness, see Laura J. Miller, "Family Togetherness and the Suburban Ideal," *Sociological Forum* 10, no. 3 (1995): 393–418.

16. On the crafting of white settings, see Annie Gilbert Coleman, "The Unbearable Whiteness of Skiing," *Pacific Historical Review* 65 (November 1996): 584.

17. David Sibley, *Geographies of Exclusion: Society and Difference in the West* (London: Routledge, 1995), xi.

18. Coleman, "Unbearable Whiteness of Skiing," 586.

19. Ibid., 589, 592.

20. *House and Home,* November 1956, 25.

21. On white dominance of the architectural profession, see Kathryn Anthony, *Designing for Diversity: Gender, Race, and Ethnicity in the Architecture Profession* (Urbana: University of Illinois Press, 2001).

22. "Push Button Home: Michigan Physician's Plush Estate Almost Runs by Itself," *Ebony,* November 1954, 42–48. By 1965, as Lynn Spigel notes, *Ebony* addressed the housing segregation issue head-on with a feature that focused on a black military officer who could not obtain housing close to his work at a key missile site in the Midwest, forcing him to commute vast distances to get to work. According to Spigel, the article used "the example of the officer at the missile site to suggest that even if blacks could buy homes in suburbia they often did not want to live in the 'monotonous' white neighborhoods with 'look-a-like' houses and shopping malls." Lynn Spigel, *Welcome to the Dreamhouse: Popular Media and Postwar Suburbs* (Durham, N.C.: Duke University Press, 2001), 156–57.

See also Hamilton J. Bims, "Housing—the Hottest Issue in the North," *Ebony*, August 1965, 93–100, which appeared in an issue titled "The White Problem in America." Andrew Wiese contends that *Ebony* "ran regular features publicizing the housing and domestic lifestyles of the nation's black elite," but he also notes that these features focused primarily on celebrities rather than on housing for ordinary, middle-class people. Wiese, *Places of Their Own*, 148–49.

23. "A Message from the Publisher," *Ebony*, November 1955, 121.

24. See, for example, Wiese, *Places of Their Own*.

25. Sibley, *Geographies of Exclusion*, 14, 24. The renderings' style was undoubtedly derived, at least in part, from European modernism of the 1920s and 1930s, which showcased domestic interiors that were characterized by a sterile, white, laboratory aesthetic; postwar houses were similarly modeled on a European social reality that was largely divested of nonwhites. Although this precedent deserves consideration, its complexity demands a separate essay. I thank Mirka Beneš for bringing this topic to my attention.

26. Joselit, "A Set Table," 25.

27. Ibid., 27, 31.

28. Among the best-known works in this corpus of literature is Catharine E. Beecher and Harriet Beecher Stowe, *The American Woman's Home; or, Principles of Domestic Science, Being a Guide to the Formation and Maintenance of Economical, Healthful, Beautiful, and Christian Homes* (New York: J.B. Ford, 1869).

29. Margaret Garb, *City of American Dreams: A History of Home Ownership and Housing Reform in Chicago, 1871–1919* (Chicago: University of Chicago Press, 2005), 186–87.

30. For an excellent study on the ways these FSA images and their circulation in popular magazines shaped American attitudes and understandings of poverty, see Finnegan, *Picturing Poverty*.

31. Stuart Hall, "The West Indian Front Room," in *The Front Room: Migrant Aesthetics in the Home*, ed. Michael McMillan (London: Black Dog, 2009), 19.

32. Davarian L. Baldwin, *Chicago's New Negroes: Modernity, the Great Migration, and Black Urban Life* (Chapel Hill: University of North Carolina Press, 2007), 29, 34.

33. The film is available for viewing on several sites online, including YouTube, at http://www.youtube.com/watch?v=-t _5wthGoWc (accessed May 31, 2012). My thanks to David Roediger for drawing my attention to this film.

34. "Ever really *look* at your place?," *Better Homes and Gardens Gardening Guide*, 6–7, Douglas and Maggie Baylis Collection [1999-4], Office Records/Clippings, Environmental Design Archives, University of California, Berkeley.

35. Ann Griffith, "The Magazines Women Read," *American Mercury*, March 1949, 273.

36. "Andrew Means: Steel City Builder," *Ebony*, January 1956, 52.

37. Leon Paul, "I Live in a Negro Neighborhood," *Ebony*, June 1956, 47. For more on white perceptions of and stereotypes about black middle-class neighborhoods, see Mary Patillo-McCoy, *Black Picket Fences: Privilege and Peril among the Black Middle Class* (Chicago: University of Chicago Press, 1999).

38. Mary Wright and Russel Wright, *Guide to Easier Living*, rev. ed. (New York: Simon & Schuster, 1954), 50.

39. On the desire to escape an "Okie" past, see also D. J. Waldie, *Holy Land: A Suburban Memoir* (New York: W. W. Norton, 1996), 172–73.

40. See Matt Wrayle and Annalee Newitz, eds., *White Trash: Race and Class in America* (New York: Routledge, 1997). On "trailer trash" see also Hurley, *Diners, Bowling Alleys, and Trailer Parks*, 251–53.

41. Wright and Wright, *Guide to Easier Living*, 135.

42. Ibid., 154, 160.

43. Suellen Hoy, *Chasing Dirt: The American Pursuit of Cleanliness* (New York: Oxford University Press, 1995), chap. 6. For more on inequality in sanitation infrastructure in postwar housing, see the discussion of postwar census data in the introduction to this volume.

44. Wright and Wright, *Guide to Easier Living*, 106.

45. Ibid., 108, 111, 113.

46. "Washable Rooms," *Life*, May 18, 1953, 76.

47. Quoted in Joseph Howland, *House Beautiful,* September 1950, 108.

48. Elizabeth Mock, *If You Want To Build a House* (New York: Simon & Schuster, 1946), 17.

49. American Trust Company, *Things To Know about Buying or Building a Home* (San Francisco: American Trust Company, 1946).

50. Laura Lawson, *City Bountiful: Urban Garden Programs in American Cities, 1890s to Present* (Berkeley: University of California Press, 2004).

51. Wayne C. Leckey, "Unusual and Modern Ideas for Living Outdoors," *Popular Mechanics,* April 1959, 176.

52. Babb, *Whiteness Visible,* 199.

4. PRIVATE WORLDS

1. *House Beautiful,* June 1950, cover.

2. For more on Gordon's connection to Cold War propaganda, see Harris, "Making Your Private World," 180–205. See also Castillo, *Cold War on the Home Front,* 112–14, 115, 118–20.

3. On the cultural construction of privacy as it relates to domestic design, see Peter Ward, *A History of Domestic Space: Privacy and the Canadian Home* (Vancouver: University of British Columbia Press, 1999).

4. For a sociological analysis, see May, *Homeward Bound.* Clifford Clark briefly notes the desire for postwar domestic privacy in *American Family Home,* 219. As a planning and design issue, privacy appears countless times in articles in shelter magazines from the period.

5. In his 1959 book *The Status Seekers,* Vance Packard cited the work of a home marketing expert named James Mills, who found that "privacy is tremendously important to people of working-class background who may have had to sleep three or four to a room sometime in their lives. They want walls around every room, and they want doors to the rooms, not entryways. The open layout characteristic of 'contemporary' houses, with rooms often divided only by furnishings, frightens them." See Daniel Horowitz, ed., *American Social Classes*

in the 1950s: Selections from Vance Packard's "The Status Seekers" (Boston: Bedford/St. Martin's Press, 1995), 62.

6. William H. Whyte, *The Organization Man* (New York: Doubleday, 1956), 337. For more on this topic, see the oral history interviews conducted and recorded in Chad M. Kimmel, "Revealing the History of Levittown, One Voice at a Time," in Harris, *Second Suburb.*

7. Ehrenhalt, *Lost City.*

8. Archer, *Architecture and Suburbia,* 95. Archer cites Leon Battista Alberti, *The Architecture of Leon Battista Alberti in Ten Books,* ed. James Leoni (London: Thomas Edlin, 1739), vol. 1, fol. 98v.

9. Archer, *Architecture and Suburbia,* 27.

10. Ibid., 51, 95, 129.

11. Ibid., 170.

12. Margaret Marsh, "From Separation to Togetherness: The Social Construction of Domestic Space in American Suburbs, 1840–1915," *Journal of American History* 76, no. 2 (September 1989): 515, 520.

13. Stilgoe, *Borderland,* 196, 198, 202, 204.

14. Quoted in Garb, *City of American Dreams,* 168.

15. Quoted in ibid., 170.

16. See Ward, *History of Domestic Space,* 97. Margaret Marsh also makes this point in her discussion of the opening up of floor plans in Victorian homes in the United States. See Marsh, "From Separation to Togetherness," 517–18, 522, 524.

17. See Ward, *History of Domestic Space,* chap. 2, esp. 48–51. For more on the origins of the establishment of private spaces within the American home, see Upton, "Traditional House and Its Enemies," 76.

18. See Graham Allan and Graham Crow, "Introduction," in *Home and Family: Creating the Domestic Sphere,* ed. Graham Allan and Graham Crow (London: Macmillan, 1989), 4–5.

19. See, for example, Gorman-Murray, "Gay and Lesbian Couples."

20. Scholarly studies based on the notion of house as a symbolic site of self-fashioning include ibid., see esp. 146–47, 150–67; Alison Blunt, "Home and Identity: Life Stories in Text and in

Person," in *Cultural Geography in Practice*, ed. Alison Blunt, Pyrs Gruffud, John May, Miles Ogborn, and David Pinder (London: Arnold, 2003), 71–87; Marcus, *House as a Mirror of Self*; Duncan and Lambert, "Landscapes of Home," 382–403; Ann Dupuis and David Thorns, "Home, Home Ownership, and the Search for Ontological Security," *Sociological Review* 46, no. 1 (1998): 24–47; McDowell, *Gender, Identity, and Place*; Daniel Miller, ed., *Home Possessions: Material Culture behind Closed Doors* (Oxford: Berg, 2001); Wise, "Home."

21. Allan and Crow, "Introduction," 4–5.

22. Lynn Spigel, *Make Room for TV: Television and the Family Ideal in Postwar America* (Chicago: University of Chicago Press, 1992), 100–101.

23. Paul Boyer, "The United States, 1941–63: A Historical Overview," in Brooke Kamin Rapaport, Kevin L. Stayton, et al., *Vital Forms: American Art and Design in the Atomic Age* (New York: Brooklyn Museum of Art and Harry N. Abrams, 2001), 52.

24. Sibley, *Geographies of Exclusion*, 78.

25. A wide range of theorists have noted the links between the creation of "home" (conceived at a variety of scales to include the idea of the nation as home or homeland) and the need to create exclusionary boundaries. See, for example, Zygmunt Bauman, *Globalisation* (Cambridge: Polity Press, 1998), 117; Mitzi Goldman, "The Fine Line Between Hatred and Home," *Communal/Plural* 5 (1997): 153; Julia Kristeva, *Nations without Nationalism* (New York: Columbia University Press, 1993), 3. See also Morley, *Home Territories*, 31.

26. Morley, *Home Territories*, 23. See also Leonore Davidoff and Catherine Hall, *Family Fortunes: Men and Women of the English Middle Class, 1780–1850* (Chicago: University of Chicago Press, 1987).

27. Morley, *Home Territories*, 34. Morley cites Peter Stallybrass and Allon White, *The Politics and Poetics of Transgression* (London: Methuen, 1986), 128–29.

28. Sibley, *Geographies of Exclusion*, 94.

29. For more on this subject, see Donald Bogle, *Toms, Coons, Mulattoes, Mammies, and Bucks: An Interpretive History of Blacks in American Films*, 4th ed. (New York: Continuum International, 2001).

30. Gotham, *Race, Real Estate*, 126, 145. See also C. Harris, "Whiteness as Property," 1710–69.

31. On the links between homeownership and citizenship, see Freund, *Colored Property*.

32. It should be noted that the kitchen was not always considered a public zone within the home. It became more public in the postwar era in part because of the lack of domestic servants. Whereas servants and their work were frequently considered in need of concealment, the housewife and her labors were to be integrated into the daily life of the house, so the postwar kitchen became more integrated into the public zones of the home.

33. Hurley, *Diners, Bowling Alleys, and Trailer Parks*, 159. Several other authors also cite *McCall's* as the source of this slogan; see, for example, Betty Friedan, *The Feminine Mystique* (New York: W. W. Norton, 1963), 48; Miller, "Family Togetherness," 394.

34. Marsh, "From Separation to Togetherness," 514, 515, 517, 524.

35. Hurley, *Diners, Bowling Alleys, and Trailer Parks*, 159.

36. Ibid., 163, 193, 278.

37. Ibid., 210, 230.

38. Alan F. Westin, *Privacy and Freedom* (New York: Atheneum, 1967), 172, 174. Westin's chapter 8 is titled "Dissolving the Walls and Windows."

39. John Cheever, "The Enormous Radio," in *The Stories of John Cheever* (New York: Vintage Books, 2000), 33–41.

40. Westin, *Privacy and Freedom*, 179–81.

41. Vance Packard, *The Hidden Persuaders* (New York: David McKay, 1957), 42.

42. Westin, *Privacy and Freedom*, 279–80.

43. Quoted in ibid., 281. Westin cites "Talk of the Town," *New Yorker*, September 21, 1957.

44. Stuart Ewen, *Captains of Consciousness: Advertising and the Social Roots of the Consumer Culture* (New York: McGraw-Hill, 1976), 208.

45. See Breines, *Young, White, and Miserable*, 9–10.

46. Breines points out that sociological texts of the 1950s, which were written by white male professionals, represent a limited perspective. She notes, however, that David Riesman's book *The Lonely Crowd* was "extraordinarily successful" in its time. See Breines, *Young, White, and Miserable*, 26, 27, 30.

47. William Roger Greeley, "Social and Visual Units," in Creighton, *Building for Modern Man*, 15.

48. For more on the discourse of individuality in the postwar period, see Timothy Mennel, "Miracle House Hoop-La: Corporate Rhetoric and the Construction of the Postwar American House," *Journal of the Society of Architectural Historians* 64, no. 3 (September 2005): 341, 357.

49. Lyman Bryson, *The Next America: Prophecy and Faith* (New York: Harper & Brothers, 1952), esp. chap. 12, "Individualism as Duty."

50. David Riesman, *The Lonely Crowd: A Study of the Changing American Character* (New Haven, Conn.: Yale University Press, 1950), 306.

51. For a refutation of the stereotype of homogeneous suburban housing, see Harris, "'The House I Live In.'"

52. Simon Frith, "British Rock and Pop," in *Visions of Suburbia*, ed. Roger Silverstone (London: Routledge, 1997), 276.

53. Riesman, *Lonely Crowd*, 307.

54. As the editors of *Fortune* magazine noted, "The modern suburbanite tries to keep down with the Joneses', or to put it more exactly, to consume no more and no less conspicuously than they. Not getting the balance just right is a source of friction, feuds, and sleepless nights in many of the newer suburban communities." See Editors of Fortune, *Changing American Market*, 80.

55. Russell Lynes, *The Tastemakers* (New York: Grosset & Dunlap, 1954), 246.

56. Karal Ann Marling has asserted that things seen advertised in the period, whether on television or in magazines, were even more intriguing to 1950s homeowners, because once purchased they existed "simultaneously in the public arena and in the private home." She notes further that "an intense need for privacy was counterbalanced by a love of public display, introspection by extroversion, the primitive and simple by the technologically complex." See Karal Ann Marling, "Designing Popular Culture in the Postwar Era," in Rapaport et al., *Vital Forms*, 208–37.

57. Sarah Williams Goldhagen and Réjean Legault, "Introduction: Critical Themes of Postwar Modernism," in *Anxious Modernisms: Experimentation in Postwar Architectural Culture*, ed. Sarah Williams Goldhagen and Réjean Legault (Cambridge: MIT Press, 2000), 15, 19.

58. See Wright and Wright, *Guide to Easier Living*.

59. Philip H. Ennis, "Leisure in the Suburbs: Research Prolegomenon," in William M. Dobriner, *The Suburban Community* (New York: G. P. Putnam's Sons, 1958), 262. See also John R. Seeley, *Crestwood Heights: A Study of the Culture of Suburban Life* (New York: Basic Books, 1956); John Keats, *The Crack in the Picture Window* (Boston: Houghton Mifflin, 1956); Whyte, *Organization Man*.

60. Keats, *Crack in the Picture Window*, 61, 169, 193.

61. Catlin and Catlin, *Building Your New House*, 162, 160.

62. Ibid., 163.

63. Rogers, *Modern House, U.S.A.*, 17, 21.

64. Elizabeth Gordon, "The Key to Pace-Setting Living," *House Beautiful*, November 1952, 212.

65. On "everday modernism" see Treib, *An Everyday Modernism*. Other terms that are sometimes used to describe this style are *soft modernism* and *middling modernism*.

66. Elizabeth Gordon, "The Responsibility of an Editor," manuscript for speech delivered to the Press Club Luncheon of the American Furniture Mart, Chicago, June 22, 1953, 14, 15, 21, Thomas Church Collection, Environmental Design Archives, University of California, Berkeley.

67. Joseph Howland, "Good Living Is NOT Public Living," *House Beautiful*, January 1950, 30.

68. Dobriner, *Class in Suburbia*, 10.

69. Sandy Isenstadt, "The Rise and Fall of the Picture Window," *Harvard Design Magazine*, Fall 1998, 30.

70. Sandy Isenstadt, "The Visual Commodification of Landscape

in the Real Estate Appraisal Industry, 1900–1992," *Business and Economic History* 28, no. 2 (Winter 1999): 65.

71. Keats, *Crack in the Picture Window*, 21, 58–59.

72. Ibid., 167.

73. Catlin and Catlin, *Building Your New House*, 150.

74. See Isenstadt, "Rise and Fall of the Picture Window," 30–33.

75. Will Mulhorn, "The Enlarging Window: Straw-in-the-Wind That Shows You the Direction in Which American House Design Is Heading," *House Beautiful*, December 1946, 286.

76. Judy Barry, "Report: To the Housewife," *Ladies' Home Journal*, November 1945, 195.

77. Federal Housing Administration, "Privacy," in *Underwriting Manual* (Washington, D.C.: Federal Housing Administration, 1952), 428-1.

78. Modernfold doors appeared in numerous publications. For an example, see Walter Murray, *Interior Decoration for Today and Tomorrow* (Hollywood, Calif.: Murray & Gee, 1946).

79. Harris, "'The House I Live In,'" 219, 220, 227, 228, 231.

80. "The U.S. Need for More Livable Homes" (first installment of a series on U.S. homes), *Life*, September 15, 1958, 62–64.

81. See Betty Jane Johnston, *Equipment for Modern Living* (New York: Macmillan, 1965), 251.

82. Catlin and Catlin, *Building Your New House*, 157.

83. *Popular Mechanics*, October 1957, 2.

84. Quoted in Thomas H. Creighton and Katherine M. Ford, *Contemporary Houses Evaluated by Their Owners* (New York: Reinhold, 1961), 61.

85. Ibid., 11.

86. John Burchard, "The Better Dream House," *Life*, September 15, 1958, 67.

87. Kennedy, *House and the Art of Its Design*, 92, 93, 95.

88. Ibid., 96.

89. Ibid., 276.

90. Sibley, *Geographies of Exclusion*, 98.

91. Morley, *Home Territories*, 20.

92. Denis Wood and Robert J. Beck, *Home Rules* (Baltimore: Johns Hopkins University Press, 1994), 61, 154.

93. Sibley, *Geographies of Exclusion*, 94.

94. Mock, *If You Want To Build a House*, 17.

95. An article in *House & Garden* in 1957 referred to the "unbearable congeniality" of the open plan thus: "The open plan, as it knocks down partition after partition, is not designed to rob us of a final refuge from the hammerings of unbearable congeniality." "Seclusion by Design: Behind a Camouflage of Screens and Walls—Blessed Solitude," *House & Garden*, January 1957, 34–39.

96. Benjamin Spock, *The Common Sense Book of Baby and Child Care* (New York: Duell, Sloan & Pearce, 1957), 379.

97. Spigel, *Make Room for TV*, 67, 68.

98. "Radio and Electronics Today," *Popular Mechanics*, November 1953, 164.

99. Richard Pratt, "Equal Rights . . . for Parents and Children," *Ladies' Home Journal*, November 1945, 190–91.

100. Promotional brochure for the Eichler X-100 house, courtesy Elaine Sewell Jones.

101. A. Quincy Jones, *House and Home*, January 1957, 142.

102. "Built-In Merchandising Lifts California," *House and Home*, July 1955, 130–31.

103. See Creighton and Ford, *Contemporary Houses*.

104. Raymond H. Harrell and James T. Lendrum, *A Demonstration of New Techniques for Low-Cost Small House Construction*, November 1952, Small Homes Council, 12/6/0/12, University of Illinois Archives.

105. "People Want Room to Enjoy the New Leisure," *House and Home*, May 1954, 134.

106. Thomas Church, "Where to Put the Playground," *House Beautiful*, September 1955, 146–49, 214–15.

107. "Homes That Achieve Most in Livability," *Life*, September 29, 1958, 60.

108. Ibid., 64.

109. "More Space Upstairs and Down," *Life*, October 6, 1958, 84, 85.

110. Ibid., 90.

111. Joseph Barry, "Free Taste: The American Style of the Future," *House Beautiful*, October 1952, 178.

5. HOUSEHOLD GOODS

1. Lizabeth Cohen, *A Consumers' Republic: The Politics of Mass Consumption in Postwar America* (New York: Alfred A. Knopf, 2003), 195.

2. Castillo, *Cold War on the Home Front.*

3. Ewen, *Captains of Consciousness*, 210–14.

4. Marina Moskowitz makes a similar point: "While material culture certainly did not create the middle class, it did identify the growing group, both to themselves and to others, on a national scale." Marina Moskowitz, *Standard of Living: The Measure of the Middle Class in Modern America* (Baltimore: Johns Hopkins University Press, 2004), 2.

5. Dell Upton reminds us "to think of the middle-class family as a group defined by acquired manners and up-to-date, constantly renewed possessions. It was imagined as a private, consuming unit, rather than a public, producing one. For this new family, the house came to be a collective, public declaration of manner and possession. And the architectural advice literature was important in making it so." Upton, "Traditional House and Its Enemies," 78.

6. Roediger, "How Old and New Whiteness," 94. See also David Roediger, "I Came for the Art: Exposing Whiteness and Imagining Nonwhite Spaces," *Art Papers*, May/June 2003, 22–27. For a perspective on the ways in which purchasing defines some black identities, see Elizabeth Chin, *Purchasing Power: Black Kids and American Consumer Culture* (Minneapolis: University of Minnesota Press, 2001). As Chin notes, "In the consumer sphere normalcy is represented by the white middle class"; 3.

7. Sara Ahmed, *Queer Phenomenology: Orientations, Objects, Others* (Durham, N.C.: Duke University Press, 2006), 150–51.

8. Babb, *Whiteness Visible*, 126, 140, 141–42.

9. Joselit, "A Set Table," 25, 27, 31.

10. Ehrenhalt, *Lost City*, 197.

11. On the idea of the home as a shelter against societal hazards, see May, *Homeward Bound*, 14.

12. On the relationship between "careful consumption" and anx-ieties, see Joanne Meyerowitz, "Beyond the Feminine Mystique: A Reassessment of Postwar Mass Culture, 1946–1958," in *Not June Cleaver: Women and Gender in Postwar America*, ed. Joanne Meyerowitz (Philadelphia: Temple University Press, 1994), 245.

13. David Sibley asserts that "a fear of difference is projected onto the objects and spaces comprising the home or locality which can be polluted by the presence of non-conforming people, activities or artefacts." See Sibley, *Geographies of Exclusion*, 91.

14. See Reimer and Leslie, "Identity, Consumption, and the Home"; P. Jackson and B. Holbrook, "Multiple Meanings: Shopping and the Cultural Politics of Identity," *Environment and Planning A* 27, no. 12 (1995): 1913–30; A. Pred, "Interfusions: Consumption, Identity and the Practices and Power Relations of Everyday Life," *Environment and Planning A* 28, no. 1 (1996): 11–24.

15. David Halberstam called this a new culture of capitalism driven by "ferocious consumerism." See Halberstam, *The Fifties* (New York: Fawcett Columbine, 1993), 506. Erika Doss also describes the age in terms of exuberant consumption. See Doss, *Benton, Pollock, and the Politics of Modernism: From Regionalism to Abstract Expressionism* (Chicago: University of Chicago Press, 1991), 332–34.

16. Fredric Jameson, "Postmodernism and Consumer Society," in *Postmodernism and Its Discontents*, ed. E. Ann Kaplan (London: Verso, 1988). See also Breines, *Young, White, and Miserable*, 105; Chin, *Purchasing Power*, 9, 38.

17. May, *Homeward Bound*, 165.

18. "Moses and the Jackals," *Life*, September 26, 1955, 49.

19. Andrew Hurley has noted that trailer parks "fixed lower boundaries of the middle majority market" in the postwar era. Although trailers often provided blue-collar families of modest means with the opportunity for homeownership, Hurley notes, "external prejudices and internal spatial constraints made it difficult for trailer park residents to present their trailer coaches as emblems of social success. Assigned a cultural niche far beyond the middle majority mainstream, trailer parks exposed the notion of a classless nation as illu-

sory and highlighted the consequences for consumers of failing to meet prevailing norms of postwar domesticity." Most significant, "in a culture that correlated racial status with social standing, trailer park dwellers who violated prevailing norms of domesticity found their whiteness constantly called into question and qualified. Thus, the labels 'white trash' and 'trailer trash' stuck to them wherever they went." Hurley, *Diners, Bowling Alleys, and Trailer Parks,* 197–98, 253.

20. See Jennifer Guglielmo and Salvatore Salerno, eds., *Are Italians White? How Race Is Made in America* (New York: Routledge, 2003).

21. "A Sociologist Looks at an American Community," *Life,* September 12, 1949, 108–19. W. Lloyd Warner was coauthor, with Marchia Meeker and Kenneth Eells, of *Social Class in America: A Manual of Procedure for the Measurement of Social Status* (Chicago: Science Research Associates, 1949).

22. Lizabeth Cohen also indicates the extent to which homeownership served as a marker of class status, such that "new homeowners made clear social-class associations with particular house types." The allocation of space within homes signaled class distinctions as well, such that having a separate and distinct dining room and living room, additional bathrooms, an attached garage, and a "rec room" all signaled status. See Cohen, *Consumers' Republic,* 208–9.

23. Rogers, *Modern House, U.S.A.,* 23, 38, 39. Although women engaged less frequently than men in published architectural criticism outside the realm of shelter magazines during this period, Kate Ellen Rogers is among the few women—along with Elizabeth Mock and Catherine Bauer—whose voices seem to have pierced the professional design ranks. She was the first editor of the *Journal of Interior Design Education Research* and chair of the Interior Design Program at the University of Missouri from 1954 until 1984. She also opened the first Knoll furniture showroom in Texas. Rogers's concern that suburban developments would turn to slums echoed the writings of well-known urban critics such as Lewis Mumford.

24. Ibid., 38.

25. See Harris, "'The House I Live In.'"

26. Russell Lynes, *A Surfeit of Honey* (New York: Harper, 1952), 32, cited in Ehrenreich, *Fear of Falling,* 38.

27. James A. Davis, "Cultural Factors in the Perception of Status Symbols," *Midwest Sociologist* 21, no. 1 (December 1958): 5. I am grateful to Harvey Choldin for bringing this article to my attention.

28. Ibid. On the other hand, *Sunset* magazine featured an article titled "How Books Add Livability . . . to Any Room" and illustrated the piece with three examples of bookshelves in frankly modern houses. The author wrote that bookshelves "give a feeling of warmth to a wall and room." *Sunset,* April 1958, 94. See also the analysis of bookshelves that appears in the novel *Revolutionary Road,* discussed in this book's introduction.

29. Davis, "Cultural Factors," 7.

30. Ibid., 2.

31. Ibid., 9–10.

32. Davis concluded that elite women were more sensitive to taste in making status judgments, whereas lower-status women were more interested in cost; he referred to taste as "essentially an elite-group cultural element." Ibid., 9, 11. Davis correctly asserted that interior decoration has different meanings at different status levels. "For the elite woman it may tend to be an intellectual exercise in demonstrating her mastery of esthetics. For the lower status woman the home is more likely to be an unplanned complex of symbols of family prestige and familism"; ibid., 6. In a separate article, Davis noted that prestige insecurity increases with the process of mobility, which helps to explain the excruciating focus on status for upwardly mobile Americans in the postwar era. See James A. Davis, "Status Symbols and the Measurement of Status Perception," *Sociometry* 19 (September 1956): 162.

33. Russell Lynes, "Highbrow, Middlebrow, Lowbrow," *Harper's,* February 1949, 19–28. The chart appeared in *Life,* April 1949. Lynes later republished the essay in his 1954 book *The Tastemakers.*

34. John Brooks, "Highbrow, Lowbrow, Middlebrow, Now: An Interview with Russell Lynes," *American Heritage,* June/July

1983, accessed June 4, 2012, at http://www.americanheritage
.com/content/highbrow-lowbrows-middlebrow-now.

35. All quotations from Packard's *Status Seekers* are found in
Horowitz, *American Social Classes*, 45, 49, 60–64.

36. Nickles, "More Is Better," 588.

37. A. Quincy Jones, summary of remarks made during a seminar
presented by Arcadia Metal Products, "The Scientific Sixties:
Effects of Changing Economic, Social and Scientific Values
upon Architecture," February 20, 1959, A. Quincy Jones papers, courtesy Elaine Sewell Jones.

38. On the museum exhibits, see, for example, George H. Marcus, *Design in the Fifties: When Everyone Went Modern* (Mu-
nich: Prestel-Verlag, 1998). See also "Good Design for 1949,"
Interiors 108 (December 1948): 114.

39. Indeed, and as the magazines recognized, many Americans
were either confused about the definition of "modernism"
as a style or made uncomfortable by it. Many of the popular
shelter magazines and design publications featured articles
intended to reassure their readers about the new style. For
more on this, see my essay "Making Your Private World," 183,
190.

40. Donald Albrecht, Robert Schonfeld, and Lindsay Stamm Sha-
piro, *Russel Wright: Creating American Lifestyle* (New York:
Harry N. Abrams, 2001).

41. Lynn Spigel, "High Culture in Low Places," in *Welcome to the
Dreamhouse*, 279, 281.

42. Editors of Fortune, *Changing American Market*, 26.

43. Ibid., 73, 74.

44. Ibid., 108, 113.

45. Ibid., 116, 117, 118, 120, 126. On the various ways in which
"modern" furniture could be interpreted, see Harris, "'The
House I Live In.'"

46. Eugene R. Beem, *Trading Stamps in the American Economy* (St.
Louis, Mo.: American Marketing Association, 1958), 8.

47. Legislative Research Council, Massachusetts, *Report on the
Use and Redemption of Merchandise Stamps* (Boston: Legislative Research Council, April 13, 1956), 3.

48. Consumer Council to the Governor, State of New York, summary transcript of representative State Conference on Store
Trading Stamps, State Capitol, Albany, October 2, 1956, 4.

49. Ibid., 11.

50. The Gold Bond stamp company, a division of the Carlson
Companies, issued its second redemption catalog as "a slick,
16-page tabloid-size supplement to the Sunday editions of the
Minneapolis Tribune, the *Des Moines Register*, and the *Dakota
Farmer* in August and September of 1955." Curtis L. Carlson,
Good as Gold: The Story of the Carlson Companies (Minneapolis: Carlson Companies, 1994), 70. See this source for more
on the trading stamp companies' histories and advertising
strategies.

51. Ibid., 66.

52. Consumer Council to the Governor, summary transcript, 21,
30.

53. Federal Trade Commission, *Economic Report on the Use and
Economic Significance of Trading Stamps* (Washington, D.C.:
Federal Trade Commission, January 1966), 39.

54. Ibid., 38.

55. Ibid., 40–41. These data come from a 1963 survey of trading stamp redemption centers. The findings of such surveys
varied to an extent. For example, in 1968, Harold Fox found
that the most popular items purchased with trading stamps
were GE steam irons, Hamilton wristwatches, decorative
bridge lamps, eggbeaters, and can openers. Sheets and pillowcases were also among the most popular items, and as a
result, "Gold Bond became the largest single buyer of sheets
and pillowcases in the entire mid-west." Harold Fox, *The Economics of Trading Stamps* (Washington, D.C.: Public Affairs
Press, 1968), 70. The Legislative Research Council study of
1956 found that 30 percent of consumers wanted electrical
appliances, 18 percent wanted kitchen utensils and dishes, 12
percent wanted folding aluminum chairs, 7 percent wanted
toys, and the rest redeemed stamps for cameras, tools, bedding, and rugs. See Legislative Research Council, *Report on
the Use*, 12.

56. Fox, *Economics of Trading Stamps*, 82.

57. Ibid., 98.

58. Ibid., 98–99.

59. Thomas J. Schlereth, "Mail Order Catalogs as Resources in American Culture Studies," *Prospects* 7 (1983): 142, 147, 154.

60. Editors of Fortune, *Changing American Market*, 197.

61. "People Want Room," 134.

6. BUILT-INS AND CLOSETS

1. On the kitchen debate, see Karal Ann Marling, *As Seen on TV: The Visual Culture of Everyday Life in the 1950s* (Cambridge, Mass.: Harvard University Press, 1994), 243–83; May, *Homeward Bound*, 163; Cohen, *Consumers' Republic*, 126; Castillo, *Cold War on the Home Front*, x–xi, 140, 158–60.

2. An exception is Karal Ann Marling, who noted, however briefly, that the new purchases, such as "power tools, snack foods and recliners" needed to be stored somewhere in the house. See Marling, *As Seen on TV*, 52.

3. Elizabeth T. Halsey, *Ladies' Home Journal Book of Interior Decoration* (Garden City, N.Y.: Doubleday, 1957), 175.

4. Federal Housing Administration, *Underwriting Manual*, secs. 429-1 through 429-6.

5. Rogers, *Modern House, U.S.A.*, 279.

6. S. Robert Anshen, "The Postwar House and Its Materials," *Arts and Architecture*, November 1945, cited in Kevin Starr, "The Case Study House Program and the Impending Future: Some Regional Considerations," in Smith, *Blueprints for Modern Living*, 139.

7. Rogers, *Modern House, U.S.A.*, 273.

8. J. R. Shipley, *Fundamentals of Interior Design*, Small Homes Council Circular Series Index Number H1.0, *University of Illinois Bulletin* 43, no. 49 (April 12, 1946); J. R. Shipley, *Interior Design*, Small Homes Council Circular Series Index Number H1.0, *University of Illinois Bulletin* 47, no. 72 (June 1950): 2, University of Illinois Archives.

9. Shipley, *Interior Design*, 3, 5, 6.

10. Ibid., 8.

11. See Regina Lee Blaszczyk, "Cinderella Stories: The Glass of Fashion and the Gendered Marketplace," in *His and Hers: Gender, Consumption, and Technology*, ed. Roger Horowitz and Arwen Mohun (Charlottesville: University Press of Virginia, 1998), 155. Vance Packard noted that the upper classes preferred "a good deal of relaxed informality . . . food typically is offered casually." See Horowitz, *American Social Classes*, 106.

12. Shipley, *Interior Design*, 8.

13. See Murray, *Interior Decoration*, 25–52.

14. Hurley, *Diners, Bowling Alleys, and Trailer Parks*, 298.

15. William W. Braham, "The Authority of the Natural: Color Palettes of the Postwar Period, 1948–1968," in *Preserving the Recent Past 2*, ed. Deborah Slaton and William G. Foulks (Washington, D.C.: Historic Preservation Education Foundation, 2000), 3-104.

16. Quoted in ibid., 3-101.

17. Ibid., 3-105.

18. An illustration of the "picnic prototype" from Russel Wright's 1951 *Guide to Easier Living* is reproduced in Albrecht et al., *Russel Wright*, 45. The very low disposition of Wright's design of the "Easier Living Coffee Table" necessitated sitting on floor cushions, and a 1948 promotional photograph for Leacock Linens that included his tableware featured a picnic on a living room floor. See Albrecht et al., *Russel Wright*, 151, 160.

19. Braham, "Authority of the Natural," 3-106.

20. For a detailed analysis of changes in the forms of kitchens in Levittown, Pennsylvania, see Curtis Miner, "Pink Kitchens for Little Boxes," in Harris, *Second Suburb*, 243–80.

21. For brief historic overviews of the relationship between women's housework and appliances, particularly in the late nineteenth and early twentieth centuries, see Cowan, *More Work for Mother*; Strasser, *Never Done*. See also Ellen Lupton, *Mechanical Brides: Women and Machines from Home to Office* (New York: Princeton Architectural Press, 1993). On the changing culture of cleanliness in the 1950s, see Hoy, *Chasing Dirt*, chap. 6. On women and domesticity, see Kathleen Anne McHugh, *American Domesticity: From How-to Manual to Hollywood Melodrama* (New York: Oxford University Press, 1999).

22. Brodkin, *How Jews Became White Folks*, 18.

23. Ibid., 55, 57. Brodkin cites Phyllis Palmer, who has suggested that "sex, dirt, housework, and badness in women are linked in Western unconsciousness and that white middle-class women sought to transcend these associations by demonstrating their sexual purity and their pristine domesticity. " See ibid., 85, and Phyllis Palmer, *Domesticity and Dirt: Housewives and Domestic Servants in the United States, 1920–1945* (Philadelphia: Temple University Press, 1989). The performance of waged domestic labor in particular marked one as nonwhite and inferior.

24. Catlin and Catlin, *Building Your New House*, 151.

25. Andrew Hurley is among the scholars who have noted the connection between modern appliances and the stigmatization of housework. See Hurley, *Diners, Bowling Alleys, and Trailer Parks*, 63.

26. Beecher and Stowe, *American Woman's Home.*

27. A 1955 advertisement for the *Guide to Easier Living* declared, "Let America's Best-Known Designer Show You How to Have a Home That Almost Runs Itself!" and "His new 1000-idea book tells how to transform your home—so you can laugh at housework!" Quoted in Robert Schonfeld, "Marketing Easier Living: The Commodification of Russel Wright," in Albrecht et al., *Russel Wright*, 162. For another example of a labor-saving study for postwar housewives, see Elizabeth M. Ranney, *Kitchen Planning Standards*, Small Homes Council Circular Series Index Number C5.32, *University of Illinois Bulletin* 47, no. 19 (October 1949): 2–3, University of Illinois Archives. The circular, funded by Hotpoint, was intended to "determine kitchen and laundry design standards for the small basementless house" to avoid handicapping the efficiency of the homemaker. The study specified optimal distances between appliances and triangulated patterns of arrangement derived from time-and-motion studies.

28. Rogers, *Modern House, U.S.A.*, 166.

29. Joy Parr, "Shopping for a Good Stove: A Parable about Gender, Design, and the Market" in Horowitz and Mohun, *His and Hers*, 180.

30. Harris, "'The House I Live In.'"

31. "Kitchen No. 3: As Compact and Detailed as a Yacht Galley," *Sunset*, September 1960, 90.

32. Elizabeth Mock's writings enforce my analysis here of the kitchen and open plans. In 1946, Mock wrote: "What about the current mania for hiding everything in closed cabinets, even to the extent of providing a collapsible top for the stove? Again, it is the superficial order of the slick, impersonal surface. . . . A kitchen is more than the sum of its gadgets. It should be large enough for at least two people to work in without tripping over each other, as even a minimum of kitchen should make allowance for part-time professional help. . . . Indeed, if your life is completely casual and servantless, perhaps you will want to expand the kitchen into one large cooking-dining-living room." Mock, *If You Want To Build a House*, 12. In these passages Mock emphasized the importance of displaying newly acquired appliances and the importance of opening the kitchen to the living rooms of the house. She used the word "casual" essentially as a code word for middle-class, servantless living.

33. Editors of Fortune, *Changing American Market*, 110.

34. Margaret R. Goodyear, Dorothy J. Iwig, F. D. Miles, Gladys J. Ward, and Virginia H. Weaver, *Planning the Kitchen*, Small Homes Council Circular Series Index Number C5.3, *University of Illinois Bulletin* 43, no. 8 (September 19, 1945): 8, University of Illinois Archives.

35. "The First Postwar House," *House Beautiful*, May 1946, 104.

36. Nickles, "More Is Better," 602.

37. "First Postwar House," 114.

38. Annmarie Adams, "The Eichler Home: Intention and Experience in Postwar Suburbia," *Perspectives in Vernacular Architecture* 5 (1995): 169.

39. "Pace-Setting News of the Year—The Sit-Down Sink," *House Beautiful*, 1954, Kitchen Clip File, Environmental Design Archives, University of California, Berkeley.

40. Goodyear et al., *Planning the Kitchen*, 2–3.

41. Murray, *Interior Decoration*, 10.

42. Ibid., 11.

43. Helen E. McCullough, *Cabinet Space for the Kitchen*, Small

Homes Council Circular Series Index Number C5.31, *University of Illinois Bulletin* 46, no. 43 (February 1949): 6, 12/6/0/10, Box 1, University of Illinois Archives. The study was also funded by Hotpoint, a manufacturer of kitchen appliances; the company undoubtedly wanted to make sure that kitchens were large enough and contained enough storage so that consumers would be encouraged to purchase more of its products.

44. Clarence W. Farrier, *Final Draft—Primary Report on Study of Storage Space Requirements for Homes* (Washington, D.C.: Federal Housing Administration, Standards and Studies Section, March 21, 1960); Rudard A. Jones, *Household Storage Study,* Small Homes Council Research Report 63-1, developed under the Technical Studies Program of the Federal Housing Administration, 1963, 20–23, Small Homes Council, Research Reports, 12/6/0/12, University of Illinois Archives.

45. Kitchen Clip File Environmental Design Archives, University of California, Berkeley.

46. Helen E. McCullough and Martha S. Schoeppel, *Separate Ovens,* Small Homes Council Circular Series Index Number C5.33, *University of Illinois Bulletin* 53, no. 36 (January 1956): 2, University of Illinois Archives.

47. Goodyear et al., *Planning the Kitchen,* 3.

48. Hurley, *Diners, Bowling Alleys, and Trailer Parks,* 231.

49. Jones, *Household Storage Study,* 14, 26, 30.

50. "Portable Household: Peripatetic Furniture Unfolds to Make One Room Do the Work of Four," *Life,* March 17, 1947, 53–56.

51. Jones, *Household Storage Study,* 14, 26, 30. This report was developed by the University of Illinois Small Homes Council under the Technical Studies Program of the Federal Housing Administration. The objective was "to review and recommend improvements in the requirements for storage facilities needed in residences of one or two living units as specified in the *Minimum Property Standards* of the FHA"; ibid., 1. A committee of specialists consulted on the report, including a homemaker, the head of the university's home economics department, a faculty member from the clothing and textiles department, a builder, an engineer, and two architects. The study was based on the Farrier Report (cited in note 44),

which "tabulated information from six inventory surveys of the possessions of a total of 4,771 families." From that survey, "computations of space required to store inventoried items" were derived. The aim of the study was to create "minimum storage standards [that would] at least meet the needs of families married five to ten years" without altering the values of homes for which the FHA had guaranteed mortgages. See ibid., 3, 4.

52. Such folding screen doors were typical again in houses constructed in Levittown, Pennsylvania. See Harris, "'The House I Live In.'"

53. Jones, *Household Storage Study,* 32, 35, 37, 45.

54. Elizabeth Cromley, "Domestic Space Transformed, 1850–2000," in *Architectures: Modernism and After,* ed. Andrew Ballantyne (Oxford: Blackwell, 2004), 182, 185.

55. "People Want Better Storage . . . and More of It," *House and Home,* May 1954, 152.

56. *Household Storage Units,* Small Homes Council Circular Series Index Number C5.1, *University of Illinois Bulletin* 50, no. 42 (January 1953): 3, University of Illinois Archives.

57. William H. Kapple, *Storage Partitions,* Small Homes Council Circular Series Index Number C5.11, *University of Illinois Bulletin* 51, no. 12 (1953), 12/6/0/10, Box 1, University of Illinois Archives.

58. Mildred Friedman, "From Futurama to Motorama," in Rapaport et al., *Vital Forms,* 174. Michael Webb likewise asserts that George Nelson first conceived of the storage wall toward the end of the war in 1944 when he was writing *Tomorrow's House* with Henry Wright (the two men were then coeditors at *Architectural Forum*). According to Webb, Nelson and Wright's storage wall design was first published in *Architectural Forum* and then in *Life.* See Michael Webb, *George Nelson* (San Francisco: Chronicle Books, 2003), 10.

59. Sandy Isenstadt, "Visions of Plenty: Refrigerators in America around 1950," *Journal of Design History* 11, no. 4 (1998): 313.

60. "A House Full of Built-Ins," *Popular Mechanics,* November 1958, 113–15. For an example of an activity wall, see also *Life,* October 4, 1954, 54.

61. On the split bathroom, see, for example, *Things to Know about Buying or Building a Home,* pamphlet, American Trust Company, circa 1946, 27, Arne and Lois Cartwold Collection [2000–11], Environmental Design Archives, University of California, Berkeley.

62. "Built-In Merchandising," 130–31.

63. "*PM* House of Built-Ins," *Popular Mechanics,* October 1960, 160.

64. The House of Built-Ins was constructed in Barrington, Illinois; Flossmoor, Illinois; Denver, Colorado; Fort Worth, Texas; Woodland Hills, California; Lubbock, Texas; Cedar Hills, Oregon; San Antonio, Texas; Seattle, Washington; South Bend, Indiana; St. Louis, Missouri; and Tulsa, Oklahoma. See ibid., 169.

65. "$75,000 Showcase," *Architectural Forum,* March 1946, 101.

66. On the development of separate spheres for parents and children in postwar homes, see chapter 4 as well as Morley, *Home Territories,* 20.

67. "$75,000 Showcase," 100.

68. On the liminal space that television occupies, see Margaret Morse, "An Ontology of Everyday Distraction: The Freeway, the Mall, and Television," in *Logics of Television: Essays in Cultural Criticism,* ed. Patricia Mellencamp (Bloomington: Indiana University Press, 1990), 193; Morley, *Home Territories,* 87.

69. See, for example, William Boddy, "The Shining Center of the Home: Ontologies of TV in the Golden Age," in *Television in Transition,* ed. Phillip Drummond and Richard Paterson (London: British Film Institute, 1985), 126. See also Morley, *Home Territories,* 88.

7. THE HOME SHOW

1. Keats, *Crack in the Picture Window,* 81.

2. Quoted in Don Shewey, "TV's Custom-Tailored 'Salesman,'" *New York Times,* September 15, 1985.

3. Spigel, *Make Room for TV*; Marling: *As Seen on TV.*

4. In addition to the works by Lynn Spigel cited here, see Hayden, *Building Suburbia,* chap. 7; Archer, *Architecture and Suburbia,* 318–20; Mary Beth Haralovich, "Sitcoms and Suburbs: Positioning the 1950s Homemaker," *Quarterly Review of Film and Video* 11 (1989): 61–83.

5. Raymond Williams, *Television: Technology and Cultural Form* (London: Fontana, 1974). Lynn Spigel's work is a notable exception. See, for example, Spigel, *TV by Design: Modern Art and the Rise of Network Television* (Chicago: University of Chicago Press, 2008).

6. Spigel, *TV by Design,* 3.

7. These statistics are from the table "Number of TV Households in America," in Television History: The First 75 Years, accessed June 7, 2012, at http://www.tvhistory.tv/Annual_TV_Households_50-78.JPG

8. As Lynn Spigel notes, television became a mass medium between 1948 and 1955. Spigel, *Make Room for TV,* 2.

9. Morley, *Home Territories,* 118.

10. National Association of Home Builders, *Plan for a Homebuilder's Public Relations* (Washington, D.C.: National Association of Home Builders, 1954), 41.

11. Spigel, *Make Room for TV,* 1.

12. See Williams, *Television.* See also Roger Silverstone, "Introduction," in Silverstone, *Visions of Suburbia,* 10.

13. Keats, *Crack in the Picture Window,* 78.

14. National Association of Manufacturers *Industry on Parade* film collection, 1950–1960, no. 507, Archives Center, National Museum of American History, Smithsonian Institution.

15. National Association of Manufacturers *Industry on Parade* film collection, Reel 38 (RV507.38), 6/20/51, Archives Center, National Museum of American History, Smithsonian Institution. The Levitts made several additional films at their second development in Bucks County, Pennsylvania. For one of these, they partnered with the Ford Motor Company to indicate the ways in which Ford trucks and tractors aided in the construction of Levittown. In another, they simply relied on the medium to broadcast the attributes of their second suburb. See, for example, *The Quiet Revolution,* Prelinger Archives, available on YouTube at http://www.youtube.com/watch?v=70CtKdw8d-0 (accessed June 7, 2012); and

"A Town Is Born: Levittown, Pennsylvania," which was part of the newsreel series *The March of Time,* available at http://www.youtube.com/watch?v=2KtoQppahfo (accessed June 7, 2012).

16. National Association of Manufacturers *Industry on Parade* film collection, *A New Way of Living!,* Reel 103 (RV507.103), 9/26/52, Archives Center, National Museum of American History, Smithsonian Institution.

17. For more on Park Forest, see Gregory C. Randall, *America's Original GI Town: Park Forest, Illinois* (Baltimore: Johns Hopkins University Press, 2000).

18. National Association of Manufacturers *Industry on Parade* film collection, Reel 101 (RV507.101), 9/12/52, Archives Center, National Museum of American History, Smithsonian Institution.

19. Script for *Blueprint for Modern Living,* December 4, 1956, 6, A. Quincy Jones papers, text file 003.0 454, courtesy Elaine Sewell Jones.

20. Ibid.

21. Ibid.

22. Richard Pinkham, letter to Carma McCarty, February 26, 1954, NBC papers, Box 123, Folder 26, Wisconsin Historical Society Archives.

23. Morley, *Home Territories,* 119.

24. Inger L. Stole, "There Is No Place Like *Home*: NBC's Search for a Daytime Audience, 1954–1957," *Communications Review* 2, no. 2 (1997): 144, 146, 147.

25. Spigel, *TV by Design,* 111.

26. Ibid., 118–19.

27. Ibid., 145.

28. Peterson, *Magazines in the Twentieth Century,* 26.

29. NBC promotional material, Clare Barrows papers, courtesy Susanna Barrows collection. Clare Barrows served as the managing editor for all three years of the "House That *Home* Built" programs. Her responsibilities included overseeing all facets of the projects, including coordination among the network, the builders, the NAHB, the Housing and Home Finance Administration, the Federal Housing Administration, and the Veterans Administration for promotion and public relations. Clare Barrows, "Resume," 10/63, Clare Barrows papers, courtesy Susanna Barrows collection.

30. Little footage of *Home* remains, but a few episodes are available for viewing at the Paley Center for Media (formerly the Museum of Television and Radio) in New York. See, for example, the April 11, 1957, episode (B:03679), which was the 807th, and the final, 893rd episode, which aired on August 9, 1957 (B:02264). One segment from 1956, featuring Charles Eames in conversation with Arlene Francis about the design of his lounge chair, is available on YouTube at http://www.youtube.com/watch?v=-MomNfLGOLg (accessed June 7, 2012).

31. Joe Culligan, memo to "All Salesmen," February 24, 1954, NBC papers, Box 123, Folder 26, Wisconsin Historical Society Archives.

32. Spigel, *Make Room for TV,* 82; clipping from *Billboard,* March 20, 1954, NBC papers, Box 123, Folder 26, Wisconsin Historical Society Archives.

33. Marjorie Trumbull served as *Sunset*'s regular *Home* show representative. NBC papers, Box 133, Folder 68, Wisconsin Historical Society Archives; see also memo dated June 12, 1956, NBC papers, Box 175, Folder 4, Wisconsin Historical Society Archives.

34. Ken Bilby, memo to Ted Rogers, April 1, 1957, NBC papers, Box 140, Folder 67, Wisconsin Historical Society Archives.

35. Dale Olmstead, letter to NBC, September 2, 1954, NBC papers, Box 280, Folder 48, Wisconsin Historical Society Archives.

36. Dick Linkroum, memo to Dick Pinkham and Mort Werner, April 8, 1955, NBC papers, Box 171, Folder 26, Wisconsin Historical Society Archives.

37. *Retailing Daily,* January 3, 1955, n.p., Clare Barrows papers, courtesy Susanna Barrows collection.

38. *Chicago Market Daily,* December 20, 1954, 1, Clare Barrows papers, courtesy Susanna Barrows collection.

39. Estimates on the cost of the *Home* set ranged from $100,000 to $250,000—a remarkably large amount for the early days

of television. See, for example, Harriet Van Horne, "Hearth Bowed Down Gets Boost on TV," *New York World Telegram and Sun*, January 28, 1954, Clare Barrows papers, courtesy Susanna Barrows collection. See also Spigel, *Make Room for TV*, 83.

40. Stole, "There Is No Place Like *Home*," 141, 143.

41. Arlene Francis, "Problems with a traveling *Home*," n.d., NBC papers, Box 175, Folder 4, Wisconsin Historical Society Archives.

42. See NBC papers, Box 247, Folder 33, Wisconsin Historical Society Archives.

43. For example, one viewer wrote to Weaver to inform him that "Poppy Cannon is married to a Negro" and that this would offend many viewers. Weaver then sent the note to executive producer Pinkham, stating, "We will watch publicity and are willing to risk letters like this." Mrs. Alice Davidson, letter to Dick Weaver, February 2, 1954, NBC papers, Box 123, Folder 26, Wisconsin Historical Society Archives.

44. Poppy Cannon, resignation letter, March 17, 1954, NBC papers, Box 168, Folder 6, Wisconsin Historical Society Archives.

45. Richard Pinkham, memo, January 5, 1955, NBC papers, Box 171, Folder 26, Wisconsin Historical Society Archives.

46. Joe Culligan, memo to Ted Cott, March 9, 1954, NBC papers, Box 567c, folder labeled *Home*, Wisconsin Historical Society Archives.

47. Pat Weaver, memo to Dick Linkroum, August 17, 1955, NBC papers, Box 125, Folder 38, Wisconsin Historical Society Archives; Beth Blossom, memo to Ellis Moore, February 10, 1955, NBC papers, Box 171, Folder 26, Wisconsin Historical Society Archives.

48. Blossom, memo to Moore.

49. James Steele and David Jenkins have called the Case Study House program "one of the most brilliantly conceived and consistently implemented public relations campaigns in American history that enmeshed *Arts and Architecture* magazine with the local broadcast media, national and international newspapers, manufacturers and advertisers." Steele

and Jenkins, *Pierre Koenig* (London: Phaidon Press, 1998), 149.

50. The house price appears in *Pacific Architect and Builder*, April 1955, 24.

51. *Southwest Builder and Contractor*, April 22, 1955, n.p. The first house built from this plan was constructed in Fullerton, California. See *Building News*, April 7, 1955. See also *House and Home*, April 1955, 77.

52. *House and Home*, April 1955, 77.

53. "Home Starts Slowly: Plans Made for Fall Showing," *House and Home*, July 1955, 70.

54. *House and Home*, June 1956, 114.

55. Don Foley, memo and brochure to staff, January 22, 1957, NBC papers, Box 401, Folder 8, Wisconsin Historical Society Archives.

56. "NBC News from *Home*," April 27, 1956, NBC papers, Box 175, Folder 4, Wisconsin Historical Society Archives.

57. Document titled "Tentative HTHB Programming," 1957, Clare Barrows papers, courtesy Susanna Barrows collection.

58. Blossom, memo to Moore.

59. Richard Linkroum, memo to HTHB staff, January 27, 1955, NBC papers, Box 391, Folder 18, Wisconsin Historical Society Archives.

60. "Best in Living at Home Calendar," November 27, 1956, Clare Barrows papers, courtesy Susanna Barrows collection.

61. Roy Porteous, memo to Ernie Fladell, December 14, 1956, NBC papers, Box 141, Folder 11, Wisconsin Historical Society Archives.

62. *House and Home*, April 1955, 77.

63. *House and Home*, July 1955, 70.

64. Memo labeled "Confidential: For use of *Home* clients only," n.d., NBC papers, Box 391, Folder 18, Wisconsin Historical Society Archives.

65. According to Robert McLaughlin, at least twenty builders constructed the Jones and Emmons plan. For his list, see McLaughlin, "Eichler, Jones, and Drummond: When National TV Put Eichler at Center Stage with the Ambitious 'House That *Home* Built' Program." Eichler Network,

accessed June 7, 2012, at http://www.eichlernetwork.com/article/house-home-built.

66. Weaver, memo to Linkroum.

67. Dee Vestal, memo to Ed Vane, February 3, 1955, NBC papers, Box 391, Folder 18, Wisconsin Historical Society Archives.

68. John McCardle, memo to network sales staff, February 7, 1955, NBC papers, Box 391, Folder 18, Wisconsin Historical Society Archives.

69. Vestal, memo to Vane.

70. Murray Heilweil, memo to Jim Hergen, February 3, 1956, NBC papers, Box 401, Folder 8, Wisconsin Historical Society Archives.

71. Stole, "There Is No Place Like *Home*," 148.

72. Script for *Home*, April 17, 1957, Clare Barrows papers, courtesy Susanna Barrows collection.

73. John Hartley, *Uses of Television* (New York: Routledge, 1999), 94, 95, 97, 99, 100, 103.

74. Robert Beuka, *SuburbiaNation: Reading Suburban Landscape in Twentieth-Century American Fiction and Film* (New York: Palgrave Macmillan, 2004), 191.

8. DESIGNING THE YARD

1. Donald Katz, *Home Fires: An Intimate Portrait of One Middle-Class Family in Postwar America* (New York: HarperCollins, 1992), 64, 71, 106.

2. Many books, magazines, and newspaper articles in this period were devoted to instruction about basic landscape installation, maintenance, and horticulture. See, for example, Robert S. Malkin, *How to Landscape Your Own Home* (New York: Harper, 1955). This book, like so many others of the time, instructed first-time homeowners on what to do with the land surrounding their houses and included very detailed instructions for how to draw designs on paper, how to build fences, how to install plants, and how to maintain them. Most postwar newspapers included at least a weekly column on residential gardening, such as the one authored by Thomas Church for the Sunday *San Francisco Chronicle* and Abraham Levitt's "Gardening Chats" column, which ran weekly in the *Levittown Times*.

3. Nicolaides, *My Blue Heaven*, 26, 29, 228, 230, 186–87.

4. For a good overview of the history of the development of this particular American landscape aesthetic, see Christopher Grampp, *From Yard to Garden: The Domestication of America's Home Grounds* (Chicago: Center for American Places, Columbia College, 2008), chaps. 1–5.

5. On Garrett Eckbo, see Marc Treib and Dorothée Imbert, *Garrett Eckbo: Modern Landscapes for Living* (Berkeley: University of California Press, 1997); on James Rose, see Marc Treib, ed., *Modern Landscape Architecture: A Critical Review* (Cambridge: MIT Press, 1994).

6. Thomas Church, *Gardens Are for People: How to Plan for Outdoor Living* (New York: Reinhold, 1955). On the success of Church's publications and their impact, see Dianne Harris, "Writing the Modern Garden: Thomas Church as Author," in *Thomas Church, Landscape Architect*, ed. Marc Treib (San Francisco: William Stout, 2004).

7. Joseph Howland, memo to Conrad-Pyle Rose Company, April 7, 1949, Howland Papers, Environmental Design Archives, University of California, Berkeley.

8. Joseph E. Howland, "Why Does a Man Garden?," in *National Garden Supply Merchandiser and Power Equipment Dealer*, October 1951, Howland Papers, Environmental Design Archives, University of California, Berkeley.

9. Dobriner, *Class in Suburbia*, 9.

10. Stanley White, *Fundamentals of Landscape Design*, Small Homes Council Circular Series Index Number B3.0, *University of Illinois Bulletin* 44, no. 55 (May 12, 1947), University of Illinois Archives.

11. Joseph Howland, memo to Elizabeth Gordon, "Re: 1955 Garden Editorial Program," December 2, 1954, 6, Howland Papers, Environmental Design Archives, University of California, Berkeley.

12. Dell Upton, "Sound as Landscape," *Landscape Journal* 26, no. 1 (2007): 24–35.

13. Mary Alice Hines, *Real Estate Appraisal* (New York: Macmillan, 1981), 81.

14. See H. O. Lehman, "The Effect of Trees and Planting on Property Values," in *Appraisal and Valuation Manual of the American Society of Appraisers*, vol. 4 (Washington, D.C.: American Society of Appraisers, 1959), 173–76.

15. "People Want Better Storage," 152.

16. See Gary Daynes, "Cars, Carports, and Suburban Values in Brookside, Delaware," *Material Culture* 29 (Spring 1997): 3.

17. Fogelson, *Bourgeois Nightmares,* 168.

18. "Something New Is Happening at the Back Door," *House Beautiful,* April 1952, 163, 229, 232; see also "Ways to Store Garden Materials," *Sunset,* February 1947, 22. Joseph Howland thought storage was an important enough problem that it deserved its own feature article in the July 1954 issue of *House Beautiful.* Howland, memo to Gordon, 5.

19. Federal Housing Administration, *Underwriting Manual,* 418-4.

20. Ibid., 1388-1-6.

21. Ibid.

22. Avi Friedman, "The Evolution of Design Characteristics during the Post–Second World War Era," *Journal of Design History* 8, no. 2 (1995): 140.

23. Arthur A. May, "Appraising the Home: III," in *Selected Readings in Real Estate Appraisal* (Chicago: American Institute of Real Estate Appraisers, 1953), 464, 465. See also Henry Wright, "Trends in Architecture," in *Selected Readings in Real Estate Appraisal,* 500. Wright wrote: "The Contemporary house has been obstructed constantly by an overwhelming majority of mortgage lenders. Even today the policies of most lending institutions operate as a very real obstacle to the home builder, who would like to realize some of the advantages of contemporary design, because of the practical matter of obtaining financing."

24. See, for example, the 1957 issue of *House Beautiful's Practical Gardener,* which describes the Siebenthaler Garden Center in Dayton, Ohio.

25. Tom Riley, "We Built a Family Room Outdoors," *Popular Mechanics,* April 1958, 144–49, 234, 236–37.

26. Ibid., 144.

27. Ibid., 147, 148, 234, 236.

28. Leckey, "Unusual and Modern Ideas," 176, 177, 181, 186, 188. For two additional examples that include a list of the features considered essential for ordinary postwar yards, see Jay W. Hedden, "*PM*'s Landscaping Plan for the Small Yard," *Popular Mechanics,* April 1957, 147, 148, 150. Hedden's plan was for a 60-by-113-foot lot surrounding a ranch house in the Chicago suburbs. His plan included a patio for outdoor parties, play space for children, and storage space for bikes, garden tools, and patio furniture because the house had no basement or attic. Creation of an "outdoor living room" required fencing the lot. Planting was to be largely self-sustaining to permit leisure time, and Hedden recommended using the services of a landscape architect; the landscape architect that Hedden employed charged $65.00 for a planting plan. See also Harold O. Klopp, "The Test of Good Landscaping . . . That Year-Round Effect," *Popular Mechanics,* October 1959, 187, 258. Klopp told readers to plan their gardens to include three important elements. The first of these was privacy: "You'll want a section of lawn where you can sit, entertain and perhaps barbecue a picnic supper without making it necessary for the neighbors to see and hear everything that's going on. They may not enjoy it any more than you." The second element was a play area, and the third was utility: "Drying area, burning area, off-street parking space, storage nooks for building materials and compost, space for a small vegetable or fruit garden, all should be worked into the master plan with careful thought to convenience as well as design." These are just two among what were certainly dozens of similar articles that appeared in popular and shelter magazines between 1945 and 1960, and they follow the same prescriptions as those found in tastemaking and design literature from the period.

29. For another example of an article promoting nighttime activity in residential gardens, see "All Outdoors Lit Up: New

Fixtures Bring Down the Cost of Getting Dramatic Night Landscapes," *Life*, August 2, 1954, 67–69.

30. For more on this subject, see Harris, "Making Your Private World," 180–205.

31. See, for example, "Big Outdoors on a 100-Foot Lot," *Life*, November 15, 1954, 120: "One of the commandments of contemporary architecture is that the house must be opened up with big window walls and the outdoors brought indoors."

32. Editors of Fortune, *Changing American Market*, 82.

33. Beecher and Stowe, *American Woman's Home*, 91, 96. For discussion of the work of a Morris follower who shaped this tradition in California from the 1880s onward, see Harris, *Maybeck's Landscapes*; Wright, *Building the Dream*, 107. On the sleeping porch, see Elizabeth Collins Cromley, "A History of Beds and Bedrooms," *Perspectives in Vernacular Architecture* 4 (1991): 177–86. On Victorian notions of the healthful nature of outdoor activity, see Dianne Harris, "Cultivating Power: The Language of Feminism in Women's Garden Literature, 1870–1920," *Landscape Journal* 13, no. 2 (Fall 1994): 113–23.

34. Richard Pratt, "Garden through Glass," *Ladies' Home Journal*, April 1945, 40.

35. Spigel, *Make Room for TV*, 103, 104–5.

36. "*Life* Presents Landscapes and a Garden Calendar for *Life*'s Houses," *Life*, March 20, 1939, 24.

37. Klopp, "Test of Good Landscaping," 187, 258.

38. Hurley, *Diners, Bowling Alleys, and Trailer Parks*, 281.

39. Dr. Eric Deutsch, letter to A. Quincy Jones, September 28, 1950, with copy sent to *House Beautiful*, A. Quincy Jones papers, "Modern Home" file, courtesy Elaine Sewell Jones.

40. "The *PM* Indoor–Outdoor House" *Popular Mechanics*, October 1959, 144–51, 286.

41. Grampp, *From Yard to Garden*, 29, 49, 55. See also Frank J. Scott, *The Art of Beautifying Home Grounds* (New York: Appleton, 1870). Grampp also cites Leonard Johnson, *Foundation Planting* (New York: A. T. De La Mare, 1927).

42. For more on the design of gardens surrounding houses in Levittown, Pennsylvania, see Christopher Sellers, "Suburban Na-

ture, Class, and Environmentalism in Levittown," in Harris, *Second Suburb*, 287–88, 294. The 1956 promotional documentary film *The Quiet Revolution*, produced by the Ford Motor Company, shows how tractors were used to plant the grounds of Levittown houses. The film is available on YouTube at http://www.youtube.com/watch?v=7oCtKdw8d-o (accessed June 7, 2012).

43. Mock, *If You Want To Build a House*, 13.

44. Ibid., 30.

45. Howland, memo to Gordon.

46. *House and Home*, March 1954, 14–16, cited in Ackerman, "What Should Women (and Men) Want?," 9.

47. Howland, memo to Gordon.

48. Ibid., 2.

49. Ibid.

50. Christopher Grampp's study of the evolution of the American yard indicates that the dooryards of nineteenth- and early twentieth-century residences contained numerous elements related to the reproduction of daily life for families (including the cultivation of produce and space for raising farm animals) as well as to the maintenance of household sanitation. Dooryards and early backyards that belonged to immigrant and working-class Americans were work spaces, not spaces of leisure. See Grampp, *From Yard to Garden*, chap. 1.

51. Wiese, *Places of Their Own*, 75, 77–79, 86, 145–46.

52. See note 3, above.

53. White, *Fundamentals of Landscape Design*, 4–5.

54. Leckey, "Unusual and Modern Ideas," 176.

55. See, for example, Ann Bermingham, *Landscape and Ideology: The English Rustic Tradition, 1740–1860* (Berkeley: University of California Press, 1986); John Barrell, *The Dark Side of the Landscape: The Rural Poor in English Painting, 1730–1840* (New York: Cambridge University Press, 1983).

56. Andrew Jackson Downing, *A Treatise on the Theory and Practice of Landscape Gardening*, 6th ed. (New York: A. O. Moore, 1859), 433.

57. See, for example, Virginia Scott Jenkins, *The Lawn: A History*

of an American Obsession (Washington, D.C.: Smithsonian Institution Press, 1994); Georges Teyssot, ed., The American Lawn (New York: Princeton Architectural Press, 1999); Michael Pollan, Second Nature: A Gardener's Education (New York: Grove/Atlantic, 1991); Ted Steinberg, American Green: The Obsessive Quest for the Perfect Lawn (New York: W. W. Norton, 2007).

58. Federal Housing Administration, Underwriting Manual, 1368-1, 1388-5, 1388-7.

59. Leonard M. Cowley, "The Value of View," Appraisal Journal, April 1951, 239–42, reprinted in Selected Readings in Real Estate Appraisal, 458. On the importance of views, see also Isenstadt, "Visual Commodification of Landscape," 60–69; and Sandy Isenstadt, "Four Views, Three of Them through Glass," in Sites Unseen: Landscape and Vision, ed. Dianne Harris and D. Fairchild Ruggles (Pittsburgh: University of Pittsburgh Press, 2007), 213–40.

60. Lacy, Blue-Chip Black, 64, 65, 66. On the aesthetic of whiteness and privilege presented by the picturesque landscapes surrounding houses in affluent suburbs, see Duncan and Duncan, Landscapes of Privilege.

61. Homeowner's Guide: Some Information for Residents of Levittown to Help Them Enjoy Their New Homes, 1951, Levittown Collection, Bucks County Public Library, Levittown Branch.

62. Nicolaides, My Blue Heaven, 229.

63. Jenkins, The Lawn, 128.

64. National Association of Manufacturers Industry on Parade film collection, Reel 31 (RV507.31), 5/4/51, Archives Center, National Museum of American History, Smithsonian Institution.

65. National Association of Manufacturers Industry on Parade film collection, Reel 192 (RV 507.192), 6/15/54, Archives Center, National Museum of American History, Smithsonian Institution.

66. National Association of Manufacturers Industry on Parade film collection, Reel 405 (RV507.405), 7/12/58, Archives Center, National Museum of American History, Smithsonian Institution.

67. The best source on the history of the lawn sprinkler is Jenkins, The Lawn, 108–9.

68. See the segment "Soak, Don't Sprinkle!," sponsored by the Scovill Manufacturing Company, Waterbury, Connecticut, National Association of Manufacturers Industry on Parade film collection, Reel 197 (RV507.197), 7/20/54, Archives Center, National Museum of American History, Smithsonian Institution.

69. For a first-person account of homeowner installation of such an irrigation system, see the suburban memoir by David Beers, Blue Sky Dream: A Memoir of America's Fall from Grace (San Diego: Harcourt Brace, 1996), 48.

70. F. W. Ferguson, "Sambo Novel Lawn Sprinkler," Popular Mechanics, May 1949, 205. The image also appeared in an advertisement in Life, June 29, 1942, 51.

71. M. M. Manring, Slave in a Box: The Strange Career of Aunt Jemima (Charlottesville: University Press of Virginia, 1998), 111, 112.

72. Despite recent efforts at revisionist history claiming that the "Jocko" sculpture was originally a patriotic symbol of a black man who guided George Washington and his army to safety, the figure became a symbol of racist antagonism to many blacks in the United States by at least the twentieth century as it remains so today.

73. Steven C. Dubin, "Symbolic Slavery: Black Representations in Popular Culture," Social Problems 34, no. 2 (April 1987): 122–40.

74. Amy Chazkel and David Serlin, "Editors' Introduction," in "Enclosures: Fences, Walls, and Contested Spaces," ed. Amy Chazkel and David Serlin, special issue, Radical History Review 2010, no. 108 (Fall 2010): 1.

75. Ibid., 7; John Streamas, "Looking between Fences in American History," in Chazkel and Serlin, "Enclosures," Radical History Review 2010, no. 108 (Fall 2010): 161–74.

76. John R. Stilgoe, Outside Lies Magic: Regaining History and Awareness in Everyday Places (New York: Walker, 1998), 107–12.

77. Frank J. Scott, The Art of Beautifying Suburban Home Grounds

of *Small Extent* (New York: John B. Alden, 1886), 61; Grampp, *From Yard to Garden*, 55, 101.

78. Robert M. Fogelson provides a fine overview of these developments in fencing in the nineteenth and early twentieth centuries in *Bourgeois Nightmares*, 164–67. See also Paul Groth, "Lot, Yard, and Garden: American Distinctions," *Landscape* 30, no. 3 (1990): 29–35; Scott, *Art of Beautifying Suburban Home Grounds of Small Extent*, 51, 55, 107; Nathaniel H. Egleston, *The Home and Its Surroundings; or, Villages and Village Life* (New York: Harper & Brothers, 1884), 134–46.

79. For discussion of an example of restrictions against fencing in a postwar suburb, see Sellers, "Suburban Nature," 291–93. An abbreviated version of the Levittown deed restrictions appeared in the *Homeowner's Guide* given to every new Levittown homeowner.

80. See Ward, *History of Domestic Space*, 137.

81. Ibid., 147.

82. "How Our Cars Have Changed Our Gardens," *House Beautiful*, November 1956, 254.

83. As a 1949 Pace-Setter house plan caption stated: "Broad L-shape living porch shows how vitamin-conscious moderns turn toward outdoors. Because people now work indoors, outdoors is a symbol of relaxation. Re barbecue: cooking has prestige when you cook for fun." *House Beautiful*, January 1949, 57.

84. Thomas Church, *House Beautiful*, August 1948, 78; Jean Burden, "From Ordinary Back Yard to Country-Club Living," *House Beautiful*, August 1958, 72; "Mark of a MODERN House—The Paved Terrace," *House Beautiful*, November 1952, 220. Elaine Tyler May has likewise noted that "the suburban home was planned as a self-contained universe. . . . family members would not need to go out for recreation or amusements, since they had swing sets, playrooms, and backyards with barbecues at home." May, *Homeward Bound*, 171; see also Clark, *American Family Home*, 219. Andrew Hurley has argued that, ultimately, American families were pulled away from each other and into the outside world because "the vendors of mass goods and services recognized that men, women, and

children were as likely to seek refuge from the straitjacket of family hierarchies and responsibilities through their consumption activities as they were to seek togetherness. . . . the endeavor became more difficult as time wore on and the centrifugal pull of peer-group pressure and individual expression overwhelmed the centripetal lure of family togetherness." Hurley, *Diners, Bowling Alleys, and Trailer Parks*, 290–91.

85. A. Quincy Jones, *House and Home*, January 1957, 142.

86. "The Backyard—America's Most Mis-used Natural Resource," *House Beautiful*, January 1949, 37–42. See also Folder: Garden Design Plants—Alive Environment, Environmental Design Archives, University of California, Berkeley.

87. Elizabeth Gordon, "Is Privacy Your Right or a Stolen Pleasure?" *House Beautiful*, May 1960, 152, 232, 234–35.

88. "The Backyard—America's Most Mis-used Natural Resource," 37, 38, 41.

89. The X-100 received a great deal of media attention in the year of its construction, but the privacy wall itself was featured in *Concrete Masonry Review*, April 1957, 16–17.

90. Although historians such as Lynn Spigel have correctly asserted that picture windows served as essential showcases for the display of household possessions, they have largely neglected to address the privacy problems that arose in conflict with the desire for such display. See Spigel, "From Theatre to Space Ship: Metaphors of Suburban Domesticity in Postwar America," in Silverstone, *Visions of Suburbia*, 221.

91. Catlin and Catlin, *Building Your New House*, 149.

92. According to Marc Treib, the landscape architect Fletcher Steele recommended as early as 1924 that kitchens be moved to the street side of the lot in order to facilitate a greater connection between living and dining spaces and the garden. Indeed, this pattern is found in postwar housing as well, but equally numerous are houses that moved the kitchen toward the rear of the house or allowed it to span the length, from front to back, in very small houses. See Treib, "Aspects of Regionality and the Modern(ist) Garden in California," in *Regional Garden Design in the United States*, ed. Therese O'Malley and Marc Treib (Washington, D.C.: Dumbarton Oaks, 1995),

15. For an interesting analysis of actual use versus architect's intentions in an Eichler house, see Adams, "The Eichler Home," 164–78. Adams shows that despite the designer's ideas about supervision from the windows, children managed to find ways to escape their mother's watchful eye. For a detailed analysis of the placement of kitchens in Levitt houses, see Miner, "Pink Kitchens for Little Boxes," 243–80.

93. "Ways to Use Translucent Plastic Screen," *Sunset,* March 1951, 74.

94. Douglas Baylis, "Privacy Makes Better Outdoor Living: Why Fence Yourself In?," *Better Homes and Gardens,* April 1950, 48, 49, 54, 174, 175. See also Douglas and Maggie Baylis Collection [1999-4], office records/clippings, Environmental Design Archives, University of California, Berkeley. Baylis collected extensive material on fencing and wrote numerous articles about fencing for *House Beautiful, House & Garden,* and *Sunset.* See ibid., 48–49, 174–75; "For Privacy along Your Property Line: To Fence or Not to Fence?" *Sunset,* March 1954, 70–71.

95. Elizabeth Gordon, "The 12 Best Houses of the Last 12 Years," *House Beautiful,* September 1947, 89.

96. Carolyn Murray, "How an Interior Court Can 'Save' a Crowded Lot," *House Beautiful,* November 1957, 305. See also "Orientation Is More than Just a Word," *House Beautiful,* May 1961, 109; and Madelaine Thatcher, "How Public Should the Front Entrance Be?," *House Beautiful,* November 1963, 225.

97. Although, as noted above, the Levitt deed restrictions prohibited fence construction, a majority of the yards (75 percent) in the Pennsylvania development were fenced by 1977. See David Popenoe, *The Suburban Environment: Sweden and the United States* (Chicago: University of Chicago Press, 1977), 116–17.

98. "For Privacy Along Your Property Line," 70–71. See also Douglas and Maggie Baylis Collection, office records/clippings, Environmental Design Archives, University of California, Berkeley.

99. Thomas Church, *Your Private World: A Study of Intimate Gardens* (San Francisco: Chronicle Books, 1969).

100. Chazkel and Serlin, "Editors' Introduction," 1.

101. Peter Linebaugh, "Enclosures from the Bottom Up," in Chazkel and Serlin, "Enclosures," *Radical History Review* 2010, no. 108 (Fall 2010): 12.

EPILOGUE

1. Susan W. Hardwick, "Toward a Suburban Immigrant Nation," in *Twenty-first Century Gateways,* ed. Audrey Singer, Susan W. Hardwick, and Caroline B. Brettell (Washington, D.C.: Brookings Institution Press, 2008), 31.

2. A reliable source of information on the continuing struggle for fair housing is the Web site of the National Fair Housing Alliance: http://www.nationalfairhousing.org. See also the section of the U.S. Department of Housing and Urban Development Web site that deals with fair housing: http://portal.hud.gov/hudportal/HUD?src=/program_offices/fair_housing_equal_opp.

Index

Addams, Jane, 116; Hull House, 162

advertising, 15, 24, 43, 64, 68, 70, 71, 72, 75, 77, 81, 88, 124, 134, 232, 234, 242, 243, 258, 333n38, 334n50, 344n50

Ahmed, Sara, 161, 342n7

Alberti, Leon Battista, 115, 338n8

American Association to Improve Our Neighborhoods, 36

American Dream (of homeownership), viii, 7, 17, 89, 95, 133, 315

American style, 105, 112, 131, 132, 157, 294; and democracy, 132, 133

Anderson, Benedict, 60

Anshen, Robert, 189

apartments, viii, 134, 238; apartment dwelling/living, 21, 47, 91, 106, 193; crowded/crowding, 116, 140; and distinction/class status, 165, 167, 168; plots, 27, 123

appliances, 52, 71, 76, 142, 144, 164, 174, 178, 188, 209, 217, 220, 226, 232, 258, 344n55, 345n21, 346n25, 346n27, 346n32, 347n43; storage of, 195, 196, 197, 201, 202, 203, 205, 207–10, 216

Archer, John, 115, 319, 324n3, 333n21

architects/architectural profession, 3, 4, 6, 7, 8, 35, 52, 69, 71, 72, 73, 76, 83, 87, 88, 89, 91, 113, 125, 140, 173, 216, 224, 258, 279, 282; and drawing, 83–109

architects/architectural profession, eighteenth-century British, 115; and journals, magazines, publications, 73, 74, 77, 146, 190, 234

architects/architectural profession, nineteenth-century North American, 115; and sexism, 72; social conservatism, 109; and television, 235, 238, 248, 256, 259

architects/architectural profession, twentieth-century, 116; whiteness of, 95

architectural drawings. *See* representations

architecture: and construction of political, social, and economic realities, 3; corporate, 241; democratic, 35, 131; of enclosure, 312; high-style, 3, 27, 31, 52, 134; as not benign/neutral, 3, 31; political histories of, 27; and race, 3; representations of, 83–109; as rhetorical, 27; of settlement houses, 61; suburban, 166, 280; vernacular, 105, 166

Arts + Architecture magazine, 76, 189, 248, 249, 335n53, 350n49; Case Study House program, 76, 248, 249, 334n52, 350n49; John Entenza, 76

Asians, 30, 34, 81

assimilation/assimilate, viii, 18, 36, 50, 61, 92, 122, 323n2, 327n35,

330n31, 332n5; and middle class, 72, 327n34; and passing, 32, 36, 38, 54

attics, 50, 182, 185, 187, 212, 273, 280, 352n28

authenticity, 6

Babb, Valerie, 60, 61, 62, 162, 332n3, 332n5, 332n10, 338n52, 342n8

baby boom, 48, 144

basements, 50, 144, 154, 182, 185, 187, 205, 212, 215, 253, 273, 280, 289, 331n56, 346n27, 352n28

bathrooms, 44, 47, 49, 50, 52, 114, 117, 118, 139, 149, 156, 178, 201, 210, 216, 217, 221, 223, 249, 252, 253, 256, 343n22, 347n61

Bauhaus, 46, 73, 159

Baylis, Douglas (and Maggie), 73, 101, 148, 197, 290, 310, 311, 312, 356n94

Becket, Wurdeman Architects, 200, 202, 203, 205, 221, 222

bedrooms, 44, 45, 46, 47, 48, 52, 71, 86, 102, 114, 115, 117, 118, 126, 139, 140, 146, 149, 150, 151, 152, 154, 156, 200, 210, 211, 215, 216, 217, 220, 221, 222, 229, 249, 250, 252, 253, 254, 255, 256

Berger, Martin, 11, 61, 325n15, 332n4

blacks/blackness: black/white binary, 18, 23; and housing/housing developments, 17; images of, 95, 301; imagined as, 19, 38, 119; servants, 93, 300, 301; slaves, 93, 265; spaces, 38, 119; stereotypes, 37, 94, 97, 101, 298, 337n37

blockbusting, 97

body/bodies, 27, 224, 227; changing ideas about, 115; movement of, 91, 235; smells, 49; white, 134

books/bookshelves/bookcases: and coffee tables, 190; as signifiers of distinction or class, 51, 56, 57, 98, 166, 167, 168, 188, 189, 190, 210

built-ins/built-in cabinetry. See closets/cabinets/storage

California, 4, 30, 291, 312; Berkeley, 144; Lakewood, 166; Los Angeles, 154, 200, 202, 203, 205, 221, 222; Palo Alto, 308; San Diego, 137; San Mateo (Eichler X-100 House), 139, 152, 153, 238, 309; style, 27, 51, 52, 281; Van Nuys, 111

Cannon, Poppy, 239, 245, 350nn43–44; marriage to Walter Francis White (NAACP), 245

Cape Cod house, 40

carpet, 30, 46, 102, 126, 192, 193

Castillo, Greg, 160, 336n8, 338n2, 342n2, 345n1

catalogs, 1, 88, 173; trading stamp, 176, 177, 178, 180, 181, 344n50

Catlin, Mary and George, 39, 40, 129, 131, 135, 144, 195, 310, 330nn34–35, 330n38, 340n61, 341n73, 341n82, 346n24, 355n91

CBS, 241

census statistics. See homeownership

Chamber of Commerce, 36

Cheever, John, 123, 339n39

Chicago, 4, 15, 57, 79, 97, 116, 132, 162, 164, 167, 171, 238, 243, 250, 251, 257, 281, 284, 286; Black Belt, 98

children/children's spaces, 40, 47, 48, 52, 56, 59, 61, 75, 79, 85, 99, 109, 118, 121, 124, 126, 128, 131, 132, 144, 146, 148–54, 156, 161, 186, 200, 210, 211, 220, 223, 236, 250, 254, 256, 264, 269, 272, 274, 277, 279, 281, 293, 299, 302, 304, 305, 307, 309, 310, 312, 323

Church, Thomas Dolliver, 24, 73, 91, 103, 154, 268, 290, 312, 341n106, 351n2, 351n6, 355n84, 356n99

citizenship, vii, ix, 11, 132, 323n2; and consumption, 105; and homeownership/property ownership, ix, 1, 2, 12, 14, 21, 31, 57, 60, 64, 85, 99, 237, 297, 302, 313, 339n31; and privacy, 113, 121

civil rights movement/civil rights era, 11, 17, 35, 91, 109, 317

class: blue-collar, viii, 21, 69, 95, 106, 165, 192, 198, 205, 342n19; distinctions, 22, 23, 112; as a fluid category, 22; and house types, 164–65; lower economic, 32, 103, 105, 128, 135, 151, 293, 297; middle class, viii, 1, 6, 12, 14, 18, 21, 22, 39, 40, 43, 45, 51, 54, 57, 60–62, 70, 72–73, 79, 81, 85–86, 89, 91, 92, 96, 98–99, 101, 103, 105, 109, 111, 114–19, 121, 129, 132, 141, 160, 161, 163, 165, 173, 180–82, 187–88, 190–93, 196–97, 201, 205, 209, 211, 222–23, 226, 232–33, 239, 249, 259, 261, 267, 269, 272, 279, 282–84, 286, 291–92, 295, 297–98, 304, 309–11, 327n34, 332n12, 337n22, 337n37, 342nn4–6, 346n23, 346n3; middle majority, 21, 85, 91, 101, 109, 113, 121, 127, 131, 136, 160, 163, 165, 181, 189, 190, 191, 227, 279, 342n19; mobility, 85, 131; stability, 21; structure, 20, 61; upper classes, 39, 61, 69, 85, 108, 116, 146, 165, 171, 191, 205, 211, 224, 243, 244, 272, 292, 295, 304, 345n11; white collar, 21, 101, 103, 171, 195–200, 203, 205, 209, 292; working class, viii, 15, 18, 21, 36, 38, 39, 64, 121, 164,

65, 77, 113, 115, 117, 121, 122, 160, 162, 174, 189, 190, 200, 205, 206, 272, 296; income/budget, 69, 174, 183, 311; mixed race, 161; needs, 49, 55, 183; nuclear, 63, 83, 91, 122; privacy, 111–57; togetherness, 2, 91, 121, 122, 123, 151, 156, 306

family rooms, 52, 74, 140, 151, 154, 214, 220, 226, 252, 254, 255, 277, 278, 286

Federal Housing Administration (FHA), 34, 140, 292; and architectural modernism, 35, 76, 89, 336n12; guidelines, 40, 44, 187; and landscape design, 274–76, 291, 296, 297; minimum house/property standards, 47, 207, 211, 276, 331n47, 347n51; mortgages/mortgage insurance/loan approvals, 36, 77, 85, 250, 257, 331n52; and redlining/racist practices, 34, 36, 37, 44, 292, 297, 329n24n27; underwriting manuals, 36, 139, 274, 291, 296, 341n77, 345n4, 352n19, 354n58

fences. *See* gardens: fences

films: *Goodbye Columbus*, 33, 38; *House in the Middle*, 98; *Imitation of Life*, 32; *Porgy and Bess*, 119; *Raisin in the Sun*, 119; *Song of the South*, 119

Francis, Arlene, 180, 239, 243, 245, 247, 248, 249, 349n30, 350n41

front porch/stoop, 38, 97, 109

furniture, 51, 74, 75, 159, 210, 216, 217, 344n45; and distinction, 56, 126, 159–63, 191–92; garden, 51, 108, 273, 274, 277, 281, 282, 291, 293, 298, 305, 352n28; Herman Miller, 46, 159, 238; washable, 103. *See also* Jews

garage/carport, 7, 44, 45, 51, 52, 55, 111, 182, 200, 202, 203, 210, 216, 217, 220, 221, 223, 226, 249, 250, 253, 254, 263, 273, 274, 298, 309, 311, 343n22

gardens, 263–313; and black suburbs, 297–98; design of, 274–77; fences, 302–13; foundation plantings, 263, 275, 286; gardeners, 52, 103, 264, 270, 298; as hobby, 109, 270; and indoor/outdoor rooms, 52, 113, 217, 256, 277–95; and lawns and lawnmowers, 9, 45, 51, 56, 96, 99, 101, 178, 182, 210, 211, 263–313; and noise, 272; and order/cleanliness, 83, 271–74; and patios, 45, 52, 97, 150, 151, 152, 153, 217, 220, 222, 242, 263–313; and racist ornaments, 264, 265, 267, 300–301; and vegetables, 55, 106, 222, 267, 270, 271, 292, 293, 310, 352n28; victory, 106, 292. *See also* furniture: garden

gender, ix, 9, 10, 20, 21, 22, 23, 27, 38, 51, 68, 79, 80, 85, 86, 87, 146, 163, 176, 181, 188, 230, 236, 239, 243, 244, 245, 260, 261

ghettoes, 32, 34, 119

GI Bill, 34

Gilroy, Paul, 20, 327n38

glass. *See* doors; windows

Gordon, Elizabeth, 24, 71, 72, 78, 112, 125, 131, 132, 290, 306, 334nn41–42, 334n44, 335n60, 335n62, 335nn63–65, 340n64, 340n66, 351n11, 355n87, 356n95. *See also* magazines: *House Beautiful*

Grampp, Christopher, 286, 287, 351n4, 353n41, 353n50, 355n77

Griffin, Marion Mahoney, 88

Griffin, Walter Burley, 88

Hall, Stuart, 18, 20, 98, 327n36, 337n31

Hariman, Robert: and John Louis Lucaites, 2, 10, 11, 324n1, 325n12, 325n13

Harris, Harwell Hamilton, 73, 80, 156

Havens House, 80

Hayden, Dolores, 61, 325n10, 332n6

heating systems, 117

Hedrich Blessing Photographers, 79, 335n61

Herman Miller. *See* furniture

heteronormative household, 80; domesticity, 54, 85, 181; heterosexual household, 62; heterosexual norms, 51, 81, 109, 117, 118, 176, 239

hi-fi *See* stereo/hi-fi

home entertaining, 99, 127, 128, 193, 196, 256, 305

homeownership, vii, 193, 223; association with white identities, citizenship, and race, 1, 2, 4, 9, 12, 14, 15, 21, 31, 43, 59, 60, 62, 64, 72, 99, 258, 266, 269, 297, 298, 326n26, 339n31; census statistics, 6, 33, 34, 50, 324n9, 328n14, 329n17, 331n54; and class/class identity, 39, 160, 230, 343n22; and cultural authority, 19; and democracy, 72, 112, 125, 127, 131, 166; and magazine subscriptions, 59–81; without servants, 101, 135, 346n32. *See also* American Dream; class

Home Owners Loan Corporation/HOLC, 34, 292

homophobia, 81

housewife, 71, 102, 208, 214, 271; as household engineer, 101, 103; as household executive/white-collar professional, 103, 195, 199–200, 201, 202, 209; housewife's labor, 103, 135, 180, 205, 206; spatial integration of, 197, 339n32; as suburban drone, 128. *See also* kitchen: desk

Housing and Home Finance Agency, 43

housing inequality, 1–25, 35; and social justice, 3, 35, 302

housing market, 3, 4, 6, 11, 12, 23, 24, 28, 30, 34, 35, 36, 43, 44, 52, 85, 95, 131, 176, 247, 252, 268, 315, 316

Howland, Joseph, 133, 134, 270, 272, 290, 338n47, 340n67, 351n7, 351n11, 352n18

Hurley, Andrew, 121, 192, 210, 330n34, 342n19, 346n25, 355n84

identity construction, 18, 113

ideology, 11, 37, 72, 118, 119, 131, 162, 294; ideological cynicism, 11–12, 265–66. *See also* Žižek, Slavoj

immigrants, vii, viii, ix, 4, 15, 18, 21, 29, 132; acquisition of citizenship, 323n2; Asians, 30, 34, 81, 327n35; and assimilation/whitening of, 18, 61, 62, 327n31, 327n34, 330n31; Chinese, 33, 54, 55; and cleanliness, 38, 39, 96, 97, 98; experience, 325n19; and gardens, 10, 263, 266, 292, 293, 353n50; and house form, 54, 55, 151; Italian, 164, 165; Jewish, 30, 96; laborers, 37; and privacy, 114, 122; suburban immigrant nation, 315; as suspicious noncitizens, 323n1; and taste, 161, 162, 163, 191; and work/workers, 195, 200, 205

individualism, 119, 126–28, 132, 135, 150, 237

individuality, 27, 60, 65, 92, 117, 125–28, 131–33, 135, 146, 157, 166, 193, 291, 297, 306, 340n48

informality, 60, 92, 191, 193, 286, 291, 345n11

intercom, 46, 111, 151, 152, 156, 182, 200, 202, 203, 217, 220, 223, 311

International Style, 72, 134, 241

Isenstadt, Sandy, 134, 135, 214, 324n3, 340nn69–70, 341n74, 347n59, 354n59

Italians, 29, 164, 165, 169, 171

Jacobson, Matthew Frye, 3, 17, 18, 32, 324n4, 325n19, 327n33, 328n12

Jews, vii, viii, 15, 17, 18, 29, 32, 36, 38, 46, 98, 162, 185, 195, 236, 323n2, 327n29, 327n34, 327n35, 331n63, 332n5; builders, 30; families, 30; identities, 23, 30, 33, 54, 162; Judaica, 54; and Kosher dishes, 46; looking Jewish, 32; modern/contemporary furniture, 168, 173; and modernism, 168, 170, 174; non-Jewish, 45; social reformers, 96; and taste, 54, 173

Jim Crow era, 15, 62, 301

Jones, A. Quincy, 24, 51, 52, 73, 137, 139, 153, 154, 173, 209, 220, 238, 248, 249, 252, 283, 306, 309, 320, 335n61, 336n12

Jones, Rudard, 324n7

Kartwold, Arne, 106–8

Keats, John, 128, 135, 229, 235, 340nn59–60, 341n71, 348n1, 348n13

Kennedy, Robert Woods, 73, 146, 147, 149, 150, 151, 334n46, 341n87

kitchen: desk, 103, 197–200, 201–3, 205; housewife's domain, 203; as laboratory/office/workshop, 197–205; oven, 45, 208, 209, 220, 250; pass-through, 121, 141, 197; range, 45, 55, 163, 201, 208, 209, 220, 250; sinks, 45, 199, 205, 206; storage/cabinets, 55, 197–208. *See also* appliances

Krushchev, Nikita, 186

Ku Klux Klan (KKK), 34

labor(ers)/work, 21, 45, 195, 196, 203, 205, 209, 274, 284, 292; and garden spaces, 107, 268, 283, 293, 295, 298, 299, 300, 310; as leisure, 180, 223, 269, 295; servants, 101, 135, 188, 200, 301; union, 37, 238, 329n38. *See also* housewife; immigrants: laborers

landscape, 10, 27; Arcadian pastoral/picturesque, 135, 267; cultural, 7, 25, 34, 43, 88; and enclosure movement, 267; and ideology, 31, 265–66; Olmsted, Frederick Law, 267. *See also* gardens

Latino/as, 29, 34, 81. *See also* Mexicans

laundry lines/clotheslines (and concealing), 42, 45, 99, 111, 263, 274, 293, 304, 310

laundry spaces/laundry rooms, 52, 55, 144, 152, 153, 201, 202, 205, 215, 216, 221, 249, 252 lawns. *See* gardens

Lee, Roger, 144, 145

leisure, 60, 92, 106–9, 125–28, 154, 163, 180, 182–83, 191, 220, 223, 256, 266–67, 269–70, 277, 279, 286, 291, 293, 295, 299, 300–302, 308, 310, 352n28, 353n50; leisure styles, 128

Levitt, Abraham, 287

Levitt, William, 8, 48, 236, 247

Levitt family of builders/houses, 6, 37, 50, 136, 141, 236, 324n8

Levittown, 48; Long Island, 166, 236, 237, 311; Pennsylvania, 140, 141, 166, 197, 198, 263, 287, 288, 296, 298, 304

lifestyle, 21, 22, 47, 60, 76, 88, 92, 95, 101, 106, 114, 117, 159, 181, 191, 220, 227, 232, 237, 243, 244, 256, 266, 272, 273, 277, 279, 281, 291, 292, 295, 299, 302, 317, 337n22

living rooms, 44–47, 54, 56, 59, 65–66, 68, 70, 107, 116–17, 121, 122, 139–41, 150–51, 154, 166–70, 178, 185–86, 190, 193, 197, 200, 210–11, 215, 220, 223–24, 230, 233, 235, 249, 250, 252, 271, 280, 282–83, 286, 305, 343n22, 345n18, 346n32, 352n28

lodgers, 116

Lucaites, John Louis. *See under* Hariman, Robert

Lynes, Russell, 127, 166; and taste/class chart, 171, 173, 340n55, 343n26, 343n33, 343n44

magazines, 59–81; advertisers/advertisements, 15, 59, 62, 64, 67–71, 91, 109, 124, 163, 231–34, 242, 258, 260, 270, 333n26, 333n28, 334n50, 350n49; *Architectural Forum*, 47, 72, 77, 223, 334n40, 347n58; *Better Homes and Gardens*, 67, 69, 73, 74, 76, 99, 101, 148, 242, 333n28, 333n38, 334n48, 335n61; and circulation rates/statistics, 67–70, 74, 75, 232, 242, 333n26, 333n27, 333n28; *Collier's*, 69; and critiques of, 66; and cultural impact, 66; *Ebony*, 61, 85, 95, 101, 336n22; and expert advice, 61, 71, 72; *Godey's Ladies Book*, 65; *Good Housekeeping*, 69, 74, 247; *House and Home*, 36, 44, 74, 75, 94, 154, 182, 212, 216, 241, 242, 250, 251, 253, 257, 273, 290, 306, 324n7, 329n27, 334n48; *House Beautiful*, 24, 54, 65, 67, 69, 71–74, 78–80, 85, 91, 105,112, 131–34, 136, 154, 157, 201, 202, 205, 206, 239, 245, 252, 270, 272, 281, 283, 284, 290, 291, 303, 305–7, 311, 333n28, 334n42, 335n61; *Ladies' Home Journal*, 65, 67, 69, 74, 149, 151, 152, 163, 279; *Life*, 47, 48, 51, 63, 64, 67, 69, 74,

76, 77, 86, 92, 95, 98, 103, 104, 121, 141, 142, 146, 156, 164, 165, 171, 173, 182, 210, 213, 281, 283, 332n14, 333n19, 333n32, 333n38, 334n49; *McCall's*, 59, 66, 69, 71, 121, 335n61, 339n33; nineteenth century, 65, 86; *Pacesetter House*, 105, 131, 132, 252, 355n83; picture, 63; *Popular Mechanics*, 4, 8, 16, 24, 47, 51, 52, 67, 69, 71, 77, 78, 95, 104, 107, 123, 144, 151, 154, 181, 182, 186, 187, 214–17, 242, 269, 277–78, 281, 284–86, 289, 292–94, 300, 309, 324n7, 333n28, 336n10; print capitalism, 60; *Printer's Ink*, 70; *Saturday Evening Post*, 64; *Sunset*, 74, 197, 242, 281, 312, 343n28349n33; women as editors of (*see also* Gordon, Elizabeth), 72; women's, 6, 54, 61, 65, 69, 70, 72, 85, 92, 95, 99, 127, 181, 190, 239, 241, 242. *See also* taste: tastemakers

Marling, Karal Ann, 230, 340n56, 345nn1–2, 348n3

Marx, Karl, 11–12, 302

mass media, viii, 13, 32, 42, 51, 121, 157, 177, 231, 306

Maybeck, Bernard Ralph, 88

material culture, 9, 20, 32, 60, 70, 87, 93, 160, 173, 265, 295, 300, 302, 322, 342n4; bric-a-brac, 191; curio cabinet, 57; and distinction, 155–83; knick-knacks, 159. *See also* appliances

McCarthyism, 125

McCarty, Bruce, 248, 253–56

merchant builders, 4, 6, 29, 36, 72, 139–41, 166, 173, 234. *See also* Levitt family of builders/houses

Mexicans, 30, 33, 329n24. *See also* Latino/as

mobility: class, 85, 131, 164, 292; economic, 164, 181; social, 62, 181; spatial, 161, 302; status, 215, 343n32; upward, 21, 40, 131, 162, 332n12

Mock, Elizabeth, 105–6, 136, 150–51, 166, 289, 338n48, 341n94, 343n23, 346n32, 353n43

model homes, 71, 76, 133, 233

modernism, 159, 168, 191, 337n25, 344n39; architectural, 35, 52, 92, 96, 109, 113, 116, 122, 140, 173, 174, 192, 214, 231, 241, 294; everyday modernism, 132, 336n12, 340n65; high-style, 98, 134; International Style, 72; middling modernism, 52, 222; soft modernism, 52, 72, 132, 336n12. *See also* Jews

modernity, 47; aesthetic/architectural, 76, 89, 91, 112, 140, 145, 173, 192, 205, 209, 310; capitalist, 302; cultural, 47, 89, 140; technological, 89, 230, 298

Mortgage Bankers Association, 36
Museum of Modern Art, 73, 174, 289

National Association for the Advancement of Colored People
    (NAACP), 34, 44, 245, 329n27
National Association of Home Builders (NAHB), 23, 36, 37, 44, 74,
    233, 247, 248,249, 252, 257, 329n27, 331n52, 349n29
National Association of Retail Lumber Dealers, 36
National Urban League, 44, 329n27
NBC. *See* television
Negro Market, 70
neighborhoods, 20, 22, 25, 32, 37, 38, 43, 91, 92, 109, 134, 164,
    264, 271, 293, 316, 329n25; homogenous (black or white)/
    conforming, 36, 37, 56, 114, 117, 127, 128, 166, 170, 272–74,
    276, 297–98, 330n31, 337n37; restricted/nonrestricted/
    exclusive, ix, 15, 29, 30, 32, 34, 36, 40, 97, 101, 330n38,
    332n12, 336n22
neighbors, 40, 42, 45, 57, 87, 91, 101, 104, 113, 114, 117, 118 125–28,
    133–35, 142, 162, 165, 171, 176, 178, 193, 264, 269–71, 274,
    277–78, 302–3, 306–8, 310–13, 336n14, 352n28
Nelson, George, 46, 159, 174, 180, 213, 347n58
New Face of America Program, 36
Nixon, Richard, 186, 187
Noguchi, Isamu, 174

O'Connor, Flannery, 38, 301, 329n30
Ohmann, Richard, 64–65, 333nn21–22; and Professional Manage-
    rial Class (PMC), 64–65, 203
Omi, Michael, 3, 13, 14, 17, 324n6, 324n21, 327n32
open plan, 45, 51, 52, 116–17, 121–22, 140–41, 154, 197, 221, 285,
    306, 346n32; forced congeniality of/frictions caused by, 121–
    22, 142, 144–46, 151, 341n95

Packard, Vance, 124, 171, 173, 190, 338n5, 339n41, 344n35, 345n11
Parade of Homes, 77
Parker, Maynard L., 24, 42, 65, 66, 67, 68, 70, 78, 83, 137, 139, 195,
    200, 201, 202, 203, 205, 212, 221, 222, 224, 226, 282, 308,
    335n60, 335n62, 335n63, 335n64, 335n65

Park Forest, Illinois, 6, 236–37, 327n29, 349n17
parlor, 115, 116, 117, 171
passing (racial), 32, 36, 38, 125
pattern books, 88, 115, 173, 234
picture windows. *See* windows
postwar economy, 112, 160, 161. *See also* housing market
prefabricated house, 236, 237, 238, 298; Wingfoot house, 129, 131
privacy: acoustical, 114, 149, 151, 156; and family zoning, 148–56;
    language of, 140; and public spaces of home, 121; and unpri-
    vacy, 119, 123; and voyeurism, 114, 127, 133, 233, 311. *See* also
    gardens: fences
property rights, 31, 119, 302, 313
property values, 6, 37, 38, 187, 270, 297, 329n24, 330n31
public housing, 17, 36, 168

quality of life, 292

race riots, 15, 298
racial codes, 37–40, 42–43, 95, 109, 329n31
racial formation, 13, 14
racial thinking, 2, 18
racism: and exoticism, 94; and minstrelsy, 93, 94, 300–301; and
    respectability, 98, 114, 119, 267; and stereotype of hypersexu-
    alization, 94; and stereotype of primitivism, 94; and stereo-
    types, 37, 64, 94, 97, 101, 103, 105, 118, 126, 166, 298, 301,
    337n37, 340n51
radiant heat, 47, 236
radio, vii, 18, 66, 75, 123, 124, 144, 146, 151, 174, 187, 199, 201, 210,
    214, 223, 224, 226, 231–34, 298, 311, 321
ranch house, 28, 48, 77, 78, 352n28
real estate agents, 35, 91, 97, 272
real estate boards, 24, 37
real estate steering, 316
recreation, 126, 127, 154, 162, 186, 211, 232, 254, 256, 265, 266,
    270, 274, 279, 293, 295, 305, 355n84; equipment storage, 51,
    211
representations: aerial views, 86, 91, 95, 336n11; axonometric view,
    83, 86, 89; bird's-eye-view, 89, 336n11; conventions, 63, 86,

99, 114, 118, 124, 144, 146, 151, 154, 157, 174, 187, 210, 214, 220, 223, 224, 226, 229–61, 264, 266, 280, 317, 340n56, 348n68, 348n8, 350n39; *Blueprint for Modern Living*, 238; *Discovery*, 238; *Home*, 239–61; "House That *Home* Built," 241, 247–61; *Industry on Parade*, 235; and "mobile privatization," 234; programs about the home, 231; and Raymond Williams, 231

tenements, 54, 96, 116, 119, 140, 192

trading stamps, 175–82; and consumer goods, 175–82; Gold Bond, 176, 344n50, 344n55; S&H, 175–81

traditional/nontraditional, 8, 9, 35, 45, 52, 89, 132, 141, 142, 154, 162, 169, 170, 174, 180, 181, 182, 191, 213, 252, 276, 293, 325n20, 336n12

trailers/trailer trash, 39, 125, 129, 164, 211, 330n34, 337n40, 342n19

United States Savings and Loan League, 36

Upton, Dell, 61, 272, 320, 332n8, 338n17, 342n5, 351n12

urban renewal, 15, 36, 43

U.S. Gypsum, 77, 258; Research Village, 79, 335n61

Van der Rohe, Mies, 116, 121

Victorian home/house, 88, 286, 338n16, 353n33; nineteenth-century home economists, 96; and separate spheres, 121

visual culture, 9, 10, 18, 24, 64, 83, 85–87, 89, 109, 320, 325n12

Walker Art Center, 174

walls, 39, 144, 169, 188, 193, 209, 212, 213, 214; glass, 52, 217, 249, 282, 286, 334n48; folding/movable/sliding, 140, 151, 279; partitions, 51, 116, 140, 141, 197; privacy, 55, 136, 137, 153, 306, 309, 311, 312; screens, 140; window, 135. *See also* closets/cabinets/storage

Weber, Max, 22

Westinghouse home, 77

White, Richard, ix, 324n5

white identity, viii, 30, 92, 103, 206

whiteness, viii, 1, 3, 4, 11–13, 18–19, 21, 23, 30, 37, 43, 57, 60, 62; and "American style," 294; and class identity, 91; and commod-ity consumption, 159–227; iconography of/representations of, 60, 62–64, 70, 83–109, 258, 297; invisibility of, 60; and its opposite, 19, 38, 94–95, 119, 161; lexicon for, 60; and magazines, 59–81; as possession, 325n19; possessive investment in, 62, 328n9; and privacy, 111–57; probationary whiteness, 32; and purity/cleanliness/sanitation, 96, 98–104, 113, 161, 210, 223; signifiers for, 19, 42, 99; and sound (containment of), 21, 40, 114, 134, 142, 144, 145, 206, 272, 3336n14; studies of, 30–32, 1–57; and television, 229–61; and women's bodies, 188; white trash/Okies, 103; and yards/gardens, 263–313. *See also* homeownership; women

white privilege, 15, 30, 31, 162, 326n26

Whyte, William H., 22, 114, 128, 338n6

Wills, Royal Barry, 77

Winant, Howard, 3, 13, 14, 17, 324n6, 325n21, 327n32

windows, 38, 45, 47, 111, 127, 156, 202, 211, 253, 279, 309, 310; cleaning, 135; coverings, 126, 136, 192; glass, 112, 279, 286; picture window, 7, 56, 71, 75, 99, 113, 127, 134–37, 140, 174, 215, 229, 234, 235, 271, 279, 280, 290, 308, 310, 355n90

women, 21, 59, 62, 65, 71, 81, 121, 167, 169, 193, 343n32; of color, 188; homemaker, 62, 107, 188; housewife-engineer/manager/white-collar worker, 101, 103, 195–206, 209, 284, 345n21, 346n23; representations of, 62, 83, 89, 195; and television, 233, 239, 241, 243, 244; and trading stamps, 175–78; Women's Congress on Housing, 255. *See also* labor(ers)/work; magazines: women's; servants; sitting to work

Wright, Frank Lloyd, 73, 88, 122

Wright, Gwendolyn, 61, 320, 324n3, 336n12

Wright, Russel and Mary, 101, 102, 127, 174, 193, 196, 295, 337n38, 345n18, 346n27

Wurster, William, 73, 91, 106

yard. *See* gardens

Yeon, John, 73

Zion, Robert, 256

Žižek, Slavoj, 11–12, 31, 61, 266, 325nn16–18

DIANNE HARRIS

is an architectural historian and director of the
Illinois Program for Research in the Humanities at
the University of Illinois, Urbana–Champaign. She is
author of *The Nature of Authority: Villa Culture, Landscape,
and Representation in Eighteenth-Century Lombardy* and
editor of *Second Suburb: Levittown, Pennsylvania.*